An Introduction to Transitional Justice

Edited by Olivera Simić

Routledge
Taylor & Francis Group

LONDON AND NEW YORK

First published 2017
by Routledge
2 Park Square, Milton Park, Abingdon, Oxon OX14 4RN

and by Routledge
711 Third Avenue, New York, NY 10017

Routledge is an imprint of the Taylor & Francis Group, an informa business

British Library Cataloguing in Publication Data
A catalogue record for this book is available from the British Library

Library of Congress Cataloging-in-Publication Data
Names: Simić, Olivera
Title: An introduction to transitional justice / edited by Olivera Simic.
Description: Abingdon; New York, NY: Routledge [2017]
    Includes bibliographical references and index.
Identifiers: LCCN 2016018270| ISBN 9781138943216 (hbk) |
    ISBN 9781138943223 (pbk) | ISBN 9781315672649 (ebk)
Subjects: LCSH: Transitional justice—History. | Transitional justice
    Methodology. | Reconciliation—Political aspects. | Reparation
    (Criminal justice).
Classification: LCC K5250.I587 2017 | DDC 340/.115—dc23
LC record available at https://lccn.loc.gov/2016018270

ISBN: 978-1-138-94321-6 (hbk)
ISBN: 978-1-138-94322-3 (pbk)
ISBN: 978-1-315-67264-9 (ebk)

Typeset in Times New Roman
by Swales & Willis Ltd, Exeter, Devon, UK

Printed and bound in the United States of America by Publishers Graphics, LLC on sustainably sourced paper.

An Introduction to Transitional Justice

An Introduction to Transitional Justice provides the first comprehensive overview of transitional justice judicial and non-judicial measures implemented by societies to redress legacies of massive human rights abuse. Written by some of the leading experts in the field it takes a broad, interdisciplinary approach to the subject, addressing the dominant transitional justice mechanisms as well as key themes and challenges faced by scholars and practitioners.

Using a wide historic and geographic range of case studies to illustrate key concepts and debates, and featuring discussion questions and suggestions for further reading, this is an essential introduction to the subject for students.

Olivera Simić is a Senior Lecturer at Griffith Law School, Australia.

Contents

CONTENTS

Notes on contributors

Annika Björkdahl is Professor of Political Science at Lund University, Sweden. Her current research includes peacebuilding with a particular focus on urban peacebuilding, and gender and transitional justice as well as international norms in International Relations. Among her recent publications is the co-edited *Rethinking Peacebuilding: The Quest for Just Peace in the Middle East and the Western Balkans* (Routledge, 2013), *Peacebuilding and Friction: Global and Local Encounters in Post-Conflict Societies* (Routledge, 2016), and *Spatializing Peace and Conflict* (Palgrave, 2016), and she has published articles in journals such as *Security Dialogue, Millennium, Peace and Change, Human Rights Review* and *Third World Quarterly.*

Susanne Buckley-Zistel is Professor for Peace Conflict Studies and Director of the Center for Conflict Studies, Philipps University, Marburg, Germany, and currently Senior Fellow at the Käte Hamburger Kolleg for Global Cooperation Research at the University of Duisburg-Essen. Her research focuses on issues pertaining to peace and conflict, violence, gender and transitional justice. She has co-edited a number of volumes including *Memorials in Times of Transition* (Intersentia, 2014), *Transitional Justice Theories* (Routledge, 2014), *Gender in Transitional Justice* (Palgrave, 2012) and *Spatializing Peace and Conflict* (Palgrave, 2016).

Agata Fijalkowski is Senior Lecturer-in-Law at University of Lancaster Law School, United Kingdom. Dr Fijalkowski completed her PhD in law at the University of London. She has published widely in the field of transitional justice. Her most recent works include the edited collection, *Transitional Criminal Justice in Post-Dictatorial and Post-Conflict Societies* (Intersentia, 2015), which stemmed from British Academy funding, and 'Musine Kokalari and the Power of Images: Law, Aesthetics and Memory Regimes in the Albanian Experience', which was published in the *International Journal for the Semiotics of Law* (2015). In addition to examining transitional justice measures in Albania, Dr Fijalkowski has written about Polish resistance fighters and the maladministration of justice in communist Europe. Her current research project explores the experience of the law through the analysis of images taken at trials in Albania, East Germany and Poland. The images have been gathered from collections at the respective national archives. The study demonstrates the way that alternative dispute solutions in certain societies highlight justice roles and document atrocities that legal proceedings are not able to approach. Dr Fijalkowski has also published on the death penalty and its abolition in post-communist Europe, and on Polish constitutional developments in *From Old Times to New Europe* (Ashgate, 2010).

Jemima García-Godos (Dr Polit.) is Associate Professor in Human Geography at the Department of Sociology and Human Geography, University of Oslo, Norway. Her broad research interest is state–society relations in post-conflict societies. Her research on transitional justice focuses on victim reparations, reparations programmes and land restitution, particularly in Latin America, with emphasis on Peru, Colombia and Guatemala. Her research has been published in *The International Journal of Transitional Justice, Journal of Latin American Studies, Human Rights Review, Nordic Journal of Human Rights* and various anthologies. Her current research focuses on the Colombian land restitution programme and the dynamics of post-conflict state–society relations. She is co-editor of *Transitional Justice and Peacebuilding on the Ground: Victims and Ex-combatants* (Routledge, 2013) and *Transitional Justice in Latin America: The Uneven Road from Impunity towards Accountability* (Routledge, 2016), and was guest editor for the *Nordic Journal of Human Rights* Special Issue on 'Land Restitution in Transitional Justice' (2010).

Lia Kent is a Research Fellow at the Australian National University's (ANU) RegNet School of Regulation and Global Governance. She has research interests in the areas of transitional justice, memory studies, peacebuilding and gender studies, with a geographic focus on Timor-Leste. Much of her work is concerned with the discursive struggles that take place in post-conflict societies over questions of remembrance, reconciliation and justice, and what these reveal about the dynamics of political identity formation. Lia is the author of *The Dynamics of Transitional Justice: International Models and Local Realities in East Timor* (Routledge, 2012) and numerous articles in journals including *The International Journal of Transitional Justice, Human Rights Quarterly* and the *International Feminist Journal of Politics*. Lia is currently working on a three-year project funded by an Australian Research Council Discovery Early Career Researcher Award entitled *After Conflict: Local Memories and Peacebuilding in Timor-Leste and Aceh.*

Rachel Kerr is a Senior Lecturer in War Studies at King's College London. Her research interests are in the area of law and war, in particular war crimes and transitional/post-conflict justice, and she co-directs the War Crimes Research Group at King's. Her books include: *The International Criminal Tribunal for the Former Yugoslavia: Law, Diplomacy and Politics* (Oxford University Press, 2004); *Peace and Justice: Seeking Accountability after War* (Polity, 2007), with Eirin Mobekk, *The Military on Trial: The British Army in Iraq* (Wolf Legal Publishers, 2008), and *Prosecuting War Crimes:*

Lessons and Legacies of 20 Years of the International Criminal Tribunal for the Former Yugoslavia (Routledge, 2013), co-edited with James Gow and Zoran Pajic. Her most recent projects have focused on the role of visual evidence in war crimes prosecutions, and legal and ethical challenges of technological and scientific innovations and non-obvious warfare. In 2009–10, Dr Kerr was a Fellow at the Woodrow Wilson International Center for Scholars in Washington, DC, and in 2011–13, she was a Visiting Research Associate at the Centre for International Policy Studies, University of Ottawa, Canada. She is currently a co-chair of the London Transitional Justice Network.

Johanna Mannergren Selimovic is a Senior Research Fellow at the Swedish Institute of International Affairs. Her research concerns peacebuilding with a special interest in transitional justice, politics of memory, everyday peace and gender. She is currently involved in two research projects: *Gender-Just Peace and Transitional Justice*, and *Divided Cities – Challenges to Post-Conflict Peacebuilding and Development*. Her work has been published in journals such as *Security Dialogue, The International Journal of Transitional Justice, Third World Quarterly, Peacebuilding*, and *Conflict, Security and Development*.

Anja Mihr currently replaces the Franz Haniel Chair of Public Policy at the University of Erfurt, Germany. She has been Assoc. Professor at the Netherlands Institute of Human Rights (SIM), University of Utrecht, Netherlands, and is founder and Program Director of the Humboldt-Viadrina Center on Governance through Human Rights in Berlin, Germany. Mihr has been Head of the Rule of Law department at The Hague Institute for Global Justice, and carried out a number of Visiting Professorships for Human Rights such as at Peking University Law School in China together with the Raoul Wallenberg Research Institute on Human Rights, Lund University. She was the European Program Director for the European Master's Degree in Human Rights and Democratization (E.MA) at the European Inter-University Center for Human Rights in Venice (EIUC), Italy. She received her PhD in Political Sciences from the Free University in Berlin, Germany, in 2001. Mihr has published a number of books and articles on international human rights regimes, human rights education, transitional justice, European human rights system and non-state actors.

Andrew G Reiter (PhD, University of Wisconsin-Madison) is Assistant Professor of Politics and International Relations at Mount Holyoke College, where his teaching and research focus on conflict resolution, post-conflict peacebuilding and transitional justice. He has published widely on these topics and is the author of *Fighting Over Peace: Spoilers, Peace Agreements, and the Strategic Use of Violence* (Palgrave Macmillan, 2016) and co-author of *Transitional Justice in Balance: Comparing Processes, Weighing Efficacy* (United States Institute of Peace Press, 2010). Reiter is co-founder of the Transitional Justice database and a member of the Transitional Justice Research Collaborative, projects that have developed global datasets of transitional justice mechanisms.

Olivera Simić is a Senior Lecturer with the Griffith Law School, Griffith University, Australia, and a Visiting Professor with UN University for Peace, Costa Rica. Her research engages with transitional justice, international law, gender and crime from an interdisciplinary perspective. Olivera's latest edited collection is *Transitional Justice and Reconciliation: Lessons from the Balkans*, with Martina Fischer (Routledge, 2015). Her latest monograph is *Surviving Peace: A Political Memoir* (Spinifex, 2014). Olivera is currently working on her monograph *Silenced Victims of Wartime Sexual Violence* (Routledge, 2017) and guest-edited a special issue of the *Human Rights Review* on 'Engendering Transitional Justice' (2016).

Lavinia Stan is Chair of the Department of Political Science at St Francis Xavier University, Canada. A comparative politics specialist, she has published mostly in the areas of democracy and democratisation, with a focus on post-communist Eastern Europe. Her main areas of interest are transitional justice, and religion and politics. Stan is the author, co-author, editor or co-editor of eleven books, including *Encyclopedia of Transitional Justice* (Cambridge University Press, 2012), *Transitional Justice in Post-Communist Romania* (CUP, 2014), and *Post-Communist Transitional Justice* (CUP, 2015) as well as *Religion and Politics in Post-Communist Romania* (Oxford University Press, 2007) and *Church, State and Democracy in Expanding Europe* (OUP, 2011). A former member of the Scientific Council of the Institute for the Investigation of Communist Crimes in Romania, and chair of the Wildavsky Award Committee of the American Political Science Association, Stan has served as President of the Society for Romanian Studies since January 2014, and as an Associate Editor for the peer-reviewed *Women's Studies International Forum* since 2009.

Lars Waldorf is Senior Lecturer at the Centre for Applied Human Rights and York Law School at the University of York. He practised as a civil rights and poverty lawyer in the US for nine years. He then reported on genocide trials at the International Criminal Tribunal for Rwanda (2001) and ran Human Rights Watch's field office in Rwanda (2002–04). He has authored numerous publications on both transitional justice and Rwanda. He has co-edited three books: *Remaking Rwanda: State Building and Human Rights after Mass Violence* (University of Wisconsin Press, 2011); *Localizing Transitional Justice: Interventions and Priorities after Mass Violence* (Stanford University Press, 2010) and *Disarming the Past: Transitional Justice and Ex-Combatants* (SSRC, 2009). He also guest-edited a special issue of the *International Journal of Human Rights* on 'Legal Empowerment in Transitions' (2015).

Preface

Transitional justice is a relatively new field of scholarly inquiry, although its processes and mechanisms are a few centuries old. Thinking and researching about the ways in which communities, peoples and states respond to mass human rights violations was initially appropriated by lawyers and legal scholars, but the field quickly attracted the interest of experts in other disciplines, such as anthropology, psychology, politics, international relations, and peace and conflict studies. Transitional justice has become an integral component of these intersecting fields, which contribute, shape, influence and sometimes present challenges to each other. Over the past three decades, the discipline has grown into its own body of literature and research, and scholars, practitioners and policy makers have established their unique approaches to studying and researching transitional justice. The discipline has become an increasingly popular subject of teaching too at undergraduate and postgraduate courses around the world.

Yet despite the rapidly growing field, an introductory textbook in this field that could serve as a fundamental teaching tool has been missing. *An Introduction to Transitional Justice* seeks to fill this niche, hopefully providing a useful means for study, in particular for those seeking an understanding of the essential concepts and mechanisms that are of importance in illustrating transitional justice practices in different regions of the world.

Faced with the challenge of identifying a required text for my students that would include all introductory concepts and mechanisms in the field, I started imagining an ideal textbook. I spent considerable time thinking about what such a textbook would look like; a book that could be used for teaching purposes in courses worldwide and that would be accessible, scholarly and attractive to students. I also hoped that the book could be developed in such a way that it could also be useful to policymakers and others who wished to grasp key concepts in this fascinating field of inquiry. Knowing the depth and the breadth of the discipline, I had doubts whether such a project was feasible, or whether it might prove overly ambitious. I decided to test my idea by asking leading experts in the field, residing in different parts of the globe, what they thought of the proposition, and about their insights into what such a textbook, if ever produced, should include.

The content of the textbook you have in front of you is a result of numerous consultations with my colleagues, and valuable suggestions that were put forward by several Routledge peer reviewers. This feedback elucidated key issues that most teachers cover during a regular course semester and led me to invite some of the leading experts in the field to write content on particular mechanisms or processes.

The idea to produce an introductory textbook on transitional justice is not, however, entirely new. In the course of researching whether to write this book, I discovered that a few scholars had already contemplated such an idea, but due to their busy lives, none had yet been able to realise the project.

Many colleagues with whom I consulted about putting together a textbook were enthusiastic, and confirmed that it would assist enormously in their teaching and in conveying key ideas in the field. Due to the absence of a textbook, teachers have needed to compile their own sets of readings, and bring together varied ground-breaking works, journal articles and book chapters to form an *ad hoc* reading pack to be used by students. This textbook is not meant to replace the other scholarly texts, but simply to compress some of the main ideas and present them to students in a plain yet scholarly and engaging language that will expand the students' abilities to think critically about the field. Indeed, I hope that students and teachers will continue to use other articles and sources (including movies, theatre and other forms of art) to enrich their knowledge, and to elaborate and provoke further thinking and interest in this burgeoning field of study.

As with any project, compromises have had to be made in terms of depth and breadth, such as balancing the desire to include a wide plethora of topics with the publishers' expectations that the textbook would not increase in size unduly. In form, the book is not an orthodox textbook, due to the field's interdisciplinary nature and our effort to bring various disciplines in conversation through each chapter. The book aims to be the first introductory set text for students, introducing them to some of the core concepts and ideas set out in, what I believe are, foundational chapters; giving students a platform from which to further explore and understand more specific and narrow topics of inquiry.

The chapters in the textbook follow a similar structure: introduction, development of the idea/concept/mechanism, challenges and controversies, case studies that are used to illustrate key principles and how they have been used in real life (so students will not feel that mechanisms have been discussed in a vacuum), a summary of the chapter, conclusion, tutorial questions or questions for discussion, and suggested reading/films/arts that contain primary and secondary sources that the authors believe are relevant to support a knowledge and an understanding of each area. The last section of each chapter is a bibliography that compiles references used throughout the chapter. Only a few chapters deviate from this structure due to the specific nature of their discussion.

We hope that students will find this textbook valuable for their studies and that it will bring to life a subject that at heart lies within the relationships between victims and perpetrators and state/community. We also hope that once the main concepts and ideas are grasped, and their practical effect is fully understood, transitional justice will emerge as an intriguing subject to pursue further.

I am grateful to all of the contributors, experts in the field, for seeing the importance of producing this first edition of a transitional justice textbook, and for accepting my invitation to write without hesitation. In producing this book, the authors have drawn upon their experiences in teaching and researching in the field over many years.

In compiling the textbook, I have been assisted by a number of individuals. Many people have contributed their ideas, writing and support. I would like to thank all of the scholars who gave valuable inputs regarding the content and the Routledge peer reviewers. I would also like to thank the team at Routledge, and in particular Laura Muir, for their enthusiasm, encouragement and support of the idea of writing this textbook. Lastly, I am thankful to Stojan and Andrej for their unwavering patience and love.

Olivera Simić,
Brisbane, October 2016

Chapter 1

An introduction to transitional justice

Anja Mihr

1.1 Definition

Transitional Justice is a concept and a process that encompasses a number of different legal, political and cultural instruments and mechanisms that can strengthen, weaken, enhance or accelerate processes of regime change and consolidation. Transitional justice measures can foster or hamper successful transition or reconciliation processes, and there is not automatic guarantee for a certain outcome. Transitional justice measures can be politically instrumentalised, used or abused, and the process outcome depends on a variety of different actors involved. The process, as such, is inter-generational, and the measures are multiple.

The United Nations refers to transitional justice measures as a set of judicial and non-judicial instruments and mechanisms such as trials, truth commissions, vetting and lustration procedures, memorials, reparations, restitutions or compensations, and even amnesty and rehabilitation laws that redress the legacies of massive human rights abuses either during war, occupation, dictatorships or other violent and suppressive conflicts and situations. These measures include criminal and political procedures and actions, as well as various kinds of institutional reforms such as security sector reforms or constitution-building. These measures aim to facilitate civil or political initiatives during transition and transformation processes. In the hands of political and civil actors, such initiatives can lead to reparations, legal, security sector or institutional reforms. Whatever combination of measures is chosen by the government or by civil society actors during transition processes, they ought to be in conformity with international human rights standards and obligations in order to have any positive impact on democratic institution-building.[1]

---

1 United Nations, 'Guidance Note of the Secretary-General: United Nations Approach to Transitional Justice' (10 March 2010).

Consequently, the field and the array of transitional justice measures and its actors are wide and large. They can include asking private enterprise and companies to issue apologies and compensations for enslaved workers during wartimes, or disappeared labour unionists during the Apartheid regime in South Africa and during military dictatorships in Latin America. They can involve war criminals being trialled by international, hybrid or national tribunals or local courts after an armed conflict, war or genocide has ended. Victims of human rights abuse may receive reparations or compensations according to the wrongdoings they had to endure during suppression, war or dictatorships. Memorials, for example, are erected to acknowledge these wrongdoings and atrocities, and to serve as a warning to future generations. Lustration and vetting procedures aim to shed light on who was responsible to what extent during times of injustice and suppression. Thus, transitional justice measures are multiple and range from memorials to trials, from apologies to amnesty laws but, nevertheless, serve the same purpose. Governments and civil actors use them to delegitimise the past regime and to legitimise the new, ideally democratic, regime, and thus transitional justice measures only trigger reforms and change to the extent to which the actors involved want them to affect, for example, institutional reforms during transition and transformation periods.

Transitional justice measures can be divided into different categories: procedural, interpersonal, and informational justice measures, such as trials, truth commissions, reconciliation programmes, vetting, lustration, security sector reforms, apologies, reparations, compensations or memorials and many different ways of dealing with the past. They are aiming to lead to distributive and restorative justice, often referred to as establishing the rule of law.[2] Justice is meant in an institutional sense to build up (democratic) institutions for the future, based on the (bad) experience of the past, and less so in philosophical terms. Overall, transitional justice measures aim to prevent society and their institutions, such as political regimes, to repeat the wrongdoings of the past which led to suppression, war or personal losses and grievances.

Generally speaking, transitional justice is more forward- than backward-looking, and has become a driver for regime consolidation both in post-conflict and transition countries. The whole process attains to demystify and delegitimise the past, and legitimise and strengthen the future and present political or societal structures or regime. Transitional justice can – but does not automatically have to – contribute to (re-)building trust in institutions and among divided societies, former combatants, enemies or ethnic, linguistic or religious groups. Some mechanisms aim to reconcile societies and their former opposing parties,

---

2 Hague Institute for the Internationalisation of Law, 'Measuring Access to Justice in a Globalising World: Final Report' (Tilburg University and Utrecht University, 2010).

others focus more on building trust in institutions, and others again seek to acknowledge and remember past injustice through memorials, compensations or apologies.

In analytical terms, transitional justice measures aim at dealing with an unjust or atrocious past in order to delegitimise its responsible leadership (on all levels) and political system, and at the same time these measures aim to re-establish and legitimise a new political, and hopefully better, but certainly different, regime.[3] Transitional justice measures can affect both autocratic and democratic regime change and consolidation. The example of reparations, apologies, lustrations, trials or commissions of inquiry used by Australian, Canadian, Japanese and German governments over the past decades have proved that transitional justice is multifunctional and aims to find effective ways of dealing with an unjust past, even though these events have occurred decades ago. The purpose here is to increase and leverage the civic and political trust in their institution and society.

The way transitional justice measures contribute to change and consolidation is best illustrated through a mutual reinforcing process between the different measures and the institutions they aim to build or strengthen, such as commissions of inquiry, memorials, lustration, security sector reforms, amnesties or trials, and their contribution to building trust in political institutions such as courts, parliaments, municipalities, public administration, education systems or security forces. This mutual reinforcement between measures and institutions can strengthen democratic institution building by enhancing the quality and thus effectiveness of (democratic) institutions, but it can also strengthen a regime that becomes autocratic or dictatorial. The main difference between the two ways is that the first is an inclusive transitional justice process and the second an exclusive one.

An inclusive transitional justice process aims to include all parties or members that were involved in the previous conflict or dictatorship, may they be victims, bystanders or perpetrators, regardless of their political or social status, religious or ethnic background. This process allows putting blame and responsibilities on all sides, not just on those who lost the preceding war or the violent conflict. With this inclusive process, the new political regime in place also illustrates that they aim to make politics different and more democratic than the previous regime. With such an approach, they also delegitimise the previous regime, which usually was a discriminatory and exclusive one. In contrast to this, the exclusive transitional justice process usually selects victims and perpetrators, that is to say those whom the current government portrays as victimisers of the previous regime and thus enemies of the current political justice. This is winner's justice. Although it

---

3 Ruti G Teitel, *Globalizing Transitional Justice* (Oxford University Press, 2014).

is hardly ever possible to be fully inclusive because often victims and perpetrators cannot or do not want to cooperate, it is important to keep the door open for future generations who might want to talk to each other despite the fact that their parents and grandparents had been opposing parties, or either victims or victimisers. Generally speaking, there is no fully-fledged inclusive or exclusive transitional justice process in this world; however, some governments have leaned more to inclusiveness, others more to exclusiveness, which has made a difference in how transitional justice has contributed to stabilising and consolidating new political regimes.

1.2 Transitional justice measures

Transitional justice measures thus include the simple acknowledgement by political actors of previous wrongdoings; that is, through history or truth commissions, apologies or the establishment of memorials and memorial days. Additionally, acknowledgement can be carried out through initiating and responding to public debates, producing films and documentaries, publishing literature or novels about the past, introducing past wrongdoings and historical facts in school textbooks, conducting scientific research and allowing researchers access to archives, media involvement, or naming victims and alleged perpetrators. These acts can include novels, films, blogs, social networks, media or any civil society initiative for certain actions.

Different from acknowledgement, restorative measures can be summarised as acts that involve reparation, restitution, rehabilitation or compensation for victims of expropriation, eviction, imprisonment or illegal killings. Its advantage is that it can be easily assessed through qualitative data and has, therefore, been the subject of intensive investigation in numerous case studies. Alongside substantive and financial compensation or restoration, it includes ways and means for establishing working relationships between former combatants in public institutions, such as via quota systems, reconciliation and reintegration programmes to political prisoners of the former regime, restoring and maintaining memorials, or the public exhumation of mass graves. Although restorative measures such as compensation have been proven to be very effective in terms of victim satisfaction, they are only one part of transitional justice measures. These measures have to be connected to a larger profile of transitional justice, which acknowledges and quantifies the personal loss of lives or years of living under suppression across time. Otherwise, it would lose its meaning for future generations. For example, Rule 150 of the Hague Convention on Reparations from 1948 has become customary international law and is applicable to all countries and societies. It implies that the responsible state is obliged to make full reparations for the injury caused by the internationally recognised wrongful act; once again a measure focusing on victims.[4] Restoring Armenian churches in Turkey, Buddhist temples in Cambodia or synagogues in Germany after war and genocide can be directly linked to the Hague Convention from 1948 and state obligations to restore and acknowledge past wrongdoings.

Nevertheless, most prominent in the transitional justice debate are criminal justice measures such as trials, tribunals or vetting procedures according to international human, public, criminal or humanitarian law. Criminal justice is predominantly focused on perpetrators, and so are vetting measures or lustration policies of civil servants and public officers. International norms and instruments, such as international human rights covenants and treaties, help to lay down the legal framework to establish tribunals and a new national court system aiming to establish the rule of law in a country. So does generally the judiciary dealing with cases of the past. Criminal justice also aims to combat impunity, to establish and reform security, and to condemn or probe perpetrators of the former regime. The International Criminal Court (ICC) and the Rome Statute of 1999 have added significantly to this concept, with emphasis being placed on individual accountability being equal to state accountability with respect to past injustices. In this context, retributive justice is defined by the retroactive clause that perpetrators should only be charged under the laws of the past regime, unless they commit crimes against humanity, such as genocide, systematic rape or torture.

Surprisingly or not, silencing the past through *de facto* amnesty laws or so-called rehabilitation laws are the most common measures that governments in transition apply to deal with the past. They are among the most disputed ones, too. These measures include amnesty laws or informal 'silence pacts': that is, agreements among old and new political elites and governments shortly before and after transition takes place, as was the case in post-authoritarian Argentina or post-Franco Spain in the 1970s and 1980s. They also include reintegration and rehabilitation measures, laws and actions to fully or partly pardon victimisers, re-educate and reintegrate them in the state sector, in particular in the security sector and public administration.

Most amnesty laws that are issued after a regime change has taken place include the release of all political prisoners, thus emptying the prisons of the previous regime, including all those who were either against or somewhat collaborating with the previous regime. For example, the Spanish amnesty laws of 1977 during

---

4 International Committee of the Red Cross, Geneva Convention for the Amelioration of the Condition of the Wounded and Sick in Armed Forces in the Field (First Geneva Convention), 12 August 1949, 75 UNTS 31 (entered into force 21 October 1950) 'Article 51'; UN Educational, Scientific and Cultural Organisation (UNESCO), Convention for the Protection of Cultural Property in the Event of Armed Conflict, 14 May 1954, 'Article 38'.

the post-Franco regime exempted all those who had been politically active before the regime change, including Franquistas, and thus protected the old Franco-elite from facing litigation. In the 1980s in many Latin American countries in transition, former military elites 'issued themselves' extensive amnesty laws prior to passing power to a new civil and democratic government, in order not to be held accountable for their past wrongdoings. Amnesty laws are sometimes issued through informal agreements or national legislation and are therefore not immediately regarded as impunity measures. Amnesties imply that perpetrators surrender and may be seen as having committed crimes of some sort without (yet) having been punished. It also allows perpetrators to testify in front of truth commissions or other commissions of inquiry without fearing long-term prison sentences. Other ways of issuing *de facto* amnesties are 'reintegration' and 'rehabilitation'

Table 1.1 **Categories of transitional justice measures (samples)**

Acknowledgement	Restoration	Criminal Justice	Amnesties
History commissions	Reparation	Application of international human and humanitarian law	Blanket or conditional amnesties
Truth commissions	Restitution	Criminal justice	Silence pacts
Apologies	Compensation for past injustice	Tribunals and ad hoc tribunals	Rehabilitation programmes
Memorials	Quota and affirmative action	Trials	
Public debates	Restoration of historical sites	Security system reform	
Film	Exhumation of mass graves	Condemnation or probation	
Literature		Vetting and lustrations	
Schoolbooks			
Scientific research open archives			
Media involvement			
Symbolic naming of victims and perpetrators			

laws, such as in post-war Germany after 1949 and in many post-communist coun-tries in Central and Eastern Europe after 1990, to reintegrate or rehabilitate, for example, lawyers and technocrats of the previous regime, by reinstating them in the new offices with new titles.

Effects of these transitional justice measures are inter-generational and show their positive or negative effect only after 20-plus years when a new generation of (democratically) trained administrators and technocrats replace former judges, politicians or military, and a civil society is strong enough to support the new democratic regime and its values. Those regimes that do not enjoy a significant replacement of old elites after some time often remain fragile and turn back to their authoritarian rules and values, such as those seen in post-Soviet Russia, Hungary, Rwanda and Venezuela. Common to the latter is that they opted for an exclusive transitional justice process during most of their transition time after dictatorship, genocide or military coups.

In the early years of transition up to ten years, transitional justice measures are mainly used by political actors for tactical reasons, such as to make conces-sions to international donors, to victim groups or as part of foreign policy.[5] Only after 20-plus years with a new generation entering the political and technocratic arena do these societies reach the level of becoming morally capable to empatheti-cally face their past and use the past as a constant reminder to legitimise the new and different political regime.

1.3 State of the art

The term transitional justice was coined in the 1980s and 1990s with the first truth and reconciliation commissions during the democratisation processes in Latin America, and later by the vetting and lustration procedures, trials and reparation policies that were issued in Eastern Europe, the Balkans and sub-Saharan Africa.[6] Over the past few decades, the concept of transitional justice has undergone dramatic changes in its definition and spectrum. The term was first connoted as a notion describing the transition process in the early 1980s at the time of the Latin American transition process, in particular in Chile and Argentina; and in the 1990s, the war in Yugoslavia, the end of Apartheid in South Africa, after the genocide in Rwanda and the collapse of the Soviet Union and its satellite states.

---

5 Nicole Deitelhoff and Klaus Dieter Wolff, 'Business and Human Rights: How Corporate Norm Violators Become Norm Enterperneurs' in Thomas Risse, Stephen C Ropp, and Kathryn Sikkink (eds), *The Persisting Power of Human Rights, From Commitment to Compliance* (Cambridge University Press, 2013) 227.
6 Paige, Arthur, 'How "Transitions" Reshaped Human Rights: A Conceptual History of Transitional Justice' (2009) 31 *Human Rights Quarterly* 321.

With the establishment of the International Criminal Tribunal to the Former Yugoslavia (ICTY) in 1992–1993, and later the Criminal Tribunal for Rwanda (ICTR) in 1994, the legal basis for international jurisdiction became prominent in the transition debate and has since dominated the discourse. The international community, development agencies, UN and European Union (EU) institutions, tried to look for ways to guarantee peaceful means to transit from autocracy and violence to peace and democracy, or to stabilise existing regimes. International or hybrid tribunals were seen as one way ahead to introduce international law and standards into the transitional justice process later in Sierra Leone and Cambodia. During the developments of the early 1990s, that reference was made to the post-war trials in Nuremberg in the 1940s and an attempt was made to create similar tribunals for other post-conflict societies. These trials intended to shift arbitrary justice to civil justice based on human rights, using international jurisdiction and the international treaty-based human rights framework. Interestingly enough, the Tokyo Tribunals (1946–1948) on war crimes by Japan have often been criticised as a negative example of transitional justice, although they had a significant effect on the Japanese post-war democratisation process in the 1950s and on universal jurisdiction as it stands today. Instead, the focus on Nuremberg as a positive example also wrongly leads to the assumption that the Tokyo Trials had little effect on democracy or regime change, which is not the case. Both trials had different effects on the re-establishment of the legal and political regime and, moreover, on the judicial system in Japan and West Germany. However, they were just one part of the contribution to the bigger picture of transitional justice and regime consolidation.

With the end of the Apartheid regime in South Africa in the early 1990s and with the massive transition processes in Eastern Europe, and the Rwanda Genocide in 1994, the massive demand for more transitional justice mechanisms emerged – assuming that trials and commissions of inquiry alone would aid to prevent perpetrators from committing mass atrocities or at least punish those who had done so. Nevertheless, it soon became evident that there is more to transitional justice than punishing perpetrators, compensating victims and expelling public servants from their positions. The Rome Statute for the International Criminal Court (ICC) in 1999 was thus a result of these developments. It has set legal standards for criminal justice and reparation procedures in response to massive human rights violations and crimes against humanity. Since around 2000, the Rome Statute and the subsequent UN guidelines for transitional justice dramatically influenced the scope of transitional justice as we know it today.

In 2006, and during the subsequent years, the UN passed a set of general guidelines on transitional justice, and in 2009, the UN General Assembly called for the 'International Year of Reconciliation', with the aim of calling upon all countries, democracies and those in transition to democracy (which is the majority) to contribute to peaceful and stable transitions and transformations through transitional justice measures.[7] To name but a few non-governmental agencies and actors in this field are the German International Development and Cooperation Agency (GIZ), the US Agency for International Development (USAID), the International Center for Transitional Justice (ICTJ) and Open Society Institute or Africa Trust supporting transitional justice across borders. Thousands of other agencies, non-governmental organisations (NGOs) or civil society (CS) followed the example and established advisory bodies to consult private and public agents of transitional justice on the pathways to justice – although with different outcomes and effects. In some cases, these transformations happen suddenly; in others, they may take place over many decades, even after democracies have been more or less consolidated.[8]

The concept of transitional justice has, since its establishment, reached out to powerful international allies. Many international organisations such as the UN, later the EU, the Organization for American States (OAS), the African Union (AU) and the World Bank published reports, and in 2011 the first *World Development Report on Conflict, Security and Development*, which included a clear link between transitional justice and societal and democratic development.[9] It supports many transitional justice projects and measures in emerging democracies. National development agencies are pivotal partners in this process as they finance commissions, tribunals, institutional reforms or memorials around the world. International NGOs, often led by diaspora or victims of one's country, present reports or initiate public debates. They intend to lead to more public awareness and consciousness about the wrongdoings of the past. This shapes the political culture in a country to be more self-reflective and self-critical, and thus more open for pluralism and democratic compromises, and therefore less tolerant to radical and dictatorial movements.

1.4 Balancing transitional justice measures and realpolitik

Any transitional justice process is about balancing the demand for truth and justice on the one side and the demand for adequate condemnation of perpetrators on the other side. *Realpolitik* is often at odds with transitional justice measures and, in particular, the claims of victims who seek justice rather than rule of law.

---

7 United Nations, *Addendum 61st Session of the United Nations General Assembly*, UN Doc A/61/L.22/Add.1 (20 November 2006).
8 International Center for Transitional Justice, *Home Page* (2015) ICJT <https://www.ictj.org>.
9 Pablo de Greiff, 'Transitional Justice, Security, and Development' (Security and Justice Thematic Paper, World Bank, 2010).

However, transitional justice never attains justice in a philosophical or ethical sense, but rather in an institutional one, when increasing or leveraging the trust in public institutions and, by doing so, strengthening the rule of law in any given country. *Realpolitik* means real day-to-day politics and decision-making by policymakers and their daily concerns. Whereas transitional justice is a concept and a process with medium- to long-term impact, *realpolitik* are the politics and policymaking of everyday life. When using transitional justice measures as political tools to trigger regime change and consolidations, executive and legislative powers believe that responding to victims' or victimisers' claims and demands for commissions, trials, memorials and vetting procedures will be directly relevant to the current political changes.[10] When Ruti Teitel[11] or Priscilla Hayner[12] analysed transition periods in the 1980s and 1990s in Africa and Latin America, they came to the conclusion that transitional justice processes may have relevance for social and political stability in the countries, and thus provide the foundations to build up and strengthen political and civil institutions, such as an independent judiciary, and make civil society stronger. All argue that none of the concepts of the rule of law, constitution-building and institution-making can be understood without drawing at least some links to transitional justice measures and procedures. For example, Priscilla Hayner adds that truth commissions, during the period of transition and transformation, are essential for justice and accountability of young democracies and thus any democratisation and consolidation process.

Martha Minow observed that after mass atrocities and human rights violations, in the second half of the twentieth century, historical memory, narratives, memorials, recognition, truth commissions and forgiveness are somewhat interlinked when re-establishing societal trust, but due to a lack of research there is little evidence yet that they contribute to democracy.[13] The lack of global comparative, multi-level studies on transitional justice measures and their possible impact is one of the reasons why as of today there is little evidence that transitional justice has a direct causal effect or impact on democracy. But it does contribute to regime consolidation either way. One of the most profound works on the possible effect of transitional justice on democracies is done by James Gibson, in which he reviews the Truth and Reconciliation Commission (TRC) and transitional justice

---

10 A James McAdams, *Transitional Justice and the Rule of Law in New Democracies* (University of Notre Dame Press, 1997).

11 Ruti G Teitel, 'Transitional Justice Globalised' (2008) 2 *International Journal of Transitional Justice* 1.

12 Priscilla B Hayner, *Unspeakable Truths: Facing the Challenge of Truth Commissions* (Routledge, 2002).

13 Martha Minow, *Between Vengeance and Forgiveness, Facing History after Genocide and Mass Violence* (Beacon Press, 1988).

process in South Africa.[14] He emphasises that truth or rather facts about the past contribute to reconciliation, which in and of itself relates to the trust that people build up in (new) institutions. It is, therefore, important to aim for an inclusive transitional justice process and put the blame or responsibility onto all sides and all of those members of societies who violated the law of human rights – regardless of their social, political, religious or ethnic background.[15] Even though this is far from what we see in current transitional justice processes and thus far from *real-politik*, governments ought to politically aim for an inclusive transitional justice process and even litigate those who might be among their best friends and party members.

Based on current studies thus far, no systematic evidence has shown that trials, tribunals and legal punishment would lead to a peaceful society. What is known is that it is a mix of legal, political and historical measures that can have an effect on leveraging trust of the citizen in new political institutions and among victims and victimisers. The simplest way to describe the current state of the art is that all theoretical and conceptual endeavours in the area of transitional justice studies combine theories of justice and theories of democracy with those of trans-formation and new institutional legitimacy. In short: transitional justice is about transformation towards institutional and societal change, and consolidation based on the legal and political concept of justice. Stephen Winter states that transitional justice can contribute to stopping cycles of violence by improving the legitimacy of (new) state institutions. In order to do that, peoples' claims for justice need to be addressed.[16] One way of doing so is by using transitional justice instruments and mechanisms to turn the vicious circle of violence and suppression into a virtu-ous one of peace and free development. The division of transitional justice meas-ures into punitive, historical, reparatory, administrative or constitutional ones, as Ruti Teitel does in her first approach to defining transitional justice, is a helpful categorisation to understand how cumulative the effect of measures can be on institutional and societal development.[17]

In line with these observations of transitional justice processes around the world, James McAdams, for example, has long opted for a prudent and thus slow transitional justice process, referring to its longer-term, rather than shorter-term, impact. To have realistic expectations on what transitional justice measures can do or not, it is probably the best guidance in this process. Political proclamations

---

14 James L Gibson, *Overcoming Apartheid: Can Truth Reconcile a Divided Nation?* (HSPC Press, 2004).

15 James L Gibson, 'The Contribution of Truth to Reconciliation, Lessons from South Africa' (2006) 50 *Journal of Conflict Resolution* 409.

16 Stephen Winter, *Transitional Justice in Established Democracies: A Political Theory* (Palgrave Macmillan, 2014) 225.

17 Teitel, above n 11.

for trials, truth commissions, reparations and even amnesties ought to be carefully negotiated with former elites of the previous regime.[18] Trials in particular can become a dangerous intervention during transition processes if they are issued in a biased way. Although they have a particular relevance to democracy because they aim to (re-)establish and strengthen the rule of law, they can be perceived as a tool of vengeance in the hands of new political elites in their alleged 'crusades to root out the dictator' and become caught up in legal disputes that have little, if anything, to do with the realisation of justice, let alone (de)legitimisation of the previous regime.[19]

Interestingly enough, trials and amnesty laws are the most disputed among transitional justice scholars and yet the most prominent transitional justice instruments in this debate. Little doubt is left that amnesty laws can lead to a culture of impunity and are thus contrary to one of the main goals of transitional justice, to hold perpetrators of past injustice accountable for their wrongdoings. But at the same time, they can serve as a helpful tool to reintegrate former perpetrators into the new political regime, if they are conditional and not blanket.

Ruti Teitel, however, emphasises how criminal justice responds to the predecessor regime's repressive rule and thus has a delegitimising effect, and how amnesty laws hamper this process of delegitimisation.[20] She links the establishment of international criminal law and justice, such as that exercised by the ICC in The Hague (since 2002), and the earlier tribunals to former Yugoslavia (1993–2015) and Rwanda (1994–2014), as well as the hybrid tribunals to Sierra Leone, Cambodia or Lebanon since 2004, to the fact that these trials put facts and figures to the wrongdoings of former political and military elites. The European Court of Human Rights (ECtHR) in Strasbourg and the Inter-American Court of Human Rights in Costa Rica have also addressed allegations of human rights violations in a transitional justice context over the past few decades in their specific regions, and often urged transition countries to conduct more domestic and local trials to come to terms with past perpetrators.[21]

Despite the discussions about how much of each of the different transitional justice measures to use, and at what stage of regime transformation and consolidation, frankly speaking, today's transitional justice measures are seen as a mix of judicial and non-judicial, official and non-official mechanisms, instruments, strategies and approaches to acknowledge the wrongs of the past, either within a divided and conflict-torn society or with neighbouring countries. Transitional justice aims to be part of an ongoing (de-)legitimisation process seeking to bring

---

18 McAdams, above n 10, xii.
19 Ibid x.
20 Teitel, above n 11, 1.
21 Lieselotte Viaene and Eva Brems, 'Transitional Justice and Cultural Contexts: Learning from the Universality Debate' (2010) 28 *Netherlands Quarterly of Human Rights* 199.

former conflicting parties or divided societies together into functioning relationships through political partnerships by using democratic institutions to address the challenges of a once divided and conflict-torn society.

1.5 Regional differences

Over the past two decades, almost half of all countries globally applied some measures that qualify as transitional justice measures, which underlines the current trend to correlate these measures with regime change worldwide, ranging from the Fiji islands to Sri Lanka, Germany, South Africa, and from Argentina to Canada.[22] No geographical region is exempted. In Turkey, for example, transitional justice measures were seen as a revival of international criminal law to solve long-standing and perpetuating conflicts that destabilised democratic efforts in the 1990s. Transitional justice measures were not only applied to the Kurds, who had suffered decades of war and suppression by the Turkish military, but also to help re-establish the foreign trade and political relationships with Armenia. On the African continent the AU and its various treaties, as well as the incentives given by the African court, the Truth and Reconciliation Commission in South Africa, or the Rwanda Tribunal and the Special Court for Sierra Leone, had a spillover effect on other transitional justice processes elsewhere on the continent. The Inter-American Court in Costa Rica has proven through its judgments and decisions since the 1990s that it can interfere in, hamper, and slow transitional justice processes among its member states in respect to reparations and forensic truth finding such as in Brazil, Chile or Guatemala.

In Europe, there is a normative legal and political framework with different international organisations that framed transitional justice and the democratisation process throughout the continent. That framework consists of the EU and the Council of Europe (CoE), as well as the Organization for Security and Cooperation in Europe (OSCE). The latter has more influence in transitional justice in post-communist Eastern and Central European countries. These international organisations aim to be complementary, and their legal and politically binding status, mandates, treaties and policies are often used as a reference point to conduct domestic trials on former elites in post-communist countries or in post-war Balkan countries. The EU, and in particular the European External Action Service (EEAS) of the EU is today one of the strongest promoters and funders of transitional justice measures around the world. By its financial and political means it supports civil society initiatives for memorials, truth commissions, trials and tribunals, memorials and other instruments of acknowledgement and criminal justice.

---

22 Lavinia Stan and Nadya Nedelsky, *Encyclopedia of Transitional Justice* (Cambridge University Press, 2013).

1.6 Effect and impact of transitional justice

A widely debated aspect of transitional justice is that of its effect or impact on regime consolidation and on democracy in particular. As explained above, there is no clear evidence on a linear causal effect of transitional justice measures and democracy, but we see that actors in countries in transition use or misuse these measures to consolidate their regime type.

Regardless of the possible use or misuse of transitional justice measures, what we often find in transition countries is the desire among citizens for peace, justice and truth after violent conflicts as a common phenomenon among all societies. This momentum and catharsis after war and suppression often leads to the claim for more democracy and rule of law. If used in an inclusive way by all civil and political actors, transitional justice measures can strengthen institution-building over a longer period. In that case, transitional justice measures and (new) institutions can mutually reinforce themselves. By doing so, the various actors and institutions use truth commissions, trials, vetting procedures, memorials, rehabilitation programmes or reparations to connect to the citizens, victims and victimisers alike, and rebuild trust in institutions, and to show that the new legislative and judicial powers perform according to international human rights standards rather than in a biased and arbitrary way. In order to do that, a common narrative about what happened in the past is pivotal to get the transitional justice process started in the first place.

Elazar Barkan stresses that only with a common narrative about the past will societies overcome historical injustices and join the same path into the future. Without a minimum consensus of what happened in the past, no trial, no apology, no memorial and no vetting process could be installed effectively and thus contribute to delegitimising the past regime or legitimising the future regime. This narrative, some call it 'truth', shapes new identities in society that help to 'democratise' and thus share an understanding of historical memory.[23] In line with Barkan, a narrow or biased understanding of historical facts has often led to enduring injustice, and as we see in post-Soviet Russia or in Cambodia – despite some transitional justice measures – today, a non-pluralistic and democratic society.

Spinner-Halev has been arguing that if the past remains untouched, history commissions, trials or vetting procedures are denied, and a culture of impunity is established, the 'white spots' can easily lead to new myths in society that again can lead to acts of vengeance or false and arbitrary justice, and thus new

---

23 Elazar Barkan, *The Guilt of Nations: Restitution and Negotiating Historical Injustices* (Johns Hopkins University Press, 2000).

outbreaks of violence.[24] As Hazan emphasises, without a minimum agreement from all sides, that 'something went wrong' in the past and that one has to agree at least on some common denominatives, a transitional justice process should not even be considered as it would be a waste of time and money.[25] Without the political will and a critical mass supporting the process, its effect or impact will be zero.

Consequently, those actors who dominate the historical narratives or determine the facts of the past often expressed by virtue of the numbers of deaths and casualties can easily manipulate and use them for further acts of vengeance and crimes.

In the end, the rapidly developing field of transitional justice research has put forward multiple-country case studies with examples of best practices and processes. Not surprisingly, some of the major recent publications in this area are those on societal transition,[26] on the performance of tribunals and hybrid courts,[27] victimisation and reconstruction,[28] truth and reconciliation commissions,[29] the impact of apologies[30] or amnesty and impunity,[31] the importance of historical

---

24 Jeff Spinner-Halev, 'From Historical to Enduring Injustice' (2007) 35 *Political Theory* 574.

25 Pierre Hazan, 'Measuring the Impact of Punishment and Forgiveness: A Framework for Evaluating Transitional Justice' (2006) 88 *International Review of the Red Cross* 19.

26 Neil J Kritz (ed), *Transitional Justice: How Emerging Democracies Reckon with Former Regimes* (United States Institute for Peace, 2004) vol I: General Considerations. McAdams, above n 10. Lorna McGregor and Kieran McEvoy, *Transitional Justice from Below, Grassroots Activism and the Struggle for Change* (Hart Publishing, 2008). Jiri Priban, Pauline Roberts and James Young, *Systems of Justice in Transition: Central European Experiences since 1989* (Ashgate Publishing Limited, 2003). Lavinia Stan, *Transitional Justice in Eastern Europe and the Former Soviet Union, Reckoning with the Communist Past* (Routledge, 2008).

27 Mark A Drumbl, *Atrocity, Punishment, and International Law* (Cambridge University Press, 2007). Maria Jose Falcon y Tella and Fernando Falcon y Tella, *Punishment and Culture, to Punish?* (Martinus Nijhoff Publishers, 2006). Andreas O'Shea, *Amnesty for Crime in International Law and Practice* (Kluwer Law International, 2004).

28 Paul Rock, *Constructing Victims' Rights: The Home Office, New Labour and Victims* (Oxford University Press, 2004). Heather Strang, *Repair or Revenge: Victims and Restorative Justice* (Oxford University Press, 2001).

29 Mark Freeman, *Truth Commissions and Procedural Fairness* (Cambridge University Press, 2006). Teresa Godwin Phelps, *Shattered Voices Language, Violence, and the Work of Truth Commissions* (University of Pennsylvania Press, 2004). Robert I Rotberg and Dennis Thompson, *Truth Versus Justice, The Morality of Truth Commissions* (Princeton University Press, 2000).

30 Mark Gibney et al, *The Age of Apology, Facing Up to the Past* (University of Pennsylvania Press, 2008).

31 Charles Villa-Vicencio and Erik Doxtader, *The Provocations of Amnesty, Memory, Justice and Impunity* (Africa World Press, 2003).

memory and justice,[32] reparations[33] and on reconciliation processes in general,[34] as well as amnesties.[35]

Critical theorists argue that democratic regime change aims to create more inclusive societies, and thus institutions and political systems that allow for equity rights, independent executive, legislative or judicial powers. Whatever incentives, measures or mechanisms help to reach this (new) political order and to overcome old, traditional, violent and ineffective ways of governance, they are seen as a positive contribution.[36] Transitional justice measures are one series of many measures that can contribute to better ways of governance.

I do not want to put too much weight on the political will of elites and citizens during the early stage of transition, but their will and willingness to change does matter substantially during transition periods, because the impact of transitional justice measures depends on who uses them for what purpose.[37] If transitional justice measures fail to include all societal groups and direct blame on all sides while also commemorating all victims equally, but instead only include those that are close to the new political elites, these measures will not meet their target to reintegrate divided, distrustful or war-torn societies.[38]

On the other hand, transitional justice can weaken and impede regime consolidation due to the permanent reminder of the past injustice, increasing sentiments of revenge, placing blame on only one side or group of perpetrators or conversely none at all, excluding certain groups from the decision-making process or ignoring their claims, such as the Kurds in Turkey, the Roma in Hungary, the forced

---

32 Alexandra Barahona de Brito, Carmen Gonzaléz-Enríquez and Paloma Aguilar, *The Politics of Memory: Transitional Justice in Democratizing Societies* (Oxford University Press, 2001). Barkan, above n 23, 63–90.

33 Charles KB Barton, *Restorative Justice – The Empowerment Model* (Hawkins Press, 2003). Declan Roche, *Accountability in Restorative Justice* (Oxford University Press, 2003).

34 Karen Brounéus, 'Rethinking Reconciliation Concepts, Methods, and an Empirical Study of Truth Telling and Psychological Health in Rwanda' (Uppsala University – Department of Peace and Conflict Research, 2008). Mohammed Abu-Nimer, *Reconciliation, Justice and Coexistence, Theory and Practice* (Lanham Lexington Books, 2001). Daniel Bar-Tal and Gemma H Bennink, 'The Nature of Reconciliation as an Outcome and as a Process' in Yaacov Bar-Siman-Tov (ed), *From Conflict Resolution to Reconciliation* (Oxford University Press, 2004) 11. Karen M Poremski and Amy Benson Brown, *Roads to Reconciliation, Conflict and Dialogue in the Twenty-First Century* (ME Sharpe Inc, 2005). Mark Howard Ross, 'Ritual and the Politics of Reconciliation' in Yaacov Bar-Siman-Tov (ed), *From Conflict Resolution to Reconciliation* (Oxford University Press, 2004) 197. Jeff Spinner-Halev, 'Education, Reconciliation and Nested Identities' (2003) 1 *Theory and Research in Education* 51.

35 Freeman, above n 29.

36 Christoph Humrich, 'Critical Theory' in Siegfried Schieder and Manuela Spindler, *Theories of International Relations* (Routledge, 2014) 269.

37 Anja Mihr, 'Transitional Justice and Quality of Democracy' (2013) 7 *International Journal of Conflict and Violence* 298.

38 James L Gibson, 'The Contribution of Truth to Reconciliation, Lessons from South Africa' (2006) 50 *Journal of Conflict Resolution* 409.

child-soldiers in Sierra Leone or the abducted children in Argentina during dictatorship and war. Instead, these exclusive actions are reinforcing the past regime and lead to acts of vengeance, and that reintegrates the culture of violence and mistrust which is the soil on which autocracies flourish. For example, Turkey's inability to come to terms with the Armenian Genocide has led to a closure of borders and restriction of trade with Armenia and thus impedes diplomatic and economic relationships.

Equally, in their studies on Latin American transition processes, de Brito, Gonzaléz Enríquez and Aguilar could not find any direct correlation or causal effect, let alone direct impact between transitional justice and democracy.[39] However, according to them, the successful democratisation process in some countries depended on the inclusiveness and equality of society, to which economic development, balance of power, inclusion of old and new elites and representatives of civil society organisations, and thus transitional justice measures, played an important role. Yet, these measures can only contribute to consolidate a regime if certain conditions are met, such as equal participation of all stakeholders involved, adherence to international human rights laws and standards, the continuing quest for independent legislative and judiciary powers, and comprehensive inclusion of citizens and constituencies.

The assumption that transitional justice measures increase the level of trust in newly established institutions has been strongly defended in recent years. Different surveys to measure trust in institutions have shown that there is an incremental correlation between civic trust and the level of institutional performance. Nonetheless, civic trust implies that the person who trusts, for example, to trust again the victimiser who tortured prisoners in police custody or the judge who once issued decisions loyal to a dictatorial regime freely transfers assets to this institution, without controlling their actions or having the possibility of retaliating. This is in fact often not the case in post-dictatorial societies where mistrust is widely spread, as was the case in Chile or Poland. There must also be a potential gain or incentive for the 'trust-inexperienced' citizens to engage with institutions that they have never trusted before. In this case a criminal judgment on past justice spoken through an international court or tribunal (ideally, of course, by a national court), aims to give such positive example and shows that institutions can work in favour of citizens. Symbolic acts of reconciliation or commemorations, for example, of the Holocaust among Israeli and German leaders, or an official apology of the Spanish government towards the victims of the Franco regime, can re-establish trust of victims and survivors in the new institutions, or the new or successor regime of the one that once oppressed them. Transitional justice

---

39 de Brito, Gonzaléz-Enríquez and Aguilar, above n 32.

measures thus can work as catalysts, tools or incentives to slowly develop trust in new institutions and thus consolidate regime change.[40]

In order to measure effective pathways to regime consolidation, the decisions by an independent judiciary also need to be enforced under supervision of impartial courts and police. Justice thus theorises the role of the state and/or comparable local, domestic and international governance institutions that encompass a proper democratic process.[41] But Campell also highlights that to settle political disagreements through court-centred disputes alone would fail to strengthen formal and administrative justice.[42] A mix of transitional justice measures is needed to reach the anticipated trust.

More authors argue along the same lines, such as Nevin T Aiken, for example. He highlights that transitional justice measures need to be associated with real and tangible change in the socio-economic conditions of former antagonists and thus social justice, for example through compensations or reparations, and not only criminal justice. Thus, socio-economic and legislative reforms go hand in hand. Particularly, reparations are determined to reach out to citizens and victims through compensation.[43] Aiken uses the example of South Africa after the end of the Apartheid regime, where reparation and other socio-economic benefits related to past injustice were offered as one direct way to engage (new) governmental institutions with citizens. By doing so, they acknowledged past wrongdoings and at the same time delegitimised the previous unjust Apartheid regime. Reparations were closely bound up with questions of justice and a way to counterbalance for victims the potential 'justice deficit' caused by the granting of conditional amnesties to perpetrators.[44] The latter was the result of a negotiated deal between state institutions and victimisers in order to convince them to testify at least 'something' in front of the Truth and Reconciliation Commission, such as in South Africa in the late 1990s.

Yet, the use of too many or too few transitional justice measures, too soon or too late in time, may also spoil effective transition process as well as reconciliation. To keep the balance of interest and consequences among trials, apologies, memorials or reparations is hard to achieve.[45] The constant urge

---

40 Jurgen Schupp and Michael Naef, 'Measuring Trust: Experiments and Surveys in Contrast and Combination' (Discussion Paper No 4087, Institute for the Study of Labor, 2009) 3.

41 Tom Campbell, *Justice* (Palgrave Macmillan, 2010).

42 Ibid 256.

43 Nevin T Aiken, *Identity, Reconciliation and Transitional Justice: Overcoming Intractability in Divided Societies* (Routledge, 2013).

44 Ibid 185.

45 Interestingly enough the UNO, the EU, the OAS and the AU in their mission statements have never glorified those who started or won wars (as was previously the case), but instead acknowledge those nations that suffered in their grief to establish peace and welfare for all. This indicates that the first paradigm shift had already occurred in 1945 and then again in 1990 after the end of the Cold War.

for more justice, truth or atonements can put much pressure on both old and new elites, on victimiser and victims alike, and encourage spoilers to hamper successful transition to democracy or better governance. Domestic and international stakeholders involved in the transition process have to balance and eventually constrain public interests, in order to reach an inclusive and pluralistic decision-making process. Any public interest is composed of all members of societies, some of them victims and others, victimisers. Transitional justice measures are tools to balance public interest after times of conflict and violence. Sometimes they aim at retributive justice, sometimes at restoring socio-economic equality, and sometimes at seeking truth. Martha Minow has highlighted already, in one of the first books on transitional justice, the importance of balancing transitional justice measures, and states that 'truth and justice are not the same'.[46]

1.7 Transitional justice in transition and transformation periods

Transition in a more narrow sense is the normative and institutional change from one regime to another one in the first four to five years after the end of a regime; that is to say, formal transition from one regime type to another by, for example, changing a constitution. Transformation is the medium- and long-term alteration and consolidation of a regime and society in political and socio-economic terms. This period can take decades or even a generation and longer, and it aims to change and consolidate a certain political culture, behaviour and institutions. Transitional justice measures can influence both processes in the short- as well as in the medium- and long-term. During each period, they have a different effect or impact. During the earlier phase of transition, transitional justice measures serve above all as delegitimisation tools. During the long-term transformation process, they have a legitimising effect in favour of the new political regime.

During transition and regime change, constitution and institution building is pivotal, and transitional justice measures can help to do that as we have seen in post-conflict or post-authoritarian regimes. International governmental organisations such as the UN, the Organisation for Economic Co-operation and Development (OECD), the AU, NATO, or the EU give incentives from the outside. In most cases of transition, international actors firmly supported market economies and democracy, and adhered to international law standards, making an effort to join international organisations in order for the new political regime

---

46 Minow, above n 13, 9.

to reintegrate faster in the international community, and in reverse to control and orchestrate their transition process.[47]

What has all this to do with transitional justice? Well, during the first years of the transition periods, the emergence from authoritarian or suppressive rule is often accompanied by sweeping changes in the governance system. The new regime is very fragile; institutions are to be built and citizens usually do not trust the new regime, yet. Most countries in transition opt for a democratic model and create new institutional structures such as courts, a parliament and a government based on fundamental (human and freedom) rights in their constitutional set-up.

To set up institutions on paper or as brick buildings does not say anything about the way in which these institutions, such as public administration, parliaments or courts perform, let alone their quality. Nevertheless, these new (democratic) institutions are put in place to ensure a minimum level of the rule of law and the protection of human rights, usually manifested in their constitutional set-ups. But what can be noted is that transitional justice measures make their most positive contribution in strengthening these weak institutions if they become tools in the hands of civil society, such as victim groups, to channel their claims for acknowledgement, justice or economic development.

Thus, regime change during early transition or transformation periods is a process of a series of negotiations and compromises between actors, such as political parties, victim groups, victimisers or international organisations, often with different interests and resources. Regime change is consolidated when new political rules are in place, which often include rules for transitional justice, such as the willingness to set up reparations, trials, lustrations or amnesties and others, and to which all involved parties and actors compromise and adhere.[48] Thus, depending on how these rules really reflect societal set-ups and interest, how inclusive or exclusive they are, determines whether a regime change leans more toward democracy or autocracy.

1.8 Theory of transitional justice

Due to a lack of a confined transitional justice theory, we can only summarise the efforts and attempts currently underway to develop a theory of transitional justice.

---

47 The long-term aspect of TJ measures has been stressed by the UN Special Rapporteur on the promotion of truth, justice, reparation and guarantees of non-recurrence: Pablo de Greiff, *Report of the Special Rapporteur on the Promotion of Truth, Justice, Reparation and Guarantees of Non-Recurrences*, UN Doc A/HRC/24/42 (28 August 2013).

48 Julian Brückner, 'Transitionsansatz' in Raj Kollmorgen, Wolfgang Merkel, and Hans-Jürgen Wagener (eds), *Handbuch Transformationsforschung* (Springer VS, 2014) 90.

To mention but a few are the efforts by Winter,[49] Dube,[50] Grodsky,[51] Hansen,[52] or Caney.[53] Based on the facts, case studies and measures mentioned above, most of these authors share the basic theoretical link of transitional justice to the concept of justice by Rawls,[54] and to other existing theories such as the theories of transition, transformation, justice or reconciliation. They use the normative concept of justice and argue that transitional justice measures contribute to transforming societies and establishing a new normative benchmark of justice based on human rights, which also serves as a ground for democracies.

Caney, for example, explains why a potential theory of transitional justice is normatively rooted in the concept of global justice. Global justice is based on universal human rights norms and standards without which, ideally, no transitional justice and no democracy process can take place. Winter argues that a theory of transitional justice can answer those who criticise by arguing that transitional justice consists of helpful tools for new and established democracies, because democracies attain continuing legitimacy through citizens, and transitional justice measures can resolve the burden to seek it.[55] He aims to develop a political theory based on a theory of legitimacy and regime change and states that transitional justice legitimates the new (state) order by declaring that, despite necessary continuities, political institutions will henceforth bear a very different character.[56] In all these theoretical concepts, the role of citizens and participation is pivotal. They are the ones that legitimate institutions or not, and therefore programmes, such as transitional justice, which improve institutional performance and thus legitimise them.[57] State institutions learn to respond to citizens' claims to redress wrongdoings in a way that makes it more respectful of new human rights abiding values.

1.9 Ways ahead for transitional justice

Transitional justice is a short-, medium- and long-term process that allows the introduction of political, legal or historical transitional justice measures such

---

49 Stephen Winter, 'Towards a Unified Theory of Transitional Justice' (2013) *International Journal of Transitional Justice* 1.
50 Siphiwe Ignatius Dube, 'Transitional Justice Beyond the Normative: Towards a Literary Theory of Political Transition' (2011) 5 *The International Journal of Transitional Justice* 177.
51 Brian Grodsky, 'Re-Ordering Justice: Towards a New Methodological Approach in Studying Transitional Justice' (2009) 46 *Journal of Peace Research* 819.
52 Thomas Obel Hansen, 'Transitional Justice: Towards a Differentiated Theory' (2011) 13 *Oregon Review of International Law* 1.
53 Simon Caney, *Justice Beyond Borders: Political Theory* (Oxford University Press, 2006).
54 John Rawls, *Theory of Justice.* (Harvard University Press, 1971).
55 Winter, 'Towards a Unified Theory', above n 49, 3.
56 Winter, *Transitional Justice*, above n 16, 17.
57 Ibid 22.

as commissions of inquiry, trials, reparations, memorials and more, as well as legal, judicial or political instruments composed of international human rights law, and constitutional reforms, with the aim of triggering and supporting regime transition and transformation. Transitional justice measures are used by political and civil actors to delegitimise the past regime and to legitimise the new regime. Setting up trials, ad hoc tribunals, or issuing restorative justice laws in the context of reparations or compensations ought to be seen as measures that support longer-term regime consolidation based on active civil society that learns to trust again in institutions that have long betrayed it. But no transformation process will entirely depend on transitional justice measures. Transitional justice measures are complementary to other socio-economic reforms and thus do not alone lead to societal shifts or changes. Yet, although these measures are non-partisan by nature, they depend on the political will and ambition by the actors involved in the transitional justice process and thus have deep political consequences for society.

Yet transitional justice measures are pivotal for societal transformation in the long run. Transformative justice is a term often used in this context over the past years. In the future, it will be more difficult for societies and their governments to deny claims for justice and the instalment of transitional justice measures even decades after the war or the atrocities have ended. They are seen as catalysts or tools for political and societal change, but no guarantee for democratic change. We have seen over the past two to three decades that even decades or a century after atrocities took place, governments in established democracies such as Australia, Japan, the United Kingdom, France and Canada, are asked to respond appropriately to the past injustices by issuing apologies, setting up trials or commissions of inquiry, or compensate victims and their descendants as much as 70 years after the crimes have occurred. Transitional justice in the third and fourth generation are not the exception anymore but rather the rule, as we see in post-World War II Germany or Austria. Transitional justice measures are willingly employed tools to transform and strengthen society and its institutions, and therefore the call for 'transformative justice' instead of transitional justice is not heard.

And there is more to it in international terms. International pressure or the incentives to use transitional justice such as by the OAS, AU or EU and UN are not to be underestimated in any transition and transformation process. To install transitional justice measures is often a requirement for international loans or memberships in international organisations. In order to join the EU, for example, many countries and former member states of Yugoslavia were urged to collaborate with the ICTY and issue a number of transitional justice measures in order to have accession talks or receive EU development funds, such as Slovenia, Croatia, Bosnia-Herzegovina, Serbia or Macedonia. Similarly, in 1994 the new Rwandese government had to collaborate closely with the ICTR in order to receive financial support from third countries and the World Bank. These examples show that international incentives or conditions on the side, and the wish of these governments to integrate and be part of the international community are not to be underestimated as an incentive for transitional justice.

But regardless of by which means governments are driven to install a transitional justice process, during transition these political actors have to be mindful of the fact that memory is fortunately a dynamic process, which also involves forgetting, and that each generation interprets the events of the past on its own. Pierre Hazan has stressed that unless there is no public or citizen-driven transparency, or a monitoring procedure to bring about transitional justice measures, these measures may prove ineffective and instead become a convenient alibi for inertia.[58] Such transparency and monitoring procedures can only be guaranteed if democratic institutions are set on paper and work somewhat effectively, because only if fundamental freedom rights are guaranteed can they leave room for participation of societal and political actors on all sides. This includes victims, bystanders and victimisers at the same time. Thus, democratic institutions must be formally in place in order to implement any transitional justice effort and to move ahead with transformation of a society.

1.10 Discussion and tutorial questions

1) Discuss the pros and cons of the possible effect that transitional justice measures can have for democracies as well as for authoritarian regimes.

2) Discuss recent case studies and examples of countries or societies in which restorative or retributive transitional justice measures have led to negative or positive consequences for peace, stability and equality.

3) Discuss among your peers how the political, legal or theoretical concept of transitional justice has developed over the past three decades, and what have been the major steps or pathways during its evolution. Use different regional examples and country case studies: for example, compare the Latin American transitional justice process with those in Eastern Europe. Compare, for example, security sectors and military reforms and reparation programmes in sub-Saharan Africa with those in South America, and determine whether they had any impact on institution building in the respective countries.

---

58 Pierre Hazan, 'Measuring the Impact of Punishment and Forgiveness: A Framework for Evaluating Transitional Justice' (2006) 88 *International Review of the Red Cross* 19.

Suggested reading

Cook, Karen S, Russell Hardin, and Margaret Levi, *Cooperation without Trust* (Russell Sage Foundation Series on Trust, 2005).

Corradetti, Claudio and Nir Eisikovits (eds), *Theorizing Transitional Justice* (Ashgate, 2015).

Hazan, Pierre, *Judging War, Judging History, Behind Truth and Reconciliation* (Stanford University Press, 2010).

Mihr, Anja (ed), *Transitional Justice: Between Criminal Justice, Atonement and Democracy* (SIM Special No 37, Utrecht University Press, 2012).

Olson, Tricia D, Leigh A Payne, and Andrew G Reiter, *Transitional Justice in Balance, Comparing Processes, Weighing Efficacy* (United States Institute of Peace, 2010).

Teitel, Ruti G, *Globalizing Transitional Justice, Contemporary Essays* (Oxford University Press, 2014).

Thompson, Janna, *Taking Responsibility for the Past, Reparation and Historical Justice* (Blackwell Publishing, 2002).

van der Merwe, Hugo, Victoria Baxter, and Audrey R. Chapman (eds), *Assessing the Impact of Transitional Justice, Challenges for Empirical Research* (United States Institute of Peace, 2009).

Winter, Stephen, *Transitional Justice in Established Democracies: A Political Theory* (Palgrave Macmillan, 2014).

Bibliography

Abu-Nimer, Mohammed, *Reconciliation, Justice and Coexistence, Theory and Practice* (Lexington Books, 2001).

Aiken, Nevin T, *Identity, Reconciliation and Transitional Justice: Overcoming Intractability in Divided Societies* (Routledge, 2013).

Arthur, Paige, 'How "Transitions" Reshaped Human Rights: A Conceptual History of Transitional Justice' (2009) 31 *Human Rights Quarterly*.

Barkan, Elazar, *The Guilt of Nations: Restitution and Negotiating Historical Injustices* (Johns Hopkins University Press, 2000).

Bar-Tal, Daniel and Gemma H Bennink, 'The Nature of Reconciliation as an Outcome and as a Process' in Yaacov Bar-Siman-Tov (ed), *From Conflict Resolution to Reconciliation* (Oxford University Press, 2004).

Barton, Charles KB, *Restorative Justice – The Empowerment Model* (Hawkins Press, 2003).

Brounéus, Karen, *Rethinking Reconciliation Concepts, Methods, and an Empirical Study of Truth Telling and Psychological Health in Rwanda* (Uppsala University – Department of Peace and Conflict Research, 2008).

Brückner, Julian, 'Transitionsansatz' in Kollmorgen, Raj, Wolfgang Merkel, and Hans-Jürgen Wagener (eds), *Handbuch Transformationsforschung* (Springer VS, 2014).

Campbell, Tom, *Justice* (Palgrave Macmillan, 2010).

Caney, Simon, *Justice Beyond Borders: Political Theory* (Oxford University Press, 2006).

de Brito, Alexandra Barahona, Carmen Gonzaléz Enríquez, and Paloma Aguilar, *The Politics of Memory: Transitional Justice in Democratizing Societies* (Oxford University Press, 2001).

de Greiff, Pablo, 'Transitional Justice, Security, and Development' (Security and Justice Thematic Paper, World Bank, 2010).

de Greiff, Pablo, *Report of the Special Rapporteur on the Promotion of Truth, Justice, Reparation and Guarantees of Non-Recurrences*, UN Doc A/HRC/24/42 (28 August 2013).

Deitelhoff, Nicole and Klaus Dieter Wolff, 'Business and Human Rights: How Corporate Norm Violators Become Norm Enterperneurs' in Risse, Thomas, Stephen C Ropp, and Kathryn Sikkink (eds), *The Persisting Power of Human Rights, From Commitment to Compliance* (Cambridge University Press, 2013).

Drumbl, Mark A, *Atrocity, Punishment, and International Law* (Cambridge University Press, 2007).

Dube, Siphiwe Ignatius, 'Transitional Justice Beyond the Normative: Towards a Literary Theory of Political Transition' (2011) 5 *The International Journal of Transitional Justice*.

Falcon y Tella, Maria Jose and Fernando Falcon y Tella, *Punishment and Culture, to Punish?* (Martinus Nijhoff Publishers, 2006).

Freeman, Mark, *Truth Commissions and Procedural Fairness* (Cambridge University Press, 2006).

Gibney, Mark, Rhoda E Howard-Hassmann, Jean-Marc Coicaud, and Niklaus Steiner, *The Age of Apology, Facing Up to the Past* (University of Pennsylvania Press, 2008).

Gibson, James L, *Overcoming Apartheid: Can Truth Reconcile a Divided Nation?* (HSPC Press, 2004).

Gibson, James L, 'The Contribution of Truth to Reconciliation, Lessons from South Africa' (2006) 50 *Journal of Conflict Resolution*.

Godwin Phelps, Teresa, *Shattered Voices Language, Violence, and the Work of Truth Commissions* (University of Pennsylvania Press, 2004).

Grodsky, Brian, 'Re-Ordering Justice: Towards a New Methodological Approach in Studying Transitional Justice' (2009) 46 *Journal of Peace Research*.

Hague Institute for the Internationalisation of Law, *Measuring Access to Justice in a Globalising World: Final Report* (Tilburg University and Utrecht University, 2010).

Hansen, Thomas Obel, 'Transitional Justice: Towards a Differentiated Theory' (2011) 13 *Oregon Review of International Law*.

Hayner, Priscilla B, *Unspeakable Truths: Facing the Challenge of Truth Commissions* (Routledge, 2002).

Hazan, Pierre, 'Measuring the Impact of Punishment and Forgiveness: A Framework for Evaluating Transitional Justice' (2006) 88 *International Review of the Red Cross*.

Humrich, Christoph, 'Critical Theory' in Siegfried Schieder and Manuela Spindler (eds), *Theories of International Relations* (Routledge, 2014).

International Center for Transitional Justice, *Home Page* (2015) ICJT ‹https://www.ictj.org›.

International Committee of the Red Cross, Geneva Convention for the Amelioration of the Condition of the Wounded and Sick in Armed Forces in the Field (First Geneva Convention), 12 August 1949, 75 UNTS 31 (entered into force 21 October 1950) 'Article 51'.

Kritz, Neil J (ed), *Transitional Justice: How Emerging Democracies Reckon with Former Regimes* (United States Institute for Peace, 2004) Volume I: General Considerations.

McAdams, A James, *Transitional Justice and the Rule of Law in New Democracies* (University of Notre Dame Press, 1997).

McGregor, Lorna and Kieran McEvoy, *Transitional Justice from Below, Grassroots Activism and the Struggle for Change* (Hart Publishing, 2008).

Mihr, Anja, 'Transitional Justice and Quality of Democracy' (2013) 7 *International Journal of Conflict and Violence*.

Minow, Martha, *Between Vengeance and Forgiveness, Facing History after Genocide and Mass Violence* (Beacon Press, 1988).

O'Shea, Andreas, *Amnesty for Crime in International Law and Practice* (Kluwer Law International, 2004).

Poremski, Karen M and Amy Benson Brown, *Roads to Reconciliation, Conflict and Dialogue in the Twenty-First Century* (ME Sharpe Inc, 2005).

Priban, Jiri, Pauline Roberts, and James Young, *Systems of Justice in Transition: Central European Experiences since 1989* (Ashgate Publishing Limited, 2003).

Rawls, John, *Theory of Justice* (Harvard University Press, 1971).

Roche, Declan, *Accountability in Restorative Justice* (Oxford University Press, 2003).

Rock, Paul, *Constructing Victims' Rights: The Home Office, New Labour and Victims* (Oxford University Press, 2004).

Ross, Mark Howard, 'Ritual and the Politics of Reconciliation' in Yaacov Bar-Siman-Tov (ed), *From Conflict Resolution to Reconciliation* (Oxford University Press, 2004).

Rotberg, Robert I and Dennis Thompson, *Truth Versus Justice, The Morality of Truth Commissions* (Princeton University Press, 2000).

Schupp, Jurgen and Michael Naef, 'Measuring Trust: Experiments and Surveys in Contrast and Combination' (Discussion Paper No 4087, Institute for the Study of Labor, 2009).

Spinner-Halev, Jeff, 'Education, Reconciliation and Nested Identities' (2003) 1 *Theory and Research in Education*.

Spinner-Halev, Jeff, 'From Historical to Enduring Injustice' (2007) 35 *Political Theory*.

Stan, Lavinia, *Transitional Justice in Eastern Europe and the Former Soviet Union, Reckoning with the Communist Past* (Routledge, 2008).

Stan, Lavinia and Nadya Nedelsky, *Encyclopedia of Transitional Justice* (Cambridge University Press, 2013).

Strang, Heather, *Repair or Revenge: Victims and Restorative Justice* (Oxford University Press, 2001).

Teitel, Ruti G, 'Transitional Justice Globalised' (2008) 2 *International Journal of Transitional Justice*.

Teitel, Ruti G, *Globalizing Transitional Justice* (Oxford University Press, 2014).

United Nations, *Addendum 61st Session of the United Nations General Assembly*, UN Doc A/61/L.22/Add.1 (20 November 2006).

UN Educational, Scientific and Cultural Organisation (UNESCO), Convention for the Protection of Cultural Property in the Event of Armed Conflict, 14 May 1954, 'Article 38'.

United Nations, 'Guidance Note of the Secretary-General: United Nations Approach to Transitional Justice' (10 March 2010).

Viaene, Lieselotte and Eva Brems, 'Transitional Justice and Cultural Contexts: Learning from the Universality Debate' (2010) 28 *Netherlands Quarterly of Human Rights*.

Villa-Vicencio, Charles and Erik Doxtader, *The Provocations of Amnesty, Memory, Justice and Impunity* (Africa World Press, 2003).

Winter, Stephen, 'Towards a Unified Theory of Transitional Justice' (2013) *International Journal of Transitional Justice*.

Winter, Stephen, *Transitional Justice in Established Democracies: A Political Theory* (Palgrave Macmillan, 2014).

Chapter 2

The development of transitional justice

Andrew G Reiter

2.1 Introduction

Transitional justice has ancient roots. For centuries states have undertaken the difficult task of engaging past violence. Yet it is also a modern phenomenon dramatically shaped by recent transformations in international relations. This chapter traces the development of transitional justice, beginning with prominent historical examples of societies emerging from war. The discussion then shifts to the international response to World War II that ushered in a new era of individual criminal accountability. Beginning in the mid-1970s, the world experienced a massive wave of democratisation – termed the 'third wave' – that was marked by significant innovation in transitional justice.[1] These transitioning states enacted sweeping amnesty laws to provide stability, operated novel truth commissions to uncover information about the past, created programmes to provide reparations to individual victims, and instituted lustration laws to limit the influence of perpetrators on government and politics. Transitional justice went through another transformation following the end of the Cold War, in what some have termed a 'fourth wave' of democratisation,[2] as justice once again became prominent on the international stage, leading to the creation of new tribunals to handle war crimes and the development of new global norms of accountability. Finally, the chapter takes stock of the field today, in which transitional justice has become a permanent component of any domestic or international response to atrocities.

---

1 This followed two previous waves that occurred from 1828–1926 and 1943–1962. Samuel P Huntington, *The Third Wave: Democratization in the Late Twentieth Century* (University of Oklahoma Press, 1999).
2 Renske Doorenspleet, *Democratic Transitions: Exploring the Structural Sources of the Fourth Wave* (Lynne Rienner Publishers, 2005).

2.2 The historical roots of transitional justice

As long as societies have emerged from conflicts and transitioned from one regime to another they have been engaging in activities we would now consider transitional justice mechanisms. Scholars have identified transitional justice occurring at least as far back as early Athens. In 411 BC, the new democratic regime pursued policies of retribution against the ousted oligarchy, but enacted an amnesty law and pursued policies of reconciliation following the defeat of a second oligarchic regime.[3]

Transitional justice also played a key role in many of the most prominent global events of recent centuries. Following the defeat of France in 1814, the victorious coalition of European powers forcibly exiled Napoleon Bonaparte to the island of Elba, only to see him escape less than a year later. After defeating him for good in the summer of 1815, the victors chose to imprison Napoleon on the island of Saint Helena in the Atlantic Ocean, under British guard. He remained there until his death in 1821.

The end of the US Civil War in 1865 was marked by the extension of an official Proclamation of Amnesty and Pardon by President Andrew Johnson on May 29 to those who had participated in the Southern rebellion. The government also engaged in the policies of Reconstruction aimed at transforming and rebuilding the South after the war, though most consider the attempts having failed in effectively reintegrating and rehabilitating the region.

The end of World War I would also involve important transitional justice decisions on the part of the victors. The Treaty of Versailles famously included the War Guilt Clause that forced Germany to admit to being the cause of the global conflict. Moreover, the treaty required Germany to pay war reparations, to the tune of US$33 billion (or the equivalent of over US$400 billion today). These reparations were a source of tension within Germany and between Germany and the victors of World War I, particularly France, and are widely considered a contributing factor to the rise of Adolf Hitler in Germany and the advent of World War II just two decades later. Germany took out a considerable number of loans in the 1920s to pay reparations, the last of which was not fully paid off until 2010.[4]

In general, all of the early transitional justice efforts focused primarily on immediate retribution through executions and exiles, or were centred on broad amnesty policies geared towards enabling societies to simply move on from past

---

3 Jon Elster, *Closing the Books: Transitional Justice in Historical Perspective* (Cambridge University Press, 2004).

4 Olivia Lang, 'Why Has Germany Taken So Long to Pay Off Its WWI Debt?', *BBC News* (online), 2 October 2010 <http://www.bbc.com/news/world-europe-11442892>.

violence. Following World War II, however, transitional justice would take on a new form, with 'justice' taking prominence and a shift in focus from national level efforts to policies aimed at individual perpetrators and victims.

2.3 The Nuremberg Trials

The foundations of modern transitional justice emerged following the global devastation of World War II. A militaristic Japan engaged in an aggressive expansion of its empire throughout East Asia beginning in 1937, and Germany, led by Hitler and his Nazi Party, proceeded to invade and conquer most of Europe. In 1945, both Germany and Japan were finally defeated by a coalition of powers (the 'Allies') led by the United States, the Soviet Union, and the United Kingdom, but not before over 50 million people were left dead. More than any war before it, World War II was also marked by its impact on civilians, who were often caught between advancing armies and targeted in mass bombing campaigns of cities. The world was further outraged as more evidence of the Holocaust – the extermination of over 11 million people, 6 million of them Jews, by the Nazi regime – began to be uncovered.

In the wake of this devastation, the victorious allies engaged in extensive debates about what to do with those believed to be responsible for wartime atrocities. With the failures of the collective responsibility approach used after World War I fresh in their minds, and viewed as one of the causes of World War II, the Allies decided to pursue individual criminal responsibility in a public trial that would demonstrate democratic notions of justice to the world. The International Military Tribunal at Nuremberg (referred to as the Nuremberg Trials) began operation in November 1945 and was jointly run by the United States, the Soviet Union, the United Kingdom, and France. In the Pacific, the United States also took the lead in adopting a similar process – the International Military Tribunal for the Far East (referred to as the Tokyo War Crimes Tribunal) – for trying Japanese political and military leaders.

The Nuremberg Trials, representing the first true collaborative effort at international justice, became the foundation for modern international criminal law. Overall, 20 former Nazi political and military leaders were convicted at Nuremberg (three were acquitted). The trials created the legal concept of crimes against humanity that is still in use today, and the legal reasoning used in the trials directly influenced the Genocide Convention (1948), Universal Declaration of Human Rights (1948), Geneva Conventions (1949), and many other human rights treaties signed in subsequent decades. The Nuremberg Trials also served as the inspiration for the eventual creation of a permanent international court to handle cases of war crimes and crimes against humanity (see below).

The Nuremberg Trials, however, were not without controversy. By creating new categories of law, the Allies were essentially convicting individuals of crimes that were not crimes when they were committed. Other important decisions made by the tribunal, including which defendants to charge, were made on predominantly political rather than legal grounds.[5] The trials were denounced by some as nothing more than victors' justice, since the Allies quietly ignored their own crimes committed during the war, particularly the atrocities perpetrated by the Soviet Union, which began the war by invading Poland, the Baltic States, and Finland as an ally of Germany. In the end, 'it is clear that the Nuremberg prosecution was primarily intended to justify and legitimate Allied intervention in the war'.[6] Yet, while partially politically motivated and inherently flawed, the Nuremberg Trials served to dramatically shift the manner in which the world would respond to atrocities, and the notion of individual criminal responsibility would be picked up again by the international community following the end of the Cold War (see below). In the interim, transitional justice shifted to the domestic level, where individual states struggled to deal with atrocities committed by their own authoritarian regimes. Transitional justice in this context took on a new complexity, since the perpetrators were often important actors who remained influential long after leaving power.

2.4 Transitional justice in the 'third wave'

For two decades beginning in the mid-1970s, the world witnessed a dramatic surge of countries transitioning from authoritarian rule to democracy. Beginning with the Carnation Revolution in Portugal in 1973 until the aftermath of the collapse of the Soviet Union in the early 1990s, well over 50 countries transitioned in what Samuel Huntington has termed the 'third wave' of democratisation.[7] In the wake of the human rights violations carried out by exiting dictators, military governments, and one-party regimes, each new democracy was forced to make difficult choices about how to engage the past. Immediate transitional justice decisions were often determined by the relative power of former authoritarian actors, as many states faced a trade-off between justice and peace.[8]

In cases where the outgoing regime was defeated or significantly weakened, new democracies were more ambitious in their pursuit of justice for past wrongs. In Greece, for example, a weak military junta ruled from 1967 to 1974 before its failed attempt to take over Cyprus. Turkey invaded Cyprus to expel the

---

5 Richard Overy, 'The Nuremberg Trials: International Law in the Making' in Philippe Sands (ed), *From Nuremberg to The Hague: The Future of International Criminal Justice* (Cambridge University Press, 2003) 1, 7–8.

6 Ruti G Teitel, 'Transitional Justice Genealogy' (2003) 16 *Harvard Human Rights Journal* 69, 73.

7 Huntington, above n 1.

8 Chandra Lekha Sriram, *Confronting Past Human Rights Violations: Justice vs Peace in Times of Transition* (Frank Cass, 2004).

Greek forces, undermining the military regime and leading to the restoration of democracy. The new Greek government subsequently undertook a massive purge of those with ties to the former regime from the government and military, and proceeded to put over 400 former regime leaders on trial. The highest-ranking officers were sentenced to death (commuted to life sentences) in August 1975.[9] Argentina attempted to take a similar approach with its outgoing military regime, but soon faced a backlash and had to reverse course with a series of amnesties and pardons (see case study).

In other cases, however, authoritarian regimes carefully negotiated their transitions from power, and amnesty laws severely limited the ability of any new regime to engage the past. In Brazil, for example, the military regime enacted an amnesty in 1979, and after a gradual transition beginning in 1985, the amnesty was incorporated into the 1988 constitution. Despite challenges by victims' groups and human rights proponents, the amnesty prevented any trials of members of the military regime for over three decades, and in April 2010, the Supreme Court reaffirmed the law, citing its historical context and role as a catalyst for democratisation.[10] Other countries too felt that amnesties and forgetting the past were necessary for peace and democratic stability. In Spain, a pact of forgetting, or '*pacto del olvido*', negotiated by elites but widely accepted by society, has reigned from its transition in 1978 to present.[11] The 1973–1985 Uruguayan military regime ended as a result of the Naval Club pact between the military and political parties. The new regime issued two major amnesty laws in 1985 and 1986. Human rights organisations attempted to overturn the amnesty provisions, but they were upheld by popular vote in a 1989 referendum and again in a 2009 plebiscite.[12] There was a strong perception within Uruguay that human rights trials could jeopardise the democratisation process.[13]

Faced with restrictions on pursuing justice, many democracies in the 'third wave' shifted their attention to other transitional justice mechanisms that would achieve some lesser level of accountability for perpetrators or address the needs

---

9 Nicos C Alivizatos and P Nikiforos Diamandouros, 'Politics and the Judiciary in the Greek Transition to Democracy' in A James McAdams (ed), *Transitional Justice and the Rule of Law in New Democracies* (University of Notre Dame Press, 1997) 27.

10 Nina Schneider, 'Impunity in Post-Authoritarian Brazil: The Supreme Court's Recent Verdict on the Amnesty Law' (2011) 90 *European Review of Latin American and Caribbean Studies* 39.

11 Madeleine Davis, 'Is Spain Recovering Its Memory – Breaking the Pacto del Olvido?' (2005) 27(3) *Human Rights Quarterly* 858.

12 Luis R Roniger and Mario Sznajder, 'The Legacy of Human Rights Violations and the Collective Identity of Redemocratized Uruguay' (1997) 19(1) *Human Rights Quarterly* 55, 57.

13 Alexandra Barahona de Brito, 'Truth, Justice, Memory, and Democratization in the Southern Cone' in Alexandra Barahona de Brito, Carmen González-Enríquez, and Paloma Aguilar (eds), *The Politics of Memory: Transitional Justice in Democratizing Societies* (Oxford University Press, 2001) 119.

of victims. This was mirrored by a shift in those working on and studying transitional justice, as a field dominated by lawyers and legal scholars opened up to the social sciences and humanities more broadly. In Eastern Europe and the former Soviet Union, with Communist parties often still strong, new democracies largely eschewed trials in favour of lustration processes, whereby those with links to the former regime were removed from and/or banned from holding positions of power within the new government. Some countries, such as the Czech Republic, took an aggressive approach, publicising secret files to expose those responsible for past crimes, dismissing members of the government and security services, and enacting stringent laws regarding eligibility for government service. Other countries, however, took a softer approach, publicising officials' pasts but allowing them to stay in office (Hungary) or granting individuals the right to confess their past complicity and remain in government if the testimony was truthful (Poland).[14] Many of these countries, for example Romania, also had to deal with the tricky issue of property restitution for land and dwellings confiscated by the state during Communist rule.[15]

A novel approach to transitional justice also began to develop during this time in Latin America: the truth commission. These temporary institutions aimed to investigate and report on past human rights violations, thereby delivering some accountability for the crimes while also providing healing and closure for victims. The first major truth commission was the National Commission on the Disappeared (CONADEP), established in Argentina in 1983. Other prominent commissions in Uruguay and Chile followed, and in 1992 the United Nations funded and administered the Commission on the Truth for El Salvador, agreed upon as part of the peace process that ended the country's long running civil war. The widespread publicity of the South African Truth and Reconciliation Commission (TRC), which began in 1995, led to a global expansion in the adoption of this mechanism. The South African TRC, which investigated the crimes of Apartheid, was notable for its integration of amnesty into the truth-telling process: perpetrators would not be punished if they participated in the proceedings and told the truth about the past. In many cases, truth commissions led directly to reparations programmes for victims, and spurred grassroots efforts to construct monuments and memorialise the past.

Overall, while trials occurred in several notable cases, domestic transitional justice processes during the 'third wave' were mostly victim-focused, as new democracies feared the instability that could result from attempting to bring

---

14 Roman David, *Lustration and Transitional Justice: Personnel Systems in the Czech Republic, Hungary and Poland* (University of Pennsylvania Press, 2011).

15 Lavinia Stan, 'The Roof over Our Head: Property Restitution in Romania' (2006) 22(2) *Journal of Communist Studies and Transition Politics* 180.

perpetrators of past crimes to justice. The end of the Cold War, however, would bring about dramatic changes in international politics that led to a resurgence of justice worldwide.

2.5 A new era of international justice

Throughout the Cold War, civil wars raged throughout the world, with opposing parties receiving significant financial and military support from the two global superpowers: the United States and the Soviet Union. While atrocities were widespread, the geopolitics of the time resulted in little international reaction. The fall of the Soviet Union and the end of the Cold War led to more upheaval as ethnic tensions, held at bay by externally supported regimes, were now released. Yet at the same time, there were now fewer strategic incentives to block international interventions into these conflicts. The United States and other regional powers became more active in intervening in armed conflicts, and United Nations peacekeeping took a prominent role in ending wars and maintaining peace after their termination. In this environment, international justice took on a renewed purpose as the international community hoped to solidify new international norms and deter future human rights violations.

The first impetus for a renewed approach to international justice came shortly after the Cold War ended, when ethnic conflict broke out in the former Yugoslavia. Lasting from 1991 to 1995, the war left nearly 100,000 dead and opposing sides engaged in orchestrated ethnic cleansing. Military intervention by the North Atlantic Treaty Organization was necessary to stop the conflict, giving the major international powers a vested interest in post-war politics and preventing a renewal of violence. In addition, over 8,000 Muslim Bosniaks were massacred in Srebrenica, Bosnia and Herzegovina in 1995, and the occurrence of a genocide in Europe, despite the Nuremberg Trials and pledges that such atrocities would never happen again, forced the international community to respond. In 1993, the UN established the International Criminal Tribunal for the former Yugoslavia (ICTY) to try violations of the laws of war, genocide and crimes against humanity committed during the conflict. The ICTY is still in operation and has indicted 161 individuals, from all sides of the conflict, to date, including high-profile leaders of various warring parties. Slobodan Milošević, the president of Serbia, was the first sitting head of state to be indicted for war crimes.

A second crisis soon confronted the international community in 1994 when 800,000 Rwandans (mostly Tutsi) were killed in a genocide that lasted just 100 days. There was widespread horror at the atrocities, with much of the killing done with machetes. Moreover, the powerful states avoided intervening to stop the violence, and the UN, which had a presence in Rwanda, also failed to act. After the violence ended, the UN responded by creating the International Criminal

Tribunal for Rwanda (ICTR) in 1994. The court concluded its operation in 2015, having indicted 93 individuals. The ICTR made history with its judgment against Jean-Paul Akayesu on 2 September 1998, where it delivered the first international verdict for the crime of genocide and also established the role of rape as a means of perpetrating genocide. Overall, both international tribunals succeeded in helping to expose the extent of and responsibility for past crimes, and in putting justice back on the international agenda.

The international tribunals, however, were not without their shortcomings. Their ad hoc nature placed a considerable burden on the UN in creating each institution from scratch. Their locations – in The Hague, Netherlands and Arusha, Tanzania respectively – made them distant from the populations they were aiming to influence. Despite having a much wider mandate than the Nuremberg Trials, the tribunals could still not get over the claims that they were meting out victors' justice.[16] Finally, there was significant donor fatigue as many states questioned whether the tribunals were worth it, given their high costs. The ICTY, for example, is now in its 22nd year, maintained a staff of approximately 1,200 at its height, and has cost nearly $2 billion – or roughly $14 million per trial.[17]

Given these issues, in the wake of further conflicts with varying degrees of international intervention the UN took a new 'hybrid' approach to international justice. These were combined international and domestic efforts held in the countries in which the violations occurred. The UN would provide some funding and contribute international judges and lawyers, but the country in question would also shoulder some of the burden and provide its judges and lawyers. The hope was that these efforts would be cheaper, provide quicker results, help build the rule of law domestically, and allow the local populations to see justice being done.

There were four major hybrid tribunals created in just a five-year span from 1999 to 2003. Following East Timor's independence struggle from Indonesia, which ended with a UN-brokered peace and intervention, the Special Panels of the Dili District Court operated from 2000 to 2006, indicting nearly 400 individuals for rape, murder, and torture committed in East Timor in 1999. In the aftermath of the Kosovo War in 1999, the UN provided assistance to the operation of the Kosovo judicial system, including granting the Special Representative of the Secretary-General the authority to establish 'Regulation 64 panels' that removed the most controversial cases of war crimes from domestic courts to specially

---

16 Victor Peskin, 'Beyond Victor's Justice? The Challenge of Prosecuting the Winners at the International Criminal Tribunals for the Former Yugoslavia and Rwanda' (2005) 4(2) *Journal of Human Rights* 213.

17 Robert M Hayden, *From Yugoslavia to the Western Balkans: Studies of a European Disunion, 1991–2011* (Brill, 2013) 278.

created three-judge panels comprised of at least two international judges. The deadly civil war in Sierra Leone, which left over 50,000 dead, led to a request by the government of Sierra Leone in 2000 for the creation of the Special Court for Sierra Leone to prosecute those who bear the greatest responsibility for serious violations of international humanitarian law during the war. The court was established in 2002 and completed its work in 2013, convicting nine individuals, including former Liberian President Charles Taylor, who became the first African head of state to be convicted of war crimes. Finally, after years of negotiation, the UN and Cambodia agreed to create the Extraordinary Chambers in the Courts of Cambodia in 2003. Funding issues delayed its start until 2007, but the court subsequently indicted five individuals of the former Khmer Rouge regime, three of whom have been convicted.

While an improvement in some ways from the ICTY and ICTR efforts, the hybrid approach suffered from its own problems. The tribunals had difficulty merging international and domestic laws and practices, local resistance and a lack of cooperation on the ground hindered investigative and enforcement efforts, and most were underfunded and understaffed, limiting their effectiveness. In East Timor, for example, the Special Panels were unable to bring most perpetrators to trial since they resided in Indonesia, which had no interest in cooperating. In addition, many continued to deride the ad hoc nature of the institutions, and momentum continued to mount for the creation of a permanent international criminal court.

2.6 The International Criminal Court

In 1998, the UN General Assembly convened a five-week conference in Rome, Italy to draft a convention for the creation of an international tribunal to prosecute individuals accused of genocide and other serious international crimes. On July 17, the Rome Statute was adopted, outlining a new International Criminal Court (ICC). States ratified the treaty over the ensuing years, reaching a total of 60 signatories and bringing the statute into force on 1 July 2002. The permanent court, based in The Hague, has jurisdiction over crimes against humanity, genocide, and war crimes committed on or after 1 July 2002 in member states or in situations referred to the Court by the UN Security Council.

To date, the Court has opened investigations into nine cases. In 2003, Uganda, a state party, referred the situation of the Lord's Resistance Army (LRA) to the Court. The Prosecutor opened an investigation into the case in 2004 and in July 2005 issued the Court's first arrest warrants for five senior leaders of the LRA, including Joseph Kony. In 2004, another state party, the Democratic Republic of Congo, referred crimes committed in its territory to the Court, and Thomas Lubanga, former leader of the Union of Congolese Patriots militia, became the first person to be arrested under a warrant issued by the Court in 2006 and the first person to be convicted by the Court in 2012 when he was sentenced to 14 years in prison for abducting children to serve as soldiers. In a case referred by the UN Security Council, the ICC issued an arrest warrant in 2009 – the first for a sitting head of state – for Sudanese President Omar al-Bashir for crimes committed in Darfur. Soon after, Laurent Gbagbo, President of Côte d'Ivoire, became the first head of state to be taken into custody by the Court when he was arrested and extradited in 2009. During the 2011 Libyan Civil War, the UN Security Council once again referred a case to the Court, and within days the prosecutor issued several arrest warrants, including for President Muammar Gaddafi and his son Saif al-Islam. Gaddafi was killed in the conflict shortly after, and al-Islam is currently being tried in Libya, which has refused repeated requests from the ICC to turn him over. Other cases are ongoing in Kenya, Central African Republic, and Mali.

There is no doubt that the creation of the ICC represents a dramatic and positive shift in international relations. A permanent body now exists with the sole purpose of prosecuting serious international crimes, and has demonstrated that even heads of state are not beyond its reach. Yet despite its impressive achievements in just over a decade of operation, the Court has been heavily criticised.[18] First, many question the extent to which the court truly is international. As of today, 123 states have ratified the convention, yet many of the world's most important states remain outside of it. These include the world's largest and most powerful states, such as the United States, China, Russia, India, and Indonesia, as well as nuclear powers Pakistan, North Korea, and Israel. How effective can the court be if a large percentage of the world's population is not covered, and the strongest militaries and largest arms suppliers remain above the law? Moreover, all nine cases the ICC has investigated have been in Africa, leading to many questions about the global reach of the Court and leading to a backlash on the continent.[19] Recently, in June 2015, Sudan's al-Bashir, indicted by the ICC in 2009, attended an African Union summit in South Africa, whose government refused to arrest him despite being obligated by the Rome Statute to do so. Finally, despite many high-profile cases, the Court so far has only delivered two convictions, raising similar questions to those raised about previous ad hoc tribunals regarding the institution's costs and effectiveness. While only time will tell if these issues will end up being temporary stumbling blocks or symptoms of insurmountable problems, the ICC nevertheless represents a landmark development in international relations that has reshaped views on justice and accountability worldwide.

---

18 David Bosco, *Rough Justice: The International Criminal Court in a World of Power Politics* (Oxford University Press, 2014).

19 Adam Taylor, 'Why So Many African Leaders Hate the International Criminal Court' *Washington Post* (online), 15 June 2015 <https://www.washingtonpost.com/news/worldviews/wp/2015/06/15/why-so-many-african-leaders-hate-the-international-criminal-court/>.

2.7 The 'justice cascade' and universal jurisdiction

The creation of the ICC was not only an institutional response to the problems associated with ad hoc tribunals, but also part of a larger global normative shift towards accountability for human rights violations. Scholars Ellen Lutz and Kathryn Sikkink first coined the term 'justice cascade' in 2001 to describe this transformation, defining it as a 'rapid shift toward recognizing the legitimacy of human rights norms and an increase in international and regional action to effect compliance with those norms'.[20] The emergence of a global transitional justice advocacy network of tightly linked domestic activists and international non-governmental organisations pushed often-recalcitrant states to pursue accountability for past human rights violations. The transitional justice network was part of a broader human rights advocacy network and an even larger transformation in international norms toward greater protection of human rights. These norms have become increasingly codified in a range of legally binding treaties and conventions, including the Genocide Convention, the International Convention Against Torture, and the Geneva Conventions.[21] In addition, the European and Inter-American Courts on Human Rights, in interpreting and enforcing regional conventions, have made key rulings regarding the duty of states to investigate and prosecute past human rights violations.[22]

As a result of the justice cascade, countries everywhere in the world have increasingly pursued trials in the wake of human rights violations.[23] While amnesties are still used, they have shifted, from 'broader to more tailored, from sweeping to qualified, from laws with no reference to international law to those which explicitly try to stay within its strictures'.[24] Perhaps no development signifies this global shift more than the emergence of the concept of universal jurisdiction. Under this legal concept: 'Certain crimes are so universally agreed to be heinous, so potentially disruptive of international peace, and so difficult for states to adequately prosecute on account of potential links to state officials or other powerful people that all states have the right to try anyone accused of them.'[25]

---

20 Ellen Lutz and Kathryn Sikkink, 'The Justice Cascade: The Evolution and Impact of Foreign Human Rights Trials in Latin America' (2001) 2(1) *Chicago Journal of International Law* 1, 4.

21 Diane F Orentlicher, 'Settling Accounts: The Duty to Prosecute Human Rights Violations of a Prior Regime' (1991) 100(8) *Yale Law Journal* 2537.

22 Naomi Roht-Arriaza, 'State Responsibility to Investigate and Prosecute Grave Human Rights Violations in International Law' (1990) 78(2) *California Law Review* 449, 471–72.

23 Kathryn Sikkink, *The Justice Cascade: How Human Rights Prosecutions Are Changing World Politics* (Norton, 2011).

24 Naomi Roht-Arriaza and Lauren Gibson, 'The Developing Jurisprudence on Amnesty' (1998) 20(4) *Human Rights Quarterly* 843, 884.

25 Naomi Roht-Arriaza, 'The Multiple Prosecutions of Augusto Pinochet' in Ellen L Lutz and Caitlin Reiger (eds), *Prosecuting Heads of State* (Cambridge University Press, 2009) 77, 80.

The landmark case in the development of universal jurisdiction was that of former Chilean dictator Augusto Pinochet. After taking power in a coup in 1973, Pinochet ruled Chile until 1989 when he unexpectedly lost a plebiscite on his rule and was forced to allow democratic elections. While Pinochet stepped down, he remained commander-in-chief of the armed forces and became a senator for life. The military remained a powerful political player and Pinochet handpicked many of the senators and Supreme Court justices, all working to prevent any significant efforts into holding perpetrators accountable for human rights abuses committed during Pinochet's regime. In Spain, however, the Spanish Union of Progressive Prosecutors filed a case in a Spanish federal court against members of the former military regime in Argentina for the detention and disappearance of Spanish citizens. The case, under the direction of Judge Baltazar Garzón, later grew to examine the coordination of Latin America's authoritarian regimes in carrying out these crimes (known by the regimes as 'Operation Condor'), including Chile and Pinochet. In March 1998, Garzón issued arrest warrants for Pinochet and 38 other individuals associated with Chile's authoritarian regime.

Despite the ongoing Spanish case, Pinochet travelled to London in October 1998 for medical treatment. Alerted to his travel by Amnesty International, Garzón responded by issuing an international arrest warrant for Pinochet. British police served it on October 17, and he was placed under house arrest. Pinochet would remain there for 502 days during a hotly contested legal battle, until he was finally released and allowed to return to Chile on grounds of ill health. The Spanish case, however, proved to be a catalyst for efforts within Chile to bring accountability for the authoritarian regime's crimes.[26] Aided by strong support from domestic human rights organisations, Chilean judge Juan Guzmán declared that missing person cases should be considered kidnappings rather than homicides and thus were ongoing crimes, creatively circumventing the existing amnesty law.[27] Over 1,000 cases have been opened in Chile,[28] and Pinochet himself was indicted and charged multiple times, though he was never convicted prior to his death in 2006.

While there have been few cases tried under the concept of universal jurisdiction, the Pinochet case represented a landmark change in international human rights discourse, and the legal concept that some crimes extend beyond state sovereignty continues to shape transitional justice decisions – visible in prosecutions at the international ad hoc tribunals and the ICC.

---

26 David Pion-Berlin, 'The Pinochet Case and Human Rights Progress in Chile: Was Europe a Catalyst, Cause or Inconsequential?' (2004) 36(3) *Journal of Latin American Studies* 479.

27 Francesca Lessa et al, 'Overcoming Impunity: Pathways to Accountability in Latin America' (2014) 8(1) *International Journal of Transitional Justice* 75, 91–92.

28 For up-to-date information, see Instituto de Investigación en Ciencias Sociales, 'Latest Human Rights Statistics for Chile' <http://www.icso.cl/observatorio-derechos-humanos/cifras-causas-case-statistics/>.

2.8 The permanency of transitional justice

Over the past two decades, transitional justice has become a permanent feature of any response to human rights violations, expanding and normalising into what Ruti Teitel has called a 'steady-state' phase.[29] Many international and domestic non-governmental organisations have formed in response to the steady demand for transitional justice mechanisms, including the International Center for Transitional Justice, which was founded in 2001. The UN also now considers transitional justice to be a key component of its toolkit for responding to atrocities, and in 2010 the Secretary-General released a guidance note outlining the organisation's position.[30] As a result of these developments, transitional justice processes have played a prominent role in resolution of civil wars in many countries over the past decade, including Liberia, Burundi, the Democratic Republic of Congo, Nepal, and Afghanistan. Ongoing peace negotiations to end Colombia's 50-year conflict have also focused on the transitional justice response, and include provisions for special tribunals, an amnesty, and reparations for victims.[31]

The civil wars and toppling of dictators associated with the Arab Spring beginning in 2010 have featured key debates on transitional justice, and just as in the third wave, domestic conditions have led to divergent approaches.[32] Tunisia, for example, has been relatively free of its authoritarian shadow, as dictator Zine el-Abidine Ben Ali fled the country for exile in Saudi Arabia. The new regime has pursued trials of Ben Ali, several government officials, and numerous high- and low-ranking officers in the security forces for crimes committed during the uprising and protests in 2010–2011. A Tunisian court sentenced Ben Ali to life imprisonment for inciting violence and murder. In 2014, the government also established the Truth and Dignity Commission to examine past violence. In contrast, Ali Abdullah Saleh carefully negotiated his exit from power in Yemen and secured an amnesty as a precondition for stepping down. Soon after, he opened a museum to commemorate his own 33-year rule and has remained influential in politics. In 2015, an insurgency of Shia Houthi forces, loyal to Saleh, captured the capital, and the country has been embroiled in civil war since. In Egypt, the new regime has tried former dictator Hosni Mubarak,

---

29 Teitel, above n 6.

30 United Nations, 'Guidance Note of the Secretary-General: United Nations Approach to Transitional Justice' (10 March 2010).

31 Sibylla Brodzinsky, 'FARC Peace Talks: Colombia Nears Historic Deal after Agreement on Justice and Reparations', *The Guardian* (online), 23 September 2015 <http://www.theguardian.com/world/2015/sep/24/farc-peace-talks-colombia-nears-historic-deal-after-agreement-on-justice-and-reparations>.

32 Kirsten Fisher and Robert Stewart (eds), *Transitional Justice and the Arab Spring* (Routledge, 2014).

but the military has closely controlled transitional justice efforts and prevented any attempts to expose its role in human rights violations.

Meanwhile, countries that transitioned long ago continue to revisit their violent pasts, engaging in what scholars have termed 'post-transitional justice'.[33] Former Peruvian dictator Alberto Fujimori was convicted for his use of military death squads against suspected terrorists during his rule and sentenced to 25 years in prison in 2009. Likewise, in 2012, former Guatemalan military leader Efraín Rios Montt was found guilty of committing genocide and crimes against humanity during the country's long civil war. After 30 years of silence, Spain finally took the first steps to engage the abuses of its past with the enactment of the Historical Memory Law in 2007, which recognised victims on both sides of the Spanish Civil War and condemned the regime of Francisco Franco that followed. Poland recently instituted a new reparations programme and enacted a new law on the dissemination of objects depicting fascism or communism in 2009. If history is any indication, those countries transitioning and engaging in transitional justice for the first time today will almost certainly still be revisiting their violent pasts decades from now.

Case study: Argentina

Perhaps no country illustrates the development of transitional justice over the past half-century better than Argentina. The country was prominent in the wake of Nuremberg as many Nazis fled to its sympathetic shores. Most famously, Adolf Eichmann, one of the key architects of the Holocaust, was captured in Argentina in 1960 by Mossad, Israel's intelligence service, and publicly tried in Israel. Found guilty of war crimes, he was hanged in 1962.[34] Argentina would experience its own extensive human rights violations at the hands of a military regime that took power in 1976. In its effort to combat those on the political left in the context of the Cold War, the military enacted a highly repressive regime that imprisoned and tortured citizens, and 'disappeared' an estimated 15,000 people, often disposing of their bodies in the ocean in what became known as the Dirty War. The defeat of the regime by the British in its failed attempt to take control of the Malvinas/ Falkland Islands forced the military to allow elections and step down from power in 1983 – but not before passing a self-amnesty law (the National Pacification Law) to prevent themselves from being tried for crimes. The new democratic regime, however, led by President Raul Alfonsín, a human rights lawyer, quickly worked to engage the past, creating the CONADEP to investigate past violence in 1983. Its final report, entitled *Nunca Más* [*Never Again*], confirmed at least 9,000 disappearances at the hands of the former regime. Shortly after taking power, the new government annulled the National Pacification Law, and trials

---

33 Cath Collins, *Post-Transitional Justice: Human Rights Trials in Chile and El Salvador* (Penn State University Press, 2011).

34 Hannah Arendt, *Eichmann in Jerusalem: A Report on the Banality of Evil* (Viking Press, 1963).

of members of the former regime, including the ruling junta, began, culminating in thousands of convictions. Resistance within the military, however, began to grow, and in 1986 the government, under threat, sought to limit prosecutions by passing the Full Stop Law, which gave prosecutors sixty days to bring any further cases to trial. In 1987, a series of junior officer revolts (the Carapintada rebellion) forced the government to pass the Law of Due Obedience, which exempted lower-ranking members of the military from prosecution. The election of Carlos Menem in 1989 led to a series of presidential pardons, including of the former military junta. By 1990, Argentina thus found itself blocked from holding trials, and with those who had been convicted now free.[35] In this vacuum, victim-centred mechanisms thus began to take centre stage. In 1992, the National Commission for the Right to Identity was created and began working with the National Genetic Databank to reunite children of the disappeared, who had often been given to military families, with their extended families. From 1994 to 2000, the government also paid out over $750 million in reparations to victims of the Dirty War. Strong civil society pressure to renew the pursuit of justice began to emerge in the early 2000s, and new President Néstor Kirchner annulled the amnesty laws in August 2003. The Supreme Court validated the nullification and declared the amnesties unconstitutional in 2005. Kirchner also overturned the previous presidential pardons, paving the way for renewed prosecutions, which continue in domestic courts today.

2.9 Summary

Transitional justice has undergone a dramatic transformation over the past century. For centuries, policies were often directed at states or societies as a whole, such as the reparations Germany was forced to pay after World War I, or involved swift executions or exiles of opposing leaders. Following World War II, the international community set a new precedent of providing judicial accountability for individual responsibility in mass atrocity by establishing the Nuremberg Trials. While the Cold War prevented further international response, individual states embarked on a significant period of innovation, enacting a wide range of transitional justice mechanisms aimed at healing victims and reconciling divided societies. The emergence of new human rights norms in the post-Cold War world then led to a new wave of international justice via the creation of several important ad hoc tribunals, the legal development of the concept of universal jurisdiction, and the eventual establishment of the ICC. Now transitional justice has become a staple of all efforts to transition from authoritarianism to democracy, and from armed conflict to peace. While power politics continues to play a role, and mechanisms

---

35 Par Engstrom and Gabriel Pereira, 'From Amnesty to Accountability: The Ebb and Flow in the Search for Justice in Argentina' in Francesca Lessa and Leigh A Payne (eds), *Amnesty in the Age of Human Rights Accountability: Comparative and International Perspectives* (Cambridge University Press, 2012) 97.

have varied significantly in their levels of success, there is now a growing consensus that engaging the past is necessary for societies to heal and move forward following episodes of political violence.

2.10 Discussion and tutorial questions

1) What have been the most significant developments in transitional justice? What explains the major shifts in approach following World War II and again after the Cold War? What types of changes do you anticipate for transitional justice in the future?

2) What major factors shape domestic transitional justice decisions? What do we mean by states having to choose between peace or stability and justice?

3) What is the 'justice cascade'? What important events provide evidence of its existence? Is there contrary evidence that suggests the norm is not as strong as many think?

4) Since the Nuremberg Trials there has been an effort to make international justice universal. Yet international tribunals have been accused of enacting victors' justice and the major powers in the world continue to remain outside of the ICC's jurisdiction. To what extent do you think accountability for past human rights violations has become universal? Will power politics always trump justice, or do you think this barrier can be overcome?

Suggested reading

Bass, Gary J, *Stay the Hand of Vengeance: The Politics of War Crimes Tribunals* (Princeton University Press, 2000).

Bosco, David, *Rough Justice: The International Criminal Court in a World of Power Politics* (Oxford University Press, 2014).

Elster, Jon, *Closing the Books: Transitional Justice in Historical Perspective* (Cambridge University Press, 2004).

Kritz, Neil J (ed), *Transitional Justice: How Emerging Democracies Reckon with Former Regimes*, 3 volumes (United States Institute of Peace Press, 1995).

Nedelsky, Nadya and Lavinia Stan (eds), *The Encyclopedia of Transitional Justice*, 3 volumes (Cambridge University Press, 2012).

Teitel, Ruti G, *Transitional Justice* (Oxford University Press, 1999).

Suggested film

Nuremberg (Directed by Yves Simoneau, Turner Home Entertainment, 2001)

Bibliography

Alivizatos, Nicos C and P Nikiforos Diamandouros, 'Politics and the Judiciary in the Greek Transition to Democracy' in A James McAdams (ed), *Transitional Justice and the Rule of Law in New Democracies* (University of Notre Dame Press, 1997).

Arendt, Hannah, *Eichmann in Jerusalem: A Report on the Banality of Evil* (Viking Press, 1963).

Bosco, David, *Rough Justice: The International Criminal Court in a World of Power Politics* (Oxford University Press, 2014).

Brodzinsky, Sibylla, 'FARC Peace Talks: Colombia Nears Historic Deal after Agreement on Justice and Reparations', *The Guardian* (online), 23 September 2015 ‹http://www.theguardian.com/world/2015/sep/24/farc-peace-talks-colombia-nears-historic-deal-after-agreement-on-justice-and-reparations›.

Collins, Cath, *Post-Transitional Justice: Human Rights Trials in Chile and El Salvador* (Penn State University Press, 2011).

David, Roman, *Lustration and Transitional Justice: Personnel Systems in the Czech Republic, Hungary and Poland* (University of Pennsylvania Press, 2011).

Davis, Madeleine, 'Is Spain Recovering Its Memory – Breaking the Pacto del Olvido?' (2005) 27(3) *Human Rights Quarterly*.

de Brito, Alexandra Barahona, 'Truth, Justice, Memory, and Democratization in the Southern Cone' in Alexandra Barahona de Brito, Carmen González-Enríquez, and Paloma Aguilar (eds), *The Politics of Memory: Transitional Justice in Democratizing Societies* (Oxford University Press, 2001).

Doorenspleet, Renske, *Democratic Transitions: Exploring the Structural Sources of the Fourth Wave* (Lynne Rienner Publishers, 2005).

Elster, Jon, *Closing the Books: Transitional Justice in Historical Perspective* (Cambridge University Press, 2004).

Engstrom, Par and Gabriel Pereira, 'From Amnesty to Accountability: The Ebb and Flow in the Search for Justice in Argentina' in Francesca Lessa and Leigh A Payne (eds), *Amnesty in the Age of Human Rights Accountability: Comparative and International Perspectives* (Cambridge University Press, 2012).

Fisher, Kirsten and Robert Stewart (eds), *Transitional Justice and the Arab Spring* (Routledge Press, 2014).

Hayden, Robert M, *From Yugoslavia to the Western Balkans: Studies of a European Disunion, 1991–2011* (Brill, 2013).

Huntington, Samuel P, *The Third Wave: Democratization in the Late Twentieth Century* (University of Oklahoma Press, 1999).

Instituto de Investigación en Ciencias Sociales, 'Latest Human Rights Statistics for Chile' ‹http://www.icso.cl/observatorio-derechos-humanos/cifras-causas-case-statistics/›.

Lang, Olivia, 'Why Has Germany Taken So Long to Pay Off Its WWI Debt?', *BBC News* (online), 2 October 2010 ‹http://www.bbc.com/news/world-europe-11442892›

Lessa, Francesca, Tricia D Olsen, Leigh A Payne, Gabriel Pereira, and Andrew G Reiter, 'Overcoming Impunity: Pathways to Accountability in Latin America' (2014) 8(1) *International Journal of Transitional Justice*.

Lutz, Ellen and Kathryn Sikkink, 'The Justice Cascade: The Evolution and Impact of Foreign Human Rights Trials in Latin America' (2001) 2(1) *Chicago Journal of International Law*.

Orentlicher, Diane F, 'Settling Accounts: The Duty to Prosecute Human Rights Violations of a Prior Regime' (1991) 100(8) *Yale Law Journal*.

Overy, Richard, 'The Nuremberg Trials: International Law in the Making' in Philippe Sands (ed), *From Nuremberg to The Hague: The Future of International Criminal Justice* (Cambridge University Press, 2003).

Peskin, Victor, 'Beyond Victor's Justice? The Challenge of Prosecuting the Winners at the International Criminal Tribunals for the Former Yugoslavia and Rwanda' (2005) 4(2) *Journal of Human Rights*.

Pion-Berlin, David, 'The Pinochet Case and Human Rights Progress in Chile: Was Europe a Catalyst, Cause or Inconsequential?' (2004) 36(3) *Journal of Latin American Studies*.

Roht-Arriaza, Naomi, 'State Responsibility to Investigate and Prosecute Grave Human Rights Violations in International Law' (1990) 78(2) *California Law Review*.

Roht-Arriaza, Naomi, 'The Multiple Prosecutions of Augusto Pinochet' in Ellen L Lutz and Caitlin Reiger (eds), *Prosecuting Heads of State* (Cambridge University Press, 2009).

Roht-Arriaza, Naomi and Lauren Gibson, 'The Developing Jurisprudence on Amnesty' (1998) 20(4) *Human Rights Quarterly*.

Roniger, Luis R and Mario Sznajder, 'The Legacy of Human Rights Violations and the Collective Identity of Redemocratized Uruguay' (1997) 19(1) *Human Rights Quarterly*.

Schneider, Nina, 'Impunity in Post-Authoritarian Brazil: The Supreme Court's Recent Verdict on the Amnesty Law' (2011) 90 *European Review of Latin American and Caribbean Studies*.

Sikkink, Kathryn, *The Justice Cascade: How Human Rights Prosecutions Are Changing World Politics* (Norton, 2011).

Sriram, Chandra Lekha, *Confronting Past Human Rights Violations: Justice vs Peace in Times of Transition* (Frank Cass, 2004).

Stan, Lavinia, 'The Roof over Our Head: Property Restitution in Romania' (2006) 22(2) *Journal of Communist Studies and Transition Politics*.

Taylor, Adam, 'Why So Many African Leaders Hate the International Criminal Court' *Washington Post* (online), 15 June 2015 <https://www.washingtonpost.com/news/worldviews/wp/2015/06/15/why-so-many-african-leaders-hate-the-international-criminal-court/>.

Teitel, Ruti G, 'Transitional Justice Genealogy' (2003) 16 *Harvard Human Rights Journal*.

United Nations, 'Guidance Note of the Secretary-General: United Nations Approach to Transitional Justice' (10 March 2010).

Chapter 3

International criminal justice

Rachel Kerr

3.1 Introduction

Over the course of the last 20 years or so, a powerful movement emerged to bring to justice those accused of international crimes. This movement – international criminal justice – reached its apex with the establishment of a permanent International Criminal Court (ICC), with the adoption of the Rome Statute in July 1998, and its coming into force four years later, in July 2002, ushering in a much-vaunted 'end to impunity'. The establishment of the ICC was highly significant symbolically and materially. It was the culmination of a movement that traced its origins to the military tribunals at Nuremberg and Tokyo after World War II, and was revived following a fifty-year hiatus with the establishment by the UN Security Council in 1993 and 1994 of ad hoc International Criminal Tribunals for the former Yugoslavia (ICTY) and for Rwanda (ICTR). International criminal justice also comprised a number of hybrid institutions, blending international and local law and personnel, such as the Special Court for Sierra Leone, the Extraordinary Chambers in the Courts of Cambodia, and a handful of cases brought in domestic courts under the principle of universal jurisdiction.[1]

This chapter provides a survey of the theory and practice of international criminal justice, focused on the history, development and operation of international courts. It begins with a brief historical overview, moves on to consider the purposes and goals of international criminal justice, key points of contention and controversy – in particular those revolving around the three 'great debates'

---

[1] Although the exercise of universal jurisdiction by domestic courts in cases such as Pinochet, 1998, can be placed under the rubric of international criminal justice, it is not discussed in detail here; for discussion of the principle and its application, see Andrew G Reiter, 'The development of transitional justice', in this volume.

of peace vs justice, international vs local actors and interests, and retributive vs restorative conceptions of justice. Finally, it considers the current position of international criminal justice, focusing in particular on the purported 'crisis' at the ICC.

3.2 Definition

International criminal justice implies not only the practice of prosecuting, or seeking accountability for international crimes, but also the idea that such crimes are the concern of the international community writ large. It has been articulated elsewhere as 'the response of the international community to mass atrocity'. There are different disciplinary approaches to the study of international criminal justice, including notable contributions from scholars of politics, history, sociology and psychology, as well as international law, which have significantly broadened its scope as a field of study.

International criminal justice is often conflated with the broader field of transitional justice, but it represents only one of a range of mechanisms for dealing with the legacy of past abuses in the transitional justice 'toolkit' (which also includes mechanisms such as truth commissions, reparations programmes and various kinds of institutional reforms, such as vetting and lustration). A significant difference between international criminal justice and transitional justice is that while transitional justice is focused on the relationship of justice and accountability measures and their role in fostering domestic transition, international criminal justice seeks to remove the issue of justice and accountability from the immediate politics of transition to the international arena.

It is also important to note that international criminal justice, as a form of transitional justice, is often invoked in post-conflict settings (or during conflict) and as such, both transitional justice and international criminal justice are often referred to as 'post-conflict justice' as well. The difference between the latter and transitional justice more broadly is in the nature of transition implied, with transitional justice having its roots in transitions from authoritarian to democratic rule, and post-conflict justice in transitions from war to peace. There has thus emerged an explicit link between transitional justice and peace building. In his 2004 report, 'The Rule of Law and Transitional Justice in Conflict and Post-Conflict Societies', the UN Secretary-General formally acknowledged that some form of justice is crucial for societies emerging from violent conflict, as the task of dealing with the legacy of past crimes is essential to building a more peaceful future.[2] Central to the international criminal justice project – and a key point of

---

2 UN Security Council, *The Rule of Law and Transitional Justice in Conflict and Post-Conflict Societies: Report of the Secretary-General*, S/2004/616 (23 August 2004).

contention and controversy – is the relationship to the goal of international peace and security – both implicitly and explicitly through the UN Security Council. The record has shown that the two goals are not mutually exclusive, but nor are they always mutually reinforcing.

3.3 Brief overview

The origins of international criminal justice are usually traced to the post-World War II international military tribunals at Nuremberg and Tokyo, although a much earlier precedent is often invoked: the trial of Peter von Hagenbach, Governor of Breisach, for crimes against 'the laws of God and Humanity' in 1494.[3] Von Hagenbach's trial was notable because he was tried before an ostensibly 'international' tribunal of 28 judges from across the Holy Roman Empire for a catalogue of crimes, including murder and rape, committed during military occupation, and his defence of superior orders was rejected.

However, it was the Nuremberg and Tokyo trials that marked a real watershed in international criminal justice by demonstrating that not only was accountability desirable, but that it was also feasible. It was feasible because the Allies had achieved total victory and were in occupation of Germany and Japan. The function of the trials was both backwards and forwards looking. As the 'last act of the war', the trials publicised Nazi atrocities and justified the war effort; as the 'first act of the peace', the trials were supposed to pave the way for a new order. According to US Prosecutor Robert Jackson, Nuremberg's primary purpose was 'to bring the weight of law and criminal sanction to bear in support of the peaceful and humanitarian principles that the UN was to promote'.[4]

But the Nuremberg legacy was also problematic; indeed, for some, it provoked a 'genuine moral crisis'.[5] There were a number of grounds for criticism: chief among them that it was one-sided in that the judges were all from the victorious Allied nations, and had jurisdiction only over Nazi war criminals, deliberately avoiding scrutiny of the Allied war record, including area bombing of German cities, unrestricted U-boat warfare, allegations of the rape of German women by Allied soldiers, and Soviet war responsibility, and that it was fundamentally

---

3 The case was dug up by Georg Schwarzenberger in 1946, in support of a legal precedent for the novel category of crimes against humanity. For detailed discussion, see Gregory S Gordon, 'The Trial of Peter von Hagenbach: Reconciling History, Historiography and International Criminal Law' in Kevin Jon Heller and Gerry Simpson (eds), *The Hidden Histories of War Crimes Trials* (Oxford University Press, 2013) 13–49.

4 Cited in Rachel Kerr and Eirin Mobekk, *Peace and Justice: Seeking Accountability after War* (Polity, 2007) 6.

5 Judith Shklar, *Legalism: Law, Morals and Political Trials* (Harvard University Press, 1964) cited in ibid.

unfair in applying ex post facto law in respect of crimes against peace and crimes against humanity, in particular. The Tokyo tribunal came under fire also, and in many ways has an even more dubious legacy.[6] The accusation of 'victors' justice' levelled at the tribunal by one of its judges (Pal) in a dissenting opinion has stuck as the overarching judgment of both sets of proceedings. Its shortcomings notwithstanding, the Nuremberg legacy was highly significant for international criminal justice. Not only did it document the atrocities committed by the Nazi regime, and provide an incontrovertible documentary record of the Final Solution such that 'there can be no responsible denial of these crimes', it also showed that, on occasion, international resolve could be sufficiently compelling to uphold and enforce international law, and hold individuals criminally accountable.

After an almost fifty-year hiatus, in which proposals for a permanent international criminal court went nowhere, the Nuremberg precedent was revived with the establishment of an ad hoc International Criminal Tribunal for the former Yugoslavia (ICTY). By the time the ICTY was established, the laws applied at Nuremberg were firmly embedded in the framework of international law, with the adoption of the Nuremberg Principles by the UN General Assembly in 1950, the adoption of the 1948 Genocide Convention and the 1949 Geneva Conventions. As such, the law in 1993 was deemed 'beyond any doubt', even if, in the interim, it had not resulted in much in the way of concrete action.

Based in The Hague, the ICTY's mandate was to prosecute persons responsible for violations of international humanitarian law committed in the territory of the former Yugoslavia since 1991, the year in which the series of conflicts that made up the Yugoslav War began. The decision to establish the ICTY was taken in February 1993, in response to sustained reports of atrocities in Croatia and then in Bosnia, and the Security Council established the ICTY on 25 May 1993. The mode of establishment, as a Chapter VII measure aimed at restoring international peace and security, was highly significant, truly innovative, and had a number of important ramifications for its mandate and operation. 'International Judicial Intervention'[7] was part of a broader trend of interference in the sovereign affairs of states in order to protect human rights – a trend that also gave rise to the doctrine of the 'Responsibility to Protect'. While some welcomed this development, others, as discussed below, objected on political, pragmatic and legal grounds.

The establishment of the ICTY was followed a year-and-a-half later with the establishment of a second ad hoc International Criminal Tribunal for Rwanda (ICTR). The UN Security Council exercising its Chapter VII powers also established

---

6 Madoka Futamura, *War Crimes Tribunals and Transitional Justice: The Tokyo Trial and the Nuremberg Legacy* (Routledge, 2008).

7 This term was first used by David Scheffer, US Ambassador at Large for War Crimes: David J Scheffer, 'International Judicial Intervention' (1996) 102 *Foreign Policy* 32–51.

the ICTR, but, unlike the ICTY, the Government of Rwanda originally requested it, although they later objected to the form it took and the fact that it was based in Arusha, Tanzania, and not in Kigali. The ICTR's mandate was to prosecute persons responsible for violations of international humanitarian law in the territory of Rwanda since 1994, the year in which the genocide took place. Unlike the ICTY, however, which had jurisdiction for war crimes committed in international as well as non-international armed conflict, the ICTR's jurisdiction did not extend to grave breaches committed in international armed conflict. Another significant difference was that the ICTR's Statute, created only 18 months after the ICTY's, nevertheless constituted a leap forward in the development of international law by removing any required nexus with armed conflict for crimes against humanity. Both tribunals have contributed hugely to the development of international criminal law through their extensive jurisdiction, pushing the boundaries of international humanitarian law in important respects, including extending its application to non-international armed conflict and expanding the scope of the crime of genocide, as well as establishing rules and procedures for the prosecution of war crimes, crimes against humanity and genocide.

Arguably the most significant contribution to international criminal law was in providing a precedent, and renewed impetus, for the establishment of a permanent International Criminal Court (ICC). This was unforeseen; as David Forsythe noted, 'What started in 1993 as mostly a public relations ploy, namely to create an international tribunal to appear to be doing something about human rights violations in Bosnia without major risk, by 1998 had become an important global movement for international criminal justice.'[8] The ICC was established in July 1998 with the adoption, by 120 votes to seven (and 21 abstentions), of the Rome Statute of the International Criminal Court, and came into force four years later, with the requisite 60th ratification.[9] Like the ICTY, the ICC is based in The Hague, also home to the International Court of Justice (ICJ).

The Rome Statute was the product of protracted negotiations, followed by five weeks of intensive negotiations in Rome, and reflects the interests of key groups of states, in particular the so-called 'Like-Minded Group' (LMG) led by Canada and Australia. One significant feature of the negotiations at Rome was the influence of a transnational advocacy network of non-governmental organisations (NGOs) on the LMG in particular. The most contentious issues were the applicable law (in particular the crime of aggression), the role and responsibilities of the Prosecutor and the Court's relationship with the Security Council. The LMG

---

8 David P Forsythe, *Human Rights in International Relations* (Cambridge University Press, 2000) 211.

9 As of April 2015, there were 123 State Parties: *ICC at a Glance*, International Criminal Court <https://www.icc-cpi.int/en_menus/icc/about%20the%20court/icc%20at%20a%20glance/Pages/icc%20at%20a%20glance.aspx>.

favoured a strong court with an independent prosecutor, in direct contrast to the Permanent Five (P5) members of the Security Council who wanted the Court to be subordinate to it. A compromise (the so-called Singapore compromise) was found in the form of Articles 13 and 16 of the Statute, which provide for the Security Council to refer cases to the Court and to defer investigations, if it is in the interests of international peace and security. The independence of the prosecutor was also upheld, with the power to initiate investigations on his own initiative (*proprio motu*), subject to the jurisdictional criteria set out in the Statute.

This 'uncomfortable amalgam of near irreconcilable positions' was possibly only because the UK and France voted with the LMG, largely because not to do so would scupper the whole endeavour, to which both were strongly committed in principle. The US, meanwhile, voted against, along with six others (Libya, Israel, Iraq, China, Syria and Sudan), although it later signed up as one of the last acts of the outgoing Clinton Administration, in January 2002. The US position on the ICC has fluctuated since its establishment, from outright opposition and attempts to undermine the Court by later 'unsigning' the Statute, passing the so-called 'Hague Invasion Act' to allow for the 'rescue' of any US citizens detained by the Court, and pressurising others to resist cooperation where US citizens might be concerned, to a later policy of trying to control it via Security Council referrals, to a degree of accommodation.

Although there are circumstances in which a non-Party such as the US might find its citizens brought before the Court (for example, if the Prosecutor launched an investigation into a situation in a State Party, under its territorial jurisdiction, but in which US citizens were involved), the constraints on jurisdiction connected with the ICC's complementarity mandate make it highly unlikely. The ICC has jurisdiction over individuals (not states) for genocide, crimes against humanity and war crimes. The crime of aggression is also within the remit of the Court, but is heavily circumscribed.[10] As with the ad hoc tribunals, this includes those directly responsible for committing the crimes, as well as others who may be indirectly responsible, for example by aiding and abetting, or by failing to prevent and punish a crime under the jurisdiction of the Court.

Significantly, however, the ICC does not exercise universal jurisdiction – i.e. it cannot exercise jurisdiction against anyone, anywhere, for international crimes.[11] As a treaty-based Court, it has jurisdiction only over those States that have expressly consented. As such, the ICC may only exercise jurisdiction on

---

10 The Court may exercise jurisdiction over the crime of aggression, subject to a decision to be taken after 1 January 2017 by a two-thirds majority of State Parties and subject to the ratification of the amendment concerning this crime by at least 30 State Parties.

11 For discussion of universal jurisdiction, see Andrew G Reiter, 'The development of transitional justice', in this volume.

the basis of: a) nationality – the accused is a national of a State Party or a State otherwise accepting the jurisdiction of the Court; or b) territoriality – the crime took place on the territory of a State Party or a State otherwise accepting the jurisdiction of the Court. The only circumstance in which the Court's jurisdiction might extend beyond these bases is when a situation is referred by the Security Council, in which case the ICC has jurisdiction irrespective of the nationality of the accused or the location of the crime, but limited to the terms of the referral. The Court's jurisdiction is also limited to events taking place since 1 July 2002, the date on which the Statute came into force, or, if a State joins the Court after 1 July 2002, the Court only has jurisdiction after the Statute entered into force for that State, unless otherwise agreed.

Even where the Court has jurisdiction, it will not necessarily act. The principle of 'complementarity' provides that certain cases will be deemed inadmissible. Because the ICC's relationship to national courts is horizontal rather than vertical, as was the case with the ICTY and ICTR, it can only exercise jurisdiction in cases where national courts are either unwilling or unable to do so. The ICC thus plays a residual role, whereas national courts are the fora of first resort. It is in this context that the Prosecutor of the Court has maintained that the measure of success for the Court would be an absence, rather than a multitude, of trials. There are a number of issues with complementarity, which we'll explore in more depth below; briefly, it potentially involves the Court in determinations as to the adequacy of national judicial systems and presents a problem for the Court in obtaining cooperation – such that in cases where it has deemed that a State is unwilling to prosecute, it would seem reasonable to assume that the State in question would also be unwilling to cooperate. The other set of constraints on the Prosecutor in determining where to exercise jurisdiction are the thresholds of 'sufficient gravity' and the 'interests of justice'. This both allows for considerable discretion and, as discussed below, also exposes the Prosecutor to criticism given that neither threshold is easily quantifiable.

The other major development in the international criminal justice project was the establishment of 'internationalised' or 'hybrid' courts, with a mix of international and domestic law and personnel, such as the Special Court for Sierra Leone (SCSL), established in 2002, and the Extraordinary Chambers in the Courts of Cambodia (ECCC), which began operations in 2006, or domestic courts with elements of internationalisation such as the insertion of International Judges and Prosecutors (IJPs) in selected categories of cases in Kosovo ('Regulation 64 Panels') and specially constituted internationalised courts established within the domestic judicial system as in Bosnia (Bosnian War Crimes Chambers – BWCC) and in Timor-Leste (Serious Crimes Panels of the District Court of Dili). This new model of international criminal justice was in some ways a reaction to the perceived failings of the ad hoc tribunals, in particular relating to their huge cost, and their failure to engage local constituencies. For example, the SCSL, having learned from the ICTY's mistakes, made a more concerted effort to involve the population by way of outreach activities and benefited from its domestic location, in Freetown (rather than The Hague), yet it too found it difficult to dispel all of the misperceptions surrounding its work.

3.4 Aims and objectives

What, and whom, is international criminal justice for? The preamble to the Rome Statute states the purpose of the ICC thus: 'To put an end to impunity for the perpetrators of these crimes and thus to contribute to the prevention of such crimes.' This translates into primary goals of accountability and deterrence. These purposes are purported also to contribute to broader goals of securing peace and promoting reconciliation in societies riven by violent conflict and egregious violations of human rights. Peace, justice and reconciliation, it was argued, go hand in hand.

The establishment of the ad hoc tribunals drew an explicit link between international criminal justice and international peace and security through the use of a new tool, international criminal justice. The purpose of international criminal justice is also to provide a forum for retributive justice on behalf of the victims, and to establish individual responsibility, not collective guilt. In that sense, international criminal justice is as much for individual victims and survivors as it is for the international community writ large. But some of these goals, and purposes, may be irreconcilable.[12]

In particular, the integration of transitional justice – of which international criminal justice is one of a range of tools – into peace building activities was accompanied by a significant expansion and recasting of the goals ascribed to it, and led to considerable conceptual and analytical muddiness where goals of transitional justice associated with transitions to democracy were conflated with goals associated with transitions to peace. This created a dilemma in which inflated expectations of what international criminal justice might realistically accomplish contrasted with the ever more challenging settings in which it was implemented, in societies riven by decades of conflict and under-development with urgent security and development needs.

Another problematic aspect was the privileging of justice as an end in and of itself. This, according to Jack Snyder and Leslie Vinjamuri's analytic framework, is the approach espoused by 'legalists' who advocate transitional justice based on

---

12 Bronwyn Leebaw, 'The Irreconcilable Goals of Transitional Justice' (2003) 30(1) *Human Rights Quarterly* 95–118.

a 'logic of appropriateness'.[13] For legalists, there are important moral and legal imperatives to pursue some form of accountability. The moral imperative stems from a sense of outrage at the widespread and egregious atrocities committed during many contemporary wars, not merely an unfortunate by-product, but in many cases of genocide and ethnic cleansing, these crimes form part of a concerted strategy. The legal imperative is derived from international treaties and customary international law, specifically the obligation to prevent and punish war crimes, crimes against humanity and genocide.

Snyder and Vinjamuri identify a second set of 'pragmatists', who advocate transitional justice strategies on the basis of a 'logic of consequences'.[14] Notwithstanding any moral and legal imperative, addressing past violations makes 'good political sense'. Pragmatists stress the various means through which transitional justice can contribute to restoring peace, such as establishing individual accountability instead of collective guilt, and thus ending 'cycles of violence' from one generation to the other, deterring future violations by demonstrating an 'end to impunity', establishing a historical record that cannot easily be denied, promoting reconciliation, providing victims with a forum and means of redress, removing and/or side-lining perpetrators, reinforcing and building respect for the rule of law, and capacity-building.[15]

The goal of accountability is linked to the oft-quoted desire to 'end impunity' for massive human rights abuses. It operates in two ways. The first is stressed by proponents of criminal trials, and focuses on the goal of establishing individual criminal responsibility, thus making an individual (and not a group) accountable. By individualising guilt, responsibility is removed from the collective, which can be helpful, it is argued, in situations where blame might be placed on, for example, entire nations or ethnic groups, leading to 'cycles of violence'.

Ensuring accountability and 'ending impunity' is also closely linked to the purported deterrent function of transitional justice. Proponents of criminal trials, in particular, argue that they can play an important role in deterring future abuses. Although there is some anecdotal evidence that investigations and prosecutions underway in some cases may have had a deterrent effect, there is little to show that it has had any more than a very marginal impact, which is not surprising, given the huge gaps in enforcement.

Another claim that is made of international criminal justice is that it contributes to the establishment of a historical record, or a shared narrative, which can comprise a detailed account of the pattern of abuses and the causes of the

---

13 Jack Snyder and Leslie Vinjamuri, 'Trials and Errors: Principle and Pragmatism in Strategies of International Justice' (2003–04) 28(3) *International Security* 5–44.
14 Ibid.
15 See Rachel Kerr and Eirin Mobekk, above n 4.

conflict. Criminal trials construct this record through the introduction of evidence and in the final judgment, but this form of creating history is deeply problematic, as Richard Ashby Wilson has shown, especially because the goal of a trial is to find the guilt or innocence of an individual accused, which doesn't always translate well, especially if narratives are contested.[16] As has been clear in the former Yugoslavia, judgments and trial proceedings have been interpreted in particular ways, mediated by narratives of denial and victimhood to the extent that some of the ICTY's work can be said to have been 'lost in translation'.[17]

Finally, the capacity of international criminal justice to promote reconciliation is regarded as one of its key contributions, but it is also one of the most contentious claims. Some have argued that expanding the mandate beyond justice to include reconciliation and peace is stretching the capacity of criminal justice too far, whereas others argue that if international criminal justice cannot bring reconciliation, what is the point of it? Part of the difficulty stems from the fact that reconciliation, like 'justice' and 'peace', is a contested concept. It could be taken to mean individual reconciliation, with one's own past, or with others, or group and/or societal reconciliation. It may require active repentance from perpetrators seeking forgiveness, or may occur in the absence of such acts, as a result of processes of reintegration and reformation. Like peace, also cast as both a proximate (ending violent conflict) and final (sustainable peace) goal, it is not an end-state but rather a point on a spectrum. Moreover, the goal of retribution or redress stands in contrast to the goal of forgiveness central to interpersonal reconciliation.

3.5 Points of contention and controversy

As the above discussion illustrates, international criminal justice was not without its critics. Some challenged 'international judicial intervention' on political and pragmatic grounds, arguing that it was too selective, politically motivated, potentially destabilising and a waste of scarce resources.[18] Others argued that it unreasonably prioritised retributive over restorative justice, and international over local interests (including those of the victim/survivor communities).

These points of contention have been vigorously debated in the literature on international criminal justice. A recurring theme has been the so-called

---

16 Richard Ashby Wilson, *Writing History in International Criminal Trials* (Cambridge University Press, 2011).

17 Rachel Kerr, 'Lost in Translation: Perceptions of the ICTY in the Former Yugoslavia' in James Gow, Rachel Kerr and Zoran Pajic (eds), *Prosecuting War Crimes: Lessons and Legacies of the International Criminal Tribunal for the Former Yugoslavia* (Routledge, 2013).

18 Snyder and Vinjamuri, above n 13.

'peace vs justice' debate, which can be characterised in a number of different ways. At its core, it boils down to a contest between principle and pragmatism in so far as it revolves around whether the goals of international criminal justice – ensuring accountability and ending impunity – are sufficiently compelling in their own right to warrant mounting international criminal trials, or whether they should be considered not as absolute, but as relative goals in the context of the political context in which international criminal justice operates at both the international and domestic level.

Pragmatic critics argued that transitional justice was at best ineffective, and at worst, detrimental to the task of making and building peace. There is a risk that pursuing justice risks destabilising a fragile peace by targeting the very people on whom peace relies, leading to further violence and abuses. For a new regime, moreover, addressing the past could upset a relatively fragile new order. In post-conflict settings, the dilemma is acute in situations where the very people being pursued to account for their crimes are those on whom a nascent peace agreement depends. This dilemma was cast in stark terms in relation to the former Yugoslavia where one critic warned that pursuing justice 'risks making today's living the dead of tomorrow', by prolonging the conflict.[19] In a country engaged in the process of negotiating the end of a conflict, especially one that has raged for years or even decades, the threat of prosecution might prolong or even reignite conflict. This was the crux of the criticism levelled at the ICC when it refused to lift its indictment of Lord's Resistance Army leader Joseph Kony, in order to facilitate the 2008 Juba peace talks.

In addition to concerns about the potential risks of pursuing international criminal justice in fragile situations, critics point to its inherent shortcomings, both in terms of specific approaches and more generally questioning whether there is any appropriate way of addressing 'radical evil'.[20] Advocates and critics debate the relative merits of different approaches, setting retributive processes such as trials up against restorative processes such as truth commissions and international mechanisms versus domestic/cultural ones, often underpinned by the conviction that local/cultural approaches are somehow inherently superior. Some also stressed the risk of re-traumatising victims, who would prefer simply to forget and move on, or heightening tensions and delaying reconciliation. Rather than being cathartic for victims, testifying at courts and truth commissions can lead to a sense of re-victimisation. Others argued that pursuing justice diverts resources from other pressing needs. In a post-conflict setting with many urgent priorities

---

19 Comment, 'Human Rights in Peace Negotiations' (1996) 18(2) *Human Rights Quarterly* 249–258.
20 Carlos Santiago Nino, *Radical Evil on Trial* (Yale University Press, 1998).

and pressing needs, 'justice is a luxury'.[21] A trenchant criticism of international criminal justice is that it does not represent good value for money. It ought to cost less and deliver more.[22]

Finally, a major challenge to international criminal justice was raised on methodological grounds, based on a lack of evidence that it actually 'worked'. In 2008, the Centre for International Policy Studies (CIPS) at the University of Ottawa conducted a comprehensive review of the transitional justice field, and found that, to date, there was insufficient evidence to support any strong claims about positive or negative impacts.[23] As such, they echoed the views of Harvey Weinstein and Eric Stover who, some years earlier, had argued that 'the primary weakness of writings on justice in the aftermath of war and political violence is the paucity of objective evidence to substantiate claims about how well criminal trials or other accountability mechanisms achieve the goals ascribed to them'.[24] Moreover, as the CIPS report acknowledges, most of what we did know about the effects of transitional justice came from countries that experienced political transitions from authoritarianism to democracy. International criminal justice efforts in post-conflict societies, which are likely to have quite different experiences, may have little in common.[25] Many have echoed CIPS' call for more empirical research to move from a 'faith-based' to a 'fact-based' discussion of impacts, and the field has responded with an array of empirical studies, but a less than satisfactory consensus on the meaning of all of this for policy and practice.

Case study A: International judicial intervention – the ICTY

The dissolution of the Socialist Federal Republic of Yugoslavia (SFRY) in 1991–92 was the proximate cause of a series of conflicts in the territory that, grouped together, made up the Yugoslav War. The conflict began in Slovenia in June 1991, following that country's and Croatia's declarations of independence, moved swiftly to Croatia, and entered its bloodiest and longest phase in Bosnia in April 1992. The war in Bosnia was finally brought to an end with the Dayton Peace Agreement in November 1995. A defining element of the war in the Croatian and Bosnian theatres was the practice of 'ethnic cleansing', involving mass forced population transfers to detention centres, in which detainees were subjected to

---

21 This view was cited by the International Centre for Transitional Justice in 2006, addressing the public perception that the cost of transitional justice is high. See Rama Mani, 'Editorial: Dilemmas of Expanding Transitional Justice, or Forging the Nexus between Transitional Justice and Development' (2008) 2 *International Journal of Transitional Justice* 257.

22 Ibid.

23 Oskar NT Thoms, James Ron and Roland Paris, 'State-Level Effects of Transitional Justice: What Do We Know?' (2010) 4 *International Journal of Transitional Justice* 329–354.

24 Eric Stover and Harvey Weinstein, *My Neighbour, My Enemy: Justice and Community in the Aftermath of Mass Atrocity* (Cambridge University Press, 2008) 4.

25 Thoms, Ron and Paris, above n 23.

torture, rape, sexual assault and other inhumane treatment. In Bosnia alone, it is estimated that around 100,000 people were killed, 7–8,000 of those in a matter of days in Srebrenica in July 1995. The violence in Kosovo in 1998–99 was the Yugoslav War's 'final act'.

The establishment of the International Criminal Tribunal for the Former Yugoslavia (ICTY) was one of a series of measures taken by the international community, and it is notable because it was intended both to contribute to ending the conflict – the Tribunal was established in the midst of the worst of the violence, in May 1993 – and to restoring peace afterwards. In establishing the ICTY as an enforcement mechanism under Chapter VII of the United Nations Charter, the Security Council invoked international criminal justice as a tool of international peace and security. Its mandate was to deliver justice, deterrence and peace.

The ICTY dominated the landscape of transitional justice in the region but after 20 years of operation what has been its contribution? With regard to the first of its goals, delivering justice, the Tribunal can boast tremendous success. As of the time of writing, the Tribunal had almost completed its work, having concluded proceedings for 147 of its 161 accused. Four accused remain on trial and ten are at the Appeals stage. Among its indictees were those at the highest levels of political and military responsibility, including the Bosnian Serb political and military leaders, Radovan Karadžić and Ratko Mladić, and the former President of Serbia (and the FRY), Slobodan Milošević. Its cases reflect the broad sweep of crimes, targeting all groups, and addressing the most notorious examples of ethnic cleansing and even genocide.

A residual impact of this record of judicial success was its impact on the peace process. The Tribunal made a pragmatic contribution through the indictment of certain key individuals (including the Bosnian Serb political and military leadership), which, by ensuring their removal from political and public life, created space for change.[26] The Tribunal also had an impact on rule of law and judicial reform in the region, acting as a catalyst for the creation of specialised war crimes courts in Bosnia, Croatia and Serbia, and transferring evidence and disseminating knowledge and jurisprudence to those courts. Lastly, the Tribunal cites its wider international impact among its achievements. Most significant is its role as a precedent, proving that international criminal justice is viable, and leading to the establishment of other ad hoc international tribunals – and, in July 1998, a permanent International Criminal Court. It has also pioneered a number of significant developments in international criminal law and procedure.

But what of the Tribunal's contribution to building peace? This aspect of the Tribunal's legacy is more ambiguous and difficult to assess. As discussed above, advocates of war crimes trials argued that strategies of ensuring individual accountability (rather than collective guilt) and establishing a historical record

(continued)

---

26 Although there was unease at the time about the wisdom of such a move, in the end the publication of indictments against Radovan Karadžić and Ratko Mladić in July 1995 was instrumental in allowing for a peace agreement to be concluded because it effectively excluded them from the negotiations that led to the Dayton Peace Accords. See Rachel Kerr, *The International Criminal Tribunal for the Former Yugoslavia: Law, Diplomacy and Politics* (Oxford University Press, 2004)

(continued)

would help facilitate processes of reconciliation and thus contribute to building lasting peace. On this measure, the record of the Tribunal is less impressive: while some small signs of progress exist, narratives of denial and victimhood remain deeply entrenched, and attitudes and perceptions of the Tribunal in the region remain largely negative.[27]

Although clearly there is some way to go before the legacy of these trials can be deemed to have played a truly significant role in the process of building lasting peace in the region, there is room for cautious optimism. In particular, the scope of the Tribunal's outreach programme has transformed radically from its first faltering steps, so that it now has the potential to foster real critical engagement with the Tribunal's work. Such a result is critical because unless perceptions of the Tribunal shift over the course of the next few years, its legacy will suffer the consequences.

Case study B: Hybrid justice – the Special Court for Sierra Leone

The civil war in Sierra Leone (1991–2002) was well documented for its 'breathtaking malevolence' and 'unspeakable brutality'. In a decade of conflict, it is estimated that as many as 75,000 civilians were killed and 500,000 were displaced. Civilians were directly targeted with tactics such as amputations of hands, arms, legs and feet, sexual violence, mutilation, forced marriage, forced recruitment of children and wanton destruction of villages and towns. Even before a peace agreement was signed, the nature and extent of the atrocities committed was such that there were demands for some form of accountability. It was felt that without the designation of responsibility – at all levels – and a public acknowledgement of their roles, social structures would remain unsettled, and public faith in the solidity of the peace would be undermined. However, the Sierra Leone judicial system, destroyed by the war and by years of corruption and neglect, lacked the capacity to deal with these crimes.

In June 2000, the President of Sierra Leone, Dr Ahmad Tejan Kabbah, wrote to the Secretary-General asking for UN assistance to set up a court, and on 16 January 2002, an agreement was signed between the UN and the Government of Sierra Leone establishing the Special Court for Sierra Leone in Freetown. The Court's mandate was to prosecute those on all sides – including government forces and the Civil Defense Forces (CDF) – who bore the 'greatest responsibility' for war crimes, crimes against humanity and other violations of international humanitarian law committed in Sierra Leone since 30 November 1996 (the date of the Abidjan Accord). The Special Court was the first 'hybrid' international criminal court to be established – 'hybrid' in the sense that it involved a mixture of international and domestic law and personnel.

Transitional justice in Sierra Leone was also 'hybrid' in the sense that the Special Court operated alongside a Truth and Reconciliation Commission (TRC),

---

27 Kerr, 'Lost in Translation', above n 17.

which occupied the site next door, in Freetown, and was established following the 1999 Lomé Accords, which had offered amnesty to Revolutionary United Front (RUF) leaders, including Foday Sankoh. As such, it was a departure from the model of the ad hoc tribunals for the former Yugoslavia and Rwanda (ICTY and ICTR) on the one hand, and the ICC on the other, and was welcomed by many as a potentially more effective and efficient form of international criminal justice. But the reality was that both the TRC and the Court were under-funded, and their operation alongside one another was not without its problems, manifested in legal and political wrangling.

In total, the Court brought cases against 13 accused. Two were subsequently withdrawn following the deaths of the accused. (Foday Sankoh, Sam Bockarie (leader and battlefield commander of the RUF) and Johnny Paul Koroma (leader of the Armed Forces Revolutionary Council (AFRC)) all died before they could face justice.) The trials of three former leaders of the AFRC, two members of the CDF and of three former leaders of the RUF were completed in Freetown. The trial of former Liberian President Charles Taylor is currently in the Appeal phase in The Hague. In April 2012, Taylor was convicted on all 11 counts of aiding and abetting the commission of crimes against humanity and war crimes in Sierra Leone from 1996 to 2002.

The case has a significant role to play in establishing a record of events. The judgment in the Taylor case puts on record the litany of crimes committed by the RUF and the AFRC, both of which received material support from Taylor as leader of the National Patriotic Front of Liberia (NPFL) and as President of Liberia. These crimes include murder, rape, sexual slavery, outrages on personal dignity, conscription and enlistment of child soldiers, violence to life, health and physical or mental well-being, and other inhumane and cruel treatment. It is to be hoped that the Taylor verdict, in particular, will provide some form of redress for the victims of those crimes, and there is some evidence that it has, in particular for victims of gender-based crimes. According to one observer, the Special Court's judgments, and the Charles Taylor trial in particular, together with the report of the Sierra Leone TRC have helped raise awareness in Sierra Leone about the forms of gender-based violence that took place during the conflict, and this increased attention, coupled with local non-governmental activism, has helped in efforts to secure gender-sensitive law reform, although there is still a long way to go.

But there are also reasons to be circumspect regarding the impact of transitional justice in Sierra Leone. For some, the fact that Taylor was convicted on the lowest threshold of responsibility (aiding and abetting rather than directly ordering or participating in a joint criminal enterprise) dilutes his individual accountability. For others, the trial is viewed as part of an enterprise that is engaged in the imposition of Western values on African states and a form of 'victors' justice' (tied to criticism of the ICC in Africa). This was the critique with which Taylor's supporters in Liberia greeted the verdict, echoed by Taylor in his own statement (in which he accused the Court of being manipulated to suit US interests). In Sierra Leone, although there was jubilation, there were also mixed feelings. While some expressed a wish to move on and the need to focus on other pressing issues, others expressed disappointment that the trial (which was moved to The Hague for security reasons) had not taken place on Sierra Leonean soil.

(continued)

(continued)

These sentiments reflect the conclusions of an evaluation of the impact of the Special Court's outreach programme. In spite of much effort having been expended (especially compared to the early stilted efforts of the ICTY and ICTR), many Sierra Leoneans did not report a sense of engagement with, and ownership of, the process.[28] As was the case in the former Yugoslavia, there was dissonance between local and international expectations of the Court's contribution to restoration of peace and justice in Sierra Leone. Again, the Court's ability to communicate knowledge and understanding about its mandate and processes was somewhat stymied by a relatively hostile and, in some cases, sensationalist, domestic news coverage.

There was also confusion surrounding the respective roles of the Court and the TRC, and a lack of coordination with other aspects, such as DDR and judicial reform, and wider socio-economic problems also became intertwined with issues of the Court's legacy and impacted on perceptions. In a country ranked as the second poorest in the world (UNDP HDI), where literacy levels were low, corruption was endemic, and the justice system was defunct, the demands on international donors and on civil society organisations were high. Socio-economic inequality and corruption, as well as a lack of faith in the rule of law were at the root of the conflict. Although the Truth Commission made a number of very far-reaching recommendations addressing these two factors, most of them have yet to be followed up. A recurrent theme with regard to both mechanisms was that they represented a 'missed opportunity' to address some of these structural causes of violence.

Case study C: The ICC and Libya

As of November 2015, 23 cases in eight situations have been brought before the ICC. Four of those situations have been referred by state parties to the Rome Statute (Uganda, the Democratic Republic of the Congo, the Central African Republic and Mali). The Security Council has referred two cases (Darfur, Sudan and Libya). The Prosecutor opened investigations *proprio motu* in Kenya and Côte d'Ivoire. In addition, the Prosecutor is currently conducting preliminary examinations in respect of Afghanistan, Colombia, Georgia, Iraq (in respect of UK nationals), Guinea, Nigeria, Palestine and Ukraine.

On 26 February 2011, the United Nations Security Council decided unanimously to refer the situation in Libya since 15 February 2011 to the ICC Prosecutor. On 3 March 2011, the ICC Prosecutor announced his decision to open an investigation into the situation in Libya, which was assigned by the Presidency to Pre-Trial Chamber I. On 27 June 2011, Pre-Trial Chamber I issued three warrants of arrest respectively for Muammar Mohammed Abu Minyar Gaddafi, Saif Al-Islam Gaddafi and Abdullah Al-Senussi for crimes against humanity (murder and persecution) allegedly committed across Libya from 15 until at

---

28 Jessica Lincoln, *Transitional Justice, Peace and Accountability: Outreach and the Role of International Courts after Conflict* (Routledge, 2011).

least 28 February 2011, through the State apparatus and Security Forces. On 22 November 2011, Pre-Trial Chamber I formally terminated the case against Muammar Gaddafi due to his death. The two other suspects are not in the custody of the Court.

On 31 May 2013, Pre-Trial Chamber I rejected Libya's challenge to the admissibility of the case against Saif Al-Islam Gaddafi and reminded Libya of its obligation to surrender the suspect to the Court. On 21 May 2014, the ICC Appeals Chamber confirmed the decision of Pre-Trial Chamber I declaring the case against Saif Al-Islam Gaddafi admissible. On 11 October 2013, Pre-Trial Chamber I decided that the case against Abdullah Al-Senussi is inadmissible before the ICC as it was currently subject to domestic proceedings conducted by the Libyan competent authorities, and that Libya is willing and able genuinely to carry out such investigation. On 24 July 2014, the Appeals Chamber unanimously confirmed Pre-Trial Chamber I's decision, declaring the case against Abdullah Al-Senussi inadmissible before the ICC.

3.6 Current position

With the ICTR and ICTY now in their closing stages, the focus of international criminal justice has shifted firmly to the ICC. As of the time of writing, the ICC had opened investigations in eight situations, and a further eight were the subject of preliminary investigations. It had secured only two convictions – those of Thomas Lubanga Dyilo and Germain Katanga, both relating to the Democratic Republic of the Congo (DRC). In 13 years of operation, what are we then to make of its record, and what are its future prospects?

On the one hand, talk of an ICC in crisis might be overstated, or at least wrongheaded. As Mark Kersten has argued, the ICC is, to some extent, always 'in crisis' to the extent that it must always struggle to exist, and to operate in a world dominated by state interests, and in the midst of international politics that do not always coincide with the interests and requirements of the ICC in pursuing its justice mandate.[29] Critics cite the ICC's inability to obtain custody of Sudanese President Omar Al-Bashir, last seen in June 2015 flouting his arrest warrant with the acquiescence of South Africa, a State Party to the Rome Statute, and the collapse of some of the charges in the Kenya cases, most notably those against President Uhuru Kenyatta. In the Uganda case, only one defendant is in custody, the other two, Joseph Kony and Vincent Otti, remain at large. The ICC is also involved in a tussle with the Libyan authorities over the cases of Abdullah Al-Senussi, which was declared inadmissible at the ICC due to proceedings underway at the national level.

Supporters of the ICC, including its Chief Prosecutor, refute these criticisms, arguing that the inability of the Court to influence political decisions, and the

---

29 Mark Kersten, 'Yes, the ICC is in Crisis. It Always Has Been', *Justice in Crisis* (online), 24 February 2015 <http://justiceinconflict.org/2015/02/24/yes-the-icc-is-in-crisis-it-always-has-been/>.

fact that it is subject to them, should not be taken as a sign of weakness, and that, instead, we should look to its symbolic and practical function as an instrument of positive complementarity. That is, the fewer cases on the ICC docket, one assumes, the more that appear in national courts where impunity is combatted more effectively. Moreover, the opening (and re-opening, in 2014) of preliminary investigations in Palestine and Israel, Afghanistan, Georgia, Ukraine and Iraq (the latter concerning allegations of abuse against British forces and the former potentially including scrutiny of Israeli and US conduct, respectively) is testament to the Court's willingness to act impartially and on its own volition, and against the interests of powerful states including erstwhile champions of the Court, such as the UK.

It remains to be seen what the outcome of the current cases will be, and how the ICC will adapt in the years to come. Notwithstanding trenchant criticisms, the ICC's impending move to a shiny new building in The Hague, together with its recent activity, is testament both to an emboldened Chief Prosecutor and a Court that considers itself a permanent fixture on the international political scene. International criminal justice, it seems, is here to stay.

3.7 Summary and conclusion

The experiences of the last 20 years of international criminal justice in particular have been instructive in establishing best practice and – perhaps especially important – in identifying what not to do. Each new initiative was welcomed as offering significant improvements on the last, from the 'shiny new hammer'[30] of the ICTY to the 'magic-bullet' of the ICC. Meanwhile, high-profile trials of notorious defendants such as Slobodan Milošević at the ICTY, Charles Taylor at the Special Court and Saddam Hussein at the Iraqi High Tribunal demonstrated the pitfalls of allowing a soapbox from which these former leaders can denounce the international community, as well as highlighting the impossibility of entirely removing politics from the legal process. The ICC itself suffers from consistent and sustained criticism, including allegations of politicisation, of meddling in peace deals and of being no more than another instrument of Western imperialism in Africa.[31]

Perhaps the most significant and sustained criticism, however, is that international criminal justice has failed to deliver on its goals. International courts have contributed enormously to the development of international criminal law through their now extensive jurisprudence, and the trials themselves have ensured accountability for certain crimes, but their legacy is less auspicious in terms of impact on broader goals of peace and reconciliation. On the other hand it may be unrealistic

---

30 Scheffer, above n 7, 51.
31 Kersten, above n 29.

to expect them to do so. After all, 'If there is any moral in the story . . . it is that international criminal law cannot itself substitute for the ultimately political project of confronting past wrongs and trying to achieve national reconciliation'.[32]

3.8 Discussion and tutorial questions

1) 'There can be no peace without justice'. Do you agree?

2) Is international criminal justice inevitably 'victors' justice'?

3) Would you agree with UN Secretary-General Ban Ki-moon that the ICC is central to a 'new age of accountability'?

4) Which is more important – principle or pragmatism – in assessing the success or failure of international criminal justice?

5) Is the ICC in crisis?

Suggested reading

Bass, GJ, *Stay the Hand of Vengeance: The Politics of War Crimes Tribunals* (Princeton University Press, 2000).

Boas, Gideon, William A Schabas and Michael P Scharf, *International Criminal Justice: Legitimacy and Coherence* (E Elgar, 2012).

Bosco, David, *Rough Justice: The International Criminal Court in a World of Power Politics* (Oxford University Press, 2014).

Drumbl, Mark A, *Atrocity, Punishment and International Law* (Cambridge University Press, 2007).

Dworkin, Anthony, *International Justice and the Prevention of Atrocity* (European Council on Foreign Relations, 2014) ‹http://www.ecfr.eu/page/-/ECFR115_International_Justice_Report.pdf›.

Hazan, Pierre, *Judging War, Judging History* (Stanford University Press, 2010).

Heller, Kevin Jon and Gerry Simpson (eds), *The Hidden Histories of War Crimes Trials* (Oxford University Press, 2013).

International Criminal Court ‹https://www.icc-cpi.int/en_menus/icc/Pages/default.aspx›.

Kerr, R and Eirin Mobekk, *Peace and Justice: Seeking Accountability after War* (Polity, 2007).

Kerston, Mark, *Justice in Conflict* ‹http://justiceinconflict.org/›.

Simpson, Gerry, 'Throwing a Little Remembrance on the Past: The International Court and the Politics of Sovereignty' (1999) 5 *Journal of International Law and Politics* 133–146.

Simpson, Gerry, *Law, War and Crime* (Polity, 2007).

---

32 Tamas Hoffman, 'Trying Communism through International Criminal Law? The Experiences of the Hungarian Historical Justice Trials' in Heller and Simpson, above n 3, 247.

UN Security Council, *The Rule of Law and Transitional Justice in Conflict and Post-Conflict Societies: Report of the Secretary General*, S/2004/616 (23 August 2004).

Suggested film

The Prosecutor (Directed by Barry Stevens, White Pine Pictures, 2010) ‹https://www.nfb.ca/film/prosecutor/trailer/prosecutor_trailer/› [This documentary follows the Chief Prosecutor through the first trials of the newly formed International Criminal Court]).

Bibliography

Comment, 'Human Rights in Peace Negotiations' (1996) 18(2) *Human Rights Quarterly*.

Dockrill, Michael and Barrie Paskins, *The Ethics of War* (London: Duckworth, 1979) p. 266.

Fanthorpe, R. 'Neither Citizen Nor Subject: Lumpen Agency and the Legacy of Native Administration in Sierra Leone' (2001) 100 *African Affairs* 362–86.

Forsythe, David P, *Human Rights in International Relations* (Cambridge University Press, 2000).

Futamura, Madoka, *War Crimes Tribunals and Transitional Justice: The Tokyo Trial and the Nuremberg Legacy* (Routledge, 2008).

Gordon, Gregory S, 'The Trial of Peter von Hagenbach: Reconciling History, Historiography and International Criminal Law' in Kevin Jon Heller and Gerry Simpson, *The Hidden Histories of War Crimes Trials* (Oxford University Press, 2013).

Gow, James, Rachel Kerr and Zoran Pajic (eds), *Prosecuting War Crimes: Lessons and Legacies of the International Criminal Tribunal for the Former Yugoslavia* (Routledge, 2013).

Heller, Kevin Jon and Gerry Simpson (eds), *The Hidden Histories of War Crimes Trials* (Oxford University Press, 2013).

Hoffman, Tamas, 'Trying Communism through International Criminal Law? The Experiences of the Hungarian Historical Justice Trials' in Kevin Jon Heller and Gerry Simpson (eds), *The Hidden Histories of War Crimes Trials* (Oxford University Press, 2013).

International Criminal Court, *ICC at a Glance*, ‹https://www.icc-cpi.int/en_menus/icc/about%20the%20court/icc%20at%20a%20glance/Pages/icc%20at%20a%20glance.aspx›.

Jackson, Robert H., Chief Prosecutor at Nuremberg. International Conference on Military Trials: London, 1945. Report to the President by Mr. Justice Jackson, October 7, 1946. ‹http://avalon.law.yale.edu/imt/jack63.asp› (1 September 2016).

Kelsall, Tim, *Culture under Cross-Examination: International Justice and the Special Court for Sierra Leone* (Cambridge University Press, 2013).

Kerr, Rachel, 'Lost in Translation: Perceptions of the ICTY in the Former Yugoslavia' in James Gow, Rachel Kerr and Zoran Pajic (eds), *Prosecuting War Crimes: Lessons and Legacies of the International Criminal Tribunal for the Former Yugoslavia* (Routledge, 2013).

Kerr, Rachel and Eirin Mobekk, *Peace and Justice: Seeking Accountability after War* (Polity, 2007).

Kerr, Rachel, *The International Criminal Tribunal for the Former Yugoslavia: Law, Diplomacy and Politics* (Oxford University Press, 2004).

Kersten, Mark, 'Yes, the ICC Is in Crisis. It Always Has Been', *Justice in Crisis* (online), 24 February 2015 <http://justiceinconflict.org/2015/02/24/yes-the-icc-is-in-crisis-it-always-has-been/>.

Leebaw, Bronwyn, 'The Irreconcilable Goals of Transitional Justice' (2003) 30(1) *Human Rights Quarterly*.

Lincoln, Jessica, *Transitional Justice, Peace and Accountability: Outreach and the Role of International Courts after Conflict* (Routledge, 2011).

Mani, Rama, 'Editorial: Dilemmas of Expanding Transitional Justice, or Forging the Nexus between Transitional Justice and Development' (2008) 2 *International Journal of Transitional Justice*.

Nino, Carlos Santiago, *Radical Evil on Trial* (Yale University Press, 1998).

Report of the Secretary-General Pursuant to Paragraph 2 of Resolution 808 [on the establishment of an international criminal tribunal], S/25704, 3 May 1993.

Scheffer, David J, 'International Judicial Intervention' (1996) 102 *Foreign Policy*.

Shklar, Judith, Legalism: Law, Morals and Political Trials (Harvard University Press, 1964)

Snyder, Jack, and Leslie Vinjamuri, 'Trials and Errors: Principle and Pragmatism in Strategies of International Justice' (2003–04) 28(3) *International Security*.

Stover, Eric and Harvey Weinstein, *My Neighbour, My Enemy: Justice and Community in the Aftermath of Mass Atrocity* (Cambridge University Press, 2008).

Thoms, Oskar NT, James Ron and Roland Paris, 'State-Level Effects of Transitional Justice: What Do We Know?' (2010) 4 *International Journal of Transitional Justice*.

UN Security Council, *The Rule of Law and Transitional Justice in Conflict and Post-Conflict Societies: Report of the Secretary-General*, S/2004/616 (23 August 2004).

Wilson, Richard Ashby, *Writing History in International Criminal Trials* (Cambridge University Press, 2011).

Chapter 4

Gender and transitional justice

Annika Björkdahl and Johanna Mannergren Selimovic

4.1 Introduction

Today we know that men and women often experience violent conflicts differently and that they suffer human rights abuses, ethnic cleansing, imprisonment and injustices in different ways. Consequently, their needs for redress and justice often diverge, and what constitutes appropriate practices may differ accordingly. To accommodate this, one would expect transitional justice mechanisms to be gender-sensitive. Yet evaluations of past and present transitional justice practices show that they tend to disadvantage women in transitions to peace, justice and democracy. Transitional justice outcomes thus have serious implications for gender relations in post-conflict societies. Given these conditions, gender concerns in relation to transitional justice seek to address the disparities and inequities between men and women when it comes to access to power, opportunities and rights in transitional societies.

J Ann Tickner notes that 'too often women's experiences have been deemed trivial, or important only in so far as they relate to the experiences of men'.[1] This has long been true also for transitional justice. Against this background, the chapter provides a short overview and investigation of gender perspectives on transitional justice. We examine some of the gender implications of the 'transitional' theory of justice. As an analytical tool, gender holds the promise to ask new questions that reveal transitional justice projects as a site of power production. Thus, the project of gendering transitional justice is driven by questions such as: Where are women in transitional justice? Where is gender in transitional justice? Whose justice and justice for whom?

---

1 J Ann Tickner, 'Feminism Meets International Relations: Some Methodological Issues' in Brooke A Ackerly, Maria Stern and Jacqui True (eds), *Feminist Methodologies in International Relations* (Oxford University Press, 2006) 19.

By employing such critical perspectives, we are able to identify gaps in the transitional justice agenda – gendered justice gaps. In this chapter we focus on three gendered justice gaps – the accountability, acknowledgement and reparations gaps – and unmask transitional justice as a site for the long-term construction of a gendered post-conflict order. Although not always recognised, gender is salient in understandings of justice, whether it is (re)distributive, retributive, or restorative justice. Pertinent critique is raised against dominant practices of transitional justice for perpetuating stereotypical gender categories, for not realising its transformative potential, and for failing to address structural injustices, including the subordination of women and the feminisation of poverty in the aftermath of conflict. Furthermore, many transitional justice processes are unable to respond to women's calls for justice, acknowledge women's different experience of violent conflict, counter the persistent culture of impunity for violence against women in times of war and its continuity in times of peace, and recognise women doing justice in informal ways, in marginalised spaces, and through unconventional methods.

The chapter begins by defining and conceptualising the role of gender analysis in transitional justice and what it means to add gender to transitional justice. Then follows a brief historical overview of the policy and practice accomplishments and shortcomings so far. We raise key points of contention, and in the case study of Bosnia-Herzegovina (BiH), zoom in on gendered justice gaps connected to accountability, acknowledgement and reparation.

4.2 A gender perspective on transitional justice

In order to gender transitional justice we need to first grasp the concept of gender, and second, we need to rethink the whole transitional justice project by reading it through a gender lens. Such an undertaking no doubt goes beyond a focus on women. Gender is a complex, multi-layered and contested concept, and we want to acknowledge that there is a difference between 'women' and 'gender'. Gender does not solely mean women, although this is often how gender is understood. Narrow understandings of gender thus risk conflating the notions of 'gender' and 'sex,' making 'gender' mean the same as biological 'sex'. To understand gender in this way limits our ability to capture the dynamic relations of power between the identities of men and women that the concept of gender entails. Instead, our point of departure is that 'gender is a constructed and contingent set of assumptions about female and male roles'.[2] Such a definition of gender brings

---

2 Hilary Charlesworth, 'Feminist Methods in International Law' (1999) 93 *American Journal of International Law* 379.

to the fore the socially and culturally constructed identities of men and women, and women's prevalent subordination to men as key to gender hierarchies.[3] This chapter employs gender as a relational concept that more broadly informs an understanding of power, exclusion and marginalisation.

A gender perspective can inform transitional justice theory about structural relations of power that go largely unrecognised. Gender analysis, then, is a way of exploring the forms that dominance and subordination take in transitional justice processes and how these processes reproduce gender hierarchies in the transitional society. It reveals that un-gendered transitional justice practices tend to re-entrench gender hierarchies by ignoring women or circumscribing their presence to passive victims in need of protection. Furthermore, a gender analysis demonstrates that doing justice is often a conflictual process. Much is at stake as different claims about past injustices stand against each other. Through a gender lens, transitional justice is revealed as a site of power production where the judicial cannot be separated from the political, and where the justice of the victor is implemented. Enriched by a gender approach, the research on transitional justice can begin to investigate the gendered dynamics of transitional justice institutions, processes and mechanisms, and explore the role women and men play in processes of doing justice.

Gender norms shape our ways of thinking about what constitutes a crime, what constitutes a victim and what constitutes appropriate ways of doing justice.[4] A gendered reading of legal accountability measures discloses inherently subjective demarcations of what constitutes a crime and who is regarded as a victim.[5] Thus, gender cannot be accommodated within transitional justice as a descriptive category for victims. It is clear that transitional justice processes, tools, and mechanisms must not perpetuate stereotypical gender categories, but should rather unmask and challenge them. By employing a gender perspective we are able to rethink what constitutes a crime and how that is mediated by gendered norms.

Transitional justice practices aim to right wrongs in the past, institutionalise the rule of law and new juridical and normative frameworks in the present, as well as prevent the recurrence of violence and future harm. A gender perspective assists us in identifying different and continuous dynamics in pre-conflict times, in the midst of conflict, and in post-conflict times. The continuities of violence that spill over from wartime to peacetime demonstrate that gendered transitional justice must be both backward-looking and forward-looking. It is

3 See Marysia Zalewski, 'Well, What Is the Feminist Perspective on Bosnia?' (1995) 71(2) *International Affairs* 338.
4 Susanne Buckley-Zistel and Ruth Stanley, *Gender in Transitional Justice* (Palgrave, 2012).
5 Katherine M Franke, 'Gendered Subjects of Transitional Justice' (2006) 15(3) *Columbia Journal of Gender & Law* 16.

backward-looking in the sense that it seeks to identify and address hitherto ignored abuses in the past, and forward-looking in the sense that it can be a transformative vehicle for women's participation and the building of a gender-just peace. Furthermore, research demonstrates that ensuring greater gender equity is significantly connected to preventing the outbreak and relapse of violent conflict.[6] To gender transitional justice processes helps to connect peace and justice.

4.3 Overview – accomplishments and shortcomings

Over the last 25 years, activists, practitioners and policymakers have worked hard and consistently to address gender inequalities in retributive justice such as prosecutions and trials. This work has developed in conjunction with the efforts that brought UN resolution 1325 (UNSCR1325) into being in 2000.[7] The resolution and concomitant resolutions are part of the UN Women, Peace and Security agenda, and aim to ensure women's involvement in all aspects of post-conflict reconstruction and peacebuilding, as well as redress for the abuse of women's rights. These efforts have resulted in a new normative and judicial framework. Equal rights and equality before the law are now among the basic principles articulated in various international laws on human rights, including the Covenant on Civil and Political Rights, the Covenant on Economic, Social, and Cultural Rights, the Convention on the Elimination of All Forms of Discrimination against Women (CEDAW), the Convention on the Rights of the Child, the Rome Statute of the International Criminal Court, the Basic Principles on the Right to Remedy and Reparation for Victims of Gross Violations of International Human Rights Law and Serious Violations of International Humanitarian Law, the Beijing Declaration and Platform for Action, and UNSCR 1325. These new rights-based frameworks provide important impetus for gendering transitional justice. Thus the aims of the broader transitional justice agenda are anchored in an evolving normative framework. In what follows we give a brief overview of the gains made in the gendering of transitional justice from three central aspects: accountability, reparation and acknowledgement.

---

6 Valerie Hudson, Bonnie Ballif, Mary Caprioli, and Chad F Emmet, *Sex and World Peace* (New York: Columbia University Press, 2014); Mary Caprioli, 'Gender Equality and State Aggression: The Impact of Domestic Gender Equality on State First Use of Force' (2003) 29(3) *International Interactions* 195–214.

7 United Nations Security Council Resolution, SC Res 1325, UN SCOR, 4213th mtg, UN Doc S/RES/1325 (31 October 2000).

4.3.1 Gendering accountability

The first, main focus of the Women, Peace and Security agenda was the specific issue of conflict-related sexual violence. Although historically such violence against women has always been prevalent, it has been ignored, severely under-reported, and normatively understood as a side-effect of war. The issue was taken seriously for the first time through the international legal instruments that developed in the beginning of the 1990s to fight a culture of impunity. Through the consistent pressure and expertise of grassroots women activists, and individuals in elite organisations such as the UN and governments, international law and jurisprudence have made significant advances over the last two decades. Important breakthroughs were made by the two ad hoc tribunals set up to address war crimes in the former Yugoslavia and in Rwanda. The International Criminal Tribunal for the former Yugoslavia (ICTY), established in 1992, was the first tribunal to specifically list war rape as a crime against humanity, and there have been several convictions for gender-based violence, such as, for example, the case against Dragoljub Kunarac in which the accused was convicted for the crime of slavery.[8]

The International Criminal Tribunal for Rwanda (ICTR), established in 1994, followed suit with its 1998 judgement of Jean-Paul Akayesu, a mayor in one of the provinces in Rwanda, who became the first person in an international court to be convicted of rape. In the case it was further recognised that rape formed a significant part of the Rwandan genocide, and also for the first time rape and other gender-based violence were identified as crimes against humanity.[9]

The permanent International Criminal Court (ICC) with a seat in The Hague has built upon the work of the two ad hoc tribunals. The treaty that established the court and governs it, the Rome Statute, refers to gender-based violence as a possible war crime. This was the first time the term 'gender' was used and defined in an international criminal law treaty. However, opinions vary widely about the definition of 'gender' adopted in the Rome Statute, and include some sharp criticism. Some critics describe it as 'narrow',[10] and having 'limited trans-formative edge',[11] thus incapable of transforming gender inequality, challenging gender hierarchies and establishing gender equality. Still, the Court provides a

---

8 *Prosecutor v Kunarac, Kovac and Kukovic* (International Criminal Tribunal for the Former Yugoslavia, Trial Chamber, Case No. IT-96-23-T&IT-96-23/1-T, 22 February 2001) <http://www.icty.org/x/cases/kunarac/tjug/en/ kun-tj010222e.pdf>.

9 *Prosecutor v Akayesu* (International Criminal Tribunal for the Former Yugoslavia, Trial Chamber I, Case No. ICTR-96-4-T, 2 September 1998) <http://unictr.unmict.org/sites/unictr.org/files/case-documents/ictr-96-4/trial-judgements/en/980902.pdf>.

10 Brenda Cossman, 'Gender Performance, Sexual Subjects and International Law' (2002) 15 *CAN. J.L.* and *JURIS.* 281, 283.

11 Hilary Charlesworth and Christine Chinkin, *The Boundaries of International Law: A Feminist Analysis* (Manchester University Press, 2000) 335.

more detailed definition of gender-based violence, which includes not only rape but also sexual slavery, enforced pregnancy, enforced sterilisation and enforced prostitution. Thus, article 7(3) of the Rome Statute has gender-sensitivity built into its structural and discursive logic.

The developments in international law have no doubt broken new ground and laid a solid, legal base. Yet actual convictions are few and scattered, especially when read in conjunction with the continued prevalence of sexual violence in conflict. The advances risk remaining isolated at the international level as it has proved troublesome to make gender-sensitive legislation move into local and national courts, which arguably more directly affect women's lives than geographically distant international courts. Further, the majority of victims in post-conflict countries – women as well as men – do not have access to formal institutions but instead must seek justice in traditional or informal courts where patriarchal norms tend to be entrenched. It is not uncommon that rape is treated not as a criminal act but as a problem that should be dealt with informally within the family. This might mean 'solving' the issue by forcing the woman to marry the person who raped her.[12]

Hence widespread impunity for conflict-related sexual violence continues, and the gap between the number of convictions and estimations of violence is staggering. Insights are growing that it is not just a matter of getting the right legislation and jurisprudence in place. It is also important to consider what possibilities women have to seek justice and to take active part in justice processes. This is a central issue in the gender policy adopted by the ICC in 2014 under the auspices of the prosecutor of the ICC, Fatou Bensouda, and developed in conjunction with a network of civil society actors. The policy has a two-fold aim – to strengthen the capacity of the prosecutor to investigate perpetrators and also, importantly, to integrate a gender perspective in all the operations of the Court.[13] In the work of the ICTR and the ICTY, it has become increasingly clear that witness protection schemes are inadequate for women who take considerable risks to testify, and who often stand alone without support from their own communities; also that there is a lack of psychosocial support for dealing with the particular traumas associated with sexual violence. An integrated gender perspective highlights such failings and identifies impediments to women's possibilities to take part in legal proceedings. It helps to ask crucial and concrete questions such as: Do witnesses

---

12 Nahla Valji, *A Window of Opportunity: Making Transitional Justice Work for Women* (October 2012) United Nations Entity for Gender Equality and the Empowerment of Women <http://www. unwomen. org/~/media/Headquarters/Attachments/Sections/Library/Publications/2012/10/06B-Making-Transitional-Justice-Work-for-Women.pdf>.

13 Office of the Prosecutor, 'Sexual and Gender-Based Crimes' (Policy Paper, International Criminal Court, 5 June 2014) <https://www.icc-cpi.int/iccdocs/otp/OTP-Policy-Paper-on-Sexual-and-Gender-Based-Crimes--June-2014. pdf>.

have to travel a long way to reach courts to give testimony – journeys that may come with grave security risks? Do women have to leave their children unattended, and does this hinder them from witnessing? Do they have access to their own funds to pay for a bus ticket? In the end such practical concerns deeply affect possibilities for ending impunity for gender-based violence.

4.3.2 Gendering reparations

In the 2011 United Nations Secretary-General's Report on the Rule of Law and Transitional Justice in Conflict and Post-Conflict Societies, reparation is singled out as the 'most victim-centred justice mechanism available'.[14] The shift from a focus on perpetrators to the needs of victims holds the potential to redress the complex and diverse gendered experiences and violations of both men and women. While there is growing knowledge of how women and men experience conflicts in different ways and often have different needs for reparation, there is a lot of work to be done when it comes to designing reparations programmes so that they redress women more fairly and efficiently. Recommendations and legislation about measures for redress are often an outcome of truth commissions and other public hearings. Gendered analyses and recognition of women's needs for redress have moved to the top of the agenda in these fora, yet we can see that the actual implementation of recommendations remains scattered and inadequate. When it comes to funding, compensation to women victims is not prioritised in the bleak socio-economic situation in post-conflict societies.

Reparation holds the potential to address the full scope of violations of a gendered nature and understand the issue of conflict-related sexual violence in conjunction with other losses from which women disproportionally suffer. These include gendered consequences of forced displacement, disease and poverty as a consequence of the conflict. Reparation schemes can help them get justice and improve their post-conflict situation. Yet without knowledge about gender dynamics in the societies in question, reparation schemes may exacerbate injustices. For example, in some settings the paying of large one-time compensation to women may be detrimental to them, as they may not get to keep the money for themselves. Here, agencies have sometimes opted for pension schemes or support in setting up income-generating projects as a means of compensation.[15] Again, a gender analysis may also reveal that practical obstacles can seriously hinder women's access to justice schemes, such as continued levels of insecurity.

---

14 *The Rule of Law and Transitional Justice in Conflict and Post-Conflict Societies: United Nations Secretary-General's Report*, UN Doc S/2011/364 (12 October 2011) 8 <http://www.un.org/en/ga/search/view_doc.asp?symbol=S/2011/634>.

15 Ruth Rubio-Marín, 'Reparations for Conflict-Related Sexual and Reproductive Violence: A Decalogue' (2012) 19(1) *William & Mary Journal of Women and the Law* 72.

Concerning the specific issue of conflict-related sexual violence, reparation programmes are an opportunity to couple the global fight to end impunity for perpetrators of sexual violence with locally grounded victim-centred attention to compensation. Medical services providing, for example, fistula operations, psychosocial help, and monetary compensations are pointed out as essential parts of a comprehensive reparations programme.

In line with the UNSCR1325 focusing on women's participation, reparation schemes are also opportunities for acknowledging and strengthening civil society networks that engage with redress and compensation. In societies shattered by conflict, such organisations have often taken on the burden of providing psychosocial support, setting up microcredit schemes that can help women build up economic independence, and organising for just compensation. This is yet another aspect of the transformative, forward-looking potential of reparation as part of transitional justice. Channelling collective compensation through local groups may strengthen involvement of civil society groups, and strengthen voices and women's engagement in society. Such reparations would allow 'survivors to travel the road from victims to agents of change'.[16] Strengthening women's agency in these matters is key to building a more gender-just peace from which both men and women may benefit.[17] The use of collective compensation is a way of protecting women who may be harmed by exposure.

4.3.3 Gendering acknowledgement

For the above measures to be conducive to the long-term building of a gender-just peace, a change of norms is needed. Only legislation or compensation is not enough, as many victims of sexual violence continue to suffer from ostracisation, women's and men's experiences of war are not taken equally into consideration, and many women experience that their suffering is shrouded in silence.[18] Among the established transitional justice mechanisms, truth commissions are considered a potentially effective tool for breaking silences, providing acknowledgement and ultimately changing norms. In reality, women's experiences have often been sidestepped. The first truth commission to include a gender perspective was South Africa's Truth and Reconciliation Commission, which actively encouraged women to come forward and testify. But the questions and expectations at the hearings tended to reduce women to their role as wives or mothers, and their testimonies consequently centred around the suffering of their husbands or sons,

---

16 Ibid 97.
17 Annika Björkdahl and Johanna Mannergren Selimovic, 'Gendered Justice Gaps in Bosnia-Herzegovina' (2014) 15 *Human Rights Review* 201.
18 Jennie E Burnet, *Genocide Lives in Us: Women, Memory, and Silence in Rwanda* (University of Wisconsin Press, 2012).

while their own experiences were ignored. Concomitant truth commissions have taken stock of the South African experience and, with varying success, tried to encompass women's voices and concerns. But statistics indicate that women seldom consider truth commissions to be safe places for giving testimonies, especially on sexual violence. In the Liberian Truth Commission only a handful of such statements were given – yet independent surveys showed that about 80 per cent of the women in the regions concerned had been subjected to such violence.[19] As discussed above in relation to criminal courts, taking on the role of the witness is fraught with uncertainty and the risk of deepening ostracisation. The need to streamline gender awareness all through operations also holds true for truth commissions.

Nonetheless, just like reparations schemes, the work of truth commissions and public hearings hold the potential to open up a discussion of structural change, and in some cases the truth commissions have taken this challenge on board. In Sierra Leone, for example, the report of the Truth and Reconciliation Commission provided a gender analysis, noted structural causes of the war, and in its recommendations pushed for radical reform in order to achieve a gender-just peace.[20]

Beyond truth commissions there are other means for state authorities to engage in acknowledgement. One such mechanism is official apologies from the state and/or its bodies such as the police or military, which could potentially have a powerful impact, both for individual victims' sense of acknowledgement, and also for broader change of societal norms. To get 'just' monetary compensation is often not considered enough by victims if not accompanied by formal and public acknowledgement. Another mechanism concerns memorialisation practices and sites for collective remembering, such as monuments, memorials and museums. What is collectively remembered and forgotten after war is typically informed by gender stereotypes. If women are commemorated at all, they are usually there as objects to be 'saved' – a one-dimensional image of the female victim that does not allow for any commemoration of women in any other roles, be it as agents of peace, as soldiers, or indeed as perpetrators.

Despite facing opposition or disinterest, many organisations have been vocal in breaking taboos, engaging in advocacy and persistent lobbying in ways that defy the stereotyping of women as passive victims. Victim and survivor organisations have engaged in debates over what transformative, gender-just peace may entail for both men and women, and they have secured funds and support for victims and survivors, and provided reparations when the state has failed to do so.

---

19 Nahla Valji, above n 12, 11–12.
20 Ibid 11.

4.4 Identifying gender-just gaps and points of contention

On a theoretical level a great number of questions remain unresolved, and it is pertinent to problematise some of the assumptions and outcomes of research so far. One issue under theoretical debate concerns the intense focus on conflict-related sexual violence. The efforts to break the impunity for these crimes and unveil the extensive harm suffered by women paradoxically risks cementing conservative gender roles of women as victims and men as perpetrators. This interest has been, and is, necessary in order to counter the historical neglect of women's war experiences, yet arguably a 'hyper-attention' to rape may reduce women's experiences to a sexual dimension.[21] Other aspects of transitional justice, such as reparations for social and economic harms, risk being side-lined if attention to sexual violence crimes is not part of a broader agenda of gender-sensitive reparations. Reparation programmes are usually not designed with an explicit gender dimension, which would mean including compensation to women as well as an understanding of the wider impact on gender roles that reparation programmes may have. Feminist activists and scholars continue to point out that post-conflict societies often fail to do justice to the victims of conflict-related sexual violence, and the need to redress women more fairly and efficiently.

The intense focus on women victims goes hand in hand with one of the unexplored caveats in transitional justice: male victims of rape and other types of gender-based violence. In general we know very little about the scope of conflict-related sexual violence against men, and the subject seems highly taboo and shrouded in shame.[22] When testimonials in courts or truth commissions reveal violence against men in the form of, for example, genital mutilation or enforced intercourse, it is common that this violence is not labelled as 'sexual'. There are many vocal women's organisations working to help women victims, but hardly any civil society actors focusing on male victims, thus deepening the sense of shame and stigma.[23] Importantly, sexual violence against both men and women reinforces patriarchal patterns of male domination and female submission. Male victims have most commonly been subject to male violence, and the sexual violence may be performed in order to reduce them to feminised victims and strip them of masculinity, according to the logic of detrimental and conservative gender stereotypes.

---

21 Alice M Miller, 'Sexuality, Violence Against Women, and Human Rights: Women Make Demands and Ladies Get Protection' (2004) 7(2) *Health & Human Rights*, cited in Ruth Rubio-Marín, above n 15, 73.

22 Dubravka Zarkov, *The Body of War* (Duke University Press, 2007).

23 United Nations High Commissioner for Refugees, *Working with Men and Boy Survivors of Sexual and Gender-Based Violence in Forced Displacement* (July 2012) United Nations <http://www.unhcr.org/refworld/ pdfid/5006aa262.pdf>.

Recently, critical questions have been raised about the invisibility of women as perpetrators of war crimes. The conceptual lens of gender-sensitive transitional justice tends to zoom in on women's harms and suffering of injustices during conflict, and attempts to identify gendered tools and mechanisms in order to respond to women's calls for justice and to right past wrongs. This is clearly an important leap forward for transitional justice, but it also perpetuates patriarchal understandings of gender roles where women are victims and men are perpetrators.[24] Female perpetrators are obscured and their crimes often remain unpunished. Recent feminist research now unpacks these stereotypical gender categories, and raises questions about when women become perpetrators, why, and under what conditions. This research seeks to make visible women who employ violence or facilitate the conditions for the perpetration of violence, their crimes and their reception by society. The ICTY verdict against Biljana Plavšić, former President of the Bosnian entity Republika Srpska, for crimes against humanity, and the ICTR verdict against Pauline Nyiramasuhuko, the former Rwandan Minister of Family and Women Affairs, for genocide, are definitive examples of indirect violence on a genocidal scale. They reveal that women at times, and under certain circumstances, depart from the role as passive, fragile and innocent victims and become perpetrators.

Another set of questions concerns the tendency in transitional justice to compartmentalise the harms suffered during the conflict, thus ignoring the gendered continuities of violence[25] across conflict and post-conflict social and political orders. In the above outline it was indicated that peace does not always bring security to women. These dynamics need to be better understood in order to deepen our understanding of the role transitional justice can play for post-conflict transformations. Impunity norms continue even after transitional justice has been implemented and, while violence in the public sphere is selected for accountability, violence committed in the private sphere is ignored. How, then, can transitional justice mechanisms be made relevant to women who continue to suffer from violence and insecurity in the post-conflict period? Such critical thinking opens up a critique of the dichotomy between 'private' and 'public', and 'before' and 'after' violence.

The search for more inclusive transitional processes has brought a growing interest in community-based transitional justice processes. Many gains can be made from more locally grounded approaches. The Gacaca Courts, a local judicial body

---

24 Laura J Shepherd, 'Introduction: Rethinking Gender, Agency and Political Violence' in L Åhäll and LJ Shepherd (eds), *Gender, Agency and Political Violence* (Palgrave, 2012); Laura Sjoberg and Caron E Gentry, *Mothers, Monsters, Whores: Women's Violence in Global Politics* (Zed Books, 2007).
25 Cynthia Cockburn, *The Line: Women, Partition and the Gender Order in Cyprus* (Zed Books, 2004).

in Rwanda that tried over one million suspected '*génocidaires*' is one well-known and increasingly discussed tool of transitional justice. A critical, gender-informed approach reveals that bottom-up processes may at times privilege exclusionary and conservative politics and values, as noted in the example above, concerning how rape has been dealt with in traditional courts. Support to such informal institutions may thus bring gender implications that so far remain largely unexplored.[26] At the same time, external criticism is often rejected in order to safeguard 'traditional' values. This argument is valid if one considers 'traditional' practices as static and incapable of change, but an alternative view on such practices as always evolving and non-static opens up a transformative dialogical path. Further, external donors who accept gender inequality in the name of tradition should seriously consider why '(w)omen's rights continue to be yielding rights'.[27]

There is also a need to think critically about assumptions on the role played by commemoration, truth commissions and other mechanisms to enforce norms, build knowledge of the past and construct shared narratives of the past. Far from smooth processes towards reconciliation, such struggles around what is to be remembered and what is to be forgotten are highly gendered processes whereby power relations are produced and maintained. In many post-conflict societies, peace comes with a conservative backlash for women, and we need to more deeply understand the dynamics whereby gender identities are being reconstructed, reconfigured and redefined through interactions between the transitional justice discourse and nationalism, culture and religion. So far, transitional justice mechanisms have done little to put forward alternative readings of women's and men's roles in society, and have had only limited impact on cultures of shame and gendered silences. Going beyond established mechanisms for acknowledgement may be one path towards a more multi-dimensional rendering of women's and men's roles and experiences of war. A welcome task for transitional justice research would be to widen the scope of investigations to include also the narratives constructed in the arts, in media and in popular culture. These arenas may be far more important than truth commissions for challenging misogynist norms and practices.[28]

---

26 Catherine O'Rourke, 'The Shifting Signifier of "Community" in Transitional Justice: A Feminist Analysis' (2008) 23(2) *Wisconsin Women's Law Journal* 269.

27 Sirkku K Hellsten, 'Transitional Justice and Aid' (Working Paper No. 2012/06, UNE-WIDER, January 2012) 19.

28 Laura McLeod, Jovana Dimitrijević and Biliana Rakočević, 'Artistic Activism, Public Debate and Temporal Complexities: Fighting for Transitional Justice in Serbia' in Peter D Rush and Olivera Simić (eds) *The Arts of Transitional Justice: Culture, Activism, and Memory after Atrocity* (Springer, 2014) 25–42; Catherine Ramírez-Barat (ed), *Transitional Justice, Culture and Society: Beyond Outreach* (International Center for Transitional Justice and Social Science Research Council, 2014); Vikki Bell, *The Art of Post-Dictatorship: Ethics and Aesthetics in Transitional Argentina* (Routledge, 2014).

Stories emerging from film makers or artists make space for a more multi-dimensional understanding not only of harms suffered by women, but also of women as agents. One such film is *Grbavica: Esma's Secret*, directed by Jamila Žbanić, in which a resourceful woman in post-war BiH navigates the silences around war rape and confronts her own secrets.[29] To trace such agency in mechanisms for redress, not only offers women a reparative sense of recognition as victims as well as the possibility of being active participants in political and social transformation. Such fictional stories encourage further analysis of cultural engagements as a potentially fruitful and little-explored aspect of transitional justice in a broad sense.

In sum, transitional justice should not only be understood as a backward-looking tool for dealing with war crimes, but as a forward-looking opportunity for larger societal transformation. Searching for gender in transitional justice processes provokes new questions concerning its transformative power. Can it affect social and economic inequality? Can it change hierarchies and norms? The following case study analyses the multi-dimensional transitional justice process in BiH from such a perspective.

Case study: Gendered justice gaps in Bosnia-Herzegovina

During the 1992–1995 war between Bosniaks, Bosnian Croats and Bosnian Serbs, Bosnia-Herzegovina (BiH) witnessed large-scale violence and war crimes, ethnic cleansing and displacement, mass rapes and other forms of sexual violence directed against women, men and children. The BiH transitional justice process has been slow and arduous, and constantly hampered by the ethnonationalist centrifugal powers with little agreement on the past, present or future. The transitional justice process has moved from being mostly an external affair with the ICTY as its central mechanism to an internal domesticised process at the War Crimes Chamber of Bosnia's State Court. The new National Strategy for War Crimes Processing aims to process all war crimes until 2023. The strategy is complemented by the Transitional Justice Strategy, which is in its draft stage and focuses on truth seeking, reparations and reform of institutions.[30]

Despite the fact that BiH has an institutional structure for gender mainstreaming, most of the transitional justice programmes are not gender-sensitive. It is clear that the legal framework of BiH has not adequately addressed the issue of the gendered gaps concerning accountability, acknowledgement and

(continued)

29 *Grbavica: Esma's Secret* (Directed by Jamila Žbanić, Tanja Aćimović, 2006).
30 There is also a state-level law on Missing Persons, and in its draft stages is a programme of assistance for women victims of war rape, sexual violence and torture 2013–2016.

(continued)

reparation. Public awareness and interest, as well as overall social status of the survivors of crimes related to sexual violence in conflict, is at a low level. The phenomenon of conflict-related sexual violence is still perceived as a private matter, even though it is formally recognised as a public problem and a human rights issue. The survivors of conflict-related sexual violence are still not sufficiently protected, and their rights guaranteed by the Bosnian laws are not fully respected. The high level of violence registered in present day BiH, partly manifested in increased and more severe cases of domestic violence, can to a certain extent be traced to the experience of violence during the conflict.

Gender and accountability

A core aspect of transitional justice in BiH, as in many post-conflict societies, is the legal accountability mechanisms set up in order to end impunity, increase security, and change values through the prosecution of individual war criminals. The accountability process in BiH has to a large degree been defined by the ICTY, which began its proceedings in 1992 when war was still ongoing. The convictions for rape as a crime against humanity in the ICTY have been seminal for the development of international law, and some key individuals have been convicted. Nevertheless, the general recognition of these crimes in BiH has overall been very low, partly because the ICTY's verdicts have been used by ethnonationalist entrepreneurs to entice divisionism and the tribunal's work is therefore read as inherently biased.[31] As the ICTY now moves to a close, the domestic legal system in BiH is taking over through the War Crimes Chamber of Bosnia's State Court, as well as courts at the subnational entity levels. A gender analysis of the court's work so far raises serious concerns. The domestic system has generated only a couple of convictions and a handful of ongoing trials, and the legal framework is inconsistent with international standards and jurisprudence of international courts. Prevailing insecurities, partly due to the impunity of war crimes, means that women who do participate take certain risks. Several witnesses have been threatened, and programmes for witness protection are either non-existent or very marginal. It is clear that criminal justice provides women not just with relief, but also pain as they have to revisit past sufferings. By coming forward to testify, Bosnian girls and women may bring social shame on themselves and their family. Whatever good may come out of the ordeal is offset by the risks of being met with incredulity, being blamed for the rape or having their experiences trivialised. At the same time, it is noticeable that the women who, despite these obstacles, decide to come forward and testify, do it out of a strong sense of wanting to make a difference and contribute as agents of change towards a peace that brings security and acknowledgement for all. In a rare interview-based report on women witnesses, it is noted that the strongest reasons among women and girls for giving testimony were 'to make the perpetrator accountable for what he did and to see

---

31 Johanna Mannergren Selimovic, 'Challenges of Postconflict Coexistence: Narrating Truth and Justice in a Bosnian Town' (2015) 36 *Political Psychology* 231–242. Jelena Subotić, *Hijacked Justice: Dealing with the Past in the Balkans* (Cornell University Press, 2009).

him punished, to prevent other women and girls from being raped, and to tell what really happened'.[32]

Gender and acknowledgement

While the particular harms suffered by women in the Bosnian war – as rape victims – have been turned into a global, emblematic image of that war, these experiences have been silenced in the national and local context, only invoked in the abstract as a symbol of the Bosniak nation's collective hurt and suffering. Thus, we find that there is an important gendered acknowledgement gap. This gap could be addressed if acknowledgement practices were to provide a space for women victims and acknowledge harms suffered such as war rapes in infamous rape camps, like the one at the Vilina Vlas Hotel in Višegrad.[33] But the ethnonationalist divisionism that continues to haunt BiH two decades after the end of the war means that plural accounts of the past are not accepted, and that contentions over war crimes are constantly refuelled. Truth commissions have been a popular tool in many transitional societies, but it has proved difficult to establish such a commission in the deeply politically and socially fractured society of BiH. Instead, commemoration practices and memory discourses have become important as means of acknowledging the past. In these practices and discourses, women's experiences of injustices and harms, but also their agency, are often excluded, marginalised or forgotten in the memory work and commemoration practices on all 'sides'. Military 'war heroes' are celebrated, and women are written out of the post-war narratives. This is reflected in the continued denial of the rape camps and in the contestation concerning the verdicts of war rapes delivered by the ICTY, despite the fact that the tribunal has been seminal in stating that conflict-related sexual violence may constitute a crime against humanity. Public silence therefore still engulfs the rape camps in BiH, and claims for acknowledgement are interpreted as part of ethnonationalist reconfigurations of the political. According to the same logic, the interethnic work that women have performed as peacebuilders is met with suspicion and opposition. Such attempts to 'build bridges' may paradoxically be perceived as a threat by those who continue to regard 'the other side' with suspicion and believe separation is necessary in order to prevent war from breaking out again.

Nonetheless, critical voices that challenge the status quo have found other arenas for critical debate. The arts and popular culture have developed into alternative realms for raising the concerns that formal institutions have

(continued)

---

32 Medica Mondiale, "'. . . and that it does not happen to anyone anywhere in the world": The Trouble with Rape Trials – Views of Witnesses, Prosecutors and Judges on Prosecuting Sexualised Violence during the War in the Former Yugoslavia' (Medica Mondiale, December 2009) 52.

33 Olivera Simić and Zala Volcic, 'In the Land of Wartime Rape: Bosnia, Cinema and Reparations' (2015) 2(2) *Griffith Journal of Law and Human Dignity* 378–396; Zala Volcic and Olivera Simić, 'Geographies of Crime and Justice in Bosnia and Herzegovina' in Annika Björkdahl and Susanne Buckley-Zistel (eds), *Spatializing Peace and Conflict: Mapping the Production of Places, Sites and Scales of Violence* (Palgrave, 2016).

(continued)

failed to raise. Films such as *Grbavica: Esma's Secret*, depicting a rape victim who deals with post-war life in Sarajevo as a resourceful but struggling single mother, and the short documentary film *Red Rubber Boots*[34] about a mother's ceaseless mourning as she searches excavation sites for remains of her lost child, are interesting examples. The international film *In the Land of Blood and Honey*,[35] which frames the topic of the rape camps with a love story across ethnic borders, sparked a lot of controversy, which in itself opened up a debate on the voice of rape victims, raising contentious questions around who could speak for them, and who had the right to control their stories.[36] These fictional stories have complicated and challenged the narrow role for women in the post-conflict context. Clearly, we need to look beyond acceptable or 'appropriate' victimhood for women, and these unconventional ways of acknowledging harms can contribute to expanding the transitional justice agenda.

Gender and reparations

The gendered reparation gap that we notice in BiH is caused by a gender bias inherent in many rights systems, and magnified by the absence of women in the design and implementation of reparation programmes. Reparation is recognised as the transitional mechanism that can make the most concrete difference for victims. It includes a diversity of measures with far-reaching effects on societies and individual lives, including individual economic compensation, collective projects of reconstruction, as well as provisions for victims' access to education, health services and pensions. Reparations can address social and economic dimensions of violence such as the feminisation of poverty that war often brings. Contrary to expectation, reparations have played a negative role in reconciliation processes in BiH. First, determining who is a victim and who is a perpetrator is a deeply contested process. Recognition of victimhood is highly political as it is viewed as a micro negotiation of the nature of the war, and it has socio-economic consequences, as identified victims are eligible claimants for reparations. In BiH, different victim groups such as associations for camp inmates, relatives of missing persons, and women subjected to sexual violence are divided along ethnic lines making it difficult to join forces and advocate for state-level reparations programmes. Second, reparations have also divided victims and survivors within the ethnic communities. As a consequence, victims of conflict-related sexual violence have unintentionally been pitched against camp survivors. Thus, that victims/survivors of conflict-related sexual violence should deserve reparations is not all that is at stake in reparations for harms suffered. Further, state-reparations programmes are insufficient, and women organisations must step in to deliver reparations such as medical care, psychotherapy, trauma treatment and various other approaches to healing, while promoting gender awareness and addressing domestic violence – so called 'everyday rape'. These efforts

---

34 *Crvene Gumene Čizme* (Directed by Jasmila Žbanić, Deblokada, 2000).
35 Directed by Angelina Jolie, GK Films, 2011.
36 Valerie Hopkins, '"Angelina Jolie Touched Our Souls": Bosnian Rape Victims Have Their Say', *The Guardian* (online), 15 December, 2011 <http://www.guardian.co.uk/film/filmblog/2011/dec/15/angelina-jolie-bosnia-rape-victims>. Accessed 16 August 2016.

demonstrate that women in BiH engage with transitional justice both as subjects and objects.

Lessons learned from BiH

The three gendered justice gaps have unmasked transitional justice as a site for the long-term construction of the gendered post-conflict order. The gendered justice gaps in BiH point to women's presence, participation and agency in 'doing justice', and illustrate that women engage with the transitional justice project both as objects and subjects. The analysis has brought to the fore a number of paradoxes illustrating women's sense of injustice and the failure to meet their calls for justice. First, the number of war crime cases that involve sexual violence are extremely low; all the while the fight against impunity remains a top priority. Security issues remain a problem for witnesses in the domestic court system, and it is clear that the international gains concerning the criminalisation of conflict-related sexual violence are not made permanently, but under constant negotiation. Second, the post-war narratives marginalise women's experiences, as victims but also as combatants, perpetrators and peacemakers. Third, the victims of conflict-related sexual violence remain socially and economically marginalised, and there have been no comprehensive reparations programmes to redress the human rights violations. Fourth, complicated legal frameworks, institutional complexity and the absence of rights for victims of wartime rape have impeded access to care, despite awareness that unhealed war traumas lead to deterioration of survivors' wellbeing and health. Fifth, state service for victims of conflict-related sexual violence has largely been absent, and in the meantime women's organisations have stepped in to assist the victims. In BiH, as in many other places, a gender-just peace thus remains a distant goal. The gendered accountability gap, acknowledgement gap and reparations gap remain, and they seem to reinforce each other, as do the patriarchal, religious and nationalist discourses that impede efforts to address these gaps.

4.5 Conclusion

Research has only begun to investigate how and why the multi-faceted transitional processes develop along exclusionary trajectories that do not overcome gender inequality, but may even exacerbate it. Many caveats remain – for example, we know little of the impact of such mechanisms as vetting, official policies of apology, and the societal remembering and forgetting through remembrance practices. Reparation as a tool for transitional justice needs to be closely analysed to understand how it affects women's socio-economic position. Also, there is a need to trace how the intense focus on sexual crimes might have counterproductive effects on wider questions of gender justice. Interactions and friction between different transitional justice mechanisms, as well as actors and stakeholders – international, national and local – within the same post-conflict context have hardly been studied; a lacuna of the transitional justice literature at large.

Most importantly, a gendering of transitional justice offers the possibility to rethink basic ideas of transitional justice. It generates some crucial questions to ask of the transitional justice project in its backward- and forward-looking dimensions: what were the gender relations that existed before the conflict? What were the specific experiences of violence for men and women? How can they be addressed, and what consequences do these measures have on men's and women's lives? How does the conflict affect present-day gender relations?

Through such explorative work, transitional justice processes can help improve gender relations and work towards an emancipatory, gender-just peace where the peace dividend is realised in the everyday. Clearly, such peace is not simply the reconstruction of the pre-war situation. Rather, it is transformative and provides for social justice and equity. It is a peace that contributes to a fundamental shift in the provision of specific rights related to women's gender roles, to a transformation of gender relations in society, and to a redefinition of hierarchies. Such peace is the outcome of a transformative process including both gendered peacebuilding and transitional justice processes.

4.6 Summary

This overview of gender and transitional justice started with the observation that men and women experience different harms and injustices. Thus, transitional justice tools and mechanisms need to be gender-sensitive. By employing a gender perspective we think differently about what constitutes a crime, what constitutes appropriate ways of doing justice and what constitutes a victim. Evaluations of past and present transitional justice practices show that they are highly political, gendered and tend to reinforce the disadvantages that women face in transitions to peace, justice and democracy. Over the last two decades, consistent efforts to address impunity for conflict-related sexual violence have resulted in an international legal framework for dealing with these crimes. However, convictions remain few and scattered, and the track record of domestic courts is discouraging. In acknowledgement processes women are often regarded only as victims of conflict-related sexual violence, or as witnesses of human rights abuses of male family members. Little attention is paid to their agency as, for example, peacemakers or perpetrators. Yet women engage with transitional justice processes both as objects and subjects. This is particularly clear in efforts of reparative justice. Reparation holds the potential to address the full scope of violations of a gendered nature and understand the issue of conflict-related sexual violence in conjunction with other losses from which women disproportionally suffer. At the same time, sexual violence directed against men needs to be investigated further. In sum, by gendering transitional justice processes, they can work towards an emancipatory, gender-just peace where the peace dividend is realised by both men and women.

4.7 Discussion and tutorial questions

1) Which transitional justice mechanism do you think holds most promise to contribute to a gender-just peace? Why?

2) How can transitional justice address stigma around sexual violence?

3) Do you think the criticism against many locally based informal mechanisms is valid?

4) What does a gender-just peace entail, in your opinion?

Suggested reading

Buckley-Zistel, Susanne and Ruth Stanley (eds), *Gender in Transitional Justice* (Palgrave, 2011).

Mibenge, Chiseche Salome, *Sex and International Tribunals: The Erasure of Gender from the War Narrative* (University of Philadelphia Press, 2013).

Rubio-Marín, Ruth (ed), *The Gender of Reparations: Unsettling Sexual Hierarchies while Redressing Human Rights Violations* (Cambridge University Press, 2009).

Suggested films

Crvene Gumene Cizme (Red Rubber Boots) (Directed by Jasmila Žbanić, Deblokada, 2000).

Grbavica: Esma's Secret (Directed by Jamila Žbanić, Tanja Aćimović, 2006).

In the Land of Blood and Honey (Directed by Angelina Jolie, GK Films, 2011).

We Women Warriors (Tejiendo Sabiduría) (Directed by Nicole Karsin, Todos Los Pueblos Productions, 2012).

Bibliography

Bell, Vikki, *The Art of Post-Dictatorship: Ethics and Aesthetics in Transitional Argentina* (Routledge, 2014).

Björkdahl, Annika and Johanna Mannergren Selimovic, 'Gendered Justice Gaps in Bosnia-Herzegovina' (2014) 15 *Human Rights Review*.

Buckley-Zistel, Susanne and Ruth Stanley (eds), *Gender in Transitional Justice* (Palgrave, 2011).

Burnet, Jennie E, *Genocide Lives in Us: Women, Memory, and Silence in Rwanda* (University of Wisconsin Press, 2012).

Caprioli, Mary, 'Gender Equality and State Aggression: The Impact of Domestic Gender Equality on State First Use of Force' (2003) 29(3) *International Interactions* 195–214.

Charlesworth, Hilary, 'Feminist Methods in International Law' (1999) 93 *American Journal of International Law*.

Charlesworth, Hilary and Christine Chinkin, *The Boundaries of International Law: A Feminist Analysis* (Manchester University Press, 2000) 335

Cockburn, Cynthia, *The Line: Women, Partition and the Gender Order in Cyprus* (Zed Books, 2004).

Cossman, Brenda, 'Gender Performance, Sexual Subjects and International Law' (2002) 15 *CAN. J.L.* & *JURIS.* 281, 283.

Crvene Gumene Cizme (*Red Rubber Boots*) (Directed by Jasmila Žbanić, Deblokada, 2000).

Franke, Katherine M, 'Gendered Subjects of Transitional Justice' (2006) 15(3) *Columbia Journal of Gender & Law*.

Grbavica: Esma's Secret (Directed by Jamila Žbanić, Tanja Aćimović, 2006).

Hellsten, Sirkku K, 'Transitional Justice and Aid' (Working Paper No. 2012/06, UNE-WIDER, January 2012).

Hopkins, Valerie, '"Angelina Jolie Touched Our Souls": Bosnian Rape Victims Have Their Say', *The Guardian* (online), 15 December 2011 ‹http://www.guardian.co.uk/film/filmblog/ 2011/dec/15/angelina-jolie-bosnia-rape-victims›.

Hudson, Valerie, Bonnie Ballif, Mary Caprioli, and Chad F Emmet, *Sex and World Peace*. (Columbia University Press, 2014).

In the Land of Blood and Honey (Directed by Angelina Jolie, GK Films, 2011).

McLeod, Laura, Jovana Dimitrijević and Biliana Rakočević, 'Artistic Activism, Public Debate and Temporal Complexities: Fighting for Transitional Justice in Serbia' in Peter D Rush and Olivera Simić (eds) *The Arts of Transitional Justice: Culture, Activism, and Memory after Atrocity* (Springer, 2014).

Mannergren Selimovic, Johanna, 'Challenges of Postconflict Coexistence: Narrating Truth and Justice in a Bosnian Town' (2015) 36 *Political Psychology*.

Medica Mondiale, '" . . . and that it does not happen to anyone anywhere in the world": The Trouble with Rape Trials – Views of Witnesses, Prosecutors and Judges on Prosecuting Sexualised Violence during the War in the Former Yugoslavia' (Medica Mondiale, December 2009) ‹http://www.medicamondiale.org/fileadmin/redaktion/5_Service/Mediathek/Dokumente/English/Documentations_studies/medica_mondiale_and_that_it_does_not_happen_to_anyone_anywhere_in_the_world_english_complete_version_dec_2009.pdf›

Office of the Prosecutor, 'Sexual and Gender-Based Crimes' (Policy Paper, International Criminal Court, 5 June 2014) ‹https://www.icc-cpi.int/iccdocs/otp/OTP-Policy-Paper-on-Sexual-and-Gender-Based-Crimes—June-2014.pdf›.

O'Rourke, Catherine, 'The Shifting Signifier of "Community" in Transitional Justice: A Feminist Analysis' (2008) 23(2) *Wisconsin Women's Law Journal*.

Ramírez-Barat, Catherine (ed), *Transitional Justice, Culture and Society: Beyond Outreach* (International Center for Transitional Justice and Social Science Research Council, 2014).

Rubio-Marín, Ruth, 'Reparations for Conflict-Related Sexual and Reproductive Violence: A Decalogue' (2012) 19(1) *William & Mary Journal of Women and the Law*.

Rush, Peter D, and Olivera Simić (eds), *The Arts of Transitional Justice: Culture, Activism, and Memory after Atrocity* (Springer, 2014).

Shepherd, Laura J, 'Introduction: Rethinking Gender, Agency and Political Violence' in L Åhäll and LJ Shepherd (eds), *Gender, Agency and Political Violence* (Palgrave, 2012).

Simić, Olivera and Zala Volcic, 'In the Land of Wartime Rape: Bosnia, Cinema and Reparations' (2015) 2(2) *Griffith Journal of Law and Human Dignity*.

Sjoberg, Laura, and Caron E Gentry, *Mothers, Monsters, Whores: Women's Violence in Global Politics* (Zed Books, 2007).

Subotić, Jelena, *Hijacked Justice: Dealing with the Past in the Balkans* (Cornell University Press, 2009).

Tickner, J Ann, 'Feminism Meets International Relations: Some Methodological Issues' in Brooke A Ackerly, Maria Stern and Jacqui True (eds), *Feminist Methodologies in International Relations* (Oxford University Press, 2006).

United Nations, *The Rule of Law and Transitional Justice in Conflict and Post-Conflict Societies: United Nations Secretary-General's Report*, UN Doc S/2011/634(12October2011)<http://www.un.org/en/ga/search/view_doc.asp?symbol=S/2011/634>.

United Nations High Commissioner for Refugees, *Working with Men and Boy Survivors of Sexual and Gender-Based Violence in Forced Displacement* (July 2012) United Nations <http://www.unhcr.org/refworld/pdfid/5006aa262.pdf>.

United Nations Security Council Resolution, SC Res 1325, UN SCOR, 4213th mtg, UN Doc S/RES/1325 (31 October 2000).

Valji, Nahla, *A Window of Opportunity: Making Transitional Justice Work for Women* (October 2012), United Nations Entity for Gender Equality and the Empowerment of Women <http://www.unwomen.org/~/media/Headquarters/Attachments/Sections/Library/Publications/2012/10/06B-Making-Transitional-Justice-Work-for-Women.pdf>.

Volcic, Zala and Olivera Simić, 'Geographies of Crime and Justice in Bosnia and Herzegovina' in Annika Björkdahl and Susanne Buckley-Zistel (eds), *Spatializing Peace and Conflict: Mapping the Production of Places, Sites and Scales of Violence* (Palgrave, 2016).

Zalewski, Marysia, 'Well, What Is the Feminist Perspective on Bosnia?' (1995) 71(2) *International Affairs*.

Zarkov, Dubravka, *The Body of War* (Duke University Press, 2007).

Cases

Prosecutor v Akayesu (International Criminal Tribunal for the Former Yugoslavia, TrialChamberI,CaseNo.ICTR-96-4-T,2September1998)<http://unictr.unmict.org/sites/unictr.org /files/case-documents/ictr-96-4/trial-judgements/en/980902.pdf>.

Prosecutor v Kunarac, Kovac and Kukovic (International Criminal Tribunal for the Former Yugoslavia, Trial Chamber, Case No. IT-96-23-T&IT-96-23/1-T, 22 February 2001) <http://www.icty.org/x/cases/kunarac/tjug/en/kun-tj010222e.pdf>.

Chapter 5

Truth and reconciliation commissions

Agata Fijalkowski

'Do you want to remember, or to forget?'[1]

5.1 Definition and key components (truth/reconciliation/commission)

How can we define a truth and reconciliation commission (TRC)? The three main elements of truth, reconciliation and commission carry broad responsibilities and expectations. In her study on truth commissions, Hayner notes:

> A truth commission (1) is focused on the past, rather than ongoing events; (2) investigates a pattern of events that took place over a period of time; (3) engages directly and broadly with the affected population, gathering information on their experiences; (4) is a temporary body, with the aim of concluding a final report; and (5) is officially authorised or empowered by the state under review.[2]

As we shall see, as Hayner rightly suggests, it is vital not to define truth and reconciliation commissions too narrowly. It is also immediately apparent that a commission is distinct from a governmental human rights body or from a judicial commission of inquiry. In fact, truth commissions have been created under many names. A brief historical overview is needed before going on to the purpose of these bodies. A better understanding of the key components will arise when a closer look is taken at the criteria needed for a commission's actual operation. This chapter will focus on key questions concerning their work and refer to important examples throughout the discussion.

---

1 Priscilla B Hayner, *Unspeakable Truths: Transitional Justice and the Challenge of Truth Commissions* (Routledge, 2nd ed, 2011) 1.
2 Ibid 11–12.

5.2 Brief historical overview

The first truth commission was established in Argentina in 1983. It was known as the National Commission on the Disappeared (CONADEP). The term 'truth commission' would emerge later. CONADEP was created in response to the individuals who disappeared following an intense and brutal government campaign against subversives. When the military forces seized power in 1976, the communists became the main targets for elimination, resulting in some 10,000 to 30,000 people arrested, tortured, and killed. The bodies were disposed of with the purpose of never being found. As a result, families were in anguish at not knowing the fate of the victims. Before acquiescing to popular elections (as discussed in Chapter 6 on 'Amnesty') and a return to civilian rule, the military granted themselves immunity from prosecution and also promulgated a decree ordering the destruction of all documents concerning this violent government campaign of disappearance.

CONADEP was created under Raúl Alfonsín's presidency (1983–1989). President Alfonsín carefully selected the ten members of the commission, which was, after an initial resistance, assisted by non-governmental organisations (NGOs). CONADEP would receive no cooperation from the Argentine armed forces. In terms of its operation, the Commission held no public hearings. The Commission's profile, however, was very public, in the sense that the Commission's existence and function were known to most people and were widely discussed in the media. CONADEP collected 7,000 statements over a nine month period, and documented 8,960 individuals who had disappeared. Importantly, among those interviewed were 1,500 persons who could provide details about the conditions of detention and methods of torture, which aided the commission in identifying the detention centres. Some 365 torture centres were uncovered.[3]

When the commission released a full report, *Nunca Más* (*Never Again*), to the president, it was a top seller, and a publication that was in demand.[4] Parts of the report contained critical information that was presented to the prosecution, which was key to the trial of several of the military juntas – indeed, five were successfully charged and imprisoned. However, the prosecution's momentum was short-lived; even those convicted were pardoned by incoming president Carlos Menem.[5] In 1995, information was provided by one of the key perpetrators involved in death flights, where detainees were drugged and dropped

---

3 Ibid. 46.

4 *Nunca Más, Report of the Argentine Commission on the Disappeared* (Farrar, Straus & Giroux, 1986) and Emilio Crenzel, 'Argentina's National Commission on the Disappearance of Persons: Contributions to Transitional Justice' (2008) 2 *International Journal of Transitional Justice* 173–191.

5 Hayner, above n 1, 46.

from airplanes into the sea. Also that year, the commander-in-chief of the army publicly acknowledged the crimes of the Dirty War.[6] In 1998, criminal trials began for cases of kidnapping (these were excluded from amnesty).[7] In 1999, full investigations were carried out to publicly identify the individuals responsible, before applying for amnesty. In 2001, the highest court held the amnesty provisions unconstitutional. In 2003, the Argentine parliament, supported by political will, overturned the amnesties with retroactive effect. By 2009, 1,400 individuals were charged for crimes of the Dirty War and 68 per cent were convicted by 2011.[8] Thus, it can be said that Argentina arguably paved the way for such commissions.

The next important example is Chile. Here we see 'truth commission' appear as part of the name of the body itself: National Commission on Truth and Reconciliation. The military coup in Chile in September 1973 characterised 17 years of dictatorial rule under General Augusto Pinochet. During this time, independent organisations challenged almost every case of illegal detention or disappearance in court. The national courts rarely supported claims against the regime's actions. Yet the work of the independent organisations was invaluable, as they kept clear records of the individuals detained or 'disappeared'. Despite the repressive rule, it is important to note that Pinochet was a popular figure in a conservative, right-wing Chilean society. The changes Pinochet made before civilian rule took over are discussed in the chapter on 'Amnesty'. These changes constrained the leadership of civilian rule. Yet President Patricio Aylwin (1990–1994) set up a National Truth and Reconciliation Commission that comprised eight members, four of whom were supporters of Pinochet. The Commission's mandate was to investigate 'disappearances after arrest, executions, torture leading to death committed by government or people in their service, as well as kidnappings and attempts on the life of persons carried out by private citizens for political reasons'.[9] The mandate, however, did not include cases of torture that did not result in death. The practices of torture were described in some detail in the Commission's report, but only after the setup of a second commission in 2003 (under President Ricardo Lagos) was there a specific focus on torture survivors.

The 1990 Commission only had nine months to conclude its findings. During that time the Commission was able to conduct more thorough

---

6 'Dirty War' refers to the campaign by the Argentine government against suspected dissidents and subversives.

7 Ibid 47.

8 Hayner, above n 1, 47.

9 Decree Establishing the National Commission on Truth and Reconciliation, Supreme Decree No. 355, Chile (25 April 1990) reprinted in Neil J Kritz (ed), *Transitional Justice: How Emerging Democracies Reckon with Former Regimes* (US Institute of Peace, vol 3, 1995) 102.

investigations of its small number of cases, using the invaluable work of independent organisations. It was focused on developing as complete a picture as possible of the violations of human rights that occurred. It had no power to subpoena, and it received little cooperation from the armed forces. When the report was released in 1991, its 1,800 pages provided a powerful indictment against the Pinochet regime. The report confirmed that 95 per cent of the violations were ascribed to state agents and 4 per cent to leftist groups. In the aftermath of its release, President Aylwin asked for forgiveness from the victims, and emphasised the need for forgiveness and reconciliation, asking the armed forces to recognise the victims' plight. Pinochet responded with a detailed expression of disagreement with the Commission's report. The report was not as widely publicised as the Argentine one. Any discussions about reconciliation petered out. It was not until Pinochet's arrest in London in 1998 that the issue of past human rights violations could be discussed openly and widely.[10] The Spanish judge requesting Pinochet's extradition used the Commission's report, while the national prosecuting authorities used the report in building their cases.[11]

5.3 Purpose

A truth commission is a specific category for dealing with the past. Although meant to be independent, they can have an uneasy relationship with the law, in particular with criminal justice. There are several important questions about operations and management that determine a commission's competence and ultimately its effectiveness.

Many commissions have been created by presidential decree. The executive selects its members and sets the commission's mandate. The classic examples are that of Argentina and Chile. One argument for this way of establishing a commission is that it is less time consuming than relying on parliament to pass the relevant legislation. Ideally, a commission should see public engagement and debate as part of the transitioning process and ownership. This latter element refers to individual or collective ownership over the process of revisiting the past; it is also about being involved in how this past (or predecessor state's history) should form part of the transitioning state's future. Examples of commissions set up through presidential actions are Argentina, Chad, Chile, Haiti, Sri Lanka and Uganda. With the exception of Argentina

---

10 See, for example, David Sugarman, 'The Pinochet Case: International Criminal Justice in Gothic Style' (2001) 64 *Modern Law Review* 933.
11 By end of 2009, 779 former officials were charged with human rights crimes. Over 200 were convicted. Ibid.

and Chile, where the civilian presidents took advantage of public support, the remainder of the examples had little public debate on the commission's terms.

Other truth commissions are created through peace accord. One important example is Sierra Leone, discussed later in this chapter. Other examples include El Salvador, Guatemala, Liberia, the Democratic Republic of Congo and Kenya. The El Salvadoran and Guatemalan commissions were administered by a UN Office, and had members appointed by the UN, but did not operate as UN bodies *per se*. For example, in terms of identity, the Guatemalan Commission was 'located in a no man's land between domestic and international law'.[12] In most cases the terms of agreement were outlined in the national legislation.

Many commissions suffer from weak management. The head of the commission is an important post, and one that should be headed by a respected and impartial individual. The selection of the members of the commission is an under-appreciated process. In many cases the selection of members has been done too hastily, and with little consultation. One of the best examples of a strong commission, based on their independence and knowledge, is in Ecuador, where a number of commissioners came from non-governmental organisations, in order to ensure that human rights activists worked with military representatives on the commissions.[13] In Guatemala, members were selected from a list proposed by presidents of national universities.[14]

Commissions can be international, in both commission members and staff. In El Salvador, for example, the three commissioners and 25 staff members were all foreign.[15] As noted above, the commission was set up under UN administration. The Commission tried to avoid hiring anyone with previous experience of working on El Salvadoran human rights issues, as such familiarity might have suggested a bias that could have affected the neutrality of the commission. Importantly, most El Salvadorans agreed that an El Salvadoran-staffed truth commission was not possible. They insisted that there were no El Salvadorans with the authority and political neutrality needed for the job. It was unlikely that a national commission would have been able to function otherwise. Witnesses would have perhaps been intimidated into giving testimony to fellow El Salvadorans because of their inability to trust the confidentiality of the process. This was evidenced in events that transpired after the creation of the follow-up commission looking into death

---

12 See Hayner, above n 1, 211. See also *Agreement on the Establishment of the Commission to Clarify Past Human Rights Violations and Acts of Violence That Have Caused the Guatemalan Population to Suffer*, UN Doc A/48/954/S/1994/751, Annex II (23 June 1994).

13 Hayner, above n 1, 68–69.

14 Ibid 32–35.

15 Ibid.

squads.[16] The Commission recommended the removal of members of the armed forces from their positions as a result of human rights abuses. In addition, the confidential report recommended that over a hundred persons should be removed from the armed forces. The members of the Commission received death threats, and two of the three left the country.

Other truth commissions have created a mixed model of national and international staff, while some countries exclude foreigners because the situation under investigation is too complex for outsiders, or because the national pool from which to select staff is sufficient. Funds are relevant to the kind of commission that is set up. As we shall see below, where resources, in the form of individuals with the requisite knowledge as well as the physical space, are not available nationally, financial support from an international organisation is critical. It does not, however, always produce effective results.

One of the most important questions about commission work is when it should start. A quick start has its advantages. The political momentum and popular support for such an initiative are highest at the point of transition, or initial beginning, when a new government takes power or an armed conflict has ended. An early start can also hold off immediate reforms and other measures of accountability, providing the government with time to reflect, plan and strengthen institutions integral to the transitional justice initiative. For example, one of the main contributions of the Chilean Commission was giving President Aylwin a year of grace. In certain contexts, this time is needed to ensure measures are in place for the transitional justice mechanism to work. This allowed democratic institutions adequate space to work for one year before having to deal with past crimes and human rights violations. As noted by some scholars, a quickly created commission can be the 'centerpiece of a newfound peace' and one that 'often tests the boundaries of the new regime' and the willingness of authorities to cooperate with an independent investigation.[17]

It is vital to keep the tenure of the truth commission short. Very few are longer than two years. Extending the tenure runs the risk of losing momentum, focus, and both political and public attention. Outlining a work plan, collecting and organising the documents, receiving and processing testimony from thousands of victims, selecting representative cases, completing investigations and finalising a report in a two-year period is undoubtedly a challenge. However, it is useful if the report comes out when there is still the momentum of transition, and reconciliation is a real prospect. This can occur when there are public

---

16 For background on the conflict see Martha Doggett, *Death Foretold: The Jesuit Murders in El Salvador* (Georgetown University Press, 1993) and Teresa Whitfield, *Paying the Price: Ignacio Ellacuría and the Murdered Jesuits of El Salvador* (Temple University Press, 1995).

17 Hayner, above n 1, 215.

calls for change and a public trust in this transitional justice measure. This way, the recommendations made by the commission have a better chance of being implemented. For example, the Commission of Inquiry for Uganda was created in 1986. But this Commission was given no time limit and, as a result, it concluded its work nine years later.[18] By then the public had lost interest in the Commission's work.

Most truth commissions base their work on testimonies gathered from thousands of victims, witnesses and perpetrators. The findings can be standardised to reveal trends and patterns that would otherwise be unknown. If resulting in no fine, imprisonment, or other judicially imposed punishment, a truth commission's findings may negatively affect the persons and institutions named as responsible for abuses. To assign responsibility for killings or torture to one sector of the military or police might or should have implications for the future of the force, and the culpability of the commanding officer. Reparations or other initiatives will be affected by the commission's conclusions about who the victims were, whether they were apolitical citizens caught up in the repression, or politicised supporters of armed rebels, or members of certain ethnic, regional or political groups. The standard of proof of past commissions has varied considerably. For example, the El Salvadoran Commission created a table setting out standards of proof for its individual findings. The thresholds identified levels of overwhelming evidence, or conclusive evidence to support its findings; substantial evidence, or very solid evidence to support the commission's findings; and sufficient evidence, or more evidence to support the commission's findings.[19]

Many truth commissions are established with or after a reparations programme. Even when quite substantial, many reparations programmes alone do not generally satisfy the victims' need for a wider understanding of the events in question. Some individuals understandably might feel a lack of respect in the presumption that a cash payment might be sufficient in compensating for their pain. The manner in which the programme is carried out will help determine how it is received.

In Brazil, the government set up a reparations programme in 1995, a decade after the end of military rule. The Commission was to provide approximately US$100,000 to each family in some 135 cases of disappearances. (In the case of *Velásquez Rodríguez*,[20] the Inter-American Court of Human Rights awarded a lump sum to the next of kin of the victim or to the family.) The Commission also had powers to conduct investigations into these cases, and this included exhumations. The result was an acknowledgement of the facts and 'rescuing

18 Ibid 97–99.
19 Ibid 222.
20 *Velásquez Rodríguez*, decision from 29 July 1988, Inter-Am Ct HR (ser C) No. 4 (1988).

historical truths and collective memory was deemed by many as the most relevant contributions of the process[es]'.[21] However, with full disclosure of the truth not forthcoming, owing to the lack of political will, there has been continued pressure to establish a follow-up commission to fulfil the task that many families are still yearning for – to establish where the remains of the disappeared can be found.

These two examples point to the complexities underpinning the design of a reparations commission – and again, a universal design is simply not feasible for the same reasons as discussed in relation to truth commissions.

5.4 Points of contention and controversy

The founding terms of reference of a commission's mandate can range from a detailed exposition of competence to a short decree issued by the president. What is most important is that this is done in consultation with society, in particular with the victims and victims' families, and human rights organisations. However, as seen below, studies carried out on commissions have revealed that there is a lack of engagement with local practices, which might explain the later lack of commitment to the implementation of recommendations made by the commission. This has also resulted in calls for a template that could be adopted by states that lack the necessary support structures in terms of personnel and resources. One point of contention centres on ownership: commissions should be nationally established, unique to that place, and reflect a process and involvement of the community. This is further supported by the fact that commissions, for many places, represent the first inclusive process of policymaking in the transitioning phase towards democracy between various segments of society.[22]

One of the contentious questions concerns reconciliation itself and what it should look like. In her examination of whether reconciliation is beginning to be accepted, Hayner suggests three questions. The first question relates to the way that the past is dealt with in the public sphere. The key point is whether the people can talk about past conflicts and abuses, not only with each other, but with their former opponents. The second question concerns the basis of the relationships between former opponents – if they are based on the past or the present. The third question addresses the past or rather, which version of the past is being discussed and scrutinised. This is a paramount issue in this field of transitional justice. In the context of reconciliation, it means re-establishing relations and reconciling contradictory facts and stories. It is this third question that begs further research

---

21 Hayner, above n 1, 178.
22 Ibid 178.

in this area. Is it possible to establish a 'single universe of comprehensibility'?[23] Where conflict and violence have returned in cycles over generations, perceptions of the past can vary. This can make reconciliation difficult. Yet there is never just one truth. Each of us carries our own version of events and our own distinct memories. These may contradict each other. The process of disproving certain accounts might lead to an agreed settled account of history. There will be some facts that concern the specific time frame that are basic enough that wide acceptance of their truth is necessary before real reconciliation can take place.[24]

From the perspective of victims, there are a few conditions that are favourable and others that are necessary before reconciliation can start to become accepted. First, there must be an end to the violence or the threat of violence. Second, there should be an officially acknowledged recognition of the violent past. This should come from the perpetrators or be made by the political leaders. Third, there needs to be projects that bring the community together, which enable relationships to be rebuilt. Fourth, reconciliation should go beyond psychological and emotional processes. It also needs to address structural inequalities and material needs which, for example, the South Africa Truth Commission Report noted as necessary if there was to be any success and hope for national unity.[25] These needs have not been adequately addressed in the period following the report.[26] Finally, coming to terms with the past requires time, and expectations should be adjusted accordingly.

What about when a state decides to leave the past alone? Cambodia is known for its killing fields of the late 1970s, as is Spain and its mass graves. The Khmer Rouge government killed one to two million people, comprising up to one-fifth of the population.[27] The manner in which Cambodians have chosen to remember has been less clear.

---

23 Ibid 189. See Paulo Evaristo Arns (ed), *Brasil: Nunca Mais* (Editora Vozes, 1985) and *Torture in Brazil: A Shocking Report on the Pervasive Use of Torture by Brazilian Military Governments, 1964–1979*, trans. Jaime Wright (University of Texas Press, 1998). Also Lawrence Weschler, *A Miracle, A Universe: Settling Accounts with Torturers* (Penguin, 1990).

24 Richard J Goldstone, 'Justice as a Tool for Peace-Making: Truth Commissions and International Criminal Tribunals' (1996) *International Law and Politics* 485.

25 Volume Four of the South African Truth and Reconciliation Report is dedicated to the societal context within which the human rights violations occurred. This volume offers an exploration of the wider institutional and social environment. The Report encourages self-reflection on the part of various sectors (business and labour; the faith community; the legal community; the health sector; the media sector; prisons; the military; children and youth; and women). The South African Truth and Reconciliation Report is available at a website dedicated to the Commission's work at http://www.justice.gov.za/trc/report/ (last accessed 25 August 2016).

26 Romi Sigsworth and Nahla Valji, 'Continuities of Violence against Women in South Africa: The Limitations of Transitional Justice' in Susanne Buckley-Zistel and Ruth Stanley (eds), *Gender in Transitional Justice* (Palgrave, 2011) 115–135.

27 Hayner, above n 1, 204.

When the Khmer Rouge government collapsed in the 1980s, there was an initial interest in letting the world know about what happened. But the interest waned, and it was reported that Cambodians preferred to forget the past and many did not want to discuss it in public. Outside observers stated that among the community there was still some fear of talking about the past. Also, the Cambodian and Buddhist faith tradition tended not to confront conflict. However, the UN mission to Cambodia listed several reasons for this development, the most compelling being that many political, military and financial elites could be implicated and, since many in the current government had at one time been affiliated with the Khmer Rouge, it was felt that accommodation was the preferred choice. As a result of this 'hushed' treatment of the past, the younger generation did not know the history and in fact doubted their elders' accounts of atrocities. Instead there was more focus on the crimes at an international level. In 1994, the US passed the Cambodian Genocide Act, which provided financial support for the Office of Cambodian Genocide Investigations at the US Department of State.[28] This initiative led to the preservation of documentation that detailed the surveillance practices of the Khmer Rouge secret police and the structure of the regime.

Some of the Khmer Rouge surrendered in the late 1990s, and suddenly there was a desire to prosecute, but at the same time there was fear. People wanted to get on with their lives. A UN group of experts recommended a truth commission, but several doubted its potential success, as many former Khmer Rouge members re-entered Cambodian society. In 2003, the government and the UN signed an agreement to create a special tribunal, the Extraordinary Chambers in the Courts of Cambodia. By 2006 it was in operation, with five suspects in custody with trials ready to go. While the need to know what happened seemed to be strong among Cambodian society, it was felt that the mixed tribunal would not provide the truth. In cases such as these, the international community has an important role to play, by providing the funding and staff to ensure key mechanisms are created and can operate. However, it cannot fulfil the needs of a society that is divided, i.e. when there is a fearful silence that has been suppressed or where interests are better served by silence or by portions of the truth coming out.[29]

To meet the challenges of transitional justice, a society should investigate, establish and publicly disseminate the truth about past atrocities. The hard truth or forensic truth concerns information about the crime and what human rights

---

28 Ibid 205.
29 Hayner notes a similar experience in Mozambique: above n 1, 197–204.

were violated. There is also the emotional truth that refers to knowledge about the psychological and physical impact on the victims.[30] The rhetoric of political truth makes truth suspicious and exploited. Concrete political action to determine what happened is rare. So the way the past is used has a significant moral dimension. In other words, the political instrumentalisation of the past needs to be overcome.[31] It is this politicisation that results in public dissatisfaction and scepticism about justice. The frustration is compounded when the report's findings do not result in any meaningful outcome.

5.5 Key examples from Europe and Africa

One of the most interesting examples of a commission is the Commission of Inquiry for the Assessment and Consequences of the Socialist Unity Party (SED) Dictatorship in Germany, 1992–1994, and the Commission of Inquiry on Overcoming the Consequences of the SED Dictatorship in the Process of German Unity, 1995–1998. These German examples show a commission that is involved in more of a symbolic mission than a fact-finding one. Although the two are separate, one led to the creation of the other. In 1992, the German parliament created a Commission to investigate and document the practices of the German Democratic Republic (GDR, or East German) government from 1949 to 1989. The SED was the ruling party in the GDR. The structure of the Commission and its operation followed the country's guidelines for parliamentary commissions of inquiry. This meant that representation of political parties was equivalent to their representation in parliament as a whole. The SED successor, the Democratic Socialist Party, was represented on the commission with one member. Experts comprised 11 of the 27 members.

The East German regime is discussed differently in the literature, compared to its counterparts who were also the subject of commission inquiries. East German dictatorial rule physically repressed political opponents and dissidents, controlled freedom of movement, and imposed organised surveillance on some of its political dissidents. The Commission's mandate went beyond the scope of human rights violations to a wider inquiry into state policy and practice, which included an investigation into the structure and practice of the SED regime;

---

30 David A Crocker, 'Truth Commissions, Transitional Justice, and Civil Society' in Robert I Rothberg and Dennis Thompson (eds), *Truth v Justice: The Morality of Truth Commissions* (Princeton University Press, 2000) 99.

31 For example, this objective motivates the Regional Committee for Establishing the Facts about War Crimes and Other Gross Violations of Human Rights on the Territory of the Former Yugoslavia <http://www.recom.link>.

environmental degradation; political, mental and psychosocial repression; the role of ideology in education, literature, and daily life; Church–State relations; judicial independence; and relations between West and East Germany.[32]

Public hearings accompanied the work of the Commission. It should be noted that the Commission had no subpoena power; many former government officials who were invited to give testimony declined for fear that these would be used against them in court. Importantly, the files from the East German secret police, the Staatssicherheit, or Stasi, were made available for individual review. The files permitted those who had been victims of Stasi informers to confront them directly. This occurred in private or before television cameras. The work of the Commission was shaped by this mandate and thus distinct from a commission such as South Africa's. Plus the German Commission preceded the South African one. 'The Commission demonstrates that a victim-centred examination and discussion of the past and its legacy is possible without a large-scale testimony collection.'[33] The first inquiry's report was released in 1995 and was over 15,000 pages. The second Commission released its report in 1998. Both arguably helped to frame the highly controversial question of how to memorialise this period.

The South African Truth and Reconciliation Commission is viewed as being the strongest truth commission. Its creation, in 1995, was a response to the apartheid regime, which had lasted 45 years. During this time the African National Congress (ANC) and other groups carried out armed resistance against the apartheid state. South Africa had endured massacres, killings, torture, lengthy imprisonment of activists, and severe economic and social discrimination against its majority non-white population.

After Nelson Mandela was elected president in 1994, serious discussions took place regarding the creation of a commission. At the heart of the debate was whether to grant amnesty to perpetrators of crimes, as insisted upon by the government and military. This amnesty would then be linked to the truth commission. Civil society had an important input into the creation of the Commission. In mid-1995 parliament passed the Promotion of National Unity and Reconciliation Act. Following a public nomination and selection process, 17 commissioners were appointed with Archbishop Desmond Tutu as chair. The work officially began in 1995, but started in 1996 after some delay in investigations.

The Commission was given the power to grant individualised amnesty, search premises and seize evidence, subpoena witnesses and run a witness

---

32 Hayner, above n 1, 52–53.

33 Andrew H Beattie, 'An Evolutionary Process: Contributions of the Bundestag Inquiries into East Germany to an Understanding of the Role of Truth Commissions' (2009) 3 *International Journal of Transitional Justice* 229.

protection programme. It had a staff of 300 and a budget of US$18 million for the first two-and-a-half years.

The Commission took testimony from 21,000 victims and witnesses, 2,000 of whom also appeared in public hearings.[34] Media coverage was widespread, with a special television programme devoted to its work.

The Commission did not always make use of its strong powers. The powers of subpoena, and search and seizure were applied only a few times. It was criticised by human rights organisations for not issuing a subpoena against the Minister of Human Affairs. The Commission possibly was afraid of a violent reaction.

The greatest innovation of the Commission was its ability to grant individualised amnesty.[35] The period covered by the amnesty was 1960 to April 1994 – 7,115 applications for amnesty were received. If the crimes concerned gross violations of human rights, the applicant was required to appear at a public hearing to answer questions from the Commission, from legal counsel representing the victims or victims' families, and from the victims themselves. Amnesty was granted to those who fully confessed to their involvement in past crimes and showed them to be politically motivated. The Amnesty Committee considered a number of factors in determining whether the applications satisfied requirements. A significant factor was whether the crime was politically motivated. In fact, 4,500 applications were denied; most of them lacked a political objective. Neither an apology nor any sign of remorse was necessary to be granted amnesty, so to avoid inducing fake apologies. Of course, some perpetrators showed remorse and apologised.

There were several high-profile trials that resulted in convictions. But when the trial of the former Minister of Defence, Magnua Malan, ended in acquittal, it was felt that the threat of prosecution was not strong enough to persuade senior-level perpetrators to take advantage of the amnesty process. Several key amnesty decisions should be noted, such as the Stephen Biko case, where the admitted killers of the anti-apartheid activist were denied amnesty on the grounds that the perpetrators claimed that the death was accidental. Another controversial ruling was granting amnesty to 37 ANC leaders who applied jointly. Few details were provided. The Commission granted the group collective amnesty, a decision that was later overturned by the Cape Town High Court on the grounds that they did not make the full disclosures as required by the amnesty provisions. The actions were gross human rights violations, but no further action has been taken, owing to lack of evidence, despite calls for prosecution by former South African police and generals.[36]

---

34 Hayner, above n 1, 28.

35 Ibid 29.

36 Lovell Fernandez, 'Post-TRC Prosecutions in South Africa' in Gerhard Werle (ed), *Justice in Transition: Prosecution and Amnesty in Germany and South Africa* (BWV Berliner Wissenschafts Verlag, 2006) 65. See also Hayner, above n 1, 29–30.

The Truth Commission did have its powers and decisions challenged in court. The decisions showed the dissatisfaction felt by some as regards the amnesty laws. Cassese recognised the difficult and sensitive nature of the project during the country's transitioning.[37] In his analysis of the goals of international criminal justice, he draws our attention to the dilemma that amnesty laws present and refers us to the South African Constitutional Court case of *Azanian Peoples Organization v President of the Republic of South Africa*.[38] In this ruling from 25 July 1996, the Promotion of National Unity and Reconciliation Act Act was upheld and, within that, its amnesty laws. The Court saw the Commission as a suitable solution for a country that is transitioning from one of terror towards democracy. Cassese makes an important point here regarding the choice to establish a commission, which might not be suitable for all transitioning states. He uses the example of former Yugoslavia to indicate that perhaps a commission might not be best suited to a transition where, broadly speaking, a socialist democracy is transitioning to several ethnically-based mini-states that remain antagonistic towards each other. In this vein, however, it is worth noting a civic initiative in 2005, namely the Regional Committee for Establishing the Facts about War Crimes and Other Gross Violations of Human Rights on the Territory of the Former Yugoslavia. Known as 'RECOM', it continues to be an unfinished political project. RECOM does not include 'truth' in its name, but 'facts', in an effort to overcome political instrumentalisation and to counter the political memory of the past.[39] RECOM endeavours to create a space for victims by frequently referring to victims in its fact-finding. Facts can provide that necessary shift whereby victims become subjects with a name and story. Facts become meaningful when the victim's story is heard.[40]

Another factor that is discussed in *Azanian Peoples* concerns the difficulty of carrying out prosecutions – due to secrecy and the inability to collect the required proof to secure a prosecution. Moreover, in that case the Court asserted that amnesty, under the terms of the Act, was not awarded automatically and had to meet strict criteria. Sometimes amnesty and truth commissions are preferable to prosecutions, when the domestic system is too fragile to accommodate the trials against the threat of political instability.[41]

---

37 Antonio Cassese, 'Reflections on International Criminal Justice' (1998) 61 *Modern Law Review* 1.
38 *Azanian Peoples Organization v President of the Republic of South Africa* [1996] 4 SA 671.
39 Regional Committee for Establishing the Facts about War Crimes, above n 31. Jacqueline Nießer, 'A Truth and Reconciliation Commission that Dispenses with Truth? The Regional Committee for Establishing the Facts about War Crimes in the Yugoslav Wars' (Paper presented at the Association for Slavic, East European and Eurasian Studies Conference, Philadelphia, PA, USA, November 2015).
40 Ibid.
41 Antonio Cassese, above n 37, 4.

It should be noted that charges were brought against former president of South Africa P W Botha after he refused to appear before the Commission following a subpoena. The trial then became a forum for the Commission to present its evidence against him, which included his knowledge or approval of a long pattern of state crimes. Botha was convicted, fined and given a one-year suspended sentence. He successfully appealed to have his conviction overturned on a technicality.[42]

In another case involving former South African president F W de Klerk, the work of the Commission was temporarily blocked after de Klerk tried to stop the Commission from naming him in the report. For its part, the ANC also attempted to block the publication of the Commission's report. The ANC was not satisfied with the conclusions drawn about its past actions. When the report was formally considered by the parliament, deputy president Thabo Mbeki, speaking in his capacity as president of the ANC, announced that the ANC had serious reservations about the Commission's report – noting that its findings seemed to delegitimise the ANC's struggle for liberation. In the end, the government did not make any commitment to implement the Commission's recommendations because of these reservations.

The impact of the South African Truth and Reconciliation Commission on reconciliation has been the subject of ongoing debate. 'What remained clear to all, however, was that coming to terms with decades of abuses would take longer than a few years, and much more than speaking the truth.'[43]

The Sierra Leone Truth and Reconciliation Commission, and its work, give rise to similar concerns, as well as other factors that identify other features of the work of a truth commission. An agreement for the Sierra Leone Truth and Reconciliation Commission was found in the Lomé peace accord that ended the country's civil war in July 1999. The agreement was signed into law through the Truth and Reconciliation Act in February 2000. After some delay owing to fighting between the government and rebel fighters, a public process was initiated to secure nominations for commissioners. According to the Act, the Commission was to undertake research, receive statements and hold sessions with the aim of establishing 'an impartial historical record of violations and abuses of human rights and international humanitarian law related to the armed conflict in Sierra Leone',[44] from the beginning of the conflict in 1991 to January 2002. The Act places special emphasis on victims of sexual abuse and on children who were either victims or perpetrators (child soldiers). While the Commission was meant to be a fully independent body, it was later

---

42 Hayner, above n 1, 30–31.
43 Ibid 31–32.
44 Section 6 of the [Sierra Leonean] Truth and Reconciliation Act 2000.

decided that it would be administratively managed by the UN Office of the High Commissioner for Human Rights (OHCHR). While the OHCHR assisted with fundraising and administrative support, some questions were raised concerning the Commission's independence in making operational decisions. The operating budget was less than US$5 million; limited finds and a strict timeline reduced its scope, the taking of statements and public hearings.

It should be noted that there was strong support for the Commission's work from former combatants. Over 10 per cent of the statements came from perpetrators. The more the Commission's work became publicised, the more support it garnered. In fact, public hearings were held across the country, accompanied by 'reconciliation ceremonies', where victims and perpetrators got together, and went through a ritual ceremony to return to, and be reaccepted by, the community. Eventually the work of the Commission overlapped with that of the Special Court for Sierra Leone, created in 2002 after an agreement between the government and the UN. The Court's mandate was to prosecute those 'bearing the greatest responsibility' for crimes after November 1996.

The Commission published a four-volume report that was concluded in 2004. It included a video summary and a child-friendly version. In this way the country hoped to escape the dilemma that was common to other commissions – that of the government failing to act on the recommendations presented in the final report. The country set out to implement the recommendations. A follow-up committee was created, with national and international members, which would submit quarterly reports and supervise the plan. But these mechanisms were never made operational.

There was little commitment shown by the government. Despite slow progress and marginal success in the initiatives eventually put in place for women and children, there is hope in that the experience has led to important studies about the shortcomings of commissions. One of the most valuable insights is that commissions run counter to local understandings about healing and reconciliation, suggesting that such operations might pay attention to local practices to overcome obstacles to healing.[45]

Studies have shown that truth-telling may affect views on group security over a long-term period in post-conflict societies.[46] This is especially so in societies divided along cultural lines, where truth-telling might exert some peace-promoting influence. Of the documented truth commissions, most are in Africa,

---

45 Rosalind Shaw, United States Institute for Peace, *Rethinking Truth and Reconciliation Commissions: Lessons from Sierra Leone – Special Report 130* (February 2005).
46 David Mendeloff, 'Truth-Seeking, Truth-Telling, and Post-Conflict Building: Curb the Enthusiasm? (2004) 6 *International Studies Review* 355.

followed by Asia, the Americas and Europe.[47] These recent studies show that there is so much interest in creating new truth commissions because of their impact on transforming public discourses on memory, truth, justice and reconciliation. These new avenues are created even when the commissions seemingly produce modest changes owing to political constraints.[48] It is true that the academic scholarship is largely based on the better-known commissions. Greater attention from the international human rights advocacy community tends to focus on criminal justice. The dominance of this legal perspective may be missing the complexities and importance of parallel, non-judicial initiatives. Truth commissions directly impact thousands of victims, and the possibility of criminal justice, reforms, reparations, reconciliation and community relations. The interdisciplinary asset of the field of transitional justice should be used to carry out deeper legal analysis of truth commissions. For example, what is the link of TRCs to courts? Or, what is the impact on trauma and healing across time and regions? A recent study on the Liberian Truth and Reconciliation Commission reveals some important factors that might help explain what underpins the success of a truth commission.

The Liberian Commission was created in 2005, further to the 2003 Accra Comprehensive Peace Agreement that was concluded to address the country's legacy of human rights violations in the context of its civil wars in the period 1979 to 2003. According to Ezekiel Pajibo, 'Warring parties [in Liberia] agreed to the TRC concept because they wanted to prevent the establishment of a war crimes tribunal'.[49] One factor that might have influenced this position was the arrest in 2003 of Charles Taylor on charges of war crimes and crimes against humanity in Sierra Leone by the Special Court for Sierra Leone.

The Liberian Commission investigated violations that occurred between January 1979 and October 2003, marking the period of the final year of the Americo-Liberian rule and the inauguration of the National Transitional Government for Liberia.[50] The composition of the Commission included nine commissioners: three from civil society, two from political parties, one from the UN, and one from the Economic Community of Western African Societies. Out of nine, four women were in the Commission for gender balance. Gender is often neglected in the transitional justice process, and scholars have argued that

47 Tricia D Olsen, Leigh A Payne and Andrew G Reiter, *Transitional Justice in Balance: Comparing Processes* (United States Institute of Peace, 2010).

48 Onur Bakiner, *Truth Commissions: Memory, Power, and Legitimacy* (University of Pennsylvania Press, 2015). See also Bakiner, Onur, 'Truth Commission Impact: An Assessment of How Commissions Influence Politics and Society' (2014) 8 *International Journal of Transitional Justice.*

49 Ezekiel Pajibo, 'Civil Society and Transitional Justice in Liberia: A Practitioner's Reflection from the Field' (2007) 1 *International Journal of Transitional Justice* 287.

50 Carla de Ycaza, 'A Search for Truth: A Critical Analysis of the Liberian Truth and Reconciliation Commission' (2013) 14 *Human Rights Review* 189.

transitional justice mechanisms require a change in procedures (such as member-ships on truth commissions) to address this inequality.[51] Due to the absence of adequate funding and resources, the Commission did not have the expertise to make a solid legal evaluation of the cases. The final report of the Commission was made in 2008, when it was presented to the Liberian legislature. It contains four volumes. One of the most unique contributions was the Commission's inclu-sion of the diaspora community throughout the report. This is the first of its kind. The involvement of the community was paramount, as thousands fled the con-flict, creating large communities in West Africa, Europe and the United States. Their contribution included outreach, statement taking, report writing and being present at the public hearings.

Another unique contribution of the Commission was the Palava Hut Forum as a complementary tool for justice and national reconciliation. The Commission recommended that the process be based on traditional dispute-resolution mecha-nisms. The Palava Hut process was used in pre-settler Liberia. It was convened by elders to settle community matters. Traditionally, a confession was sought for the wrongful deed, followed by an apology for the wrong committed, forgiveness from the victim, and cleansing rituals and restitution. This sanction was limited to lesser crimes only, and not available for international crimes. Significantly, the informal justice system had more support and trust than the formal court system. The Liberian Commission Report also included an investigation of economic crimes, as the exploitation of resources was one of the primary causes underpin-ning the conflict. The Report sets out an extensive definition of the crimes, as well as a list of individuals and corporations that the Commission holds respon-sible for economic crimes.

The Liberian Commission's work has made an invaluable contribution to the mapping of human rights abuses. As part of its mandate it conducted the National Conflict Mapping Survey which identified the emerging conflict issues that had the potential to undermine the peace process, and that would influence the 'conflict sensitive' policy recommendations it would make. Despite the difficul-ties, the Liberian Commission succeeded in making an original and important contribution to our understanding of transitional justice and its many mecha-nisms. It succeeds in advancing our critique about the role of the law in the area, and acknowledging the vital role that non-legal actors and other forms of knowl-edge have to play in the area of reconciliation.[52]

---

51 Vasuki Nesiah et al, International Center for Transitional Justice, *Truth Commissions and Gender: Principles, Policies and Procedures: Report* (July 2006).

52 Kieran McEvoy, 'Beyond Legalism: Towards a Thicker Understanding of Transitional Justice' (2007) 34 *Journal of Law and Society* 411.

5.6 Summary

This chapter has considered the definition of a truth and reconciliation commission, and that its key components of truth, reconciliation and commission carry a broad plethora of responsibilities and expectations.

The founding terms of reference of the commission's mandate can range from a detailed exposition of competence to a short decree issued by the president. What is most important is that this is done in consultation with society, in particular the victims and victims' families, human rights organisations, and key independent actors. However, as seen above, studies carried out on commissions have revealed that there is a lack of engagement with local practices, which might explain the later lack of commitment to the implementation of the recommendations made by the commission. Also, this has resulted in calls for a template that could be adopted by states that lack the support structures. Another controversial and highly significant point arises in relation to ownership: commissions should be nationally established, unique to that place and reflect a process, which involves the community. Commissions, for many places, are the first inclusive process of policymaking in the transitioning phase towards democracy, between various segments of society. This begs the question of whether a general standard model is even possible.

Certainly more studies need to be carried out with respect to the commissions that have been created, with a view to answering the question of why there is so much interest in creating new truth commissions. Academic scholarship is largely based on the better-known commissions. On the part of the international human rights advocacy community, criminal justice predominates. The dominance of this legal perspective lacks an appreciation of the complexities and importance of parallel, non-judicial initiatives. Truth commissions affect victims and the wider community, as well as the various aspects of the criminal justice process and related non-judicial mechanisms. The interdisciplinary asset of the field of transitional justice should be used to carry out deeper legal analysis of truth commissions. For example, what is the link to courts? Or, what is the impact on trauma and healing across time and regions? The contemporary examples of commissions, such as Sierra Leone and Liberia, bring us close to such an understanding.

5.7 Discussion and tutorial questions

1) Should a truth commission be national, international or a mix? What considerations are important to bear in mind?

2) When should the work of the commission begin?

3) How long should it carry on?

4) Should there be a general, universal template to assist in the setting up of a commission?

5) What should be done with the commission's findings (e.g. prosecution)?

6) What is the role of the international community in the establishment of TRCs?

Suggested reading

Blair, James T, 'From the Numbers Who Died to Those Who Survived: Victim Participation in the Extraordinary Chambers in the Courts of Cambodia' (2009) 31 *University of Hawaii Law Review*.

Braithwaite, John, Valerie Braithwaite, Michael Cookson and Leah Dunn, *Anomie and Violence: Non-truth and Reconciliation in Indonesian Peacebuilding* (Australian National University E Press, 2010).

Collins, Cath, 'Chile 2014 ¿Una Nueva Medida de lo Posible? Verdad, Justicia, Memoria y Reparaciones Pos Dictadura' (Research Paper No. 15–07, Transitional Justice Research Institute, 25 September 2015) [trans Chile 2014 – New Possibilities for Post-Dictatorship Truth, Justice, Memory and Reparations].

Simić, Olivera and Peter D Rush (eds), *The Arts of Transitional Justice* (Springer, 2012).

Soares, Patrícia Pinto, 'Positive Complementarity: Fine-Tuning the Transitional Justice Discourse? The Cases of the Democratic Republic of Congo, Uganda and Kenya' in A Fijalkowski and R Grosescu (eds), *Post-Dictatorial and Post-Conflict Transitional Criminal Justice* (Intersentia, 2015).

Sullo, Pietro, 'Punishing Mass Atrocities: Penological Developments in the Aftermath of the Rwandan Genocide' in A Fijalkowski and R Grosescu (eds), *Post-Dictatorial and Post-Conflict Transitional Criminal Justice* (Intersentia, 2015).

Stovel, Laura, *Long Road Home: Building Reconciliation in Sierra Leone* (Intersentia, 2010).

Suggested films

A Long Night's Journey into Day (Directed by Deborah Hoffman and Francis Reid, Francis Reid Productions, 2000).

Beasts of No Nation (Directed by Cary Fukunaga, Princess Grace Foundation, 2015).

Cry Freetown (Directed by Sorious Samura, CNN Productions, 2000).

Life Does Not Lose Its Value: Father Berton and the Former Soldiers of Sierra Leone (Directed by Wilma Massucco, Bluindaco Productions, 2012).

Suggested plays

Eclipsed (Written by Danai Gurira, opened 2015).

Bibliography

Articles/books/reports

Bakiner, Onur, *Truth Commissions, Memory, Power, and Legitimacy* (University of Pennsylvania Press, 2016).

Bakiner, Onur, 'Truth Commission Impact: An Assessment of How Commissions Influence Politics and Society' (2014) 8 *International Journal of Transitional Justice*.

Beattie, Andrew H, 'An Evolutionary Process: Contributions of the Bundestag Inquiries into East Germany to an Understanding of the Role of Truth Commissions' (2009) 3 *International Journal of Transitional Justice*.

Brasil: Nunca Maís (Paulo Evaristo Arns (ed), Editora Vozes, 1985).

Brazil Archdiocese of São Paulo, *Torture in Brazil: A Shocking Report on the Pervasive Use of Torture by Brazilian Military Governments, 1964–1979* (Jaime Wright trans, University of Texas Press, 1998).

Cassese, Antonio, 'Reflections on International Criminal Justice' (1998) 61 *Modern Law Review*.

Crenzel, Emilio, 'Argentina's National Commission on the Disappearance of Persons: Contributions to Transitional Justice' (2008) 2 *International Journal of Transitional Justice*.

Crocker, David A, 'Truth Commissions, Transitional Justice, and Civil Society' in Robert I Rothberg and Dennis Thompson (eds), *Truth v Justice: the Morality of Truth Commissions* (Princeton University Press, 2000).

Doggett, Martha, *Death Foretold: The Jesuit Murders in El Salvador* (Georgetown University Press, 1993).

Fernandez, Lovell, 'Post-TRC Prosecutions in South Africa' in Gerhard Werle (ed), *Justice in Transition: Prosecution and Amnesty in Germany and South Africa* (BWV Berliner Wissenschafts Verlag, 2006).

Ferrara, Anita, *Assessing the Long Term Impact of Truth Commissions: The Chilean Truth and Reconciliation Commission in Historical Perspective* (Routledge, 2014).

Goldstone, Richard J, 'Justice as a Tool for Peace-Making: Truth Commissions and International Criminal Tribunals' (1996) *International Law and Politics*.

Hayner, Priscilla B, *Unspeakable Truths: Transitional Justice and the Challenge of Truth Commissions* (Routledge, 2nd ed, 2011).

McEvoy, Kieran, 'Beyond Legalism: Towards a Thicker Understanding of Transitional Justice (2007) 34 *Journal of Law and Society*.

Mendeloff, David, 'Truth-Seeking, Truth-Telling, and Post-Conflict Building: Curb the Enthusiasm?' (2004) 6 *International Studies Review*.

Nesiah, Vasuki, et al, 'Truth Commissions and Gender: Principles, Policies and Procedures', *International Center for Transitional Justice* (July 2006).

Nießer, Jacqueline, 'A Truth and Reconciliation Commission That Dispenses with Truth? The Regional Committee for Establishing the Facts about War Crimes in the Yugoslav Wars' (Paper presented at the Association for Slavic, East European and Eurasian Studies Conference, Philadelphia, PA, USA, November 2015).

Nunca Más, Report of the Argentine Commission on the Disappeared (Farrar, Straus & Giroux, 1986).

Olsen, Tricia D, Leigh A Payne and Andrew G Reiter, *Transitional Justice in Balance: Comparing Processes* (United States Institute of Peace, 2010).

Orentlicher, Diane, 'Settling Accounts: The Duty to Prosecute Human Rights Violations of a Prior Regime' (1991) 100 *Yale Law Review*.

Pajibo, Ezekiel, 'Civil Society and Transitional Justice in Liberia: A Practitioner's Reflection from the Field' (2007) 1 *International Journal of Transitional Justice*.

Shaw, Rosalind, United States Institute for Peace, *Rethinking Truth and Reconciliation Commissions: Lessons from Sierra Leone – Special Report 130* (February 2005).

Sigsworth, Romi and Nahla Valji, 'Continuities of Violence against Women in South Africa: The Limitations of Transitional Justice' in Susanne Buckley-Zistel and Ruth Stanley (eds), *Gender in Transitional Justice* (Palgrave, 2011).

Sugarman, David, 'The Pinochet Case: International Criminal Justice in Gothic Style' (2001) 64 *Modern Law Review*.

Weschler, Lawrence, *A Miracle, A Universe: Settling Accounts with Torturers* (Penguin, 1990).

Whitfield, Teresa, *Paying the Price: Ignacio Ellacuría and the Murdered Jesuits of El Salvador* (Temple University Press, 1995).

Ycaza, Carla de, 'A Search for Truth: A Critical Analysis of the Liberian Truth and Reconciliation Commission' (2013) 14 *Human Rights Review*.

Cases

Azanian Peoples Organization v President of the Republic of South Africa [1996] 4 SA 671.

Velásquez Rodríguez, decision from 29 July 1988, Inter-Am Ct HR (ser C) No. 4, (1988).

Legislation

Decree Establishing the National Commission on Truth and Reconciliation, Supreme Decree No. 355, Chile (25 April 1990) reprinted in Neil J Kritz (ed), *Transitional Justice: How Emerging Democracies Reckon with Former Regimes* (US Institute of Peace, vol 3, 1995).

Other

Agreement on the Establishment of the Commission to Clarify Past Human Rights Violations and Acts of Violence That Have Caused the Guatemalan Population to Suffer, UN Doc A/48/954/S/1994/751, Annex II (23 June 1994).

Regional Committee for Establishing the Facts about War Crimes and Other Gross Violations of Human Rights on the Territory of the Former Yugoslavia ‹http://www.recom.link›.

Sierra Leonean Truth and Reconciliation Act 2000

South African Truth and Reconciliation Report is available at a website dedicated to the Commission's work at http://www.justice.gov.za/trc/report/

Chapter 6

Amnesty

Agata Fijalkowski

6.1 Introduction

The topic of amnesty is a vital one in transitional justice scholarship. As a political tool it has historically provided the state the means to suppress dissent, compromise with its enemies and protect its own state agents implicated in crimes. In terms of transitional justice, which concerns the ways in which the state addresses its predecessor state's crimes, it has a more poignant meaning that can seemingly go against calls for justice.

Amnesty might not be all that it seems. A closer study of amnesty offers an important means to explore more critically the legal measures concerning extradition, or those resulting in impunity – both of which come to the fore as victims and states try and reconcile the demands of justice and the demands of peace. This particular debate concerning its goals – peace or justice – has gone on for some time.

In recent years, however, a change can be seen. For example, there has been another prominent shift protecting state agents from criminal prosecution. What is more surprising is the location of the change – namely the United States (US). The US has traditionally maintained a position which holds that the non-extradition of its citizens – and those of its allies – is strictly adhered to in the name of peace.[1] The US is not alone in its approach, a position that is the subject of ongoing consideration.[2]

Nonetheless, in August 2015, a US federal court set to rule on an extradition request made by Spain for Innocente Orlando Montano Morales. Morales is a

---

1 Helen Duffy, *The 'War on Terror' and the Framework of International Law* (Cambridge University Press, 2nd ed, 2015) 456–664.
2 Neil Boister, 'International Tribunals for Transnational Crimes: Towards a Transnational Criminal Court?' (2012) 23 *Criminal Law Forum* 295.

former Vice Minister of Defence for El Salvador who allegedly gave the order to execute several Jesuits, including an important intellectual figure, Rev. Ignacio Ellacuría – an important intellectual and leftist representative in the country, who brokered the peace process between the government and the Farabundo Martí National Liberation Front (FMNLF).[3] The executions took place in November 1989. Morales and 19 others have been charged with the murder of six priests, their housekeeper and her daughter. Five of the six priests were Spanish citizens, thus leading to the Spanish request. Many of the perpetrators of human rights atrocities committed during the 12-year civil war that ceased in 1992 remain free in El Salvador, because national amnesty laws protect them. But even this is changing. In 2016 it was reported that the exhumations taking place at El Mozote have resulted in a reassessment of the current amnesty laws. The importance of El Mozote is what occurred there, over a three-day period in December 1981. Soldiers from the Salvadoran army shot hundreds of unarmed men, women and children in the village of El Mozote and surrounding areas. This was the worst atrocity committed during the 12-year-long conflict between leftist guerrillas and El Salvador's right-wing government, in which circa 75,000 Salvadorans died. No one has been held accountable for the massacre or any crimes committed during the war. The amnesty law, passed in 1993, protected perpetrators on both sides of the conflict from prosecution. Significantly, the country's reconciliation process has been viewed as archetypal. Both sides disarmed, the army diminished in size and the security forces became the civilian police. After the civil war ended in 1992, over a six-month period, a UN Truth Commission investigated 'serious acts of violence'; 85 per cent were made against the army, paramilitary groups and right-wing death squads.[4] (Truth commissions are discussed in Chapter 5 'Truth and reconciliation commissions'.) In this Commission's report the FMNLF, noted above, was blamed for the 1989 events discussed at the start of this chapter. Importantly, demands for justice were made in 1990 when relatives of the El Mozote massacre filed a suit with the Inter-American Court of Human Rights. The Inter-American Court of Human Rights ruled that El Salvador's government investigate the massacre, punish the perpetrators, and compensate the victims.[5] Efforts to challenge the 1993 amnesty law continue, as

---

3 Jonathan Katz, 'US Wants Former Salvadoran Ally to Face Justice in 1989 Massacre', *The New York Times* (online) 13 September 2015 <http://www.nytimes.com/2015/09/14/world/americas/us-wants-former-salvadoran-ally-to-face-justice-in-1989-massacre.html>, last accessed 24 August 2016. For background on the conflict see Martha Doggett, *Death Foretold: The Jesuit Murders in El Salvador* (Georgetown University Press, 1993) and Teresa Whitfield, *Paying the Price: Ignacio Ellacuría and the Murdered Jesuits of El Salvador* (Temple University Press, 1995).

4 'Digging for Justice', *The Economist* (London), 2 January 2016, 25–26.

5 *El Mozote Massacre v El Salvador*, decision from 2 March 2006, Case 10.720, Report No. 24/06, Inter-Am Ct HR, OEA/Ser.L/V/II.124 Doc 5 (2006).

the El Salvadoran Supreme Court considers a constitutional challenge to the law.[6] In neighbouring Guatemala, a UN-backed commission to investigate corruption has resulted in prosecutions for human rights atrocities to be brought against officials from the former dictatorship, including the former dictator Efraín Ríos Montt.[7] The trial started in January 2016.[8]

It should be noted that Spain has arguably led the way in seeking justice (by way of criminal prosecution) in cases where its citizens have been victims of human rights atrocities. This in itself is ironic, as Spain adopted a policy of forgetfulness (*Pacto de Olvido*) concerning Spanish rule under the dictator General Francisco Franco (1939–1975).[9] Both the Latin American experiences, and the contemporary Spanish response to those military dictatorships' human rights abuses, form an important part of the discussion about amnesty.

This brief introduction draws our attention to several critical factors and concepts, which give rise to questions concerning which types of crimes were the human rights atrocities; the time period during which they were committed and whether statutes of limitations apply; who the perpetrators are and who were the victims; and finally, whether the expectations of victims and democracy, in relation to achieving peace and meeting the demands of justice, have been satisfied. To begin this exploration, let us start with the definition. It is not possible to provide a comprehensive overview of amnesty and amnesty laws. Instead, this chapter will focus on key questions concerning this mechanism and refer to important examples throughout the discussion.

6.2 Definition

'Amnesty' originates from the Greek word 'amnestia', which means 'forgetfulness', or 'oblivion'.[10] The use of amnesty throughout history was part of an

---

6 'Digging for Justice', above n 4, 25–26.

7 Montt was president of Guatemala from 1982 to 1983. The charges against Montt are genocide and crimes against humanity. These proceedings are a retrial, after the Guatemalan Constitutional Court overturned his conviction in 2013. 'Guatemala Court: Former Dictator Can be Tried but Not Sentenced', *The Guardian* (online), 25 August 2015 <http://www.theguardian.com/world/2015/aug/25/guatemala-rios-montt-genocide-trial-not-sentenced>.

8 *Ríos Montt's Trial: The Ultimate Test for Guatemala's Justice System* (8 January 2016) Amnesty International <https://www.amnesty.org/en/latest/news/2016/01/rios-montt-s-trial-the-ultimate-test-for-guatemala-s-justice-system/>.

9 Paloma Aguilar, 'Justice, Politics and Memory in the Spanish Transition' in Alexandra Barahona de Brito, Carmen González Enríquez and Paloma Aguilar (eds), *The Politics of Memory and Democratization* (Oxford University Press, 2001) 92–118.

10 Norman Weisman, 'A History and Discussion of Amnesty' (1972) 4 *Columbia Human Rights Law Review* 520. See also Louise Mallinder, *Amnesty, Human Rights and Political Transitions* (Hart Publishing, 2008) 3–7.

approach that could now be described as a utilitarian position vis-à-vis the past.[11] A utilitarian position subscribes to the view that decisions are made with the common good in mind. In this vein, amnesty is a promise to desist from committing crimes, from murder to other unspeakable atrocities, and whereby the victims and wider society are asked to forget the past actions of such individuals or organisations and move on for the common good. The trade is made in the name of achieving stability. However, for critics, it comes at the cost of losing truth and justice.[12] Indeed, for these commentators amnesty is politicised, because amnesty is used to silence the crimes and protect the perpetrators under the guise of policies that claim to address the past injustices of the predecessor regime.[13] The measure has come to epitomise an obstacle to justice. In fact, amnesties that recommend blanket, unconditional immunity no longer seem to be the favoured approach in a time where a new norm of accountability for human rights violations is replacing the traditional practice of amnesty. Significantly, the growth in transitional justice scholarship coincides with the calls for accountability and proposals, in some contexts, for limited, conditional amnesties as a means towards peace and reconciliation. To gain a further, critical understanding of this controversial measure it is helpful to consider selected cases of amnesty along its respective timeline and to map its key points in order to reveal more about local and universal approaches and contexts regarding justice and peace.

6.3 Brief historical overview

Early forms of amnesty date back to Ancient Greece. Amnesty was, and continues to be, a practice that has been introduced and supported by the executive, and it constituted a variety of measures, such as pardons, restoring voting rights, suppressing dissent, or exacting revenge for past actions of disloyalty. These measures have been noted in the state practice of the United Kingdom (for political prisoners), France (exemptions as a way of punishing disloyalty), and the US (restoring voting rights). These historical examples are referred to as pure amnesties, where there is a true pardon and no change to the relevant law. As will be discussed below, the control over forgetting and forgiveness is an important component of sovereignty.[14] Several scholars note that '[t]he historical granting of amnesties as a means to secure post-conflict peace and stability and

---

11 See Jeremy Bentham, *An Introduction to the Principles of Morals and Education* (Clarendon Press, 1996) first published in 1789.
12 Michael Scharf, 'The Letter of the Law: The Scope of International Legal Obligation to Prosecute Human Rights Crimes' (1996) 59 *Law and Contemporary Problems* 41.
13 Mallinder, *Amnesty, Human Rights and Political Transitions*, above n 10, 319–353.
14 Paul Ricouer, *Memory, History, Forgetting* (University of Chicago Press, 2003).

its relationship to "stateness" is relevant'.[15] In fact, the issue of sovereignty is one that stands in the way of reconciling the goals of justice and peace. This occurs in cases where the state fails to bring the matter of amnesty to the wider public discourse, and ignores the needs and wishes of the victims.

Developments in Latin America are unavoidable when studying or examining amnesty. This relates to the human rights atrocities that occurred in the region. In the 1970s, amnesties, as a sort of makeshift practice, were granted to those involved in the planning, murder and/or torture that characterised the region's military dictatorships.[16] Argentina, Chile, El Salvador, Guatemala and Uruguay were joined by other states in the 1990s, namely Cambodia, Haiti and South Africa – in that each had 'granted amnesty to members of the former regime that commanded death squads that tortured and killed thousands of civilians within their respective countries'.[17] The United Nations supported the negotiations for granting amnesty as a means of restoring peace and a democratic government in four cases: Cambodia, El Salvador, Haiti and South Africa. Thus we have national, regional, and universal approaches and involvement in transitional governments. Their involvement might explain the location of amnesty in national policies.

6.4 Purpose

The end of World War II, and the Nuremberg and Tokyo Trials mark the alteration in state practice as concerns holding individuals accountable for war crimes and crimes against humanity. Suddenly a category of crimes was created that was no longer protected by a statute of limitations (or a law that prohibits criminal prosecution for crimes that were committed a specified number of years ago). Since World War II a range of treaties have been ratified that have had a notable impact on the development of the current approach towards amnesty; specific treaties will be discussed shortly. It is worthwhile mentioning that at this point an international duty to hold perpetrators accountable is identified. Later, with the arrest of the Chilean dictator Augusto Pinochet in the late 1990s, the notion of universal jurisdiction is on the table; this notion claims that states or international organisations, such as international courts, can claim criminal jurisdiction over an accused person regardless of where the alleged crime was committed, or

---

15 Kieran McEvoy and Louise Mallinder, 'Amnesties, Punishment and the Calibration of Mercy in Transition' (2012) 39 *Journal of Law and Society* 410 (published as Research Paper No. 12–07, Transitional Justice Institute, 8 September 2012).

16 Naomi Roht-Arriaza (ed), *Impunity and Human Rights in International Law and Practice* (Oxford University Press, 1995). See also Jorge Correa Sutil, 'Dealing with Past Human Rights Violations: The Chilean Case after Dictatorship' (1992) 67 *Notre Dame Law Review* 1455.

17 Scharf, above n 12, 1.

regardless of the accused's nationality, country of residence, or any other relation with the prosecuting body. Spain, and later Belgium, came to the fore with the application of universal jurisdiction. It is the actions of the Spanish judge, Baltazar Garzón, which gives rise to pertinent questions about judicial culture and what underpins moves to challenge sovereign positions on the issue of amnesty.[18] Equally noteworthy are courts and their interpretation of relevant statutes that provides for successful requests for extradition – such as the US development noted at the start of the chapter. Pinochet certainly marked a watershed moment. The case gave rise to discussions about the aims of international criminal justice, and heated debates about what 'seeking justice' entails. Ironically, the location of victims in this constellation was, and continues to be, opaque.

6.5 Points of contention and controversy

For many, amnesty laws are equivalent to impunity (exemption from punishment).[19] This view asserts that such laws present an obstacle to the right of redress, the rule of law and the deterrence of human rights violations.[20] Since the late 1990s, the UN has taken the position that amnesties preventing the prosecution of persons charged with war crimes, genocide, crimes against humanity and other gross violations of human rights are inconsistent with state obligations under numerous ratified treaties and UN policy. It is a position that might also be incompatible with emerging principles of customary international law. Amnesty would come to haunt, as a legitimate feature of transnational polices, the UN and its international positions noted above after the establishment of the International Criminal Tribunal for former Yugoslavia and the International Criminal Tribunal for Rwanda, as well as the International Criminal Court (ICC).

On that note, both France and the US introduced provisions that enable the state to recuse the ICC's jurisdiction over war crimes concerning their own nationals.[21] Columbia attempted to use similar means when it sought to protect its paramilitary squads from future prosecution. Under Article 124 of the Rome Statute it was possible to suspend the jurisdiction of the ICC for a period of seven years. Such approaches thus created a separate legal regime for war crimes by locating them, for example, under a separate title in the criminal code (such as

---

18 David Sugarman, 'Courts, Human Rights and Transitional Justice' (2009) 36 *Journal of Law and Society* 272 and by the same author, 'The Pinochet Case: International Criminal Justice in the Gothic Style?' (2001) 64 *Modern Law Review* 933. See also Lisa Hilibink, *Judges Beyond Politics in Democracy and Dictatorship: Lessons from Chile* (Cambridge University Press, 2007).

19 Mallinder, above n 10, 319–353.

20 William Bourdon, 'Prosecuting the Perpetrators of International Crimes' (2005) 3 *Journal of International Criminal Justice* 434.

21 Ibid. See also Helen Duffy, above n 1, 456–664.

the case of France). The result is that they are covered by the statute of limitations. For example, the French definition of war crimes also left open lacunae; it rejected inserting Article 8 of the Rome Statute,[22] which concerns war crimes, or the definitions of grave breaches of the Geneva Conventions of 1949 and of the First Protocol, which the state is bound by. France withdrew its declaration in 2008, and Columbia, in 2009. In 2015 the Assembly of States Parties or ASP (comprised of representatives of states that have ratified and acceded to the Rome Statute) moved to delete Article 124.[23]

Granting amnesty to those suspected of war crimes does not answer calls for justice; that is achieved through holding the perpetrators of these crimes accountable. Proponents of amnesties would argue that the move to enacting amnesty legislation avoiding prosecutions and aaccountability is based on achieving peace, especially in post-conflict reconstruction. However, any sort of progress requires addressing and resolving the past. Amnesties seem to merely postpone the manifestation of discontent. They should only have a limited application and meet stringent conditions before being used.

6.6 Amnesty laws

Many countries have passed amnesty laws, referring to specific events in the country's history, for war crimes or crimes against humanity, or for wider categories of crimes that include these two crimes.[24] The arguments for and against a decision to grant amnesty cannot avoid a consideration of whether there is a duty to prosecute. In other words, there is a difference between a policy decision (which many assert is a poor one) and a decision that violates international law.[25]

There are several international legal instruments to note when considering the assertion that there is a duty to prosecute. Because we are dealing with treaties, Article 27 of the Vienna Convention on the Law of Treaties needs to be noted, whereby '[a] party may not invoke the provisions of its internal law as justification for failure to perform a treaty'.

The 1949 Geneva Conventions comprise four instruments that were negotiated in 1949 to codify the international rules concerning the treatment of prisoners

---

22 Rome Statute of the International Criminal Court, opened for signature 17 July 1998, 2187 UNTS 90 (entered into force 1 July 2002) at <http://legal.un.org/icc/statute/romefra.htm>.

23 Assembly of States Parties to the Rome Statute of the International Criminal Court, Res ICC-ASP/14/Res.2, 14th sess, 11th plen mtg (adopted 26 November 2015).

24 Antonio Cassese et al, *Cassese's International Criminal Law* (Oxford University Press, 3rd ed, 2013) 309. The most comprehensive study to date notes that between 1979 and 2010 an average of 12.25 amnesty laws were enacted each year around the world. See McEvoy and Mallinder, above n 15, 4.

25 Scharf, above n 12, 41. Diane Orentlicher, 'Settling Accounts: The Duty to Prosecute Human Rights Violations of a Prior Regime' (1991) 100 *Yale Law Journal* 2537.

of war and civilians in occupied territory.[26] The Geneva Conventions enjoy being one of the most ratified in the world. Each of the conventions includes a specific list of grave breaches for which there is an individual criminal liability, and for which states have a resultant duty to prosecute. These grave breaches are war crimes and include wilful killing, torture, or inhuman treatment, including biological experiments, wilfully causing great suffering or serious injury to body or health, extensive destruction of property not justified by military necessity, wilfully depriving a civilian of the rights of a fair and regular trial, and unlawful confinement of a civilian. State parties to the Geneva Conventions have an obligation to search for, prosecute and punish perpetrators of grave breaches – unless they decide to hand over the individuals for trial by another State Party. It should be noted that the duty is limited to the context of international armed conflict. In the commentary on the Conventions, the obligation to prosecute is discussed as absolute.[27]

The Convention on the Prevention and Punishment of the Crime of Genocide, which entered into force on 12 January 1951, has also been widely ratified. The Convention provides an absolute obligation to prosecute individuals responsible for genocide (as defined in the Convention).[28] The Convention applies only to those who have the specific intent to destroy a substantial portion of the population of a target group. Also, the victims must constitute one of the groups included in the document, namely national, ethnic, racial or religious. Political groups were intentionally excluded from the Convention's definition.[29]

---

26 Geneva Convention for the Amelioration of the Condition of the Wounded and Sick in Armed Forces in the Field (First Geneva Convention), adopted 12 August 1949, 75 UNTS 31 (entered into force 21 October 1950); Geneva Convention for the Amelioration of the Condition of the Wounded, Sick and Shipwrecked Members of Armed Forces at Sea (Second Geneva Convention), adopted 12 August 1949, 75 UNTS 85 (entered into force 21 October 1950); Geneva Convention Relative to the Treatment of Prisoners of War (Third Geneva Convention), adopted 12 August 1949, 75 UNTS 135 (entered into force 21 October 1950); Geneva Convention Relative to the Protection of Civilian Persons in Time of War (Fourth Geneva Convention), adopted 12 August 1949, 75 UNTS 287 (entered into force 21 October 1950); Protocol Additional to the Geneva Conventions of 12 August 1949, and Relating to the Protection of Victims of International Armed Conflicts (Protocol I), adopted 8 June 1977, 1125 UNTS 3 (entered into force 7 December 1978); Protocol Additional to the Geneva Conventions of 12 August 1949, and Relating to the Protection of Victims of Non-International Armed Conflicts (Protocol II), adopted 8 June 1977, 1125 UNTS 609 (entered into force 7 December 1978); Protocol Additional to the Geneva Conventions of 12 August 1949, and Relating to the Adoption of an Additional Distinctive Emblem (Protocol III), adopted 8 December 2005 (entered into force 14 January 2007). For full text and commentaries see the *Treaties and Customary Law*, International Committee of the Red Cross <https://www.icrc.org/en/war-and-law/treaties-customary-law>.

27 Theodor Meron, *Human Rights and Humanitarian Norms as Customary Law* (Clarendon Press, 1989) 215.

28 For the full text see the United Nations Human Rights Office of the High Commissioner at <http://www.ohchr.org/EN/ProfessionalInterest/Pages/CrimeOfGenocide.aspx>.

29 Further discussion of this point is outside the scope of this chapter.

The Convention against Torture and Other Cruel, Inhuman or Degrading Treatment or Punishment entered into force on 26 June 1987.[30] Many of the actions committed in the examples cited in this chapter would be captured by this definition. The Convention requires that each State Party criminalises all acts of torture in its domestic law, establishes competence over offences in such cases where the perpetrator is a national of the state, and if such a state does not extradite the perpetrator, the Convention requires it to submit the case to its competent authorities for the purpose of prosecution.

The Committee against Torture, in a case concerning Argentine amnesty laws, decided in 1990 that communications submitted by Argentine citizens on behalf of their relatives who had been tortured by the state's military authorities were inadmissible, as Argentina had ratified the Convention after the amnesty laws had been enacted.[31] The Committee, in its dictum, stated that '[e]ven before the entry into force of the Convention against Torture, there existed a general rule of international law which *should* oblige all states to take effective measures to prevent torture and to punish acts of torture'.[32] The Committee intentionally used 'should' in an effort to show that its claim was aspirational and not a statement of binding law.[33]

Although human rights conventions do not specifically mention the duty to prosecute, the position taken by some commentators[34] is that to ensure rights implies a duty to prosecute the perpetrators. For example, to ensure the right to life obliges the state to conduct an effective investigation into a killing to determine if it was lawful or unlawful.

The Human Rights Committee's pronouncements on the issue have not been conclusive. The Committee monitors the implementation of the 1966 International Covenant on Civil and Political Rights (ICCPR), in force since 1976. The Committee has urged states to prosecute (Surinam), told states to bring violators to justice (Uruguay) and stated that amnesties are generally incompatible with ensuring that the rights set in the ICCPR are meaningful.

Even the case of *Velásquez Rodríguez*[35] cannot be read as ensuring a duty to prosecute. This case concerned the unresolved disappearance of Manfredo Velásquez in September 1981. The Inter-American Court of Human Rights was

---

30 For the full text see the United Nations Human Rights Office of the High Commissioner at <http://www.ohchr.org/EN/ProfessionalInterest/Pages/CAT.aspx>.
31 Scharf, above n 12, 47.
32 Decision on Admissibility from 23 November 1989, Regarding Communications Nos 1/1988, 2/1988 and 3/1988 (OR, MM and MS v Argentina), Report of the Committee Against Torture, UN GAOR, 45th sess, Supp No 44, Annex VI, UN Doc A/45/44 (1990) 111.
33 Scharf, above n 12, 48.
34 Orentlicher, above n 25. See also M Cherif Bassiouni, 'Searching for Peace and Achieving Justice: The Need for Accountability' (1996) 59 *Law and Contemporary Problems* 9.
35 Decision from 29 July 1988, Inter-Am Ct HR (ser C) No. 4 (1988).

presented with testimonies indicating that he had been tortured and killed by the Honduran security services. The Court relied on Article 1(1) of the 1969 American Convention on Human Rights to ensure the rights enumerated in it.[36] It then went on to find the Honduran government to be in breach of its duties under the Convention. In the aftermath of *Velásquez*, the Inter-American Commission took another look at amnesty laws in the case of El Salvador, Uruguay and Argentina. In all three instances, the Commission held that the amnesty laws were not compatible with the American Convention's right to a remedy (Article 25) and right to a judicial process (Article 8), read in conjunction with Article 1's obligation to ensure rights. The Inter-American Commission went further in 1996 by holding that Chile's approach to self-amnesty failed on two grounds: (1) Chile did not succeed in conducting an investigation that specifically identified all individual perpetrators which, as a result, made it almost impossible to establish any such responsibility before the civil courts; (2) Chile failed to take punitive action against the perpetrators.[37]

Several commentators have noted that there is a customary international law duty to prosecute perpetrators of crimes against humanity, and that granting amnesty to such individuals violates international law.[38] As noted above, the Nuremberg proceedings marked an important moment for international crimes. The Charter of the Nuremberg War Crimes Tribunal was the first international instrument in which crimes against humanity were codified. The linkage to war and whether such a connection between crimes against humanity and war would be required by international law, or merely by its Charter, has been a subject of dispute. Although the jurisprudence of the International Criminal Tribunal for the former Yugoslavia indicated that the nexus requirement need not be with armed conflict.[39]

Despite the promulgation of the Declaration on Territorial Asylum, there is no state practice that is propounded; rather there is an advisory role on the part of the General Assembly.[40] The Declaration is often cited by some commentators as being the earliest international recognition of a legal obligation

---

36 The American Convention has been in force since 1978. The jurisprudence of the Inter-American Court has influenced the case law of the European Court of Human Rights in its interpretation of the 1950 European Convention on Human Rights in similar areas, such as disappearances. Mallinder, *Amnesty, Human Rights and Political Transitions*, above n 10, 164–165, 272–273, 424–428.

37 *Garay Hermosilla et al v Chile*, decision from 15 October 1996, Case 10.843, Report No. 36/96, Inter-Am Ct HR OEA/SerI/V/II.95 Doc 7, Rev, 156 (1997).

38 Scharf, above n 12, 41–61.

39 Ibid 53. See *Prosecutor v Duško Tadić /a/k/a 'Dule'*, decision from 2 October 1995, Decision on the Defence Motion for Interlocutory Appeal on Jurisdiction, UN Tribunal for the Protection of Persons Responsible for Serious Violations of International Humanitarian Law Committed in the Territory of the Former Yugoslavia since 1991, Case No. IT-94-1, 72.

40 Scharf, above n 12, 57.

to prosecute perpetrators of crimes against humanity.[41] Equally, no sooner had the term 'crimes against humanity' been first coined with respect to the massacres of Armenians during World War I than the international community agreed amnesty for the Turkish perpetrators.[42] Likewise in 1962, France and Algeria decided against trying persons who committed atrocities during the Algerian war.[43] In 1971, following the Bangladeshi war, India and Bangladesh agreed not to prosecute Pakistanis charged with genocide and crimes against humanity in exchange for political recognition of Bangladesh by Pakistan.[44] Finally, the Security Council can, through a Chapter VII resolution, create binding obligations on states to bring those responsible for international crimes to justice.[45]

6.7 Examples of amnesty laws across the world

In order to understand amnesty laws, we may look at the Chilean experience and the *Miguel Ángel Sandoval Rodríguez* case.[46] The case highlights three factors key to the controversy of amnesty laws: statute of limitations, murder and impunity. This case, which is critiqued more for what it did not say than for what it did, is an excellent starting point to a discussion that brings us to present day developments. The *Sandoval* case concerned a forced disappearance. Sandoval was a member of the Leftist Revolutionary Movement (*Movimiento de Izquierda Revolucionaria*). In 1975, the Chilean Directorate of National Intelligence abducted Sandoval and detained him at a secret detention camp (Villa Grimaldi). There he was tortured and later disappeared.

The decision of the Chilean Supreme Court in 2005 comes after a series of forced disappearance cases that the Court reopened after dismissal by the military courts.[47] In this unanimous decision, the Court held that the crime of aggravated abduction equates to a crime of forced disappearance as set out in international human rights law and international criminal law. The Court reaffirmed the supremacy of international law in the domestic legal order.

---

41 UN General Assembly, Declaration on Territorial Asylum, GA Res 2312 (XXII), 22 UN GAOR Supp (No 16) 81, UN Doc A/6716 (1967).

42 Scharf, above n 12, 52. Also M Cherif Bassiouni, *Crimes Against Humanity in International Criminal Law* (Cambridge University Press, 2014).

43 Mallinder, above n 10, 50–53.

44 Ibid 130.

45 Scharf, above n 12, 59.

46 *Juan Contreras Sepulvada y Otros (Crimen) Casaci*ón Fondo y Forma, Corte Suprema, 517/2004, Resolución 22267, decision 17 November 2004 (so-called '*Sandoval* Case').

47 Fannie Lafontaine, 'No Amnesty or Statute of Limitation for Enforced Disappearances: The *Sandoval* Case before the Supreme Court of Chile' (2005) 3 *Journal of International Criminal Justice* 469.

What is noteworthy about this case is that the Court maintained that amnesty is no bar to investigation, nor is it a bar to the application of criminal sanctions. The 1978 Chilean amnesty law is referred to as a self-imposed or self-proclaimed amnesty law or blanket amnesty law that is wide in scope and incorporated into the constitution.[48] In addition to granting amnesty to 'all persons who committed, as perpetrators, accomplices or conspirators, criminal offences . . . between 11 September 1973 to 10 March 1978' defendants in the cases claimed protection under the statute of limitations, as sufficient time had passed to bar any proceedings against them. The Court rejected both positions on the grounds that the crime of aggravated abduction was continuous in nature and therefore not completed within the period set out in the amnesty law. The supremacy of international law overrode any incompatible domestic law.

The following is an overview of developments in selected states that shape the position with respect to amnesty and amnesty laws.

6.7.1 Afghanistan

Afghanistan has a history of amnesties, beginning in 1979 with the amnesty issued by the Soviet-backed revolutionary forces, which asserted that the amnesty was a 'humanitarian act'. The move, like the assertion, was propaganda. In more recent years, the plan adopted by the Afghan government for peace – the 2005 Action Plan for Peace, Justice and Reconciliation – led to the drafting of a bill providing for blanket amnesty for human rights violations and war crimes in Afghanistan for the period 1978 to 2001. The idea underpinning the move was to offer immunity to members of the Taliban (save for crimes against humanity) and in an effort to weaken the organisation. The attempt was not successful. Although the bill was not formally enacted as law, it continues to be a contentious issue, and for many it is highly politicised and an abuse of power. The 2007 National Reconciliation Charter granted amnesty to warlords, many of whom entered politics and were in the government.[49] Human Rights Watch has stated that the 2007 law that provides amnesty to perpetrators of war crimes and crimes against humanity should be repealed.[50]

6.7.2 Algeria

Algeria is an important case study. After achieving independence in 1962, the country's post-colonial experience is one that cannot ignore the effect and

---

48 Ibid. See also Mallinder, *Amnesty, Human Rights and Political Transitions*, above n 10, 230.
49 Mallinder, above n 10, 133.
50 *Afghanistan: Repeal Amnesty Law* (10 March 2010) Human Rights Watch <https://www.hrw.org/news/2010/03/10/afghanistan-repeal-amnesty-law>.

legacies of French rule and France's approaches to its own past in relation to its actions against those fighting for independence. In 1989 Algeria adopted a new constitution that set up a collision between Islamic-backed parties and military forces when the government stepped in, under military pressure, to cancel a second round of elections that would have resulted in the Islamic Salvation Front (FIS) gaining absolute majority. The conflict that resulted in the 1990s is referred to as the 'Dirty War' (*la sale guerre*), during which time an estimated 100,000–150,000 people were killed.[51] It was not until the 1999 Civil Harmony Law that the security situation stabilised. The 2005 Charter for Peace and Reconciliation aimed towards negotiations between the disparate groups. The Charter also provided for amnesty. The key provision, Ordinance No. 06–61 was enacted into law in 2006. It amnestied the Islamic fighters who were engaged in the fighting, but excluded those involved in massacres, rapes, and using explosives in public areas. The applicants are required to make individual applications and surrender arms.[52] It is worth noting that an ad hoc committee on disappearances was created in 2003, but the 2005 mandate did not provide for compensation to the victims.

6.7.3 Argentina

In 1995 the chief of the Argentine army apologised to the nation for the military's crimes during the Dirty War, and in 2004 the then president also asked for forgiveness 'for the shame of a democracy which stayed silent on those atrocities during the past twenty years'.[53] These measures of atonement have been accompanied by amnesties. For example, following the report by the National Commission for Forced Disappearances (CONADEP), the country saw a series of trials of the high-ranking military leaders in the mid-1980s. In 1986, however, under the Raúl Alfonsín regime (1983–1989), the government passed two amnesty laws in order to prevent further trials. Law No. 23, 492, or the 'full stop law', set a 60-day deadline for the initiation of new prosecutions. When that law did not prevent the prosecution of large numbers of defendants, Law No. 23, 521, or the 'due obedience law' was passed, which granted automatic immunity from prosecution to all members of the military, save for the high commanders. The 'due obedience law' was deemed constitutional by the Argentine Supreme Court in 1987. In 2001, however, a disappearance case was reopened against two police agents who were accused of the torture and 'disappearance' of

---

51 Mallinder, above n 10, 69–71.
52 Ibid 181.
53 Scharf, above n 12, 47–48.

a Chilean-Argentine couple. This ruling resulted in more prosecutions.[54] Under Carlos Menem (1989–1999), the leaders of the military dictatorship were pardoned. Despite the calls for justice led by the Mothers of the Plaza del Mayo, the leaders remain free. The 2005 Argentine Supreme Court ruling overturning the amnesty laws did not extend to this group.[55] However, in 2007, after a series of challenges, the Supreme Court, in a vote of 4 to 2, found that the pardons granted by President Menem were unconstitutional.[56] Under Néstor Kirchner and Cristina Fernández de Kirchner, a presidential decree from 2007 authorised former and then in post-government military, police and government officials to reveal state secrets if called to testify at human rights trials. Presidential Decree No. 606 created a Truth and Justice programme responsible to the Chief Cabinet of Ministers.[57] But the slow rate of progress of prosecutions resulted in criticisms of the judiciary on the part of the human rights community.

6.7.4 Sierra Leone

Sierra Leonean history and culture is key to understanding the Civil War (1991–2002) and subsequent efforts to achieve peace, justice and reconciliation. Achieving a sense of justice following a conflict characterised by extreme brutality and the widespread use of child soldiers needs to be considered in this context.[58] Up until independence, the country's diverse population largely coexisted peacefully across ethnic, cultural and religious differences.[59] All this changed after 1961, when intergroup relationships came to be influenced by different actors fighting for political power.[60] The Peace Accord came to an end with the 1997 military coup. Negotiation efforts resulted in the conclusion of the 1999 Lomé Peace Agreement. However, this was supplanted by more fighting before hostilities finally ceased in 2002. The presence of a criminal tribunal and a Truth and Reconciliation Commission ((TRC), discussed in Chapter 5 on 'Truth and Reconciliation Commissions') is important. In addition

---

54 The *Barrios Altos* case is important. In 2001 the Inter-American Court of Human Rights declared two Peruvian amnesty laws to be incompatible with the American Convention on Human Rights. *Barrios Alto v Peru*, decision from 30 November 2001, Inter-Am Ct HR (ser C) No. 87 (2001).

55 Kathryn Sikkink, *Justice Cascade: How Human Rights Prosecutions are Changing World Politics* (Norton, 2011) 79.

56 This meant that the accused in this case, General Santiago Omar Riveros, could be tried for kidnappings, torture and disappearances.

57 Louise Mallinder, 'The Ongoing Quest for Truth and Justice: Enacting and Annulling Argentina's Amnesty Laws' (Working Paper No. 5, Beyond Legalism: Amnesties, Transition and Conflict Transformation, May 2009).

58 Laura Stovel, *Long Road Home: Building Reconciliation in Sierra Leone* (Intersentia, 2010) and Mallinder, above n 10, 336–337.

59 Stovel, above n 58.

60 Ibid.

to various restorative and reintegrative measures, the Lomé Peace Agreement included a highly controversial blanket amnesty that nevertheless failed to stop the Revolutionary United Front's continued military activity, including egregious human rights atrocities against civilians. Laura Stovel observes that the incorporation of the Sierra Leone TRC in the Lomé Peace Agreement, more than being an expression of strong political endorsement of this option, was a way of 'making the amnesty and power sharing deal palatable to the people of Sierra Leone'.[61] The amnesty was not accepted by the UN to include crimes against humanity or acts of genocide for the purposes of the organisation.[62] Whereas the Truth and Reconciliation Commission was included in the Lomé agreement, the Special Court for Sierra Leone was first established in 2002 by agreement between the Sierra Leone government and the UN. Unlike the international criminal tribunals of Rwanda and the former Yugoslavia, the Special Court for Sierra Leone is a hybrid tribunal acting to connect a national and international court. Instead of being imposed by the UN, the Special Court for Sierra Leone was established on the initiative of, and in cooperation with, the Sierra Leonean government.[63]

6.7.5 South Africa

In 1990 negotiations between the outgoing white minority government and the incoming opposition government led by the African National Congress (ANC) began. The period was characterised by efforts to ensure a peaceful transition, which included the release of ANC political prisoners and provisions for amnesty. The Promotion of National Unity and Reconciliation Act came into effect in 1995. Amnesty would become a vital part of the process in exchange for truth. None of the parties had a monopoly over power, and the compromise was seen as necessary. The exchange was viewed as a more positive step than prosecutions. The emphasis was on a more inclusive and restorative approach

---

61 Ibid.

62 Ibid. The Democratic Republic of Congo has also been identified as a vital case study in transitional criminal justice. In 2005 the country adopted an amnesty law that extends to combatants engaged in the conflict in the eastern provinces of the North and South Kivu. The law, however, excludes war crimes, crimes against humanity, and genocide. See Patrícia Pinto Soares, 'Positive Complementarity: Fine-Tuning the Transitional Justice Discourse? The Cases of the Democratic Republic of Congo, Uganda and Kenya' in Agata Fijalkowski and Raluca Grosescu (eds), *Transitional Criminal Justice in Post-Dictatorial and Post-Conflict Societies* (Intersentia, 2015) 187.

63 Mallinder, above n 10, 336–337.

to reconciliation[64] (the Truth and Reconciliation Commission is discussed in chapter 5). The process was one in which the state took great strides in engaging wider society. Importantly, granting amnesty was seen as being more reflective of indigenous cultural traditions. For example, *ubuntu* calls for more tolerance rather than retribution. One of the leading figures in the process and an advocate of its philosophy was Archbishop Desmond Tutu.[65] The bargain of amnesty for truth requires that eligible offenders who do not apply for amnesty or who fail to comply with its conditions will face prosecution. In reality, since the TRC's closure few prosecutions have been pursued.

6.7.6 Spain

Another relevant case study, Spain, was in a civil war between the Nationalists and the Republicans from 1936 to 1939. The Nationalists won, and under General Francisco Franco they established a right-wing dictatorship that lasted until 1975. The regime was characterised by the repression, disappearances and executions of a large number of political prisoners. Already in the early 1970s, in anticipation of Franco's death, there were calls for absolute amnesty. In 1975 the first amnesty was introduced to mark King Juan Carlos's accession to the throne. The limitations of the amnesty resulted in instability and the amnesty law was revisited and extended in 1977 to all crimes committed by both government supporters and the opposition. The legacy remained largely intact until mid-2000 when mass graves of Republican supporters were excavated, which has led to the promulgation of laws prohibiting the display of symbols and signs of the dictatorship.[66] In 2013, the UN High Commissioner for Human Rights indicated that the 1977 Amnesty Law be appealed on the grounds that it violated international human rights law.[67]

6.8 Current positions

Socio-legal scholars have carried out important critical work on amnesties. The prominent position taken by these commentators is that there is no universal duty

---

64 John Dugard, 'Retrospective Justice: International Law and the South African Model', in A James Adams (ed), *Transitional Justice and the Rule of Law in New Democracies* (University of Notre Dame Press, 1997) 269–290; John Dugard, 'Is the Truth and Reconciliation Process Compatible with International Law? An Unanswered Question' (1997) 13 *South African Journal of Human Rights* 258; John Dugard, 'Reconciliation and Justice: The South African Experience' (1998) 8 *Transnational Law and Contemporary Problems* 277. Mallinder, above n 10, 167–170.

65 *Ubuntu* is about what binds human beings, it is a belief in a shared, universal connection between people. Desmond Tutu, *No Future without Forgiveness* (Rider, 1999).

66 Mallinder, above n 10, 51–53.

67 James Badcock, 'UN Tells Spanish Government it Must Atone for Franco's Crimes', *Newsweek* (New York), 21 August 2014.

to prosecute under international law. Scholars also argue that the deterrent effect of prosecution is 'oversold' and that the rationale for punishment in international justice is 'poorly theorised'.[68] The assertions in this area frame amnesty in mercy. By doing so, amnesties can become an important tool in peace-making. As seen above, the Latin American experiences were characterised by tensions between principle and pragmatism, or between the demands of justice and the demands of a peaceful transition. Studies that have compared the Argentine, Chilean and Spanish experiences point to the role of the judiciary in overcoming amnesty laws and paving the way towards accountability through prosecutions; of these three, Argentina is the most progressive.[69] One could argue that the emphasis was placed on conducting retributive trials (and also a range of non-punitive measures). The key element of these discussions is sovereignty – which recalls Paul Ricouer and his notion of commanding forgetting and forgiveness. In other words, amnesty has nothing to do with forgiveness, because it is organised (officially) and made public. In this view, the private aspect expressed in (personal) compassion plays no part.[70]

The philosophy underpinning international criminal processes ranges from retribution to deterrence.[71] The failure to punish and absence of deterrence to future generations has led scholars like Antonio Cassese to argue that impunity of architects of, for example, the Armenian genocide gave a 'nod and a wink' to Nazi leaders.[72] These debates draw on Immanuel Kant's theories.[73] Kant asserted that retribution dictates that criminals should be punished because they deserve it for what they have done. But international law has not closed the door on amnesties, despite the shift in the discourse. Instead both international and domestic law accepts a role for prosecution and amnesties in transitional justice settings. Expressive functions of punishment might involve societal disapproval of criminal behaviour.[74] Punishment carries a message of public disapproval. But any message that is expressed is likely to be a message of many voices, and potentially carry multiple and conflicting meanings. The risk is that the offender will not receive the intended message of disapproval.

---

68 McEvoy and Mallinder, above n 15, 1.
69 Paloma Aguilar Fernández, 'Jueces, Represión, y Justicia Transicional en España, Chile y Argentina' (2013) 71 *Revista Internacional de Sociologia* 281.
70 Ricouer, above n 14.
71 Daryl Robinson, 'Serving the Interests of Justice: Amnesties, Truth Commissions and the International Criminal Court' (2003) 14 *European Journal of International Law* 481.
72 Antonio Cassese, 'Reflections on International Criminal Justice' (1998) 61 *Modern Law Review* 1 and Payam Akhavan, 'Beyond Impunity: Can International Criminal Justice Prevent Future Atrocities?' (2001) 95 *American Journal of International Law* 7.
73 Immanuel Kant, *The Cambridge Edition of the Works of Immanuel Kant* (Cambridge University Press, 1996) 472.
74 McEvoy and Mallinder, above n 15, 5–9.

Transitional justice scholars argue that truth recovery is important for preventing a repetition of crimes, and contributing to healing of victims and society. In this way, the importance of truth is a corrective to the amnesia effect connected to amnesties. For these scholars amnesties have an integral role to play in transitional contexts, which embrace a restorative role in the transition. Braithwaite famously discusses 'reintegrative shaming' as a way of finding mechanisms where offenders are subject to expressions of community disapproval, which are then followed by gestures of reintegration into the community of law-abiding citizens.[75] The alternative is 'disintegrative shaming', which creates a class of outcasts. For commentators like Kieran McEvoy, a 'criminologically-informed view of transitional justice is alive to *seeing* [emphasis in original] challenges and to trying (at least) to meet them rather than simply defaulting to top–down formalism which would simply pass an amnesty act and make no effort to engage with either victims or communities'.[76] In this sense, amnesties are about closely managing transitions, appealing to notions of justice, accountability and peace.[77]

Louise Mallinder aptly notes that when approaching these questions, it is important to privilege pragmatism over an attempt to try and apply ill-suited universal models that do not speak to the complexities of the individual transitional state. Countries need to pursue their own approaches to the past, and find their own means of connecting justice and peace.[78] Progress requires a careful consideration of the past. Amnesties should only have a limited application and meet stringent conditions before being used.

6.9 Summary

This chapter has critically considered amnesty, its definition, amnesty laws, points of controversy and the current position. We note that amnesty confronts justice and peace, but it continues to be haunted by the victim's place in any policy measure.

There is no treaty prohibiting amnesties, but states have been unwilling to agree to even the mildest discouragement when presented with an explicit

---

75 John Braithwaite, *Crime, Shame and Reintegration* (Cambridge University Press, 1989) 67: 'when individuals are shamed so remorselessly and unforgivingly that they become outcasts . . . it becomes more rewarding to associate with others who are perceived in some limited or total way as also at odds with mainstream standards'. For Braithwaite, reintegrative shaming concerns the application of clear standards of conduct and punishment, with the focus on punishing the criminal act rather than the individual.

76 McEvoy and Mallinder, above n 15, 17.

77 For example, the *Belfast Guidelines on Amnesty and Accountability*, Transitional Justice Institute <http://www.ulster.ac.uk/research-and-innovation/research-institutes/transitional-justice-institute> define a framework to evaluate the legality and legitimacy in accordance with the state's legal obligations.

78 McEvoy and Mallinder, above n 15, 22–23.

prohibition in treaty law. As noted, in international humanitarian law the duty to prosecute is absolute and mandatory but the scope is limited, therefore many atrocities cannot be included. With respect to customary law, there is no evidence of state practice or *opinio juris* to suggest there is a duty of prosecution that can only be considered permissive. This allows states discretion with alternative approaches to truth and accountability. In international human rights law no treaties state an explicit duty, but there is a duty to investigate. Concerning philosophy of punishment, in the context of transitional justice the retributive potential of punishing human rights violations is limited. Prosecution is typically selective, and punishments are rarely proportionate; it might be argued that amnesty that occurs within a properly constituted setting, such as a truth commission, may be a preferred option. And the effects of deterrence are highly uncertain. In conclusion, the present perspective dictates that amnesties be viewed from a restorative perspective. Restorative amnesties can play an important role in transitioning states, facilitating an inclusive dialogue that rebuilds relationships.

6.10 Discussion and tutorial questions

This brief introduction drew our attention to several critical factors and concepts, which give rise to the following questions.

1) Why are there no treaties prohibiting amnesties?

2) Does the involvement of international actors in the transitional process affect the decision to include amnesty as part of the post-reconstruction process?

3) What do the experiences of Latin America indicate with respect to the legitimacy of amnesty laws? Consider the key rulings of the Inter-American Court of Human Rights and the Chilean Supreme Court.

4) Consider the current position of legal scholars who criticise the rationale for punishment in international criminal justice as being 'poorly theorised'. How does this position challenge classical approaches to punishment? How does this position view amnesties?

Suggested reading

Akhavan, Payam, 'The Rise, and Fall, and Rise of International Criminal Justice' (2013) 11 *Journal of International Criminal Justice*.

Ambos, Kai, Judith Lange and Marieke Werde (eds), *Building a Future on Peace and Justice: Studies on Transitional Justice* (Springer, 2009).

Blair, James T, 'From the Numbers Who Died to Those Who Survived: Victim Participation in the Extraordinary Chambers in the Courts of Cambodia' (2009) 31 *University of Hawaii Law Review.*

Henham, Ralph, 'The Philosophical Foundations of International Sentencing' (2003) 1 *Journal of International Criminal Justice.*

Igreja, Victor, 'Amnesty Law, Political Struggles for Legitimacy and Violence in Mozambique' (2015) 9 *International Journal of Transitional Justice.*

Koskenniemi, Martti, 'Between Impunity and Show Trials' (2002) 6 *Max Planck Yearbook of United Nations Law.*

Lessa, Francesca, Tricia D Olsen, Leigh A Payne, Gabriel Pereira and Andrew G Reiter, 'Overcoming Impunity: Pathways to Accountability in Latin America' (2014) 8 *International Journal of Transitional Justice.*

Méndez, Juan E, 'Accountability for Past Abuses' (1997) 19 *Human Rights Quarterly.*

Robertson, Geoffrey, *Crimes Against Humanity: The Struggle for Global Justice* (Penguin, 2012).

Teitel, Ruti, *Transitional Justice* (Oxford University Press, 2000).

Suggested films

Buenos Aires Vice Versa (Directed by Alejandro Agresti, Staccato Films, Agresti Films, 1991).

The Girlfriend (Directed by Jeanine Meerapfel, Alma Film, Jorge Estrada Mora Producciones, 1988).

Memories They Told Me (Directed by Lúcia Murat, Elixir Entretenimento, Taiga Filmes, 2013).

The Mothers of Plaza de Mayo (Directed and produced by Susana Blaustein Muñoz and Lourdes Portillo, 1985).

Olympic Garage (Directed by Marco Bechis, Amedeo Pagani, Produced by Marco Bechis, Enrique Piñeyro, Eric Heumann, 1999).

State of Siege (Directed by Costa Gavras, Reggane Films, Euro International Film, Unidis, 1972).

Bibliography

Articles/books/reports

Afghanistan: Repeal Amnesty Law (10 March 2010) Human Rights Watch <https://www.hrw.org/news/2010/03/10/afghanistan-repeal-amnesty-law>.

Aguilar Fernández, Paloma, 'Jueces, Represión, y Justicia Transicional en España, Chile y Argentina' (2013) 71 *Revista Internacional de Sociologia.*

Aguilar, Paloma, 'Justice, Politics and Memory in the Spanish Transition' in Alexandra Barahona de Brito, Carmen González Enríquez and Paloma Aguilar (eds), *The Politics of Memory and Democratization* (Oxford University Press, 2001).

Akhavan, Payam, 'Beyond Impunity: Can International Criminal Justice Prevent Future Atrocities?' (2001) 95 *American Journal of International Law.*

Badcock, James, 'UN Tells Spanish Government It Must Atone for Franco's Crimes', *Newsweek* (New York), 21 August 2014.

Bassiouni, M Cherif, *Crimes Against Humanity in International Criminal Law* (Cambridge University Press, 2014).

Bassiouni, M Cherif, 'Searching for Peace and Achieving Justice: The Need for Accountability' (1996) 59 *Law and Contemporary Problems*.

Bentham, Jeremy, *An Introduction to the Principles of Morals and Education* (Clarendon Press, 1996).

Boister, Neil, 'International Tribunals for Transnational Crimes: Towards a Transnational Criminal Court?' (2012) 23 *Criminal Law Forum*.

Bourdon, William, 'Prosecuting the Perpetrators of International Crimes' (2005) 3 *Journal of International Criminal Justice*.

Braithwaite, John, *Crime, Shame and Reintegration* (Cambridge University Press, 1989).

Cassese, Antonio, Paola Gaeta, Laurel Baig, Mary Fan, Christopher Gosnell and Alex Whiting, *Cassese's International Criminal Law* (Oxford University Press, 3rd ed, 2013).

Cassese, Antonio, 'Reflections on International Criminal Justice' (1998) 61 *Modern Law Review*.

de Brito, Alexandra Barahona, Carmen González Enríquez and Paloma Aguilar Fernández (eds), *The Politics of Memory: Transitional Justice in Democratizing Societies* (Oxford University Press, 2001).

'Digging for Justice', *The Economist* (London), 2 January 2016.

Doggett, Martha, *Death Foretold: The Jesuit Murders in El Salvador* (Georgetown University Press, 1993).

Duffy, Helen, *The 'War on Terror' and the Framework of International Law* (University Press, 2nd ed, 2015)

Dugard, John, 'Reconciliation and Justice: The South African Experience' (1998) 8 *Transnational Law and Contemporary Problems*.

Dugard, John, 'Retrospective Justice: International Law and the South African Model' in A James Adams (ed), *Transitional Justice and the Rule of Law in New Democracies* (University of Notre Dame Press, 1997).

Dugard, John, 'Is the Truth and Reconciliation Process Compatible with International Law? An Unanswered Question' (1997) 13 *South African Journal of Human Rights*.

'Guatemala Court: Former Dictator Can be Tried but Not Sentenced', *The Guardian* (London), 25 August 2015.

Hilibink, Lisa, *Judges Beyond Politics in Democracy and Dictatorship: Lessons from Chile* (Cambridge University Press, 2007).

Kant, Immanuel, *The Cambridge Edition of the Works of Immanuel Kant* (Cambridge University Press, 1996).

Katz, Jonathan, 'US Wants Former Salvadoran Ally to Face Justice in 1989 Massacre', *The New York Times* (New York) (online) 13 September 2015 <http://www.nytimes.com/2015/09/14/world/americas/us-wants-former-salvadoran-ally-to-face-justice-in-1989-massacre.html>.

Lafontaine, Fannie, 'No Amnesty or Statute of Limitation for Enforced Disappearances: The *Sandoval* Case before the Supreme Court of Chile' (2005) 3
Journal of International Criminal Justice.

McEvoy, Kieran and Louise Mallinder, 'Amnesties, Punishment and the Calibration
of Mercy in Transition' (2012) 39 *Journal of Law and Society* (published as
Research Paper No. 12-07, Transitional Justice Institute, 8 September 2012).

Mallinder, Louise, 'The Ongoing Quest for Truth and Justice: Enacting and
Annulling Argentina's Amnesty Laws' (Working Paper No. 5, Beyond Legalism:
Amnesties, Transition and Conflict Transformation, May 2009).

Mallinder, Louise, *Amnesty, Human Rights and Political Transitions* (Hart Publishing,
2008).

Meron, Theodor, *Human Rights and Humanitarian Norms as Customary Law*
(Clarendon Press, 1989).

Orentlicher, Diane, 'Settling Accounts: The Duty to Prosecute Human Rights
Violations of a Prior Regime' (1991) 100 *Yale Law Journal.*

Ricouer, Paul, *Memory, History, Forgetting* (University of Chicago Press, 2003).

Ríos Montt's Trial: The Ultimate Test for Guatemala's Justice System (8 January 2016)
Amnesty International ‹https://www.amnesty.org/en/latest/news/2016/01/
rios-montt-s-trial-the-ultimate-test-for-guatemala-s-justice-system/›.

Robinson, Daryl, 'Serving the Interests of Justice: Amnesties, Truth Commissions
and the International Criminal Court' (2003) 14 *European Journal of International
Law.*

Roht-Arriaza, Naomi (ed), *Impunity and Human Rights in International Law and
Practice* (Oxford University Press, 1995).

Scharf, Michael, 'The Letter of the Law: The Scope of International Legal Obligation
to Prosecute Human Rights Crimes' (1996) 59 *Law and Contemporary Problems.*

Sikkink, Kathryn, *Justice Cascade: How Human Rights Prosecutions Are Changing
World Politics* (Norton, 2011).

Soares, Patrícia Pinto, 'Positive Complementarity: Fine-Tuning the Transitional
Justice Discourse? The Cases of the Democratic Republic of Congo, Uganda
and Kenya' in Agata Fijalkowski and Raluca Grosescu (eds), *Transitional Criminal
Justice in Post-Dictatorial and Post-Conflict Societies* (Intersentia, 2015).

Stovel, Laura, *Long Road Home: Building Reconciliation in Sierra Leone* (Intersentia,
2010).

Sugarman, David, 'Courts, Human Rights and Transitional Justice' (2009) 36
Journal of Law and Society.

Sugarman, David, 'The Pinochet Case: International Criminal Justice in the Gothic
Style?' (2001) 64 *Modern Law Review.*

Sutil, Jorge Correa, 'Dealing with Past Human Rights Violations: The Chilean Case
after Dictatorship' (1992) 67 *Notre Dame Law Review.*

Tutu, Desmond, *No Future without Forgiveness* (Rider, 1999).

Weisman, Norman, 'A History and Discussion of Amnesty' (1972) 4 *Columbia
Human Rights Law Review.*

Whitfield, Teresa, *Paying the Price: Ignacio Ellacuría and the Murdered Jesuits of
El Salvador* (Temple University Press, 1995).

Cases

Barrios Alto v Peru, decision from 30 November 2001, Inter-Am Ct HR (ser C) No. 87 (2001).

Decision on Admissibility from 23 November 1989, Regarding Communications Nos 1/1988, 2/1988 and 3/1988 (*OR, MM and MS v Argentina*), Report of the Committee Against Torture, UN GAOR, 45th sess, Supp No. 44, Annex VI, UN Doc A/45/44 (1990).

Garay Hermosilla et al v Chile, decision from 15 October 1996, Case 10.843, Report No. 36/96, Inter-Am Ct HR, OEA/SerI/V/II.95 Doc 7, Rev, 156 (1997).

Juan Contreras Sepulvada y Otros (Crimen) Casación Fondo y Forma, Corte Suprema, 517/2004, Resolución 22267, decision 17 November 2004.

El Mozote Massacre v El Salvador, decision from 2 March 2006, Case 10.720, Report No. 24/06, Inter-Am Ct HR, OEA/SerL/V/II.124 Doc 5 (2006).

Prosecutor v Duško Tadić a/k/a 'Dule', decision from 2 October 1995. Decision on the Defence Motion for Interlocutory Appeal on Jurisdiction, UN Tribunal for the Protection of Persons Responsible for Serious Violations of International Humanitarian Law Committed in the Territory of the Former Yugoslavia since 1991, Case No. IT-94-1.

Velásquez Rodríguez, decision from 29 July 1988, Inter-Am Ct HR (ser C) No. 4 (1988).

Legislation

Rome Statute of the International Criminal Court, opened for signature 17 July 1998, 2187 UNTS 90 (entered into force 1 July 2002) <http://legal.un.org/icc/statute/romefra.htm>.

UN General Assembly, Declaration on Territorial Asylum, GA Res 2312 (XXII), 22 UN GAOR Supp (No 16) 81, UN Doc A/6716 (1967).

Treaties

1969 American Convention on Human Rights (entered into force 18 July 1978).

Convention against Torture and Other Cruel, Inhuman or Degrading Treatment or Punishment, opened for signature 10 December 1984, 1465 UNTS 85 (entered into force 26 June 1987).

Convention on the Prevention and Punishment of the Crime of Genocide, adopted 9 December 1948, 78 UNTS 277 (entered into force 12 January 1951).

Geneva Convention for the Amelioration of the Condition of the Wounded and Sick in Armed Forces in the Field (First Geneva Convention), adopted 12 August 1949, 75 UNTS 31 (entered into force 21 October 1950).

Geneva Convention for the Amelioration of the Condition of the Wounded, Sick and Shipwrecked Members of Armed Forces at Sea (Second Geneva Convention), adopted 12 August 1949, 75 UNTS 85 (entered into force 21 October 1950).

Geneva Convention Relative to the Treatment of Prisoners of War (Third Geneva Convention), adopted 12 August 1949, 75 UNTS 135 (entered into force 21 October 1950).

Geneva Convention Relative to the Protection of Civilian Persons in Time of War (Fourth Geneva Convention), adopted 12 August 1949, 75 UNTS 287 (entered into force 21 October 1950).

Protocol Additional to the Geneva Conventions of 12 August 1949, and Relating to the Protection of Victims of International Armed Conflicts (Protocol I), adopted 8 June 1977, 1125 UNTS 3 (entered into force 7 December 1978).

Protocol Additional to the Geneva Conventions of 12 August 1949, and Relating to the Protection of Victims of Non-International Armed Conflicts (Protocol II), adopted 8 June 1977, 1125 UNTS 609 (entered into force 7 December 1978).

Protocol Additional to the Geneva Conventions of 12 August 1949, and Relating to the Adoption of an Additional Distinctive Emblem (Protocol III), adopted 8 December 2005 (entered into force 14 January 2007).

Other

Assembly of States Parties to the Rome Statute of the International Criminal Court, Res ICC-ASP/14/Res.2, 14th sess, 11th plen mtg (adopted 26 November 2015).

Belfast Guidelines on Amnesty and Accountability, Transitional Justice Institute <http://www.ulster.ac.uk/research-and-innovation/research-institutes/transitional-justice-institute>.

Treaties and Customary Law, International Committee of the Red Cross <https://www.icrc.org/en/war-and-law/treaties-customary-law>.

Chapter 7

Lustration and vetting

Lavinia Stan

7.1 Introduction

Perhaps few other transitional justice methods have elicited so spirited a debate as lustration and vetting, which in the twentieth century evolved as more restrained versions of the purges that historically led to the marginalisation from public life of public servants and political luminaries who remained loyal to the deposed regimes. This chapter defines the two terms, provides a brief historical overview of the application of these reckoning practices during the twentieth century, explains why some countries have opted for lustration and vetting while others refrained from adopting these measures, and reviews five major points of contention and controversy based on the experience to date. The cases of Ukraine, the Czech Republic, Poland and El Salvador demonstrate the backward-looking and forward-looking goals of lustration and vetting, as well as the limitations of these processes in helping newly democratising countries come to terms with the legacy of the recent past.

7.2 Definition of lustration and vetting

Lustration commonly refers to 'the broad set of parliamentary laws that restrict members and collaborators of former repressive regimes from holding a range of public offices, state management positions, or other jobs with strong public influence (such as in the media or academia) after the collapse of the authoritarian regime'.[1] This transitional justice policy targets individuals holding a wide range

---

1 Monica Nalepa, 'Lustration' in Lavinia Stan and Nadya Nedelsky (eds), *Encyclopedia of Transitional Justice* (Cambridge University Press, 2013) vol 1, 46.

of public offices such as elected and nominated public officials, heads of public universities and the banking sector, national radio and television stations, judges and prosecutors, and even teachers and priests. These persons are dismissed or demoted from their positions if the courts or independent state agencies find that they had served as party leaders or secret police agents of the previous authoritarian regime, or if they fail to disclose such past activities in a special written declaration that may or may not be made public. Lustration – derived from the Latin *lustratio* (cleansing ritual) and the Czechoslovak *lustrace* (mirror or light) – is a form of vetting, a common practice in post-authoritarian countries.

Vetting refers to a wide set of processes meant to evaluate 'the integrity of individuals to determine their suitability for continued or prospective public employment'.[2] In the transitional context where vetting is enforced, integrity refers to 'a person's adherence to relevant standards of human rights and professional conduct, including her or his financial propriety'.[3] Such screening of public officials or candidates for public employment aims at determining if their prior conduct and, more importantly, (dis)respect for human rights warrant their exclusion from public office. Unlike historical purges or summary dismissals, which target individuals for their membership in or affiliation with a group (for example, a political party or the clientele of a particular leader), vetting involves assessment of individual behaviour, calls for individual review, and offers at least some procedural guarantees to the individuals placed under evaluation.[4]

Both lustration and vetting seek to re-establish civic trust and re-legitimise public institutions. That is because both can lead to institutional reform and 'the purification of state institutions from within and without'.[5] Grounded in administrative law, lustration and vetting are both forms of 'administrative justice'. At the same time, vetting and lustration are different in scope and application. Vetting always involves exclusion from employment, a dimension with which some lustration programmes (like the one in Poland) are not primarily concerned. If widely applied, lustration can modify the composition of the entire public administration, whereas no vetting programme was ever so ambitious. As Cynthia Horne suggested, 'maybe lustration is a type of vetting but not all vetting is lustration'.[6]

---

2 Alexander Mayer-Rieckh and Pablo de Greiff (eds), *Justice as Prevention: Vetting Public Employees in Transitional Societies* (Social Science Research Council, 2007) 524.

3 Ibid 548.

4 Ibid 524.

5 Jens Meierhenrich, 'The Ethics of Lustration' (2006) 20(1) *Ethics and International Affairs* 99.

6 Email communication from Cynthia Horne to Lavinia Stan, 29 November 2015.

7.3 Brief historical overview

It was only after the collapse of the communist regimes in 1989 that Central and Eastern European countries championed lustration. However, vetting has had a long history in both dictatorial and democratic countries. In democracies of Europe, North America and Australia, the police, intelligence services and armed forces routinely vet applicants, as do some governmental bodies. Throughout history authoritarian countries carefully vetted applicants seeking access to top state positions (in the state bureaucracy, the judiciary, the police, secret police and armed forces), and banned ideologically 'unreliable' individuals from accessing such posts. During times of transition from authoritarianism to democracy, vetting was conducted in Western Europe after World War II, Latin America after the ousting of military juntas, Central and Eastern Europe after the collapse of communism, Northern Africa and the Middle East after the Arab Spring, and other post-authoritarian and post-conflict settings.

Vetting procedures have been implemented in Latin America (Argentina, El Salvador), Africa (Liberia, the Democratic Republic of Congo), post-communist Europe (Bosnia-Herzegovina, Kosovo, Bulgaria, Estonia, Latvia, Lithuania, Macedonia, Romania, Serbia and Montenegro, Slovakia, Poland, Hungary, the Czech Republic and Germany), but also in other European (Greece, Germany, Belgium), post-genocidal (Rwanda) and post-authoritarian countries (Haiti, Afghanistan, East Timor). France also merits attention for its policies of *épuration* and *criblage* implemented after World War II in an effort to identify and remove Nazi collaborators from within its extensive bureaucracy. While *épuration* and *criblage* were specific to France, other de-Nazification policies – similar in their general purpose, but different in the public offices targeted for investigation and the time span of the ban – were enacted in other European countries. The list of countries that implemented vetting procedures during times of transition is certainly much longer.

Vetting applies to a country's public sector, that is, the unelected government officials who make up the state administration (or bureaucracy, as it is sometimes called). However, to date no vetting policies screened the entire public sector of a given country. For various reasons, countries have preferred to vet only some of their state institutions, assessing all or only some (usually leadership) positions in each institution. From the experience to date, we know that vetting mostly focused on institutions that were part of serious, violent human rights abuses under the previous regime – primarily institutions in the judiciary (the courts) and the state security sector (the police and the secret police). For example, the armed forces were vetted in El Salvador and South Africa, countries where they were responsible for most human rights violations. By contrast, where less violent repression took the form of collaboration with the dictatorial regime and involved large numbers of individuals working in several state institutions, vetting was wider in scope, affecting not only the state apparatus, but also universities and the media. For example, in Greece after the dictatorship of the colonels ended in 1974, vetting was more extensive in universities and the military than in the courts and the police.[7]

The first lustration provision was included in the German Unification Treaty of 1990. The Treaty allowed the communist East Germany and the democratic West Germany (which also included the Western sectors of Berlin sealed off from 1961 to 1989 by the Soviet-built Berlin Wall) to come together again in a single state. According to the lustration provision, employers could ask a specialised governmental agency for information on an employee's past involvement with the notorious Stasi (the East German Ministry for State Security). Public officials and candidates to such posts found to have provided secret information to the Stasi were not allowed to retain, or gain, public office until 2006. Other countries in the region followed suit by adopting lustration laws in order to deal with the legacy of their communist regimes: Czechoslovakia in 1991, Lithuania in 1991 and 1999, Bulgaria in 1992, Hungary and Estonia in 1994, Albania in 1995 and 1998, as well as Poland in 1997 and 2006.

Lustration is based on either accusation or confession. Accusations are based on evidence of collaboration with the former regime obtained from archival and other sources of information. Accusation-based lustration was implemented in Germany, the Czech Republic, Bulgaria and Albania. By contrast, confession-based lustration allows individuals to disclose their past collaboration with the communist regime before the prosecutor presses charges. As such, it 'resembles plea bargaining by giving the lustrati the opportunity to continue their political activity in exchange for confessing their past activity and thus proving their loyalty to the new democratic regime and removing the possibility of blackmail'.[8] Confession-based lustration sanctions only past association with the communist regime that was kept secret from the public, not collaboration to which the lustrati admit. Hungary, Poland, Lithuania and Estonia preferred this type of lustration.

Additional differences separated the lustration programmes adopted in post-communist Europe. Some programmes screened very narrow categories of post-communist officials (those working in state-owned banks and universities in Bulgaria), while other programmes screened both state institutions and civil society organisations that accepted public funds (such as priests of the dominant Orthodox Church in Romania). Some programmes investigated only past involvement with the communist secret security that compiled extensive

---

7 Dimitri Sotiropoulos, 'Swift Gradualism and Variable Outcomes: Vetting in Post-Authoritarian Greece' in Mayer-Rieckh and de Greiff, above n 2, 120–145.

8 Nalepa, 'Lustration', in Stan and Nedelsky above n 1, 47–48.

secret archives on millions of ordinary citizens in Central and Eastern Europe, while others looked for past involvement in the Communist Party leadership as well. Some lustration programmes led to job loss (in Germany and the Czech Republic), while others did not (in Slovakia and Romania). Some programmes led to temporary bans from public administration (five years in Bulgaria), while others had effects over an indefinite period of time (the Czech Republic). The nature of the communist regime, the type of exit from communism and the 'politics of the post-communist present' have determined differences among national lustration programmes.

While generating considerable controversy at home, post-communist lustration was adopted in other regions of the world. After the ousting of Saddam Hussein in 2003, Iraq implemented a broad de-Baathification program that excluded former members of Hussein's Baath Party from the public administration, the police and the army. As a result, some 400,000 individuals, mostly men who acted as breadwinners for their families, reportedly lost their jobs.[9] More recently, in May 2013 Libya's National Congress (Parliament) overwhelmingly adopted a Law of Political Isolation that aimed at banning former members of the dictatorship of Muammar Gadaffi from holding public office during transition. Gadaffi had ruled the country with an iron fist from 1969 to 2011, routinely trampling on the most basic human rights. Whatever its original purpose, the law failed to help that country's progress towards democracy.

The international community has increasingly seen lustration and vetting as desirable for post-conflict and post-dictatorial societies, suggesting rules to align these policies with the rule of law. In 2007 the International Center for Transitional Justice, an international organisation based in New York, issued a set of *Operational Guidelines* for vetting that built on the *Rule of Law Tools for Post-Conflict States. Vetting: An Operational Framework*, a document issued in 2006 by the Office of the United Nations High Commissioner for Human Rights (UNHCR). The Guidelines explain the conditions for a vetting process and risks of undesirable consequences, describe different types of vetting, outline rules to design a vetting process and present institutional reforms that must accompany vetting to ensure its effectiveness and sustainability.[10] The UNHCR document, in turn, ponders over the role of international organisations in national vetting programmes, and proposes guidelines post-dictatorial countries can use to assess the situation, define the parameters, and design vetting programmes.[11]

---

9 Beth Dougherty, 'Iraq' in Stan and Nedelsky (eds), above n 1, vol 2, 236–243.
10 International Center for Transitional Justice, 'Vetting Public Employees in Post-Conflict Settings: Operational Guidelines' in Mayer-Rieckh and de Greiff, above n 2, 546–564.
11 Office of the United Nations High Commissioner for Human Rights, *Rule of Law Tools for Post-Conflict States – Vetting: An Operational Framework* (United Nations, 2006).

7.4 Purpose – why countries opt for lustration and vetting

Lustration and vetting presumably offer a series of benefits that make them appealing to new democracies. Before reviewing the most important such purposes, note the peculiar position of many post-conflict and post-authoritarian countries. By the time they underwent a regime change through revolutions or negotiations in the 1970s and the 1980s, Central and Eastern Europe and Latin America had lived through decades of authoritarianism that significantly altered the composition of their political, military, even economic and cultural, elites. Elite members opposing or defying the military junta or the communist authorities had been murdered, exiled, silenced, or sidelined from public life, being replaced with individuals loyal to regimes involved in egregious human rights violations. As a result, regime supporters dominated not a tiny fraction but an overwhelming majority of the public administration and state bureaucracy, the economy, mass media and universities. These public officials and luminaries acquired political, managerial and administrative experience in virtue of loyalty to the regime, personal connections, or condoning human rights abuses, more than personal merit or superior skills. Several arguments have been put forward in support of excluding these tainted elites through lustration and vetting.

First, both policies lead to personnel changes in public administration by facilitating the replacement of old elites with new ones, and inhibiting the reproduction of old elites into the new state apparatus. They represent a break between the dictatorial past and the democratic present, and 'provide opportunities for state and societal rebuilding and reconciliation, which is often deemed necessary in the wake of a conflict or authoritarian regime change'.[12] To understand why a clear break with the old regime is needed, think about the alternative to lustration and vetting, when the new government does little to prevent old elites from retaining positions of power and privilege after the regime change. In this case, the individuals who controlled the state machinery and held the most desirable positions in the society under dictatorship are also those who do so after the regime change. Such a situation would hardly convince the citizens, especially the former victims of the dictatorial regime, to trust the new democracy.

Second, lustration and vetting improve the trustworthiness of public institutions by removing individuals untrustworthy to fulfil the mandate of the new regime. Lustration in particular is linked to building trust in the government, and the society at large. Whereas the dictatorship condones human rights violations and protects perpetrators from being held accountable for their trespasses, the

---

12 Cynthia Horne, 'Vetting and Lustration', in Dov Jacobs (ed), *Research Handbook on Transitional Justice* (E Elgar, forthcoming).

new democracy demonstrates commitment to hold perpetrators accountable for past crimes by administrative justice measures. In the process, public institutions are cleansed of old elites, and new individuals with the skills required for the job and commitment to the new democracy and its human rights standards can assume those positions. Trust is key to a stable democracy, which needs its citizens to believe that the new regime works for them, not just for a narrow privileged elite unconcerned with the public good.

Third, by removing the old elites, lustration and vetting improve governmental performance and make the state machinery more accountable to the people, thus indirectly supporting democratisation. They do so by breaking the culture of impunity fostered under authoritarianism, dismantling informal networks that keep the state a prisoner to the interests of old elites, removing the possibility that those elites are blackmailed for their past, and preventing future abuses of power by tainted officials. In short, lustration and vetting are said to help improve the functionality and efficiency of the state apparatus, and make it responsive to citizens' demands. This is most evident in the case of the judiciary (which had covered the human rights abuses of the dictatorship by siding with the regime against the victims) and the armed forces, the police and the state security (which engaged in repression). In the Czech Republic, for example, lustration 'protected national security against the threat to the democratic transition posed by non-democratic old elite networks and the potential for blackmail on the part of former secret agents with access to evidence of politicians' former collaboration'.[13]

A related argument points to the extensive and ruthless corruption networks set up by former secret agents and Communist Party officials who retained their influence in the new democracy. Their corrupt behaviour is seen as a reason to lustrate them during the initial stages of post-communist transformation. Bulgaria and Romania are countries where secret officers and informers converted their communist-era political clout into political and economic advantage after 1989. In Bulgaria, the communist State Security 'privatised' itself 'after its officers launched private businesses and secured well-paid management positions in private firms set up by former communist apparatchiks. Relying on the agents' network of contacts and specialised knowledge, these firms established close ties to the emerging organised criminal groups and the budding local mafia'.[14] In Romania, former secret agents and Communist Party officials used insider information to acquire massive fortunes from the privatisation of state-owned enterprises and the property restitution process, in the process keeping

---

13 Nalepa, 'Lustration', in Stan and Nedelsky above n 1, 48.
14 Momchil Metodiev, 'Bulgaria' in Lavinia Stan (ed), *Transitional Justice in Eastern Europe and the Former Soviet Union* (Routledge, 2009) 167.

the post-communist state a captive to their interests. Their unparalleled influence over key political parties and the country's most important mass media companies and business empires allowed them to stall transitional justice, and avoid prosecution and lustration.[15]

Last, lustration and vetting are said to provide minimal justice because they exclude the former perpetrators politically, but do not prosecute them criminally. Supporters of the old regime are denied only the right to hold elected and/or nominated positions in the new democratic government, to represent the interests of the electorate in parliament, and to influence from those positions the formulation and implementation of public policy. However, they are free to engage in other activities and may become, for example, successful and rich business people, or respected academics. At the same time, the processes which enable the public identification of former perpetrators in view of banning them from public office (for example, the analysis of secret archives containing the information provided by the secret agents to the state security) help to reveal the truth about the repressive character of the ousted regime, and the nature of the crimes committed by its henchmen. For the former victims and their surviving relatives, truth revelation represents a precondition of democratisation.

7.5 Points of contention and controversy

Lustration and vetting generated considerable controversy in almost every country where they were implemented. Their supporters mention the benefits summarised above, whereas their detractors resort to some of the following arguments:

First, many analysts lament the fact that lustration and vetting claim to facilitate democratisation while in fact they deny some citizens one of their fundamental political rights: the right to be elected or nominated to public office. True, former collaborators are free to remain active in the private sector, but banning them from public office means that they cannot directly shape public policy and decide the country's future. Can a new democracy rest on such blatant discrimination? Are vetting and lustration not similar in this respect to the purges of former political, economic and cultural elites operated by the communist regime immediately after World War II? How can one expect to move away from communism when adopting the very policies that made that regime so despicable in the eyes of Central and Eastern Europeans?

Second, lustration and vetting undermine democratisation because they can easily spiral down to represent exercises of assigning collective, rather than individual, guilt. This could lead, for example, to the dismissal of all those who

---

15 Lavinia Stan (ed) *Transitional Justice in Eastern Europe and the Former Soviet Union* (Routledge, 2009).

served as communist county secretaries, irrespective of whether they were personally involved in human rights violations. Though to date most lustration and vetting programmes have included provisions designed to ascertain individual guilt based on information collected from a variety of sources, their critics remain suspicious that screening might amount to a blanket policy that insufficiently distinguishes shades of guilt.[16] When lustration and vetting lead to job loss, this charge rings truer, since both a person who briefly worked for the previous regime and a person who made a lifetime career as an authority figure of the authoritarian regime receive the same penalty: dismissal or demotion. The same is true in the case of confession-based lustration, when refusal to confess past collaboration leads to job loss for, say, a notorious prison guard responsible for human rights violations perpetrated over many years, even decades, and a young recruit of the secret police hired only months before the regime change. Since shades of guilt are not properly acknowledged, critics say, lustration and vetting are unable to bring truth and justice.

Third, lustration and vetting are also criticised for undermining, rather than facilitating reconciliation, a key goal of any successful transitional justice programme. The two policies subject people 'to loss of jobs and income, never an indifferent loss, but particularly not under circumstances, all too common in post-conflict and transitional societies, in which economies are in crisis and job creation is stagnant if not receding. The effects of such loss are particularly severe for members of the security sector, most of whom may not be particularly highly skilled or have skills that can be easily transferred to other economic activities'.[17] These economic effects, coupled with the public shaming, even opprobrium, that sometimes accompanies lustration and vetting, can turn the vetted individuals against the new democracy. How can one have a stake in the new system, if excluded from it and forced into a life of deprivation? In unstable settings like Iraq after Hussein and Libya after Gaddafi, the dismissal of many regime supporters unable to then regain employment and respect in the new state brought them closer to armed insurgent and terrorist groups threatening the very existence of the state.

Fourth, sidelining tainted public officials deprives the public administration of valuable expertise for effecting the sweeping reforms needed to turn these countries away from authoritarianism and closer to democracy. The hiring of new officials is unlikely to adequately replace this lost expertise. That is because in post-dictatorial and post-conflict countries the opposition is generally weak and

---

16 Council of Europe, Parliamentary Assembly, *Resolution 1096 – Measures to Dismantle the Heritage of Former Communist Totalitarian Systems*, 27 June 1996 <http://assembly.coe.int/nw/xml/XRef/Xref-XML2HTML-en.asp?fileid=16507&lang=en>.

17 Mayer-Rieckh and de Greiff, above n 2, 525.

inexperienced, as its members had been systematically prevented from acquiring political and administrative experience. The repression for which dictatorships were known left anti-government opponents, dissidents and critics with little room for action. These individuals might support democracy and human rights, but professionally they are less prepared than their banned predecessors, who in addition might have served the regime out of a misplaced sense of patriotism that should not be held against them by the new democratic authorities. Vetting, it is claimed, negatively affects the effectiveness of key state institutions during transition. This is particularly true when the new state security and armed forces cannot hire agents and collaborators of the former army and secret police, who represent the country's only professional military and security corps.

Fifth, other voices are raised against the use of secret archives as the main source of information for lustration. In Central and Eastern European countries where lustration extends to post-communist public officials who spied on behalf of the communist secret police, the identity of former secret collaborators is established primarily on the basis of the secret archives. Under communism, the secrecy of data collection meant that only the state security and the informers knew about it. Breaking the secrecy of the collaboration forced the secret police to abandon the informer. Since few former informers have publicly confessed their past, the only way to find out their identity is from the secret archives. However, some archives were destroyed in 1989 by secret officers eager to cover their human rights violations (communist constitutions, for instance, guaranteed the secrecy of the correspondence, which the secret police routinely infringed). Under pressure from their superiors to prove their worth, some secret officers recorded untruthful information, even reporting imaginary or dead persons as active informers, as in Romania. In that country and others, the secret archives were tampered with after 1989, with documents being added, destroyed or modified. Even if we assume that the secret archive of today is the same as the secret archive of the last day of the communist regime, remember that files present a distorted picture of communist reality. Many dissidents cannot recognise themselves in some of the secret documents, which recorded information filtered through the ideological lens of the repressive secret police. The agents did not engage in honest research designed to portray reality truthfully as they risked invalidating their decision to monitor a particular individual. Rather they sought to weed out anti-communist opposition, and to suppress attempts to challenge the state.

Case study A: Lustration in Central and Eastern Europe

Communist parties dominated Central and Eastern Europe after World War II, transforming those countries into one-party states with command, centrally planned economies. To ensure control over the society, communist authorities unleashed waves of repression carried out by extensive secret police networks.

Other parties were banned or weakened; civil society was brought under the control of the Communist Party; censorship was imposed; and former elites were arrested, persecuted, and excluded from public life. In these one-party states the Communist Party leaders occupied the top state positions (the so-called *nomenklatura*). By the late 1980s, the Communist Parties had become mass formations on which the livelihood of one-third, even half, in some countries, of the total population, depended. Party membership was essential to obtain and retain a post in public administration, the academia and the state-owned economy, and even to write the entry exam for sensitive university programmes (including sociology and philosophy).

While the 1950s and the 1960s witnessed massive arrests and ruthless persecution of opponents, the 1970s and the 1980s brought about the surveillance of vast social segments by the secret police. Full-time secret officers with military rank and part-time secret informers drawn from all walks of life collected information on millions of citizens. In East Germany, the Stasi employed 102,000 full-time officers and 174,000 unofficial collaborators in 1989. It also kept records on six million people, about one third of East Germany's 17 million citizens. In all countries, the secret police reached deep into the public administration. In Romania, for example, '90 percent of the personnel in ministries dealing with propaganda or foreign partners were Securitate collaborators', in 1989, 'the top leadership of the main ministries down to bureau heads was represented by Securitate officers whose identity was covered, residents or collaborators', and 'in every institution the party secretary, administrators and managers were all part of the Securitate information network'.[18] The situation in other communist countries was similar.

Case study B: The Czech Republic

The accusation-based Lustration Law no. 451, adopted by the Czechoslovak federal parliament in October 1991, applied to those persons who, during the communist regime (25 February 1948–17 November 1989), were members, agents and collaborators of the communist State Security (StB), owners of StB 'conspiration apartments', Communist Party officials from the district level up and members of the purge committees in 1948, among other categories. These individuals could not be employed in most elected or appointed positions in the federal and republican government levels (except member of parliament), rank above colonel in the army, and occupy management positions in state-owned enterprises, the official press agency, top positions in universities and the national radio and television, the Supreme Court, and positions of judges and prosecutors. The five-year ban was subsequently prolonged indefinitely. The Ministry of the Interior certified employees and applicants for employment, and dismissed, rejected or demoted them. Employees who shaped the intellectual content of the communication media could be screened, with their consent.

(continued)

---

18 Horia Roman Patapievici cited in Lavinia Stan, *Transitional Justice in Post-Communist Romania* (Oxford University Press, 2014) 85.

(continued)

In 1992 the Constitution Court annulled the law's application to candidates for recruitment by the StB, after investigations revealed than only about 3 per cent of 600 candidates scrutinised in 1991–1992 had actually collaborated with the secret police. Later that year, Czechoslovakia separated into the Czech and Slovak Republics. While Slovakia chose to ignore the Lustration Law because of lack of political will to implement the ban and lingering popular support for some communist policies, the Czech Republic implemented it. From 1991 to 2005, the Czech Ministry of the Interior issued as many as 451,000 lustration certificates detailing the collaboration or non-collaboration with the communist authorities of as many public officials. A mere 2 per cent of those certificates read that the person was registered under one of the law's specified categories. During the same period, the civil courts found for the plaintiff in most of the 870 suits that contested the verdict.[19]

Case study C: Poland

The Polish communist secret police (SB) arrested over 243,000 persons in 1944–1956, and facilitated the deportation of some two million Poles to the Soviet Union during the early years of the communist regime. In the 1980s, the Polish communist authorities enacted a martial law designed to weaken the Solidarity trade union, the largest opposition group in communist Central and Eastern Europe. By late 1989, the SB employed some 52,000 informers.[20]

Poland was the first country in Central and Eastern Europe to move away from communism through a popular election organised as a result of a pacted negotiation between the Communist Party officials and the opposition, represented mainly by the Solidarity. The pact, not formally supported by the people, was seen by many as amounting to amnesty for communist officials. This is why it was only in April 1997 that Poland enacted a confession-based Lustration Law that targeted the former agents and collaborators of the SB, but not the members and/or leaders of the Communist Party. According to the law, all elected state officials from the rank of deputy provincial governor upwards to the ministers, the premier and the president, as well as barristers, judges, prosecutors and public mass media leaders had to submit written declarations stating whether or not they *consciously* worked for or collaborated with the SB between 1944 and 1990. A Lustration Court checked the declarations' accuracy against the secret archives. Collaboration had to be secret, conscious and connected to the SB's operational activities. Individuals making false declarations were banned from politics for ten years and had their names published in the State Gazette. By contrast, the political careers and public image of former SB agents who acknowledged collaboration were not affected, as they retained their posts. Verdicts were subject to appeal, which was binding. Anyone found guilty of lying had to resign the office immediately.

19 Nadya Nedelsky, 'Czechoslovakia and the Czech and Slovak Republics' in Stan, above n 15, 49.
20 Stan, above n 15, 78.

By mid-1999, only 300 of all 23,000 officials asked to provide lustration statements admitted to their secret collaboration. For the following years, the Lustration Court examined very few statements, a pace that deeply dissatisfied some politicians and civil society members. Believing that confession-based lustration was unable to replace the elites and bring closure to former victims, in December 2006 the conservative Law and Justice Party proposed a radical Lustration Law that required some 700,000 citizens in some 53 authority positions (university professors and teachers, journalists, state company managers, but also individuals holding positions in the private sector born before 1 August 1972) to declare in writing whether they collaborated with the SB.[21] Individuals found to have lied could lose their jobs and be subject to a ten-year professional ban. The Constitutional Court declared the law unconstitutional in May 2007. As a result, that law was never enacted.

Case study D: Vetting public employees in transitional societies

A number of transitional societies have adopted vetting to reckon with the past. While most vetting procedures are implemented in times of transition, they differ significantly in terms of the offices they target as well as the practical effects and duration of the ban.

Case study E: El Salvador

In 1992, El Salvador concluded a twelve-year civil war that pitted the government (backed by the military) against violent guerrillas that claimed to fight in the name of democracy. The peace accords were the result of negotiations between the two sides, conducted under international supervision. Before the start of the civil war, the armed forces assumed the management of the state, used repression against those who rejected military domination and allowed the opposition very limited space. Because the military controlled most of the levers of power, 'it enjoyed a level of impunity that placed its members above the citizenry at large'.[22]

The three-pronged vetting programme aimed at transforming El Salvador into a stable democracy bound by the rule of law. Total vetting abolished an entire institution, dismissing its personnel and forbidding it from applying to the new, similar institution created by the accords. For example, the National Guard and the Treasury Police were abolished, and their members were incorporated into the armed forces. Military and police officers were subject to direct vetting, which evaluated them in order to determine who should be dismissed. Officers

(continued)

---

21 Ibid 86.
22 Ruben Zamora and David Holiday, 'The Struggle for Lasting Reform: Vetting Processes in El Salvador' in Mayer-Rieckh and de Greiff, above n 2, 81.

(continued)

could apply to the new force by being subject to an evaluation of their past conduct in addition to professional assessments. Indirect vetting, which applied to
the armed forces, the police and the judiciary, subjected the personnel to new
selection procedures in the future. For the armed forces and the police, the
peace accords included a new system for professional training of the officers,
and reforms seeking to guarantee that the institution would never again engage
in repressive behaviour.

An ad hoc Commission, which undertook the vetting *(depuración)* of the military officer corps, represents 'the first (and only) example of a Latin American
military submitting to an external civilian review panel with the power to fire or
transfer officers'.[23] The Commission evaluated each officer's past performance,
including his record of respect for human rights, professional competence and
capacity to function in the new democracy.[24] The Commission could recommend the transfer or dismissal of officers with 'serious deficiencies' in any
one of these three areas. Assessments relied on information obtained from
the individual 'service sheet' requested from the Ministry of Defense, details
about the officer's conduct received from private sources, non-governmental
organisations and foreign governments, as well as a personal interview with
the officer.

The Commission's impact was greatly restricted by time and secrecy. To
complete its evaluations within three months, the period stipulated by the peace
accords, the Commission chose to focus on the three highest echelons (including
generals, colonels and lieutenants), therefore not investigating lower echelons
that included even greater numbers of human rights offenders. Its final report,
which remained secret and was not divulged publicly, named only fifteen officers
who needed to be dismissed or transferred. The vetting of senior military officers was seen as an important component of the peace process in El Salvador,
although 'none of these officers expressed any repentance for past behaviour or
was ever brought before tribunals'.[25]

7.6 Current position

The experience to date with lustration and vetting has provided a mixed record
of the efficiency of these processes in delivering the benefits their supporters
anticipated. Neither were the shortcomings used by their critics for undermining the legitimacy of these processes as significant as anticipated. With each
new case of a democratic country that entertains the possibility of enacting such
policies, it seems that public debates bring forth with equal strength the pluses
and minuses of each policy, and that each new designed policy is only margin-
ally better in terms of practicality and morality than its historical predecessors

---

23 Ibid 89.
24 'The United Nations and El Salvador' (1995) 4 *United Nations Blue Book Series* 195.
25 Zamora and Holiday, above n 22, 96.

adopted in other settings. As post-conflict and post-dictatorial countries differ in terms of their historical evolution, the nature of the recent past, the level of repression whose legacy must be reckoned with, the type of regime change, and the post-revolutionary balance of power among political formations, it is likely that these debates will not be resolved soon.

While many countries chose to enact lustration and vetting, an equal, even larger, number of other countries retained old elites in the name of reconciliation, or effected elite change through other means. Therefore, analysts argue, lustration and vetting are not essential for the successful initiation and consolidation of democracy in post-dictatorial and post-conflict settings. After the apartheid regime was dismantled, for example, South Africa implemented only very limited vetting processes. The public service sector underwent rationalisation and demographic change, whereas charged political currents influenced the composition of political party leaderships. Only the judiciary and the state security faced significant institutional practices of personnel turnover. The Judicial Service Commission (JSC) was established to determine the composition of the courts. Within the security services, different services were first amalgamated, and vetting on grounds of loyalty to the state was later instituted.[26] It is a matter of contention whether the social and political difficulties that currently plague South Africa could have been avoided through the implementation of wider vetting processes.

The most recent case where administrative justice measures were implemented is Ukraine. After gaining independence from the Soviet Union in 1991, Ukraine sought to strengthen its ties to the European Union in the hope of gaining acceptance as a member state. In 2014, however, President Viktor Yanukovych refused to sign the agreement, at Russia's urging. After his ousting from office in February 2014 in the so-called Euromaidan Revolution, the new Prime Minister Arseniy Yatsenyuk established a Committee on Lustration within his government. In October 2014 the Ukrainian Parliament adopted a Lustration Law that instituted 'procedures for conducting checks of government officials and people nominated for government position with the purpose of deciding whether they meet certain criteria for occupying relevant post'.[27] That month, the law resulted in the removal of 39 officials, 19 of whom voluntarily renounced their positions. Among those officials were heads of central executive agencies, first deputy ministers, deputy ministers, members of national commissions and one head of the regional state administration. The ban was for ten years. By April

---

26 Jonathan Klaaren, 'Institutional Transformation and the Choice against Vetting in South Africa's Transition' in Mayer-Rieckh and de Greiff, above n 2, 146–179.
27 'Rada Passes Bill on Government Lustration in First Reading', *Interfax-Ukraine* (online), 14 August 2014 <http://en.interfax.com.ua/news/general/218428.html>.

2015, 2,000 officials of the Yanukovych regime were lustrated, of whom 1,500 quit voluntarily and 427 were dismissed.[28] Both the Ukrainian Constitutional Court and the Council of Europe criticised the law as unreasonable, as well as too broad in scope and therefore affecting too many individuals who could not be easily replaced. By contrast, Ukrainian civil society representatives criticised the slow pace of lustration and voiced their fear that lack of political will might impede the full implementation of the law.

7.7 Conclusion

Lustration and vetting are key transitional justice programmes meant to facilitate the renewal of elected and nominated structures of government, including the public administration, the judiciary, as well as the armed forces, the police and the state security sector. They fulfil a series of backward-looking and forward-looking goals that recommend them as effective transitional justice tools in countries where there is a modicum of consensus among citizens and politicians that the elites must undergo a process of renewal. When emphasising individual guilt and clearly specifying the categories of public officials to be screened, as well as the reasons and the time period for the ban, lustration and vetting policies can alleviate public concerns for fairness and accountability. Nevertheless, the experience to date with lustration and vetting is mixed, as in some cases they facilitated truth-telling, minimal justice and democratisation, while in other cases they apparently impeded them. In spite of the wide diversity of screening practices adopted all over the world, it seems that most post-conflict and post-dictatorial countries regard the screening of their most repressive state institutions (the secret police, the armed forces and the judiciary) as a necessary step in bringing closure to fragmented societies and preventing future abuses.

7.8 Summary

Lustration and vetting are key transitional justice programmes meant to facilitate the renewal of elected and nominated structures of government. While a number of new democracies in Europe, Latin America, the Middle East, Africa and Asia have adopted these programmes after World War II, other countries in transition

---

28 Alyona Zhuk, 'Critics Fear Officials Trying to Sabotage Lustration Drive', *Kyiv Post* (online) 23 April 2015, <http://www.kyivpost.com/content/kyiv-post-plus/critics-fear-officials-trying-to-sabotage-lustration-drive-38699 6.html>.

have chosen to retain tainted public officials in the name of reconciliation and social harmony. A number of arguments are put forth in support of and against lustration and vetting. Some analysts point out that the two programmes represent a break between the dictatorial past and the democratic present, improve the citizens' trust in the government and the society at large, facilitate democratisation by boosting the performance of the government and making the state machinery more accountable to the people, and provide minimal justice by punishing former collaborators. Others argue that lustration and vetting deny citizens the fundamental political rights to be elected or nominated to public office, assign collective guilt, undermine reconciliation by depriving some citizens of their jobs and income, deprive government institutions of the expertise of valuable public officials, and rely on secret archives whose reliability is questionable at best. The cases of the Czech Republic, Poland and El Salvador provide valuable insights into the way in which accusation-based and confession-based lustration as well as vetting work in practice.

7.9 Discussion and tutorial questions

1) What are the main arguments in favour of denying old elites public office after the regime change?

2) What are the main arguments against lustration and vetting?

3) In your opinion, is vetting or lustration more prone to abuse?

4) Are secret files reliable sources of information about the communist past?

5) Secret archives are important sources of information for lustration commissions. Can you think of some arguments in favour of retaining the secrecy of the secret archives (instead of opening them to the citizens) in new democracies?

Suggested reading

David, Roman, *Personnel Systems in the Czech Republic, Hungary and Poland* (University of Pennsylvania Press, 2011).

Funder, Anna, *Stasiland: Stories from Behind the Berlin Wall* (Harper Perennial, 2011).

Suggested film

The Lives of Others (Directed by Florian Henckel von Donnersmarck, Wiedemann & Berg Filmproduktion, Bayerischer Rundfunk).

Bibliography

Council of Europe, Parliamentary Assembly, *Resolution 1096 – Measures to Dismantle the Heritage of Former Communist Totalitarian Systems*, 27 June 1996 ‹http://assembly.coe.int/nw/xml/XRef/Xref-XML2HTML-en.asp?fileid=16507&lang=en›.

Dougherty, Beth, 'Iraq' in Lavinia Stan and Nadya Nedelsky (eds), *Encyclopedia of Transitional Justice* (Cambridge University Press, 2013) vol 2.

Horne, Cynthia, email communication from Cynthia Horne to Lavinia Stan, 29 November 2015.

Horne, Cynthia, 'Vetting and Lustration', in Dov Jacobs (ed), *Research Handbook on Transitional Justice* (E Elgar, forthcoming).

Interfax-Ukraine, 'Rada Passes Bill on Government Lustration in First Reading', *Interfax-Ukraine* (online), 14 August 2014 ‹http://en.interfax.com.ua/news/general/218428.html›.

International Center for Transitional Justice, 'Vetting Public Employees in Post-Conflict Settings: Operational Guidelines' in Alexander Mayer-Rieckh and Pablo de Greiff (eds.), *Justice as Prevention: Vetting Public Employees in Transitional Societies* (Social Science Research Council, 2007).

Klaaren, Jonathan, 'Institutional Transformation and the Choice against Vetting in South Africa's Transition' in Alexander Mayer-Rieckh and Pablo de Greiff (eds), *Justice as Prevention: Vetting Public Employees in Transitional Societies* (Social Science Research Council, 2007).

Mayer-Rieckh, Alexander and Pablo de Greiff (eds) *Justice as Prevention: Vetting Public Employees in Transitional Societies* (Social Science Research Council, 2007).

Meierhenrich, Jens, 'The Ethics of Lustration' (2006) 20(1) *Ethics and International Affairs*.

Metodiev, Momchil, 'Bulgaria' in Lavinia Stan (ed), *Transitional Justice in Eastern Europe and the Former Soviet Union* (Routledge, 2009).

Nalepa, Monica, 'Lustration' in Lavinia Stan and Nadya Nedelsky (eds), *Encyclopedia of Transitional Justice* (Cambridge University Press, 2013) vol 1.

Nedelsky, Nadya, 'Czechoslovakia and the Czech and Slovak Republics' in Lavinia Stan (ed), *Transitional Justice in Eastern Europe and the Former Soviet Union* (Routledge, 2009).

Office of the United Nations High Commissioner for Human Rights, *Rule of Law Tools for Post-Conflict States – Vetting: An Operational Framework* (United Nations, 2006).

Sotiropoulos, Dimitri, 'Swift Gradualism and Variable Outcomes: Vetting in Post-Authoritarian Greece' in Alexander Mayer-Rieckh and Pablo de Greiff (eds), *Justice as Prevention: Vetting Public Employees in Transitional Societies* (Social Science Research Council, 2007).

Stan, Lavinia, *Transitional Justice in Post-Communist Romania: The Politics of Memory* (Cambridge University Press, 2013).

Stan, Lavinia (ed), *Transitional Justice in Eastern Europe and the Former Soviet Union* (Routledge, 2009).

'The United Nations and El Salvador' (1995) 4 *United Nations Blue Book Series*.

Zamora, Ruben and David Holiday, 'The Struggle for Lasting Reform: Vetting Processes in El Salvador' in Alexander Mayer-Rieckh and Pablo de Greiff (eds), *Justice as Prevention: Vetting Public Employees in Transitional Societies* (Social Science Research Council, 2007).

Zhuk, Alyona, 'Critics Fear Officials Trying to Sabotage Lustration Drive', *Kyiv Post* (online), 23 April 2015 <http://www.kyivpost.com/content/kyiv-post-plus/critics-fear-officials-trying-to-sabotage-lustration-drive-386996.html>.

Chapter 8

Local transitional justice – customary law, healing rituals, and everyday justice

Lars Waldorf

8.1 Introduction

In recent years, transitional justice has increasingly embraced the local by encouraging, employing, and appropriating 'indigenous' norms, 'traditional' mechanisms, and healing rituals to repair communities affected by mass atrocities.[1] There are several factors behind this development of 'local transitional justice'.[2] First, the United Nations and other stakeholders recognised that the transitional justice 'toolkit' cannot be applied uniformly across different political and legal cultures (that is, one size does not fit all).[3] Second, these actors realised that transitional justice cannot work without 'local ownership', including community participation. Third, stakeholders were searching for more effective, more

---

1 See Rosalind Shaw and Lars Waldorf (eds), *Localizing Transitional Justice: Interventions and Priorities after Mass Violence* (Stanford University Press, 2010); Alex Hinton (ed), *Transitional Justice: Global Mechanisms and Local Realities after Genocide and Mass Violence* (Rutgers University Press, 2010); Dustin N Sharp, 'Addressing Dilemmas of the Global and the Local in Transitional Justice' (2014) 29 *Emory International Law Review* 71. Lars Waldorf, 'Mass Justice for Mass Atrocity: Rethinking Local Justice as Transitional Justice' (2006) 79 *Temple Law Review* 1.

2 There is considerable debate over terminology. This chapter uses the term 'local transitional justice' to describe 'local justice' used as transitional justice. Local justice is a broad category that embraces customary law, healing rituals, and everyday justice. Allen and Macdonald use the term 'post-conflict traditional justice' even though they acknowledge this is something of a 'misnomer': Tim Allen and Anna Macdonald, *Post-Conflict Traditional Justice: A Critical Overview* (LSE, 2013) 21. Indeed, some of the practices they describe are neither 'traditional' nor post-conflict.

3 As the former UN Independent Expert on Combating Impunity wrote: 'Given the extraordinary range of national experiences and cultures, how could anyone imagine there to be a universally relevant formula for transitional justice?' Diane F Orentlicher, '"Settling Accounts" Revisited: Reconciling Global Norms with Local Agency' (2007) 1 *International Journal of Transitional Justice* 10, 18.

efficient, and less costly justice mechanisms than internationalised tribunals and national trials. Fourth, they wanted less state-centric forms of transitional justice given the inability and unwillingness of many states to engage in meaningful accountability. Finally, transitional justice is slowly becoming more responsive to what victims and their communities actually want – which also means taking their cultural values, informal institutions, and everyday practices seriously.

Local transitional justice can take many different forms – from *magamba* spirit healers in Mozambique[4] to memory initiatives in Guatemala[5] to ritual dispute-resolution processes in Timor Leste.[6] Some focus on perpetrators, others on victims. Some are top–down, state creations while others are bottom–up, grassroots initiatives. Some are funded by international donors while others depend solely on local resources. Some are linked to formal transitional justice mechanisms (for example, trials and truth commissions) while others stand apart on their own. Despite this variation, customary law – dispute-resolution norms, rules and practices – grabbed the attention of transitional justice stakeholders in a way that other local justice initiatives, like spirit healers and community memory projects, did not. Customary law was seen as emblematic of the local, while still being recognisably law-like (that is, it consists of rule-based mediation and is sometimes codified). It was also viewed as providing both accountability and reconciliation through an emphasis on restorative justice.

While local transitional justice can be found throughout the world, the best known and most fiercely debated examples – *gacaca* in post-genocide Rwanda and *mato oput* in northern Uganda – are in Africa. This is not surprising. Over the past 23 years, Africa has been a prominent testing ground for experiments in transitional justice, including South Africa's amnesty-for-truth trade, the International Criminal Court's (ICC) prosecutions, and Morocco's collective reparations. In addition, Africa is a central arena for clashes between tradition and modernity, culture and rights, state law and customary law, and the local and the global. Furthermore, customary law plays an important role in much of Africa due to the weakness of state institutions.

This chapter examines how local norms and practices are used for transitional justice. It does not look at the broader issue of how international and national

---

4 See Victor Igreja and Beatrice Dias-Lambranca, 'Restorative Justice and the Role of *Magamba* Spirits in Post-Civil War Gorongosa, Central Mozambique' in Luc Huyse and Mark Salter (eds), *Traditional Justice and Reconciliation after Violent Conflict: Learning from African Experiences* (IDEA, 2008) 61–84.

5 See Laura J Arriaza and Naomi Roht-Arriaza, 'Weaving a Braid of Histories: Local Post-Armed Conflict Initiatives in Guatemala' in Shaw and Waldorf, above n 1.

6 See Dionisio Babo-Soares, '*Nahe Biti*: Grassroots Reconciliation in East Timor' in Elin Skaar, Siri Gloppen and Astri Suhrke (eds), *Roads to Reconciliation* (Lexington Books, 2005); Piers Pigou, *Timor-Leste: The Community Reconciliation Process of the Commission for Reception, Truth and Reconciliation* (United Nations Development Program, 2004).

transitional justice processes play out in local spaces.[7] Nor does it address recent, parallel efforts to engage with customary law to promote access to justice, legal empowerment, peacebuilding, and the rule of law.[8] This chapter begins by defining key terms. Next, it presents a brief historical overview of the thinking and practice of local transitional justice. The chapter then continues by looking at the aims, controversies, and positions around the use of local justice – topics also highlighted in the case studies of Rwanda and Uganda.

8.2 Definitions

Several concepts are helpful for understanding local transitional justice: the local, legal pluralism, customary law, and everyday justice. The local is commonly seen as the sub-national level existing below the national and international levels. This is problematic in two ways. It presumes a normative hierarchy where the local is viewed as residual, marginal, or traditional. It also suggests there are clear boundaries that separate local and global processes. Instead, it is better to conceptualise the local as a specific site of constant and mutually constitutive 'frictional engagement' between local and global norms and processes.[9]

Legal pluralism is 'a situation in which two or more legal systems coexist in the same social field'.[10] Legal pluralism exists throughout the world. In England, for example, marriage and divorce ('the same social field') are regulated not only by English law, but also by Christian, Muslim, Jewish, and Hindu law for religious believers. Legal pluralism is more pronounced in those parts of the Global South where colonial regimes imposed their law on top of or alongside pre-colonial legal orders. As a result, many post-conflict states have both formal state law and various forms of informal customary law. People will frequently 'forum-shop' among these different legal orders in an effort to gain better outcomes.

Customary law is not a cohesive, stable body of fixed rules, but rather a set of flexible and adaptive norms and practices for resolving disputes and remedying harms.[11] This enables local elites (such as community elders and tribal chiefs) to apply customary law in a discretionary manner to achieve case-specific, mediated outcomes. Customary law frequently (though not always) privileges group responsibility over individual accountability, restorative over retributive justice, and mediated over adjudicated solutions – all in the interests of restoring community 'harmony'.

---

7 See, e.g., Anne Macdonald, *Local Understandings and Experiences of Transitional Justice: A Review of the Evidence* (LSE, 2013).

8 See, e.g., Deborah Isser (ed), *Customary Justice and the Rule of Law in War-Torn Societies* (United States Institute of Peace, 2011).

9 Rosalind Shaw and Lars Waldorf, 'Introduction' in Shaw and Waldorf, above n 1, 5, 6–7.

10 Sally Engle Merry, 'Legal Pluralism' (1988) 22 *Law & Society Review* 870.

11 Customary law typically does not distinguish between crimes and torts.

Such harmony, though, is often coerced and serves elite interests. With customary law, there is also no legalistic separation between law and politics or positivistic separation between law and morality. There is a common tendency to romanticise and essentialise customary law as 'indigenous' and 'traditional' even though it was partly fashioned by colonial authorities and further re-fashioned by post-colonial regimes.[12]

States attempt to regulate customary law in one of three ways: abolition, recognition, or (partial or full) incorporation. Regardless of state efforts, most people in the world rely on customary law because it is more accessible, affordable, expeditious, and familiar than state law. Furthermore, many people (especially the poor and marginalised) associate state law with repression, inequality, and corruption. That said, customary law also suffers from numerous flaws, including elite capture, corruption, and human rights violations (particularly gender discrimination, unfair trials, and cruel, inhuman and degrading punishments).

Everyday justice is all about how ordinary people avoid, negotiate, and resolve the myriad disputes that form part of everyday life so as to co-exist. Put differently, it is how people produce justice in everyday life, drawing on their understandings of state law, customary law, spiritual practices, and normative beliefs.[13]

8.3 Historical overview

Between 2002 and 2012, there was a surge of enthusiasm for adding local justice to the globalised transitional justice 'toolkit'. This seems 'paradoxical' as it coincided with the expansion of international criminal law, especially through the ICC.[14] In fact, they are both 'part of the same process in that they seek forms of viable justice that are less directly connected with the formal authority of sovereign states – authority which may be very partial and compromised in politically fragile post-conflict circumstances'.[15] In addition, the increased use of local justice was a direct response to international criminal justice's expansion: *gacaca* was partly presented as an alternative to the UN's International Criminal Tribunal for Rwanda (ICTR or 'Rwanda Tribunal') while *mato oput* partly expressed resistance to the ICC prosecutions in Uganda.

---

12 It is important to recognise that there are different and often competing versions of customary law: 'codified customary law, judicial customary law, textbook customary law, and living customary law': Janine Ubink and Benjamin van Rooji, 'Towards Customary Legal Empowerment: An Introduction' in Janine Ubink (ed), *Customary Justice: Perspectives on Legal Empowerment* (IDLO, 2011) 10.

13 See, e.g., Austin Sarat and Thomas R Kearns, 'Beyond the Great Divide: Forms of Legal Scholarship and Everyday Life' in Austin Sarat and Thomas R Kearns (eds), *Law in Everyday Life* (University of Michigan Press, 1995) 21–62. It can be difficult to distinguish everyday justice from everyday life more generally.

14 Allen and Macdonald, above n 2, 1.

15 Ibid.

Transitional justice advocates first took notice of local transitional justice in post-conflict states that had no formal accountability mechanisms. In her influential 2001 book on truth commissions, Priscilla Hayner devoted several pages to an 'alternative means of confronting the past' in Mozambique.[16] She described how traditional healers (*curandeiros*) performed cleansing rituals to reintegrate returning soldiers and rebels back into their communities after the peace agreement and general amnesty of 1992. In one region, however, this did not prevent a subsequent outbreak of unfamiliar *magamba* spirits (the spirits of male fighters killed in the civil war) from afflicting women. In response, new spirit healers emerged who would call on the *magamba* publicly to accuse their killers and demand reparation. The resulting accusations caused fierce disputes and the spirit healer then played the role of mediator and judge. This created local, shared spaces for talking about a past that was officially ignored under the amnesty law.[17]

In other places, local justice was used to complement and legitimise national truth commissions. Sierra Leone's Truth and Reconciliation Commission was authorised to 'seek assistance from traditional and religious leaders to facilitate its public sessions and in resolving local conflicts arising from past violations or abuses or in support of healing and reconciliation'.[18] Traditional leaders participated in some district hearings outside Freetown, while several closing ceremonies involved reconstructed reconciliation rituals. However, that Commission largely avoided local rituals of swearing, cleansing, and purification, which may have limited its ability to induce confessions and effect reconciliation.[19] In its final report, the Commission acknowledged that 'it has not felt entirely comfortable relying on traditional structures to help foster reconciliation' given '[the Chiefs'] failure to explain the role they played during the war'.[20]

East Timor's Truth and Reconciliation Commission incorporated more local justice into its workings. Nearly three-quarters of its community reconciliation hearings involved adaptations of a local dispute resolution practice (*nahe biti boot*). Hearings often began with customary incantations and ended with reconciliation ceremonies that entailed chewing betel nut, sacrificing small animals, and celebratory feasting. Local ritual leaders frequently participated in the

---

16 Priscilla B Hayner, *Unspeakable Truths: Confronting State Terror and Atrocity* (Routledge, 2001) 186–195.

17 Igreja and Dias-Lambranca, above n 4, 73.

18 *Truth and Reconciliation Commission Act 2000* (Sierra Leone) pt III.6.1, §7(2).

19 Tim Kelsall, 'Truth, Lies, Ritual: Preliminary Reflections on the Truth and Reconciliation Commission in Sierra Leone' (2005) 27 *Human Rights Quarterly* 385.

20 Sierra Leone Truth and Reconciliation Commission, *Witness to Truth: Report of the Sierra Leone Truth and Reconciliation Commission* (2004) vol 3B, 438.

hearings and ceremonies. These appear to have been fairly effective as a vehicle for local reintegration.[21]

More recently, local justice was touted not as a component of truth commissions but as a transitional justice mechanism in its own right. The two mechanisms that attracted the most attention were Rwanda's *gacaca* courts and Uganda's *mato oput*. Both cases highlighted how states can control or capture local transitional justice.

8.3.1 The UN's evolving position

In his 2004 report on the rule of law and transitional justice, UN Secretary-General Kofi Annan gave qualified support to local justice:

> due regard must be given to indigenous and informal traditions for administering justice or settling disputes, to help them to continue their often vital role and to do so *in conformity with both international standards and local tradition.* Where these are ignored or overridden, the result can be the exclusion of large sectors of society from accessible justice.[22]

Unfortunately, this report did not provide any guidance on how the UN should interact with local justice that violates international human rights standards – as most does. Furthermore, the trade-off is not so much between international standards and local traditions but rather between different international human rights: the rights of non-discrimination and fair trial versus the right of access to justice.

By 2011, UN thinking had shifted somewhat. That year, UN Secretary-General Ban Ki-moon took a less absolutist human rights stance in his own report on the rule of law and transitional justice:

> In many post-conflict settings, informal justice mechanisms are the only available recourse to serve the public's justice needs. . . . the [UN] is aware of their uneven compliance with international norms and standards, and pervasive gender bias. The United Nations assists in building linkages between informal and formal systems, for example in Liberia, Nepal, Somalia, and Timor-Leste.[23]

Elsewhere, the report mentioned that 'close engagement with informal justice leaders' (among other interventions) 'has led to significant increases in convictions

---

21 Commission for Reception, Truth and Reconciliation in East Timor, *Chega! [Enough!]: Final Report* (2006) 9, 7, 18, 23–24, 27.

22 UN Security Council, *The Rule of Law and Transitional Justice in Conflict and Post-Conflict Societies: Report of the Secretary-General*, UN Doc S/2004/616 (23 August 2004) ¶36 (emphasis added). Although this has been interpreted as a partial endorsement of local transitional justice, the Secretary-General was writing here about access to justice within national justice systems.

23 UN Security Council, *The Rule of Law and Transitional Justice in Conflict and Post-Conflict Societies*, UN Doc S/2011/634 (12 October 2011) ¶39.

for violent crimes, including sexual and gender-based violence'.[24] In late 2012, three UN agencies (UNDP, UNICEF, and UN-Women) published a ground-breaking report on engaging with 'informal justice systems'.[25] The report noted that state justice systems may actually be less compliant with human rights standards than local justice, particularly when it comes to excessive (and frequently inhumane) pre-trial detention and lack of remedies.[26] It then pointed out that the

> lack of human rights compliance by [local justice] is no reason in itself for development agencies not to work with [local justice], any more than it is reason not to work with a failing formal justice system. A key consideration is whether engaging with [local justice] will strengthen the protection of human rights, which will necessarily be a gradual process of change.[27]

The report advised international actors to take a broad, rights-based approach – rather than a narrow, legalistic one – by considering whether interventions will 'enhance participation, accountability, and empowerment, whether they are grounded in human rights standards, and whether they increase protection of the most vulnerable groups'.[28] It is still too early to tell if this report has shaped UN policy and practice on using local justice for transitional justice.

8.4 Aims of local transitional justice

The goals of transitional justice keep multiplying and so become ever more difficult to achieve. Initially, transitional justice was a narrow, legalistic, and pragmatic intervention to aid democratic transitions. Today, it is called upon to end impunity, (re)establish the rule of law, improve human rights, strengthen democracy, halt mass atrocities, promote reconciliation, and transform unjust socio-economic structures.

The aims of local justice are far more modest: it seeks to restore social order by reconciling parties and placating spirits. Local justice is ill suited to

---

24 Ibid ¶37. That said, the UN Secretary-General soon reverted to insisting that local justice must meet international human rights standards: UN General Assembly, *Delivering Justice: Programme of Action to Strengthen the Rule of Law at the National and International Levels: Report of the Secretary General*, UN Doc A/66/749 (16 March 2012) ¶23.

25 Danish Institute for Human Rights, *Informal Justice Systems: Charting a Course for Human Rights-Based Engagement* (2012). The report covered not only customary law but also religious authorities, local administrators, state-regulated customary courts, and community mediation. It also contained case studies from six countries, two of which are post-conflict (Papua New Guinea and Uganda).

26 Ibid 42, 43.

27 Ibid 97. Such a pragmatic approach had been rejected by other human rights organisations. See International Council on Human Rights Policy, *When Legal Worlds Overlap: Human Rights, State and Non-State Law* (2009) ix–x, 124.

28 Danish Institute for Human Rights, above n 25, 141.

serving transitional justice's broadened goals. It is not concerned with individual accountability, the *sine qua non* of ending impunity. Local justice is often viewed as antithetical to the rule of law, human rights, and democracy because it is frequently unpredictable, discriminatory, illiberal, and elite-driven. Unlike international criminal justice, it was never meant to deal with, let alone deter, mass atrocities. Local justice is often used by older, male elites to perpetuate their social and economic status within communities. So, the only meaningful overlap in goals is reconciliation, though local justice emphasises intra- or inter-community reconciliation, whereas transitional justice sets its sights on national reconciliation.[29]

Local justice can serve transitional justice in multiple ways. It can function as a stop-gap measure until formal mechanisms are established. It can imbue national truth commissions with local legitimacy. It can supplement tribunals and truth commissions, filling the 'impunity gap' left when those mechanisms reach their limits. Or it can be a full-fledged mechanism in its own right: a more credible and efficient way to satisfy victims, reintegrate perpetrators, and repair communities.

Local justice offers several possible advantages as transitional justice. First, it usually has greater capacity and legitimacy than national justice systems and internationalised mechanisms. Second, it can be more responsive to local needs. Third, it can handle the lower-level perpetrators whose crimes do not warrant exemplary prosecutions or hearings by resource-strapped tribunals and truth commissions. Fourth, it might make it more likely that victims get some measure of restitution. Fifth, local justice may be better at grasping the complexities of local violence. Finally, it may empower local communities vis-à-vis state structures that only recently were used to commit gross human rights violations. That said, there are serious and unresolved issues with using local justice for transitional justice. For one thing, local justice depends heavily on social capital, which is badly frayed by civil war and mass atrocities. For another, it may reconstitute the very structures of subordination and exclusion that contributed to the conflict.[30]

---

29 By contrast, Luc Huyse contends there is considerable overlap in the goals of traditional conflict-resolution and transitional justice: Luc Huyse, 'Introduction: Tradition-Based Approaches in Peacemaking, Transitional Justice and Reconciliation Policies' in Huyse and Salter, above n 4, 10–13.

30 Sierra Leone's rebel forces, for example, were largely composed of youth who had been marginalised by the traditional power structures. See Sierra Leone Truth and Reconciliation Commission, above n 20, vol 3B, 343–360. At times, the Sierra Leone Commission's reconciliation ceremonies 'ritualised ex-combatants' submission to chiefs, district officers, and religious leaders': Rosalind Shaw, 'Linking Justice with Reintegration? Ex-Combatants and the Sierra Leone Experiment' in Shaw and Waldorf, above n 1, 130.

8.5 Controversy

There are two major controversies surrounding the use of local justice as transitional justice. The first concerns the stretching of local justice to deal with unfamiliar crimes (for example, genocide) and extraordinary situations (for example, civil wars) that it was never meant to handle. Such re-purposing inevitably transforms local justice into something new, which may no longer command authority or legitimacy. Two scholars ask whether it really matters if local justice is reinvented, especially if these practices prove helpful:

> Probably it does. The problem with codifying selected local practice . . . is that it takes them out of the contexts in which they have been used and adapted flexibly to specific circumstances, and it reifies them. If they are categorised and institutionalised into semi-formal judicial systems they will inevitably be very different to what they were to start with. They will lose their flexibility and will no longer have the many resonances and associations of lived ritual actions. But crucially, they will have a status that is at least partly based on their externally supported authority. They will become privileged rites and most likely the preserve of certain figures of male authority recognised by the international community or by the government.[31]

Other scholars are less perturbed by the codification and privileging of certain rites. They point out that local justice is always evolving and always partly shaped by elite interests. They also take a more functionalist approach to local transitional justice, placing the emphasis more on what works.[32]

The second controversy is whether it matters that local transitional justice violates international human rights norms. Human rights organisations have been critical of local justice for failing to respect due process, equality, and non-discrimination. According to one legal scholar, such concerns are over-stated. He contends that fair trial rights 'may well be irrelevant to procedures in traditional courts': 'If the principal aim of a hearing is to reconcile the parties, the human rights guarantees – which are aimed at protecting an accused against harsh penalties – become redundant'. While acknowledging that traditional courts discriminate against women and children, he argues that this must be balanced against other important rights – those guaranteeing access to justice and culture.[33] Other scholars note the way that local transitional justice can be, and has been, made more inclusive and equal, although this remains the exception.[34]

---

31 Allen and Macdonald, above n 2, 19.
32 See, e.g., Sverker Finnström, 'Reconciliation Grown Bitter? War, Retribution, and Ritual Action in Northern Uganda' in Shaw and Waldorf, above n 1, 147–148.
33 Tom Bennett, 'Access to Justice and Human Rights in the Traditional Courts of Sub-Saharan Africa' in Tom Bennett et al (eds), *African Perspectives on Tradition and Justice* (Intersentia, 2012), 22, 31, 32.
34 Allen and Macdonald, above n 2, 15.

Case study A: Rwanda

The 1994 Rwandan genocide was not an atavistic outbreak of tribal violence between the Hutu majority and Tutsi minority. Rather, it was a deliberate attempt by Hutu extremists to undo a negotiated peace agreement that awarded a large share of political and military power to a Tutsi rebel movement following a four-year civil war. That explains why extremists started by killing Hutu supporters of the peace agreement and ten UN peacekeepers. When the international community then evacuated most UN peacekeepers and foreign nationals, the extremists took that as a green light to accelerate their extermination campaign. Less than four months later, the Tutsi rebels defeated the Hutu extremists and formed a new government. But, by then, approximately 75 per cent of the Tutsi population (at least half a million people) had been slaughtered.

Having won a military victory, the now Tutsi-led government rejected a South African-style truth commission and insisted that only maximal prosecutions could end impunity and produce reconciliation. The regime put thousands on trial in national courts for ordinary crimes (murder, rape, assault, and theft) committed during the genocide, but, by 2001, there were over 100,000 suspects languishing in pre-trial detention. To speed up trials, it created some 11,000 community courts staffed by more than 100,000 lay judges. It named this transitional justice mechanism *inkiko gacaca* (*gacaca* courts) after the customary dispute resolution mechanism (*gacaca*). The courts were launched in 2002, but most only started functioning in 2005. Their hearings unleashed a flood of accusations and confessions. By the time the courts closed in 2012, they had tried a staggering 1.8 million cases involving over a million suspects. Two-thirds of those cases concerned theft only. The courts handed down punishments ranging from restitution awards (for theft) to life sentences (for rape).

Gacaca was widely celebrated as a homegrown alternative to the UN's costly Rwanda Tribunal, which only managed to try 70 alleged *génocidaires* between 1996 and 2014. *Gacaca* was also commonly seen as the world's most ambitious scaling up of customary law for transitional justice. However, there is considerable debate over whether *gacaca* courts reflected tradition, invented tradition, or hybridity. This is linked to a further argument over whether *gacaca* can be characterised as restorative or retributive justice.[35] These debates are complicated by the fact that very little is known about *gacaca* during pre-colonial and colonial times.

Most non-governmental organisations (NGOs) and scholars that observed *gacaca* courts in action were critical of how they operated.[36] First, the courts

---

35 For example, Clark argues that *gacaca* exemplifies hybridity: both 'a modern-traditional institution' and a mix of 'retributive and restorative functions': Phil Clark, *The Gacaca Courts, Post-Genocide Justice and Reconciliation in Rwanda: Justice without Lawyers* (Cambridge University Press, 2010) 48, 249. By contrast, Waldorf sees *gacaca* as modern and mostly retributive: Lars Waldorf, '"Like Jews Waiting for Jesus": Posthumous Justice in Post-Genocide Rwanda' in Shaw and Waldorf, above n 1.

36 See, e.g., Bert Ingelaere, *Inside Rwanda's Gacaca Courts* (University of Wisconsin Press 2016); Penal Reform International, *Eight Years On . . . A Record of Gacaca Monitoring in Rwanda* (2010); Human Rights Watch, *Justice Compromised: The Legacy of Rwanda's Community-Based Gacaca Courts* (2011); Max Rettig, '*Gacaca*: Truth, Justice and Reconciliation in Postconflict Rwanda?' (2008) 51 *African Studies Review* 25; Waldorf, above n 1.

frequently violated not only international standards but also Rwandan law governing fair trials. Second, *gacaca* constituted 'victor's justice' as courts had no jurisdiction over crimes committed by the Tutsi rebels. Third, and relatedly, *gacaca* imposed collective guilt on the Hutu majority by virtue of the fact that nearly all one million suspects were Hutu. Fourth, many Tutsi genocide survivors did not receive the restitution or compensation that *gacaca* had promised. Finally, *gacaca* did not promote reconciliation, at least in the short term. A government-commissioned, nation-wide survey found 76 per cent of genocide survivors and 71 per cent of prisoners saying that *gacaca* aggravated tensions between families.[37]

One academic insisted that *gacaca* created space for dialogic truth and hence reconciliation.[38] That ignored how the government had to coerce people just to show up to *gacaca* and how many kept silent once there. It also discounted the cultural and political constraints on public truth-telling in post-genocide Rwanda. As the researchers behind a National University of Rwanda survey found:

> the decision of potential witnesses and confessors to avoid testifying as a result of [personal] security concerns likely frustrated the production of both factual and dialogical truth. Further, the meaningful discussion and debate required to achieve dialogical truth is incompatible with silence among pertinent voices, such as prosecution and defense witnesses, the accused and victims of sexual violence.[39]

Overall, then, it does not appear that *gacaca* produced truth, justice, or reconciliation in many communities. It did, however, enable the Rwandan government to try an extraordinary number of low-level perpetrators in a very short period of time.

Case study B: Northern Uganda

Northern Uganda, particularly Acholiland, was the site of a vicious civil war between 1985 and 2008. Although Joseph Kony and his rebel movement, the Lord's Resistance Army (LRA), battled the central government in the name of the Acholi ethnic group, they quickly turned on their own community. Well before the 'Kony 2012' campaign went viral, the LRA had achieved worldwide notoriety for abducting an estimated 30,000 children and turning them into child soldiers and sex slaves. The LRA's brutality often obscured the Ugandan military's war crimes and crimes against humanity against Acholi civilians.

Uganda's government employed various half-hearted and contradictory strategies to end the war. In 2000, it enacted an amnesty law for LRA rebels

(continued)

---

37 National Unity and Reconciliation Commission, *Social Cohesion in Rwanda: An Opinion Survey, Results 2005–2007* (2008) 3.

38 Clark, above n 35.

39 Joanna Pozen, Richard Neugebauery and Joseph Ntaganira, 'Assessing the Rwanda Experiment: Popular Perceptions of *Gacaca* in Its Final Phase' (2014) 8 *International Journal of Transitional Justice* 49.

(continued)

who surrendered. In 2002, it launched Operation Iron Fist against LRA bases in southern Sudan, which caused the LRA to reinvade northern Uganda. The government also struck a deal with the ICC Prosecutor that eventually resulted in the Court issuing its first arrest warrants against the LRA leadership in 2005. When military operations and international warrants failed to capture Kony, the government went back to the negotiating table in 2006. The Ugandan President suggested granting amnesty to Kony, which prompted the ICC to remind Uganda of its legal duty to act on the arrest warrants. The peace negotiations dragged on for two years but fell apart in 2008. Before that happened, however, the government and LRA agreed to a novel combination of 'traditional justice' and national accountability, which both sides hoped would force the ICC to back off. For, under the ICC's doctrine of complementarity, the Court cannot pursue prosecutions where national states prove willing and able to do so. The preliminary agreement read in part:

> Traditional justice mechanisms, such as Culo Kwor, Mato Oput, Kayo Cuk, Ailuc and Tonu ci Koka and others as practiced in the communities affected by the conflict, shall be promoted, with necessary modifications, as a central part of the framework for accountability and reconciliation.[40]

The collapse of the peace negotiations left unanswered whether Acholi local justice would have been considered sufficient evidence of Uganda's willingness and ability to prosecute under the ICC statute.

From 2003 to 2008, Uganda was the scene of an unprecedented clash between local transitional justice and international criminal justice as various Acholi elites, religious organisations, local and international NGOs, and academics attacked the ICC's intervention for undercutting Acholi reconciliation ceremonies and thereby jeopardising peace efforts. ICC advocates responded in two ways. Human rights organisations, such as Amnesty International, criticised 'traditional' justice for promoting impunity and violating international human rights norms.[41] Others, like the anthropologist Tim Allen, challenged the authenticity and efficacy of these reconciliation ceremonies.[42] These arguments centred on the *mato oput* ceremony, in which the perpetrator's clan and the victim's clan both 'drink the bitter root' to symbolise the swallowing of their bitterness and reconciliation.

For all the controversy over *mato oput*, it has been rarely, if ever, used to reconcile the clans of former LRA fighters and their victims. This is because *mato oput* is the culmination of a protracted mediation through which the perpetrator's clan expresses repentance and pays compensation to the victim's clan.

---

40 Agreement on Accountability and Reconciliation between the Government of the Republic of Uganda and the Lord's Resistance Army/Movement, Juba, Sudan (29 June 2007) art 3.1.

41 Amnesty International, *Uganda: Government Cannot Prevent the International Criminal Court from Investigating Crimes* (16 November 2004) Amnesty International <http://www.amnesty.nl/nieuws portaal/pers/go vernment-cannot-prevent-international-criminal-court-investigating-crimes>.

42 Tim Allen, 'Bitter Roots: The "Invention" of Acholi Traditional Justice' in Tim Allen and Koen Vlassenroot (eds), *The Lord's Resistance Army: Myth and Reality* (Zed Books, 2010) 242–261. For a somewhat different perspective, see Finnström, above n 32.

Cultural leaders and elders are reluctant to request compensation from former LRA perpetrators, believing that if this is done it may deter other LRA combatants from returning. Worse, it may make the LRA doubt the sincerity of the amnesty law and seek revenge on local leaders for failing to uphold the principle of forgiveness the amnesty appears to offer.[43]

Instead of *mato oput*, returning LRA rebels typically went through various ritual cleansing ceremonies to cast off vengeful spirits of the dead. Some were group ceremonies publicly organised by Acholi elites, while others were done on an individual basis with spiritual healers.

Putting aside the debate over authenticity, there were real concerns with using *mato oput* or other practices to achieve accountability and reconciliation in northern Uganda. First, these rituals were not well understood or well supported by many Acholi who had grown up in camps for internally displaced persons. Second, these Acholi rituals were never going to be accepted or used by other war-affected ethnic groups in northern Uganda.[44] Third, the emphasis on *mato oput* treated both the conflict and reconciliation as if they were intra-Acholi affairs (that is, between the LRA and the Acholi community), ignoring the need for accountability of the Ugandan military and for national political reconciliation between the Acholi and the rest of the country. As one scholar states, 'it seems likely that the Ugandan government is interested in promoting Acholi traditional justice precisely because traditional justice may guarantee state impunity'.[45]

Since 2008, the debate between international retributive justice and local restorative justice has mostly subsided. There are several reasons for this. For one thing, the LRA was ousted from northern Uganda and peace has now taken hold. For another, it has become less and less likely that the ICC will ever manage to gain custody of Joseph Kony. Finally, the reworked Acholi rituals never became widespread practices of accountability and reconciliation. 'Not only did most local people doubt the efficacy of these public performances, many were afraid that they might even backfire; namely, because de-sacralising rituals risks incurring further spiritual affliction – a consequence that would have an effect on the entire society.'[46]

Still, the debate about whether the ICC arrest warrants promoted or hampered peace in northern Uganda continues. A former ICC employee, who worked on the LRA investigation, states that 'the facts on the ground demonstrate that since the ICC investigation began the security situation has improved dramatically, and processes to achieve a negotiated settlement have increased'.[47] But correlation is not causation, and other political events probably played a greater role.

43 Erin K Baines, 'The Haunting of Alice: Local Approaches to Justice and Reconciliation in Northern Uganda' (2007) 1 *International Journal of Transitional Justice* 110. As Baines goes on to note, 'It is therefore not only the ICC that is locally perceived as a spoiler of peace talks': ibid.

44 In 1985, however, the 'bending the spear' (*gomo tong*) ritual was used to resolve tensions between the Acholi and West Nile people. James Ojera Latigo, 'Northern Uganda: Tradition-Based Practices in the Acholi Region' in Huyse and Salter, above n 4, 106–107.

45 Adam Branch, *Displacing Human Rights: War and Intervention in Northern Uganda* (Oxford University Press, 2011) 175.

46 Barbara Meier, '"Death Does Not Rot": Transitional Justice and Local "Truths" in the Aftermath of the War in Northern Uganda' (2013) 2 *Africa Spectrum* 46.

47 Matthew Brubacher, 'The ICC Investigation of the Lord's Resistance Army: An Insider's View' in Allen and Vlassenroot, above n 42, 277.

8.6 Current positions

This section looks in turn at the relationships between local transitional justice and the ICC, the state, and the community. Events in northern Uganda caused some to worry that the ICC's complementarity regime would push states to adopt criminal trials to show they were willing and able to prosecute, and thereby preclude the ICC from exercising jurisdiction. The concern is that such 'legal mimicry' of retributive criminal trials would crowd out local transitional justice.[48] This doesn't seem to have happened. For example, the Ugandan government promised to promote local transitional justice in its 2007 agreement with the LRA.

States differ in their responses to local transitional justice. Mozambique's government was content to let the traditional healers and *magamba* spirit healers go about their work. By contrast, Timor-Leste encouraged customary dispute resolution both inside and outside truth commission proceedings. Other states seek to capture or control local justice, particularly as part of 'the battle of perceptions of wrongdoing': 'In both [the East Timor and Uganda] cases, a preoccupation with local justice (unintentionally or otherwise) protects crimes allegedly perpetrated by government officials and soldiers from scrutiny and accountability'.[49] The same is true of Rwanda, where the government used *gacaca* to entrench impunity for its own war crimes while imposing collectivised guilt for the genocide on Hutu.

Local transitional justice shapes and is shaped by community dynamics. It may encounter approval, appropriation, re-interpretation, or resistance. It may also alter, displace, or integrate ongoing practices of everyday justice. As such, the form and efficacy of local transitional justice will vary from one locale to the next.

8.7 Conclusion

The big question, of course, is whether customary transitional justice actually 'works'. Measuring the success of any transitional justice mechanism is complicated by the different metrics applied and the limited availability of cross-national data. A study that documented five African cases of local transitional justice (in Burundi, Mozambique, Rwanda, Sierra Leone, and Uganda) concluded:

> Do indigenous conflict resolution tools have an added value in times of transition? The answer is a cautious 'yes'. They are not sufficiently effective, and their legitimacy locally and internationally is not assured. The case studies have, however, demonstrated that tradition-based practices have the potential to produce

---

48 See, e.g., Mark A Drumbl, *Atrocity, Punishment and International Law* (Cambridge University Press, 2007) 141–147.

49 Allen and Macdonald, above n 2, 10.

a dividend in terms of the much-needed post-conflict accountability, truth-telling and reconciliation that is not negligible. Consequently, positive effects may be expected with regard to the more general transitional justice goals of healing and social repair.[50]

A recent overview of customary transitional justice was more equivocal: 'findings remain rather vague, inconclusive and anecdotal'.[51] This, however, is a criticism that has been levelled against transitional justice more generally.[52] What seems clear, however, is that local justice 'cannot be harnessed to the transitional justice agenda in a straightforward way'.[53]

As enthusiasm for *gacaca* and *mato oput* has waned, there has been greater interest in social practices that renegotiate the everyday.[54] One early (though not uncritical) advocate of *gacaca* later celebrated everyday justice in Burundi:

Life goes on, and social and economic relationships are re-established; beer is shared, as are benches in the church. This co-existence is a far cry from justice in any international meaning of the term but it is recognisable and, to some extent, desired, by people.[55]

There is a real danger that local transitional justice mechanisms – particularly those embraced or even imposed by the state – may delay or disrupt the re-establishment of everyday life.

8.8 Summary

Transitional justice has increasingly turned to the local. Several factors account for this. Practitioners and donors gradually realised that transitional justice 'tools' could not simply be transposed from one locale to another. Scholars and practitioners were becoming disenchanted with the Western model of retributive criminal trials, while donors balked at the expense of further internationalised criminal tribunals. In addition, stakeholders were looking for less state-centric

---

50 Luc Huyse, 'Conclusions and Recommendations' in Huyse and Salter, above n 4, 192.
51 Allen and Macdonald, above n 2, 17.
52 See, e.g., Oskar NT Thoms, James Ron, and Roland Paris, 'State-Level Effects of Transitional Justice: What Do We Know?' (2010) 4 *International Journal of Transitional Justice* 329.
53 Allen and Macdonald, above n 2, 21.
54 Erin Baines, 'Spirits and Social Reconstruction after Mass Violence: Rethinking Transitional Justice' (2010) 109 *African Affairs* 409; Lia Kent, 'Local Memory Practices in East Timor: Disrupting Transitional Justice Narratives' (2011) 5 *International Journal of Transitional Justice* 434.
55 Peter Uvin, *Life after Violence: A People's Story of Burundi* (Zed Books, 2008) 169. For similar findings, see Bert Ingelaere and Dominik Kohlhagen, 'Situating Social Imaginaries in Transitional Justice: The *Bushingantahe* in Burundi' (2012) 6 *International Journal of Transitional Justice* 46, 52–54.

and more locally-owned mechanisms. Finally, and more problematically, there was the lure of the local as some stakeholders were seduced by romanticised conceptions of local community, customary law, and restorative justice.

Local transitional justice poses four main issues. First, it is not clear how local justice can be re-purposed for transitional justice without losing its authority, legitimacy, and efficacy. Second, there are serious concerns about using local justice given how frequently it violates international human rights norms (especially due process, equality, and non-discrimination). Third, some stakeholders worry that local transitional justice can be crowded out by international actors or captured by state actors. Fourth, it remains unclear whether local transitional justice actually 'works'. All these issues are highlighted in the case studies of Rwanda and Uganda.

8.9 Discussion and tutorial questions

1) Does it matter if local justice is taken out of context to deal with mass atrocity crimes?

2) Should the UN support local transitional justice if it discriminates against women?

3) How can local transitional justice avoid being captured or compromised by state elites?

4) Should the ICC issue arrest warrants where a state has decided to forego domestic prosecutions in favour of 'traditional' healing rituals?

5) 'If victims' agency is a crucial value, does it not follow that victims should be able to opt out of these international norms [of accountability] if, say, in their culture and immediate circumstances they would prefer to reintegrate [perpetrators of atrocities] . . . through a traditional ceremony of reconciliation than to prosecute them?'[56]

Suggested reading

Allen, Tim and Anna Macdonald, *Post-Conflict Traditional Justice: A Critical Overview* (LSE, 2013) ‹http://eprints.lse.ac.uk/56357/1/JSRP_Paper3_Post-conflict_traditional_justice_Allen_Macdonald_2013.pdf›.

Duthie, Roger, 'Local Justice and Reintegration Processes as Complements to Transitional Justice and DDR' in Ana Cutter Patel, Pablo de Greiff, and Lars Waldorf (eds), *Disarming the Past: Transitional Justice and Ex-Combatants* (SSRC, 2009) ‹http://www.corteidh.or.cr/tablas/r25604.pdf›.

---

56 Orentlicher, above n 3, 19.

Shaw, Rosalind, *Rethinking Truth and Reconciliation Commissions: Lessons from Sierra Leone* (United States Institute of Peace, 2005) ‹http://www.usip.org/sites/default/files/sr130.pdf›.

Suggested films

My Neighbor, My Killer (Directed by Anne Aghion, *Gacaca* Productions, 2009) ‹http://www.gacacafilms.com/› [documentary film on *gacaca*].

Fighting Spirits (Directed by Barbara Meier, Cluster of Excellence 'Religion and Politics', University of Muenster, 2010) ‹http://www.cultureunplug ged.com/play/7988/Fighting-Spirits› [documentary film on cleansing ceremonies in Acholiland].

The Reckoning: The Battle for the International Criminal Court (Directed by Pamela Yates, Skylight Pictures, 2009) ‹http://www.pbs.org/pov/reckoning/film_description.php› [documentary film that covers the ICC in Northern Uganda].

Bibliography

Agreement on Accountability and Reconciliation between the Government of the Republic of Uganda and the Lord's Resistance Army/Movement, Juba, Sudan (29 June 2007).

Allen, Tim, 'Bitter Roots: The "Invention" of Acholi Traditional Justice' in Tim Allen and Koen Vlassenroot (eds), *The Lord's Resistance Army: Myth and Reality* (Zed Books, 2010).

Allen, Tim and Anna Macdonald, *Post-Conflict Traditional Justice: A Critical Overview* (LSE, 2013).

Amnesty International, *Uganda: Government Cannot Prevent the International Criminal Court from Investigating Crimes* (16 November 2004) Amnesty International ‹http://www.amnesty.nl/nieuwsportaal/pers/government-cannot-prevent-international-cri minal-court-investigating-crimes›.

Arriaza, Laura J and Naomi Roht-Arriaza, 'Weaving a Braid of Histories: Local Post-Armed Conflict Initiatives in Guatemala' in Rosalind Shaw and Lars Waldorf (eds), *Localizing Transitional Justice: Interventions and Priorities after Mass Violence* (Stanford University Press, 2010).

Babo-Soares, Dionisio, '*Nahe Biti*: Grassroots Reconciliation in East Timor' in Elin Skaar, Siri Gloppen and Astri Suhrke (eds), *Roads to Reconciliation* (Lexington Books, 2005).

Baines, Erin, 'Spirits and Social Reconstruction after Mass Violence: Rethinking Transitional Justice' (2010) 109 *African Affairs*.

Baines, Erin K, 'The Haunting of Alice: Local Approaches to Justice and Reconciliation in Northern Uganda' (2007) 1 *International Journal of Transitional Justice*.

Bennett, Tom, 'Access to Justice and Human Rights in the Traditional Courts of Sub-Saharan Africa' in Tom Bennett, Eva Brems, Giselle Corradi, Lia Nijzink and Martien Schotsmans (eds), *African Perspectives on Tradition and Justice* (Intersentia, 2012).

Branch, Adam, *Displacing Human Rights: War and Intervention in Northern Uganda* (Oxford University Press, 2011).

Brubacher, Matthew, 'The ICC Investigation of the Lord's Resistance Army: An Insider's View' in Tim Allen and Koen Vlassenroot (eds), *The Lord's Resistance Army: Myth and Reality* (Zed Books, 2010).

Clark, Phil, *The Gacaca Courts, Post-Genocide Justice and Reconciliation in Rwanda: Justice without Lawyers* (Cambridge University Press, 2010).

Commission for Reception, Truth and Reconciliation in East Timor, *Chega! [Enough!]: Final Report* (2006).

Danish Institute for Human Rights, *Informal Justice Systems: Charting a Course for Human Rights-Based Engagement* (2012).

Drumbl, Mark A, *Atrocity, Punishment and International Law* (Cambridge University Press, 2007).

Finnström, Sverker, 'Reconciliation Grown Bitter? War, Retribution, and Ritual Action in Northern Uganda' in Rosalind Shaw and Lars Waldorf (eds), *Localizing Transitional Justice: Interventions and Priorities after Mass Violence* (Stanford University Press, 2010).

Hayner, Priscilla B, *Unspeakable Truths: Confronting State Terror and Atrocity* (Routledge, 2001).

Hinton, Alex (ed), *Transitional Justice: Global Mechanisms and Local Realities after Genocide and Mass Violence* (Rutgers University Press, 2010)

Human Rights Watch, *Justice Compromised: The Legacy of Rwanda's Community-Based Gacaca Courts* (2011).

Huyse, Luc, 'Introduction: Tradition-Based Approaches in Peacemaking, Transitional Justice and Reconciliation Policies' in Luc Huyse and Mark Salter (eds), *Traditional Justice and Reconciliation after Violent Conflict: Learning from African Experiences* (IDEA, 2008)

Huyse, Luc, 'Conclusions and Recommendations' in Luc Huyse and Mark Salter (eds), *Traditional Justice and Reconciliation after Violent Conflict: Learning from African Experiences* (IDEA, 2008).

Igreja, Victor and Beatrice Dias-Lambranca, 'Restorative Justice and the Role of *Magamba* Spirits in Post-Civil War Gorongosa, Central Mozambique' in Luc Huyse and Mark Salter (eds), *Traditional Justice and Reconciliation after Violent Conflict: Learning from African Experiences* (IDEA, 2008).

Ingelaere, Bert, *Inside Rwanda's Gacaca Courts* (University of Wisconsin Press, 2016).

Ingelaere, Bert and Dominik Kohlhagen, 'Situating Social Imaginaries in Transitional Justice: The *Bushingantahe* in Burundi' (2012) 6 *International Journal of Transitional Justice*.

International Council on Human Rights Policy, *When Legal Worlds Overlap: Human Rights, State and Non-State Law* (2009).

Isser, Deborah (ed), *Customary Justice and the Rule of Law in War-Torn Societies* (United States Institute of Peace, 2011).

Kelsall, Tim, 'Truth, Lies, Ritual: Preliminary Reflections on the Truth and Reconciliation Commission in Sierra Leone' (2005) 27 *Human Rights Quarterly*.

Kent, Lia, 'Local Memory Practices in East Timor: Disrupting Transitional Justice Narratives' (2011) 5 *International Journal of Transitional Justice.*

Latigo, James Ojera, 'Northern Uganda: Tradition-Based Practices in the Acholi Region' in Luc Huyse and Mark Salter (eds), *Traditional Justice and Reconciliation after Violent Conflict: Learning from African Experiences* (IDEA, 2008).

Macdonald, Anne, *Local Understandings and Experiences of Transitional Justice: A Review of the Evidence* (LSE, 2013).

Meier, Barbara, '"Death Does Not Rot": Transitional Justice and Local "Truths" in the Aftermath of the War in Northern Uganda' (2013) 2 *Africa Spectrum.*

Merry, Sally Engle, 'Legal Pluralism' (1988) 22 *Law & Society Review.*

National Unity and Reconciliation Commission, *Social Cohesion in Rwanda: An Opinion Survey, Results 2005–2007* (2008).

Orentlicher, Diane F, '"Settling Accounts" Revisited: Reconciling Global Norms with Local Agency' (2007) 1 *International Journal of Transitional Justice.*

Penal Reform International, *Eight Years On . . . A Record of Gacaca Monitoring in Rwanda* (2010).

Pigou, Piers, *Timor-Leste: The Community Reconciliation Process of the Commission for Reception, Truth and Reconciliation* (United Nations Development Program, 2004).

Pozen, Joanna, Richard Neugebauery and Joseph Ntaganira, 'Assessing the Rwanda Experiment: Popular Perceptions of Gacaca in Its Final Phase' (2014) 8 *International Journal of Transitional Justice.*

Rettig, Max, '*Gacaca*: Truth, Justice and Reconciliation in Postconflict Rwanda?' (2008) 51 *African Studies Review.*

Sarat, Austin and Thomas R Kearns, 'Beyond the Great Divide: Forms of Legal Scholarship and Everyday Life' in Austin Sarat and Thomas R Kearns (eds), *Law in Everyday Life* (University of Michigan Press, 1995).

Sharp, Dustin N, 'Addressing Dilemmas of the Global and the Local in Transitional Justice' (2014) 29 *Emory International Law Review.*

Shaw, Rosalind, 'Linking Justice with Reintegration? Ex-Combatants and the Sierra Leone Experiment' in Rosalind Shaw and Lars Waldorf (eds), *Localizing Transitional Justice: Interventions and Priorities after Mass Violence* (Stanford University Press, 2010).

Shaw, Rosalind and Lars Waldorf, 'Introduction' in Rosalind Shaw and Lars Waldorf (eds), *Localizing Transitional Justice: Interventions and Priorities after Mass Violence* (Stanford University Press, 2010).

Sierra Leone Truth and Reconciliation Commission, *Witness to Truth: Report of the Sierra Leone Truth and Reconciliation Commission* (2004).

Thoms, Oskar NT, James Ron, and Roland Paris, 'State-Level Effects of Transitional Justice: What Do We Know?' (2010) 4 *International Journal of Transitional Justice.*

Truth and Reconciliation Commission Act 2000 (Sierra Leone).

Ubink, Janine and Benjamin van Rooji, 'Towards Customary Legal Empowerment: An Introduction' in Janine Ubink (ed), *Customary Justice: Perspectives on Legal Empowerment* (IDLO, 2011).

UN General Assembly, *Delivering Justice: Programme of Action to Strengthen the Rule of Law at the National and International Levels: Reports of the Secretary-General*, Un Doc A/66/749 (16 March 2012).

UN Security Council, *The Rule of Law and Transitional Justice*, UN Doc S/2011/634 (12 October 2011).

UN Security Council, *The Rule of Law and Transitional Justice in Conflict and Post-Conflict Societies: Report of the Secretary-General*, UN Doc S/2004/616 (23 August 2004).

Uvin, Peter, *Life after Violence: A People's Story of Burundi* (Zed Books, 2008).

Waldorf, Lars, '"Like Jews Waiting for Jesus": Posthumous Justice in Post-Genocide Rwanda' in Rosalind Shaw and Lars Waldorf (eds), *Localizing Transitional Justice: Interventions and Priorities after Mass Violence* (Stanford University Press, 2010).

Waldorf, Lars, 'Mass Justice for Mass Atrocity: Rethinking Local Justice as Transitional Justice' (2006) 79 *Temple Law Review*.

Chapter 9

Reparations

Jemima García-Godos

9.1 Introduction

Trials of major war criminals or former dictators charged with, for instance, crimes against humanity attract lots of media attention. We all get to see their faces on TV, often followed by archival images of situations of conflict and oppression in which they took part. When verdicts come, we all know what will happen with those found guilty. But do we know what will happen to those whose rights were violated – the victims of human rights violations? In this chapter we move our focus towards victims, as they are the main subject and actor of victim reparations.[1]

As a mechanism of transitional justice, victim reparations have emerged in recent years as a dynamic field of social and academic inquiry. 'Reparations' may seem an awkward term to use when talking about victims: how to 'repair' for the disappearance of a loved one, for torture, for internal displacement? While there might exist a common normative ground in international law on the right to reparation, the socio-political context of each country attempting to establish victim reparations will play a decisive role in shaping the conceptual framework upon which reparations are based – and this is a highly contested and political process.

This chapter starts with some basic definitions and categories for the study of victim reparations, followed by a brief historical account of victim reparations in the international human rights arena. I then move on to the discussion

---

1 Naomi Roht-Arriaza, 'Reparations in the Aftermath of Repression and Mass Violence' in Eric Stover and Harvey M Weinstein (eds), *My Neighbor, My Enemy: Justice and Community in the Aftermath of Mass Atrocity* (Cambridge University Press, 2004); Pablo de Greiff (ed), *The Handbook of Reparations* (Oxford University Press, 2006).

of some substantive issues that arise in the implementation of victim reparation programmes. In the final section, I introduce one issue that remains unresolved in the academic debate on victim reparations: the relation between transitional and distributive justice. The main message of this chapter is that in spite of their 'materiality', reparations cannot be considered mere administrative measures towards victims; on the contrary, they involve highly contested matters that bring together social processes and the interpretation of the past.

9.2 Definitions

In the context of transitional justice, there is a widespread consensus over the desirability and importance of victim reparations as an effective way to address the needs of victims[2] as well as a means to reconciliation and peace.[3] Indeed, the issue of reparations in transitional justice emerges as a way of addressing the needs and demands for redress of those who suffered some form of harm in a previous regime or during armed conflict, that is, the victims. This is what is commonly referred to as *restorative justice*, a dimension of transitional justice which focuses on the victims of human rights violations, acknowledging their suffering and needs, and attempting to restore the damage done. The underlying assumption in restorative justice is that physical, psychological and social damage must be acknowledged and addressed in order to heal and reconcile. Since restorative justice seeks to repair or restore the injustice done, victim reparations are commonly linked to restorative justice. However, victim reparations constitute only one aspect of restorative justice, as restorative justice emphasises the humanity of both victims *and* offenders, seeking to repair social relations and peace, and encouraging forgiveness and reconciliation.[4] This latter feature points to the roots of restorative justice in the roman Christian tradition. Furthermore, restorative justice has developed in Western societies as a mechanism of conflict mediation and/or conflict resolution, particularly related to criminal cases, where the participation of both victims and perpetrators is encouraged.[5] It is mainly due to its emphasis on the ultimate goal of reconciliation, which moves beyond the focus on victims, that the concept of restorative justice has been challenged as

---

2 Pablo de Greiff, 'Repairing the Past: Compensation for Victims of Human Rights Violations' in de Greiff (ed), above n 1.

3 Elin Skaar, Siri Gloppen, and Astri Suhrke (eds), *Roads to Reconciliation* (Lexington Books, 2005).

4 Martha Minow, *Between Vengeance and Forgiveness: Facing History after Genocide and Mass Violence* (Beacon Press, 1998).

5 This is the case of the European Forum for Restorative Justice, established in 2000, with the aim to help establish and develop victim–offender mediation and other restorative justice practices throughout Europe.

inadequate to address the needs of victims: what if victims do not want to forgive and reconcile?

What are, then, victim reparations? Instead of providing one specific definition, let us follow de Greiff's call for the need to distinguish between conceptualisations of reparations as used in international law and the one used by practitioners in reparation programmes. Although related to each other, these two contexts involve different choices and motivations in a conceptualisation of victim reparations.[6]

In international law, reparations refer to all sorts of reparatory measures implemented to address human rights violations suffered by victims, independently of what kind of violations we are dealing with or who the victims are. Reparations can be understood in this sense as an outcome of a judicial process: a verdict might sentence the perpetrator to a jail term, but also provide some form of reparation to the victims. This juridical definition of reparations obviously needs to be very broad, because the choices available to the judicial process need to consider all possible situations and adjust to a wide range of individual cases. Commonly, five specific forms of reparations are identified in this menu of choices: restitution, compensation, rehabilitation, satisfaction and guarantees of non-recurrence.

While restitution aims to restore the victim to the original situation before violations were committed (addressing mainly personal but also material suffering, by way of restoring rights, giving property back, or even the physical return to a place of origin), compensation refers to economically assessable damage and rehabilitation, to medical and psychological care. The categories of satisfaction and guarantees of non-recurrence make reference to broader processes and initiatives, some involving other mechanisms of transitional justice (that is, disclosure of truth, judicial and administrative sanctions) or even institutional reform.

In the context of designing specific reparation programmes, a narrow definition of reparations is needed, as it refers to a specific target group (the victims) and a specific type of human rights violation/crime. This definition does not include truth-telling, criminal justice, or institutional reform. Instead, it operates on the basis of two fundamental elements: the types of reparations provided (material and symbolic), and the forms of distribution applied (individual and collective). The narrow definition of reparations is, in a sense, an operational one, suggesting certain limits to the responsibilities of those in charge of designing reparation programmes.

Symbolic reparations include various forms of recognition and acknowledgement for the suffering of victims, such as commemorations, rituals in homage to the victims, changing the names of streets in honour of victims,

---

6 Pablo de Greiff, 'Justice and Reparations', in de Greiff, above n 1.

places of memory and apologies in the name of the nation, either as public acts or through private letters.[7] Material forms of reparation include all tangible assets which are provided to repair the harm done; this includes money (monetary compensation) and goods or services (that is, housing, working tools, health treatment). Monetary compensation might in turn be provided as a single lump sum, or a series of payments (like pensions), while restitution will involve the return of lost property. Privileged access to educational and health programmes can also be considered material reparations. There has been an expansion of the forms that material reparations may have, moving from what was previously the most dominant form of reparation (that is, individual monetary compensation) towards services, such as mental health schemes, legal counselling, physical medical treatment, scholarships, priority in housing schemes and more.

Should states provide symbolic or material reparations? There is consensus today that both forms of reparations are needed. When symbolic forms of reparations are not accompanied by other more tangible benefits, they can be interpreted by the victims as empty words with no serious commitment to redress.[8] In countries opting for monetary compensation, the challenge is not only how to measure the appropriate amount of money to be granted as reparation for specific human rights violations, but also how to restore the dignity of victims. In Argentina, monetary compensation was initially perceived by victims' families as 'blood money' offered in exchange for their silence.

One criterion that has been applied in international law to establish the size of monetary compensation is *restitutio in integrum*, that is, full restitution. There are standard methods for measurement of what 'full restitution' might be, based on the socio-economic status of the victim, future earnings and costs of living, among others. According to de Greiff, this is problematic not only because it is almost impossible to define what constitutes *full* restitution, but also because it is a mechanism designed for individual cases and therefore difficult to apply in cases of massive human rights violations, none the least due to the large amount of resources that the principle of full restitution would involve for countries that lack those resources from the outset.[9]

---

7 Symbolic reparations involve a broad scope of practices, many of which are also shared and applied by civil society, victims' organisations, NGOs, religious communities and other social actors who may want to pay homage or commemorate victims; this can be referred to as memorialisation. In the context of this chapter, shared practices are considered reparations only when carried out or implemented by the state or state actors, who have the duty to fulfil victims' right to reparation. For recent research on symbolic reparation, the arts and transitional justice, see Peter Rush and Olivera Simić (eds), *The Arts of Transitional Justice: Culture, Activism, and Memory after Atrocity* (Springer-Verlag New York, 2014).

8 Minow, above n 4.

9 de Greiff, above n 6, 456.

One way to level the choice between symbolic and material reparations is the option of *collective material reparation*, which is becoming the most preferred option for governments facing redress for massive human rights violations. The most common form of collective reparations involves the provision of basic public infrastructure, such as water and sanitation, health posts, schools, bridges and local roads. However, the distinction between reparations and development projects becomes blurred, and there are those who argue that the development responsibilities of governments can never stand as reparation for human rights violations.[10]

Regarding the form of distribution of reparation benefits, states can opt for individual or collective reparations. Ideally, a reparation programme ought to include both modalities. Most commonly, governments with limited resources prefer collective reparation schemes, while human rights activists and not a few victim organisations prefer individual reparations, based on the argument that individual suffering calls for the individual restoration of rights and dignity. Arguments in favour of one or the other form of distribution are many, and include pragmatic as well as normative and philosophical reasons. Would an individual victim of forced displacement receive the acknowledgement and redress he deserves through a collective reparation scheme providing, say, housing and public services? There are those who argue that he would, because the programme would address present needs, while others argue that the individual personal suffering is not sufficiently addressed in the collective character of the reparation.

The distinction between a juridical and an operational conceptualisation of reparations might prove useful at the analytical and operational level, yet it should also be said that the operational definition is not only grounded on the broader juridical definition, but it becomes itself a legal category which determines many aspects of the reparation involved. For this reason, the debate between international law experts and reparation practitioners and advocates seems to be more a matter of form and scope rather than content. There is no inherent contradiction between juridical and operational definitions, as they both focus on and acknowledge the victim's right to redress, and the state's duty to address the needs of victims. As we shall see later, most debates on reparations centre on the applicability and implementation of juridical definitions to specific cases, particularly those involving massive human rights violations – which is usually the case in situations of transition from armed conflict and authoritarian regimes.

---

10 This is an ongoing debate in countries where collective reparation programmes are being implemented, such as in Peru, where the author conducts research on the reparations programme. It is worth noting that there is no clear position among victim groups/beneficiaries and human rights organisations on whether or not development projects can or should be considered as an appropriate form of reparation. Different positions can be found in all groups.

9.3 Brief historical overview

Where does the term 'reparation' come from? Reparation was originally used to refer to the monetary compensation that victorious nations required from those defeated by them in war. After World War II, reparations referred also to the compensation given to the survivors of the Nazi Holocaust, by far the most comprehensive reparations effort implemented in modern history. While a similar use has been applied to compensation programmes for Japanese-Americans interned in relocation camps during World War II, and the case of Asian comfort-women for Japanese soldiers, the concept has continued to develop since World War II.[11] The term was also adopted by African-Americans seeking compensation for the enslavement of black peoples prior to the American Civil War, as well as Australian Aborigines' claims; in those particular cases, reparations are understood as a way to redress historical injustices.[12] While the literature on the Holocaust has been abundant right since the end of World War II, the literature on historical injustices has received an impetus since the end of the Cold War. According to Barkan, 'the demand that nations act morally and acknowledge their own gross historical injustices' is a novel phenomenon, resulting from the introduction of questions of morality and justice in the realm of politics.[13] These two bodies of literature share some common features with the study of victim reparations as part of transitional justice, particularly its focus on past violations and victims. The difference, however, lays more in the context in which violations where committed: World War II, colonialism (but not only), and authoritarian regimes and armed conflicts of the near past.

In the 1980s and 1990s, former military dictatorships and authoritarian regimes in Latin America, Southern and Eastern Europe underwent processes of transition to democracy, as a consequence of internal dynamics and the international political climate. The democratic transitions brought along the possibility for some form of accountability for past human rights violations. Victim reparations became part of this agenda, which grew steadily in the international arena, particularly in the realm of international law and human rights law. There are two processes which directly contributed to the consolidation of the issue of

---

11 John Torpey, 'Victims and Citizens: The Discourse of Reparation(s) at the Dawn of the New Millennium', in Koen de Feyter et al (eds), *Out of the Ashes: Reparation for Victims of Gross and Systematic Human Rights Violations* (Intersentia, 2005).

12 Elazar Barkan, *The Guilt of Nations: Restitution and Negotiating Historical Injustices* (Norton, 2000). There is abundant literature on these understandings of reparations, as is easily observed on the internet, where one can find numerous websites with resources on Holocaust and African-American reparation claims.

13 Philosophers would, of course, trace these topics back to medieval discussions about the justice of war and justice in war; thanks to Andreas Føllesdal for bringing this to my attention.

victim reparations and the enhancement of the rights of victims of human rights violations.[14] These processes were initiated at different points in time over the course of 30 years and peaked in the 1990s. In their own manner, they have both been successful in putting the issue of victim reparations on the international agenda. These processes are (i) the work with the UN's Basic Principles and Guidelines on the Right to Remedy and Reparation and (ii) the International Criminal Court's focus on victims' rights.[15]

9.3.1 Basic Principles and Guidelines on the Right to Remedy and Reparation

On December 16 2005, the General Assembly of the United Nations approved the Basic Principles and Guidelines on the Right to a Remedy and Reparation for Victims of Gross Violations of International Human Rights Law and Serious Violations of International Humanitarian Law.[16] This completed a process that started in 1988, when the then Sub-Commission on Prevention of Discrimination and Protection of Minorities (now the Sub-Commission on Promotion and Protection of Human Rights) recognised that all victims of gross violations of human rights and fundamental freedoms should be entitled to restitution, fair and just compensation, and the means for as full a rehabilitation as possible for any damage suffered.[17] This acknowledgement was followed by a 1993 study prepared by Special Rapporteur Theo van Boven;[18] this document became the basis for the Basic Principles approved in 2005.

As stated in the Preamble, the Basic Principles are directed 'at gross violations of international human rights law and serious violations of international humanitarian law which, by their very grave nature, constitute an affront to human dignity'. The Basic Principles establish that the *right to remedy* comprises two aspects: the procedural right to justice, and the substantive right to redress

---

14 The identification of these processes is based on their international presence and influence. Similar initiatives at the national level have also contributed to the advance of victims' rights in individual countries.

15 The issue of redress in the Draft Principles on State Responsibility could be considered a third track. See Jemima García-Godos, 'Victim Reparations in Transitional Justice – What is at Stake and Why' (2008) 26(2) *Norwegian Journal of Human Rights* 111–130.

16 Basic Principles and Guidelines on the Right to a Remedy and Reparation for Victims of Gross Violations of International Human Rights Law and Serious Violations of International Humanitarian Law, GA Res 147, UN GA, 60th sess, 64th plen mtg, Agenda Item 71(a), UN Doc A/RES/60/147 (adopted and proclaimed 16 December 2005) ('Basic Principles').

17 Dinah Shelton, 'The United Nations Draft Principles on Reparations for Human Rights Violations: Context and Content' in Marc Bossuyt and Paul Lemmens (eds), *Out of the Ashes: Reparation for Victims of Gross and Systematic Human Rights Violations* (Intersentia, 2005).

18 Theo van Boven, *Final Report of the Special Rapporteur: Study Concerning the Right to Restitution, Compensation and Rehabilitation for Gross Violations of Human Rights and Fundamental Freedoms*, UN Doc E/CN.4/Sub.2/1993/8 (2 July 1993).

for injury suffered due to act(s) in violation of rights contained in national or international law. According to the Basic Principles, 'remedies for gross violations of international human rights law and serious violations of international humanitarian law include the victim's right to the following as provided for under international law': equal and effective access to justice; adequate, effective and prompt reparation for harm suffered; and, access to relevant information concerning violations and reparation mechanisms.

Concerning reparation, the Basic Principles establish that 'in accordance with its domestic laws and international legal obligations, a State shall provide reparation to victims for acts or omissions which can be attributed to the State and constitute gross violations of international human rights law or serious violations of international humanitarian law.' The full and effective reparation envisaged by the Basic Principles includes: restitution, compensation, rehabilitation, satisfaction and guarantees of non-repetition (non-recurrence), introduced earlier.

The Basic Principles operate with a broad definition of reparations, one which also addresses alternative or complementary transitional justice mechanisms (that is, the right to justice, the right to truth). It is important to emphasise that the Basic Principles' focus on remedy and reparations does not exclude the right to justice, or the duty to prosecute violations that constitute crimes under international criminal law.[19] This reflects the current international trend promoting accountability for past crimes in post-conflict societies and post-authoritarian regimes,[20] while taking into account that accountability can take various forms, some aimed at fulfilling the requirements of international criminal law (prosecutions), others focusing on the needs of victims and their families (as reparations). The most recent example of this trend came in December 2016, when the Colombian government and FARC-guerrilla reached a milestone agreement on victims' rights, considered by many the most pressing issue of the peace talks' agenda.[21] Guided by principles of restorative justice, the agreement envisages a combination of judicial and non-judicial measures, a truth commission and guarantees of non-repetition. In the

---

19 Basic Principles, above n 16, section III, para 4.
20 On accountability for past crimes, see Cherif Bassiouni, 'Accountability for Violations of International Humanitarian Law and Other Serious Violations of Human Rights' in Cherif Bassiouni (ed), *Post-Conflict Justice* (Transnational Publishers, 2002); Naomi Roht-Arriaza, 'The New Landscape of Transitional Justice' in Naomi Roht-Arriaza and Javier Mariezcurrena (eds), *Transitional Justice in the Twenty-First Century: Beyond Truth versus Justice* (Cambridge University Press, 2006).
21 See *Borrador Conjunto – Acuerdo Sobre las Víctimas del Conflicto* [Common Draft – Agreement about the Victims of the Conflict] (15 December 2015)] <https://www.mesadeconversaciones.com.co/sites/default /files/borrador-conjunto-acuerdo-sobre-lasvictimas-del-conflicto-1450190262.pdf>.

Colombian case, victims' rights seem to have made their way through into the peace agreement.

The distinctions made in the Basic Principles between different forms of reparation, particularly restitution, compensation and rehabilitation, contribute to a much needed conceptual clarification in the field of victim reparations. The definitions will contribute to the operationalisation and design of specific measures in the context of reparation programmes.

Furthermore, and in spite of its status as 'soft law', since they are not legally binding, the Basic Principles provide legal support to representatives and advocates of victims' rights in national settings to the effect that victims are legally entitled to reparations.[22] Much as the Guiding Principles on Internal Displacement did for the plight of internally displaced persons in the political and humanitarian agendas, the Basic Principles constituted the beginning of a process of institutionalisation and international involvement in the issue of reparations, the rights of victims, and the design and implementation of specific reparation programmes.

9.3.2 The International Criminal Court (ICC)

The Basic Principles make explicit reference to the ICC Statute and the ICC's requirements concerning the treatment of victims of international core crimes, specifically the establishment of various forms of reparation, the creation in the ICC Statute of a trust fund for victims, and the protection and participation of victims during court proceedings. Indeed, the ICC's Statute, and Rules of Procedure and Evidence both establish a series of rights for victims of crimes that fall under its jurisdiction. One innovation in the Statute is the provision for the participation of victims during court proceedings and the chance to present their views and observations before the Court. Regarding reparations, the Court has the power to order individuals to pay reparation to other individuals, and it has the option of granting reparations individually, to a single victim, or collectively, that is, to a group of victims. Reparations may include restitution, indemnification and rehabilitation, and the Court may order these to be paid through the Victims' Fund. The ICC has two special units to ensure victims' participation. While the Victims' Participation and Reparation Section provides public information on reparation proceedings and applications, the Office of Public Counsel for Victims provides legal support and assistance to the legal representatives of victims and to victims. The institutionalisation of victim reparations as an integral part of the work of the ICC brings the rights of victims to the highest

---

22 Richard Falk, 'Reparations, International Law, and Global Justice: A New Frontier' in de Greiff, above n 1.

level, and can be expected to have a strong effect upon national criminal courts, both in protecting the right to remedy as well as fighting impunity.

A more recent development regarding victims' rights, reparation, and rehabilitation in particular is the approval of General Comment No. 3 (2012) on the Implementation of Article 14 of the Convention against Torture and Other Cruel, Inhuman or Degrading Treatment or Punishment (CAT). This general comment explains and clarifies to State Parties the content and scope of the obligations under CAT Article 14, by which State Parties have both a procedural and a substantive obligation to provide redress to victims of torture and ill-treatment.[23]

The common thread that runs across these international developments is their focus on victims, both in terms of legal status and enhancement of rights. Work along these tracks has received inputs from operational actors, such as international organisations, non-governmental organisations (NGOs) and academics alike. The influence has also gone in the opposite direction, with international legal work setting the agenda for national/regional debates and operational practices as well. Similarly, the jurisprudence of regional human rights courts has influenced and been influenced by the international debate on victim rights.[24] The drafting processes of international legal documents have involved lively academic debates, albeit confined to the field of law.[25] The transitional justice literature of the past 20 years has opened up the field for other disciplines, particularly from social science, which are contributing at the analytical and empirical level. As for research on victim reparations, the past decade has been one of expansion and prolific publication, filling a gap long lamented by those working on transitional justice.[26]

9.4 Implementing reparation programmes: points of contention and controversy

The apparent international consensus over the right to remedy and reparation for victims of human rights violations needs to be contrasted with contestation

---

23 Committee Against Torture, *General Comment No. 3*, UN Doc CAT/C/GC/3 (19 November 2012).

24 The work of the Inter-American Court of Human Rights has been particularly strong in setting precedent on the duty to repair and compensate human rights violations under international law. See Arturo J Carrillo 'Justice in Context: The Relevance of Inter-American Human Rights Law and Practice to Repairing the Past' in de Greiff, above n 1.

25 See, e.g., Christian Tomuschat, 'Individual Reparation Claims in Instances of Grave Human Rights Violations: The Position under General International Law' in Albert Randelzhofer and Christian Tomuschat (eds), *State Responsibility and the Individual: Reparation in Instances of Grave Violations of Human Rights* (Martinus Nijhoff Publishers, 1999); van Boven, above n 18.

26 This prolific development started in the mid-2000s, when seven volumes were published in the course of two years. These can be found in the 'Suggested reading' list.

around the design and implementation of specific reparation programmes. These programmes involve a series of substantive, ultimately political decisions to be taken by new regimes, and there is nothing universal about the way different countries go about taking these decisions. On the contrary, such decisions are highly contextual, depending not only on the political conditions of the post-conflict or transitional period, but also on the historical legacy of the previous regime, power structures, and even practical matters (such as the feasibility of implementation and funding). In the following sections, we discuss victim reparations by focusing on the most important decisions involved in the elaboration and implementation of reparation programmes.

9.5 Acknowledging the need for reparations

Many truth commissions may recommend the need for reparations as an integral part of a transitional justice process. This does not mean, however, that reparations will ever be implemented. In order to opt for reparations, a political regime has to first acknowledge the existence of a situation that calls for reparations, as well as the existence of people who have been harmed and are entitled to the attention of the state through various forms of reparation. Opting to provide reparations thus involves the initiation of a comprehensive and sensitive process often accompanied by high expectations among victim groups and potential beneficiaries, and volatile political commitment and public budgets. On the other hand, political will to develop and implement a reparations programme might lend popular support and legitimacy to the new regime. Having said 'yes' to victim reparations, regimes will then have to act effectively and quickly in order to prove their commitment and sustain credibility. An illustrative example is the development of the Peruvian Reparations Programme. While the legislation establishing the programme was in place in 2005, two years after the Truth Commission Report was published, the design and elaboration of the National Victims' Registry was not completed until 2011. Individual reparations could not be awarded before the Registry was complete. While this may be technically reasonable, the lapse of time was understood by victims as a lack of commitment by incumbent governments.

9.6 Defining target groups: victims and beneficiaries

Who is the subject in victim reparation programmes? In other words, who is the victim? This apparently candid question is the most important issue in victim reparations. Human rights violations are often depicted in terms of victim and perpetrator, those who have been harmed and those who have inflicted harm upon others and/or bear responsibility for the violations. In the context of repara-tions, the identification of the victim is vital, as it is he or she who will be entitled to whatever form of remedy or benefit is provided. Through the use of legal categories, reparation programmes can identify the universe of victims to which the programme is addressed, often by reference to specific types of human rights violations. In that manner, 'victims' tend to refer to all those who have suffered a specific type of violation. The most common types of violation in authoritarian regimes and armed conflict situations are, among others, murder, kidnappings, torture, forced disappearance, rape, sexual abuse, mutilation, forced draft and displacement. In other words, the victim is identified on the basis of the type of violation inflicted upon him or her.

Another way to establish who the victims are is by focusing on victimhood: what forms of suffering constitute victimhood? In his influential book *Closing the Books*, social and political theorist Jon Elster differentiates between three types of suffering, situations that are wider in scope than specific legally defined violations.[27] *Material* suffering involves the loss of real or personal property, the loss coming about either by destruction or confiscation; by personal prop-erty one refers to physical objects or financial assets. In some cases, the way the loss occurred may strengthened or delegitimise certain claims. *Personal* suf-fering refers to harm to life, body or liberty, which can take place both during and outside combat situations. *Intangible* suffering refers to the loss or lack of opportunities.

While it is important to establish the basis for the identification of a victim status with regards to access to benefits in a reparations programme, we need to remember that the same victim might have experienced multiple violations, multiple forms of suffering. This acknowledgement poses a challenge to repara-tion programmes, which will have to decide whether to provide various measures addressing different violations, or opt to focus on only one or a few specific violations. For example, what type of violation should be at the basis of an appro-priate response to an internally displaced mother of two, whose husband was murdered by paramilitaries in the Colombian countryside, and who was forced to abandon her farm? In this example, at least two violations could be used to determine the victim status of this woman: extrajudicial killing of her husband, and the forced displacement of her family. The definition of victim applied by the specific reparation programme will determine whether one single violation will take priority over the others, or whether all violations will be addressed.

As we can see, the different types of suffering call for different approaches to the issue of reparations, and new challenges arise. In most cases, the burden

---

27 Jon Elster, *Closing the Books: Transitional Justice in Historical Perspective* (Cambridge University Press, 2004) 127.

of proof is usually left to the responsibility of the claimant. The main emphasis has usually been on the need to avoid paying compensation to those not entitled, rather than to avoid denying them to those who are entitled. The demand for rigorous proof of victimisation may, for some victims, add to their burden.[28] Another aspect is the issue of citizenship or residence, as some reparation programmes may include these as a requirement for access to reparations. A state may want to provide reparations only to its own citizens, and a collective reparations programme might want to address the needs of selected populations, based on their place of origin; proving residence in that area becomes a requirement for the entitlement. Particularly in the context of intangible suffering, the debate seems to focus on what is to be considered the optimal or legitimate grounds for compensation: past suffering or present and future needs (we return to this issue in the next section). Will monetary compensation be enough to ensure that a victim not only recovers from past suffering, but also meets her present and future needs? Could these needs be better satisfied through other forms of reparation, such as property restitution? All these questions imply complex political choices.

While the identification of victims is the cornerstone of any victim reparation programme, it is necessary to problematise the dichotomy of victim/perpetrator. The human rights discourse that informs most of the transitional justice literature tends to reduce complex realities into neat, clear-cut, legalised categories.[29] However, these two categories do not cover the universe of actors that take part in armed conflict or are involved in human rights violations. Neither are the boundaries of these categories always clearly delineated. It is not uncommon to find that a single individual might have had various degrees of involvement in activities leading to human rights violations.[30] An example from Peru can illustrate this: A young man might have been recruited to join the guerrilla group Shining Path in Peru in the early 1980s, and participated in operations across the countryside, setting up flags, making incursions in small villages and calling for armed struggle among the rural population. Some of these operations resulted in the extrajudicial execution of local peasant leaders. The young man did not kill anyone himself, abandoned the guerrilla after a few months and joined the peasant patrols instead. Is this young man a perpetrator? What if a close family member was killed during a military raid – is he a victim? These alternative roles are a challenge for transitional justice processes, where clear legal identifications are the basis of the decisions that need to be taken.

---

28 Ibid 183.
29 Richard Ashby Wilson, 'Representing Human Rights Violations: Social Contexts and Subjectivities' in Richard Ashby Wilson (ed), *Human Rights, Culture and Context: Anthropological Perspectives* (Pluto Press, 1997).
30 Erika Bouris, *Complex Political Victims* (Kumarian, 2007).

Finally, and closely related to the identification of victims, is the identification of beneficiaries of reparation programmes.[31] Should reparation be limited to the victim herself, if she survived abuse? In the case of death and disappearance, it is often the closest relatives who become beneficiaries of reparations programmes. Should they also be considered as victims? Can descendants claim reparations for violations committed a generation or more ago? As we can see, the operational definitions of victims and beneficiaries bear great consequences in defining who is to be entitled to certain benefits and on what basis, and who will not.

9.7 Choosing the types of reparation

All too often national public debates on reparations tend to narrowly focus on one single issue: the size of monetary compensation, ignoring the fact that this (compensation) is only one of the many forms that reparations can take. As discussed earlier, there are two basic distinctions to be made concerning types of reparations, one regarding their form (symbolic or material), and the other concerning its distribution (individual or collective).

In choosing the most appropriate response to victims' needs, it is essential to be clear about who the victims of past human rights violations are, what types of victimhood they have experienced, and what are their current needs. The situation of amputees in Sierra Leone illustrates this clearly. The loss of a limb (or more) creates a permanent disability affecting a person's quality of life for the rest of her life, affecting her ability to perform private functions such as personal hygiene, cooking, taking care of children and taking on a job to secure her livelihood. In such a situation, lump-sum cash payments, such as the $100 reparations grant provided in Sierra Leone in the late 2000s, are ill-suited for individuals with long-term needs such as amputees. These victims are likely to require longer-term, sustained support involving different types of reparations in order to secure their livelihoods in the midst of a most difficult situation.

9.8 Operational and institutional design

Most reparation programmes are designed and operated as administrative programmes; that is, following administrative procedures in which the burden of proof is administratively set and processed by public officials. This design is appropriate for cases in which the number of potential beneficiaries is large. It is assumed that administrative procedures will be more effective and prompt than alternative mechanisms. This is only partly true, however, because the

---

31 This is not to be confused with Elster's 'beneficiaries' in the classification presented above (n 27).

operations of a reparations programme involve (i) the existence of an already identified universe of beneficiaries, properly registered and accredited in a victims' registry; and (ii) the proper set-up of specific measures to be provided to beneficiaries. Both elements cannot be taken for granted in a transitional justice context. For one, the establishment of a victims' registry poses not only logistical problems, but involves all the complex and political issues discussed earlier concerning the definition of victim. And second, the implementation of specific measures by different government agencies requires institutional coordination and cooperation as well as clear political priorities. Weaknesses in any of these elements will pose a challenge to the effective implementation of a reparation programme.

Funding is always a challenge for most public endeavours, including victim reparation programmes. Most administrative programmes are funded by public funds, often with the support of international bilateral and multilateral donors, and development cooperation agencies. While international funding is welcome and needed in many post-conflict countries, it is important to emphasise that reparation programmes can run into difficulties when trying to meet 'delivery' criteria usually applied to other forms of development cooperation. In Sierra Leone, the National Reparations Programme designed a compensation scheme towards amputee victims aiming towards the expedient delivery of funds within a year, lest funding be withdrawn. While expediency deserves praise, the scheme was problematic, as it did not take into account the long-term character of the disabilities this particular group of victims faced.

Reparation programmes are not the only way for victims to obtain reparations; judicial processes and civil litigation are also an option. While this might secure the rights of individual victims, the option of case-by-case proceedings run the risk of de-contextualising individual cases from their historical situation and collective character. The Colombian Justice and Peace process initiated in 2005 aimed to combine a judicial process with reparations for victims as an outcome of the proceedings. The scope and complexity of the process exceeded all expectations, and by December 2012 (latest official figures) only 11 cases had reached the reparations phase. Aware of the challenges ahead, the Colombian state established an administrative reparations programme in 2008, which in 2011–2012 was replaced by a more comprehensive programme of victim reparations.

9.9 Current debate: can reparations be transformative?

One of the most vibrant debates in the field of transitional justice today, bearing direct impact on victim reparations, is the one concerning the relation (or tension, for some) between transitional justice and distributive justice. Distributive justice refers to a form of justice that takes into consideration the socio-economic and political forms of distribution and access to power and resources in any given society. This understanding of justice is particularly relevant in those societies with deep socio-economic inequalities. In the framework of transitional justice, there are those who consider distributive justice to be an integral part of a transitional justice framework,[32] while others consider it to be part of the realm of politics, thus complementing but not included in the 'mandate' of transitional justice mechanisms proper. There is an increased acknowledgement, however, of the complementary role of distributive justice if the overall objective of a transitional process is sustainable peace.[33]

How does this relate to reparations? The ongoing debate on whether or not transitional justice should include a distributive justice agenda enters the reparations arena by questioning what is to be considered the optimal or legitimate grounds for victim reparations: past suffering or present and future needs? Will a monetary compensation, for example, be enough to ensure that a victim not only recovers from past suffering, but also has her present and future needs met? This is at the heart of the debate: that it is not enough to bring the victim back to her original social and economic status, often one of poverty and deprivation, but that she should be given the opportunity to improve her situation. In other words: the aim of reparations should not be limited to bringing the victim back to the original situation, but aim instead at improving not only the victim's living standards and prospects for the future, but also to transform the socio-structural conditions that fostered human rights violations in the first place. In Colombia this has been termed as 'transformative reparations' (*reparación transformadora*),[34] a principle that partly guides the current reparations and restitution programmes implemented since 2012 through Colombian Victims' Law (see Case Study B).

The tangible nature of victim reparations brings up the immediate question as to how this transformative potential can be realised and how it can be

---

32 See Roger Duthie, 'Toward a Development-Sensitive Approach to Transitional Justice' (2008) 2(3) *International Journal of Transitional Justice* 292–309; Chris Huggings, 'Linking Broad Constellations of Ideas: Transitional Justice, Land Tenure Reform, and Development' in Pablo de Greiff and Roger Duthie (eds), *Transitional Justice and Development: Making Connections* (Social Science Research Council, 2009) ch 9.

33 Pablo de Greiff, 'Articulating the Links between Transitional Justice and Development: Justice and Social Integration' in de Greiff and Duthie, above n 32, ch 1.

34 On the transformative potential of reparations in the Colombian context, see Rodrigo Uprimny and Maria Paula Saffon, 'Reparaciones Transformadoras, Justicia Distributiva y Profundización Democrática' in Catalina Díaz et al, *Reparar en Colombia: Los Dilemas en Contexto de Conflicto, Pobreza y Exclusión* (ICTJ, DeJusticia, 2009) 31–69.

operationalised. One way to think about this issue is through the selection of forms of reparations to be provided to individual victims; the focus is thus to identify or design appropriate measures that will have a lasting, positive effect in the lives of individual victims. Options might include a more generous monetary compensation or monthly pension, participation in a mental health programme, or support to return to one's place of origin and the restitution of abandoned property.

In his contribution to the debate on transitional justice and distributive justice, human rights scholar Lars Waldorf identifies socio-economic rights as an entry point, as these are particularly relevant in societies with deep socio-economic inequalities.[35] The enforcement of socio-economic rights in a transitional society is mostly considered part of everyday politics, but it could also be framed in terms of victim reparations. Recollecting the five forms of reparations identified by the Basic Principles, we can see that measures of satisfaction and guarantees of non-recurrence, involving broad measures of institutional reform, can contribute to the transformative potential of reparations at a higher, more structural level. As forms of reparation, satisfaction and guarantees of non-recurrence are still understudied, both at the empirical and conceptual level. It can, however, be expected that these two measures are possibly the ones bearing the most potential regarding the transformative character of victim reparations.

9.10 Conclusion

Victim reparations involve highly normative, ethical and political issues. Our discussion of the core issues and choices present in developing victim reparations programmes highlights the social and contested character of reparations. The conceptual clarification in this emerging field is a fairly recent development, and categories are still being challenged in the academic debate. Similarly, while consensus has been reached about the legitimacy of victims' rights to truth, justice and reparations, there is an ongoing debate over how best to address the needs of victims, both in form and content. This chapter does not provide a blueprint of the perfect reparations programme, but it does provide the student with the conceptual tools and questions needed to critically analyse the decisions behind different reparation programmes and alternatives. The take-home message is: reparations are political and must be studied in the specific socio-political context of transitional societies.

---

35 Lars Waldorf, 'Anticipating the Past: Transitional Justice and Socio-Economic Wrongs' (2012) 21(2) *Social and Legal Studies* 171–186.

9.11 Summary

The issue of reparations in transitional justice emerges as a way of addressing the needs of victims of human rights violations during authoritarian regimes or armed conflict. In spite of the international consensus over the legitimacy and need for victim reparations, these are not immediately implemented by transitional governments, mainly due to the contested nature of the demands and needs of victims. Of all the mechanisms of transitional justice, victim reparations are possibly the most tangible form of addressing victims' needs. In spite of their 'materiality', however, reparations cannot be considered mere administrative measures towards victims. On the contrary, they involve highly contested matters such as who the victims are, what are their needs and what type of responses are the most appropriate. These decisions are part of broader socio-political processes where definitions of victims and perpetrators will determine who is entitled to reparations and on what basis.

Case study A: Peru's Collective Reparations Programme

Following the Peruvian transition in 2000, a truth and reconciliation commission (*Comisión de la Verdad y Reconciliación* (CVR)) was established in 2001. The CVR's final report, delivered in 2003, included a detailed proposal for a comprehensive reparations plan. To follow up on the CVR recommendations, particularly those concerning reparations, an administrative unit was created in 2004, the High-Level Multisectoral Commission (*Comisión Multisectorial de Alto Nivel* (CMAN)). A law creating a Comprehensive Reparations Programme (*Programa Integral de Reparaciones* (PIR)) was passed first in 2005. The law also established the National Registry of Victims (*Registro Único de Víctimas* (RUV)) to be monitored by the Reparations Council (*Consejo de Reparaciones*). In addition to designing and operating the RUV, the Council developed criteria to determine whether a person or group of people can be accredited as victims. While the definitions of 'victim' and 'beneficiary' in the law, the rules of procedure, and the registry are relatively broad and inclusive, there is one important exclusion from the status of victim and thus access to reparations: former members of guerrilla groups. Independently of whether their rights have been violated, former guerrilla members cannot be entitled to reparations. This exclusion points to the political character as well as the limits of transitional justice mechanisms in post-conflict societies.

The law envisaged the creation of six reparations programmes, providing benefits to prioritised groups in the areas of health, education, housing, civil rights, symbolic reparations and collective reparations, and other measures that the CMAN might find appropriate. The Collective Reparations Programme (*Programa de Reparaciones Colectivas* (PRC)) was the first to be implemented, starting in 2007. Based on needs assessments of local communities affected by the armed conflict, the programme provided financial support for small development projects, often accompanied by a symbolic act to commemorate the victims and survivors. These projects involved basic infrastructure and productive initiatives, but also day care centres, schools and playgrounds. Some human rights organisations have criticised this type of support on the grounds that such collective reparations are not clearly distinguished from ordinary development projects. They point out that development initiatives are the duty of states under any circumstances, and therefore such projects do not embody the restorative dimension that reparations are meant to fulfil. The PRC was most active until 2011 and was for a long time the only reparations programme in operation. According to the Reparations Council, of the 5,697 communities registered as affected by the armed conflict in 2013, just 33 per cent had received collective reparations by that date.[36]

Case study B: Colombia's Victims' Law and the Land Restitution programme

Since 2005, Colombia has embarked on an unprecedented process of transitional justice, aimed at implementing mechanisms of transitional justice before the end of the armed conflict.[37] It is in that context that Colombian Law 1448 of 2011, known as the Victims' Law, addresses the issue of internal displacement and land dispossession caused by the armed conflict in the country. The law aims to facilitate the return of people who fled their homes and land due to the conflict, by giving back what was lost. With estimates between 3.5–6.6 million internally displaced people, this is an enormous task. To achieve its aims, the Colombian government has put in place a nation-wide programme of victim reparations and land restitution, operational since 2012. The land restitution programme involves a comprehensive set of regulations, legal mechanisms and procedures that brings together a multiplicity of public agencies and social actors, individuals and collectives.

The law recognises as 'victims' not only those harmed by illegal armed groups, such as paramilitaries and guerrillas, but also those victimised by the Colombian police and armed forces. Reparations can be claimed for physical, material and psychological harm since 1985, while land and property restitution applies to events occurring since 1991. Victims include those who suffered these violations independently of the status or identification of the perpetrator, as well as their closest relatives. Members of armed groups are not included in the victim category, with the exception of children and youth who demobilised while still minors. The threshold of proof to access reparations has been significantly reduced in favour of the victim, compared to previous schemes.

(continued)

---

36 Defensoría del Pueblo, *Report of the Ombudsman – A Diez Años de Verdad, Justicia y Reparación: Avances, Retrocesos y Desafíos de un Proceso Inconcluso* (2013) Defensoría del Pueblo 162.
37 Jemima García-Godos and Knut Andreas O. Lid, 'Transitional Justice and Victims' Rights before the End of a Conflict: The Unusual Case of Colombia' (2010) 42(3) *Journal of Latin American Studies* 487–516.

(continued)

The Victims' Law established new institutions for developing and implementing a national reparations programme that includes the five forms of reparations set forth in the UN Basic Principles. The new institutions include two specialised units for reparations and land restitution, a national registry of victims, a national system for victims' reparations, a national registry for usurped lands and a centre for historical memory.

The restitution programme is guided by the principles of differential treatment, progressiveness, gradual implementation, and the rights to truth, justice and integral reparation, among others. The law is explicit about the scope of victims' rights, specifically mentioning 'the right to truth, justice and reparation' and 'the right to return to one's place of origin or relocate out of free will, in conditions of security and dignity'. According to the law, formal owners, persons in possession of the land, or those using state lands who have been dispossessed or forced to abandon the land due to the armed conflict after the cut-off date are entitled to the right of restitution of land and property. The law also establishes the categories of abandonment and dispossession as bases for restitution, identifying restitution as the preferred form of reparation for victims. Restitution encompasses the return of the property lost, as well as the formalisation of legal entitlements (formal property rights). The law envisages the possibility of monetary compensation or relocation to land/property of similar characteristics to that which was lost only as a secondary measure and in cases where material restitution is not feasible.

One particular feature of the Victims' Law is its gender focus. To protect women's access to land and enhance gender equality, Law 1448 establishes preferential treatment for women in the process of land restitution. Such preferential treatment encompasses prioritisation of cases when the applicant is a woman, the general mainstreaming of gender perspectives in the administrative and judicial process, and other additional benefits.

While the restitution process requires a concerted effort, the agency responsible for moving the process forward is the specifically created Land Restitution Unit (URT), whose mandate is to design, administer and preserve a national register of abandoned and usurped lands; to gather all information and evidence of dispossession and abandonment of land and property registered by restitution claimants; to process restitution claims and formalisation procedures for abandoned lands, as well as to represent claimants before the judicial restitution authorities; and to administer compensation payments for claimants in cases where restitution is not possible. The financial costs associated with implementation of the Victims' Law are obviously high, yet are planned to be covered by state funds.

Land and property restitution is an extremely complex issue in Colombia, both for technical and administrative reasons, and because of the strong economic and political interests at stake. The coexistence of several forms of property and tenure, incomplete cadastral records, parallel registration systems, multiple registrations, and claims to the same property both concurrently and over time are among the many factors affecting implementation. Coercive practices of land expropriation and usurpation are often legalised through formal and judicial channels. The task is complicated by the presence of strong economic actors and activities on disputed lands. In addition, security challenges both to returning populations and to community leaders making restitution claims threaten progress in implementation of these measures.

Though the law precedes the initiation of peace talks between the Colombian government and FARC guerrillas, the success or failure of its implementation has great significance for Colombian society at large, as the issue of land is recognised by most actors as key for the prospects of durable peace in the country.

9.12 Discussion and tutorial questions

Read the International Organization for Migration (IOM) report *Reparations for Wartime Victims in the Former Yugoslavia: In Search of the Way Forward* (2013) (see 'Suggested reading'). The report provides a good example of a policy input for discussions and political decision-making about reparations for victims of international crimes – genocide, crimes against humanity and war crimes committed during the Yugoslav wars. Discuss with your classmates the following points:

1) What are the criteria used to identify victims and beneficiaries in the report?

2) Are there any groups that fall outside the category of victim proposed by the report? If yes, who are these, and why do you think this is so?

3) What types of reparations are suggested for implementation in the report?

4) Are there some forms of reparations that are not addressed by the report? Do you agree with this selection? Explain why.

5) The wars in Former Yugoslavia took place 20 years ago. Why do you think there is still a need to discuss victim reparations in this particular context?

6) The report was published in 2013. Do a web search and update yourself on the progress (or lack of progress) on victim reparations in the Balkan region. Present this update in class.

Suggested reading

de Greiff, Pablo (ed), *The Handbook of Reparations* (Oxford University Press, 2006).

de Feyter, Koen, Stephan Parmentier, Marc Bossuyt and Paul Lemmens (eds), *Out of the Ashes: Reparation for Victims of Gross and Systematic Human Rights Violations* (Intersentia, 2005).

du Plessis, Max and Stephen Peté (eds), *Repairing the Past? International Perspective on Reparations for Gross Human Rights Abuses* (Intersentia, 2007).

Elster, Jon (ed), *Retribution and Reparation in the Transition to Democracy* (Cambridge University Press, 2006).

European Forum for Restorative Justice website ‹http://www.euforumrj.org/›

Miller, Jon and Rahul Kumar (eds), *Reparations: Interdisciplinary Inquiries* (Oxford University Press, 2007).

Rubio-Marín, Ruth (ed), *What Happened to the Women? Gender and Reparations for Human Rights Violations* (Social Science Research Council, 2006).

Salazar, Katya (ed), Current Challenges in Seeking Justice for Serious Crimes of the Past (2013) 18 *Aportes DPLF* ‹http://dplf.org/sites/default/files/aportes_18_english_web_f inal_6_0.pdf›.

Torpey, John, *Making Whole What Has Been Smashed: On Reparations Politics* (Harvard University Press, 2006).

United Nations, *Special Rapporteur on the Promotion of Truth, Justice, Reparation and Guarantees of Non-Recurrence* (1 May 2012) Office of the High Commissioner on Human Rights ‹http://www.ohchr.org/EN/Issues/TruthJusticeReparation/Pages/Index. aspx›.

Van der Auweraert, Peter and Igor Cvetkovski, *Reparations for Wartime Victims in the Former Yugoslavia: In Search of the Way Forward* (June 2013) International Organization for Migration ‹http://www.iom.int/files/live/sites/iom/files/What-We-Do/docs/Reparations-for-Wartime-Victims-in-the-Former-Yugoslavia-In-Search-of-the-Way-Forward.pdf›.

Wemmers, Jo-Anne M (ed), *Reparation for Victims of Crimes against Humanity: The Healing Role of Reparation* (Routledge, 2014).

Wilson, Richard A and J Mitchell, 'Introduction: The Social Life of Rights' in Richard A Wilson and J Mitchell (eds), *Human Rights in Global Perspective: Anthropological Studies of Rights, Claims and Entitlements* (Routledge, 2003).

Suggested films

Impunity (Directed by Juan José Lozano, Arte, Dolce Vita Films, Intermezzo Films SA, 2010) ‹http://beamafilm.com/Impunity/#.Ve2Ymv7otaQ› [This documentary focuses on the Colombian process of transitional justice initiated in 2005 by the Law of Justice and Peace].

Paying for Justice (Directed by Guy Meroz and Orli Vilnai-Federbush, produced by Ori Dickstein, 2007) ‹http://www.ruthfilms.com/films/docs/holocaust/paying-for-justice.html›.

Reparation (Brazilian Documentary) (Directed by Daniel Moreno, Terranova Filmes, 2012) ‹https://www.youtube.com/watch?v=CgBsRvPt0OI›.

The Look of Silence (Directed by Joshua Oppenheimer, Anonymous, Final Cut for Real, Making Movies Oy, 2015) ‹http://artery.wbur.org/2015/07/29/look-of-silence›.

The Mothers of Plaza De Mayo (Directed and produced by Susana Blaustein Muñoz and Lourdes Portillo, 1985) ‹http://www.wmm.com/filmCatalog/pages/c85. shtml›.

Bibliography

Barkan, Elazar, *The Guilt of Nations: Restitution and Negotiating Historical Injustices* (Norton, 2000).

Basic Principles and Guidelines on the Right to a Remedy and Reparation for Victims of Gross Violations of International Human Rights Law and Serious Violations of International Humanitarian Law, GA Res 147, UN GA, 60th sess, 64th plen mtg, Agenda Item 71(a), UN Doc A/RES/60/147 (adopted and proclaimed 16 December 2005).

Bassiouni, Cherif, 'Accountability for Violations of International Humanitarian Law and Other Serious Violations of Human Rights' in MC Bassiouni (ed), *Post-Conflict Justice* (Transnational Publishers, 2002).

Borrador Conjunto – Acuerdo Sobre las Víctimas del Conflicto [Common Draft – Agreement about the Victims of the Conflict] (15 December 2015)] ‹https:// www.mesadeconversaciones.com.co/sites/default /files/borrador-conjunto-acuerdo-sobre-lasvictimas-del-conflicto-1450190262.pdf›.

Bouris, Erica, *Complex Political Victims* (Kumarian, 2007).

Carrillo, Arturo J, 'Justice in Context: The Relevance of Inter-American Human Rights Law and Practice to Repairing the Past' in Pablo de Greiff (ed), *The Handbook of Reparations* (Oxford University Press, 2006).

Committee Against Torture, *General Comment No. 3*, UN Doc CAT/C/GC/3 (19 November 2012).

de Greiff, Pablo (ed), *The Handbook of Reparations* (Oxford University Press, 2006).

de Greiff, Pablo, 'Justice and Reparations', in Pablo de Greiff (ed) *The Handbook of Reparations* (Oxford University Press, 2006).

de Greiff, Pablo, 'Repairing the Past: Compensation for Victims of Human Rights Violations' in Pablo de Greiff (ed), *The Handbook of Reparations* (Oxford University Press, 2006).

de Greiff, Pablo, 'Articulating the Links between Transitional Justice and Development: Justice and Social Integration' in Pablo de Greiff and Roger Duthie (eds), *Transitional Justice and Development: Making Connections* (Social Science Research Council, 2009).

Defensoría del Pueblo, *Report of the Ombudsman – A Diez Años de Verdad, Justicia y Reparación: Avances, Retrocesos y Desafíos de un Proceso Inconcluso* (Defensoría del Pueblo, 2013).

Duthie, Roger, 'Toward a Development-Sensitive Approach to Transitional Justice' (2008) 2(3) *International Journal of Transitional Justice* 292–309;

Elster, Jon, *Closing the Books: Transitional Justice in Historical Perspective* (Cambridge University Press, 2004).

Falk, Richard, 'Reparations, International Law, and Global Justice: A New Frontier' in Pablo de Greiff (ed) *The Handbook of Reparations* (Oxford University Press, 2006).

García-Godos, Jemima, 'Victim Reparations in Transitional Justice – What Is at Stake and Why' (2008) 26(2) *Norwegian Journal of Human Rights*.

García-Godos, Jemima and Knut Andreas O. Lid, 'Transitional Justice and Victims' Rights before the End of a Conflict: The Unusual Case of Colombia' (2010) 42(3) *Journal of Latin American Studies*.

Huggings, Chris, 'Linking Broad Constellations of Ideas: Transitional Justice, Land Tenure Reform, and Development' in Pablo de Greiff and Roger Duthie (eds), *Transitional Justice and Development: Making Connections* (Social Science Research Council, 2009).

Minow, Martha, *Between Vengeance and Forgiveness: Facing History after Genocide and Mass Violence* (Beacon Press, 1998).

Roht-Arriaza, Naomi, 'Reparations in the Aftermath of Repression and Mass Violence' in Eric Stover and Harvey M Weinstein (eds), *My Neighbor, My Enemy: Justice and Community in the Aftermath of Mass Atrocity* (Cambridge University Press, 2004).

Roht-Arriaza, Naomi, 'The New Landscape of Transitional Justice' in Naomi Roht-Arriaza and Javier Mariezcurrena (eds), *Transitional Justice in the Twenty-First Century: Beyond Truth versus Justice* (Cambridge University Press, 2006).

Rush, Peter and Olivera Simić (eds), *The Arts of Transitional Justice: Culture, Activism, and Memory after Atrocity* (Springer-Verlag New York, 2014).

Shelton, Dinah, 'The United Nations Draft Principles on Reparations for Human Rights Violations: Context and Content' in Marc Bossuyt and Paul Lemmens (eds), *Out of the Ashes: Reparation for Victims of Gross and Systematic Human Rights Violations* (Intersentia, 2005).

Skaar, Elin, Siri Gloppen, and Astri Suhrke (ed), *Roads to Reconciliation* (Lexington Books, 2005).

Tomuschat, Christian, 'Individual Reparation Claims in Instances of Grave Human Rights Violations: The Position under General International Law' in Albert Randelzhofer and Christian Tomuschat (eds), *State Responsibility and the Individual: Reparation in Instances of Grave Violations of Human Rights* (Martinus Nijhoff Publishers, 1999).

Torpey, John, 'Victims and Citizens: The Discourse of Reparation(s) at the Dawn of the New Millennium' in Koen de Feyter, Stephan Parmentier, Marc Bossuyt and Paul Lemmens (eds), *Out of the Ashes: Reparation for Victims of Gross and Systematic Human Rights Violations* (Intersentia, 2005).

Uprimny, Rodrigo and Maria Paula Saffon, 'Reparaciones Transformadoras, Justicia Distributiva y Profundización Democrática' in Catalina Díaz, Nelson Camilo Sánchez and Rogrigo Uprimny, *Reparar en Colombia: Los dilemas en contexto de conflicto, pobreza y exclusión* (ICTJ – DeJusticia, 2009).

van Boven, Theo, *Final Report of the Special Rapporteur: Study Concerning the Right to Restitution, Compensation and Rehabilitation for Gross Violations of Human Rights and Fundamental Freedoms*, UN Doc E/CN.4/Sub.2/1993/8 (2 July 1993).

Waldorf, Lars, 'Anticipating the Past: Transitional Justice and Socio-Economic Wrongs' (2012) 21(2) *Social and Legal Studies*.

Wilson, Richard A, 'Representing Human Rights Violations: Social Contexts and Subjectivities' in Richard A Wilson (ed), *Human Rights, Culture and Context: Anthropological Perspectives* (Routledge, 1997)

Chapter 10

Transitional justice and peacebuilding

Lia Kent

10.1 Introduction and definitions

Transitional justice is increasingly viewed as an essential component of peace-building. It is now incorporated into the mandates of many United Nations (UN) peace operations, and efforts to achieve justice, peace and democracy are treated by the UN as 'mutually reinforcing imperatives.'[1] Indeed, it is apparent that since the 1990s, the UN and other international organisations have placed the promotion of transitional justice alongside human rights, the rule of law, good governance and democratisation as a key element of peacebuilding and reconstruction interventions in post-conflict societies. This has been accompanied by efforts to develop more coordinated and integrated approaches to peacebuilding and transitional justice. At the same time, critical peacebuilding scholars sound a note of caution about the enmeshment of transitional justice within peacebuilding. They point to the liberal assumptions that underpin these interventions which, they argue, might undermine the prospects for sustainable peace.

This chapter begins with an overview of the emergence and expansion of peacebuilding, and of the growing consensus that justice is essential to long-term peace. It then highlights a number of tensions between the goals of peacebuilding and transitional justice, which complicate the view that justice and peace are mutually reinforcing. It shows how this view is further challenged by the emerging critique of liberal peacebuilding, a key aspect of which is concerned with how the externally devised and imposed nature of these interventions leaves limited space for local actors to construct their own vision of peace. This, in turn, has implications for both the legitimacy and sustainability of that peace. Building

---

1 UN Security Council, *The Rule of Law and Transitional Justice in Conflict and Post-Conflict Societies*, UN Doc S/2004/616 (23 August 2004) 1.

on the insights generated through this critique, the chapter's conclusion offers some suggestions as to how both transitional justice and peacebuilding might be reconceptualised.

10.2 Historical overview – the evolution of peacebuilding and transitional justice

The term peacebuilding is generally thought to have entered into policy discourse following the publication of UN Secretary-General Boutros Boutros-Ghali's 1992 seminal report, *An Agenda for Peace*. The report, which defined peacebuilding as 'action to identify and support structures which will tend to strengthen and solidify peace in order to prevent a relapse into conflict', marked a major shift in the international community's approach towards managing conflict.[2] In essence, this new approach went beyond an emphasis on simply bringing direct conflict to an end, and recognised that laying the foundations for sustainable peace called for a wide range of activities to rebuild conflict-affected communities, consolidate peace and prevent a recurrence of violence.

The publication of *An Agenda for Peace*, and the associated shifts in thinking about how conflict should be responded to, occurred against the backdrop of the end of the Cold War. This had ushered in a sense of new optimism about the potential for the UN Security Council to reach consensus on proposals to deploy new peace operations. This optimism was also tinged, however, by an emerging recognition that the nature of armed conflict had changed, and that while there had been a decline of wars between sovereign states, *intrastate* conflict – conflicts taking place within the borders of a single state – remained a significant problem and, according to some analysts, accounted for 94 per cent of all armed conflicts in the 1990s.[3]

The unique features of intrastate conflict posed a number of specific and profound challenges to the ways in which conflict had been traditionally understood and managed. It was recognised, for instance, that an overwhelming number of victims of intrastate conflicts were civilians.[4] Another issue was the fact that in the aftermath of intrastate conflicts, people representing different sides of the conflict are required to live together in a single jurisdiction rather than retreating to an internationally-determined frontier as in interstate conflicts. Another, more strategically driven, concern was that 'weak, failing and conflict-prone states'

---

2 See Boutros Boutros-Ghali, *An Agenda for Peace: Preventative Diplomacy, Peacemaking and Peace-Keeping*, UN Doc A/47/277-S/2411 (31 January 1992) para 21.

3 Peter Wallensteen and Margareta Sollenburg, 'Armed Conflict 1989–1999' (2000) 37 (85) *Journal of Peace Research* 632.

4 E.g. see Mary Kaldoor, *New and Old Wars: Organized Violence in a Global Era*. (2012, third edition, Polity Press) p. 106 and afterword.

might pose a threat to regional or global security.[5] Given these concerns, and an emerging realisation that traditional peace operations had not always been effective in fostering long-term peace, the UN was increasingly called upon to develop multifaceted approaches to peacebuilding that aimed to address 'underlying economic, social, cultural and humanitarian problems' that might contribute to ongoing instability.[6]

The 1990s thus saw the rapid expansion of peacebuilding missions in conflict-affected states. These missions involved a wide variety of actors, including various sections of the UN, the World Bank, and non-governmental organisations (NGOs), and promoted a broad set of programmes and activities. Unlike the so-called 'traditional' peacekeeping missions of the Cold War era, which had been expected to avoid intervening in the domestic political sphere, the mandates of these new 'multidimensional peace operations' encompassed aspects of peacebuilding and state-building (that is, the rebuilding of institutions of governance) on the basis that states required viable and functioning state authority and institutions to become stable. In addition to providing support for ceasefires, these missions engaged in efforts to demobilise former combatants and reintegrate them into society, reform the formal security sector, repatriate or resettle refugees, stabilise the economy, strengthen public service delivery and monitor or organise elections. They were also responsible for various rule of law initiatives, such as efforts to strengthen institutions of justice and police forces, draft or amend constitutions and, increasingly, support transitional justice mechanisms such as courts (international, national and 'hybrid') and truth commissions. To develop a more integrated approach to peacebuilding, the UN established a Peacebuilding Commission in 2005.

Just as the domain of peacebuilding expanded in the 1990s and began to encompass rule of law and transitional justice interventions, the domain of transitional justice also expanded. As Jeffery and Kim note, the 'transitions' included within the scope of transitional justice began to encroach into areas that had traditionally been thought of as being within the domain of peacebuilding.[7] A key shift was that, in line with the growing international awareness of the changing nature of conflict, not only were transitions from repressive regimes to democratic societies considered within the parameters of transitional justice (such as the transitions that took place in the 1980s in Latin America), but also movements from conflict to peace associated with the end of intrastate civil wars and

---

5 Dustin Sharp, 'Beyond the Post-Conflict Checklist: Linking Peacebuilding and Transitional Justice through the Lens of Critique' (2013) 14(1) *Chicago Journal of International Law* 165, 172.
6 Ibid.
7 Renee Jeffery and Hun Joon Kim, 'Introduction: New Horizons: Transitional Justice in the Asia Pacific' in Renee Jeffery and Hun Joon Kim (eds), *Transitional Justice in the Asia-Pacific* (Cambridge University Press, 2014) 5.

periods of violent instability. A simultaneous reconceptualisation of both transitional justice and peacebuilding thus occurred. As peacebuilding was redefined to 'include the pursuit of justice as a key priority', transitional justice expanded to include transitions from conflict to peace in addition to transitions from authoritarian rule to democracy.[8] These shifts began to lead to calls for peacebuilding and transitional justice programmes to be better coordinated and integrated with one another.

10.3 Purpose, aims, and assumptions

Arguments for improving coordination between transitional justice and peacebuilding are based on several assumptions. Key amongst these is the idea that establishing accountability for conflict-related human rights violations is essential to a sustainable peace. This assumption, which is reflected in the UN's 2004 report, *The Rule of Law and Transitional Justice in Post-Conflict Societies*, suggests that the vigorous and dichotomous 'peace versus justice' debate that characterised the early years of scholarship on transitional justice in the 1990s has abated. This debate, which pivoted around 'whether or not new democracies should "prosecute or punish" . . . [or] "forgive and forget" crimes committed by members and supporters of past authoritarian regimes', saw questions asked about whether some form of compromise with powerful perpetrators – including by offering them amnesties – might be necessary to secure a lasting peace. Questions were also asked about the extent to which trials might have a destabilising impact on newly democratising societies.[9] Replacing this dichotomous view was an apparent consensus that the choice between 'peace' and 'justice' was a false one, as the maintenance of peace in the long term cannot be achieved unless there is redress for grievances.

Arguments about the mutually reinforcing nature of peace and justice have become familiar in the peacebuilding and transitional justice literature. It is suggested that accountability and punishment of perpetrators will help to prevent and deter future violence, and that criminal trials will help to signal an end to a culture of impunity by indicating that 'the new political order is based on the rule of law'.[10] It is also claimed that the production of an authoritative historical record of the conflict by a truth commission will help to counter denial about the past and, in the process, make it difficult for 'conflict entrepreneurs to propagate violence-generating myths or fallacious, politicized accounts of history

---

8 Ibid.

9 Ibid.

10 Professionals in Humanitarian Assistance and Protection (PHAP), *Transitional Justice and Peacebuilding Processes* (July 2009) Peacebuilding Initiative <http://www.peacebuildinginitiative. org/>.

for political purposes, such as fomenting violence against certain sections of society'.[11] Transitional justice might also play a role in contributing to reconciliation by channelling desires for retribution and preventing popular eruptions of revenge and retaliation. Finally, it is argued that transitional justice can help to foster trust among citizens, as well as build renewed trust in state institutions.

The emergence of the view that justice is essential to durable peace has gone hand in hand with a recognition that 'no single transitional justice mechanism alone can address a post-conflict society's array of complex needs and realities.'[12] Rather than simply equating transitional justice with prosecutions, it is now argued that a range of tools, including trials, truth commissions, reparations, lustration, and even amnesties and pardons, might be needed, and can complement each other. Terms such as 'sequencing' and 'complementarity' have thus entered into the policy discourse. Complementarity encompasses the idea that some transitional justice interventions might provide the necessary support for others, while sequencing encompasses the idea that some transitional justice measures may need to be put in place before others, as not all such measures will contribute to peacebuilding at all times.

The argument for 'sequencing' is often made in respect to criminal prosecutions. Specifically, it is contended that during the early, fragile, stages of peacebuilding, it might not always be possible to conduct prosecutions, and that other mechanisms, such as truth commissions, might be more appropriate at these times, and can help to facilitate later prosecutions. For instance, the reports of truth commissions can help expose patterns of violations and raise awareness about the rights of victims that can be useful in later trial proceedings. Even amnesties (which prohibit retributive action against those who have committed criminal acts) are sometimes thought to play an initial stabilising role during a vulnerable period of transition, after which trials might be possible.

10.4 Points of contention and controversy

Despite the rhetoric that justice and peace are mutually reinforcing, there is an inherent friction between some of the goals of peacebuilding and those of transitional justice. Indeed, the 'peace versus justice' debate of the 1990s never entirely disappeared.

From a peacebuilding perspective, concerns are often raised that transitional justice initiatives – in particular prosecutions – might undermine fragile peace agreements. The threat of prosecutions may create an obstacle to former combatants laying down their weapons, or could lead those responsible for human rights

---

11 Ibid.
12 Ibid.

violations to enact coups or take up arms once more.[13] In some cases, as occurred in Timor-Leste, it is argued that the threat of prosecutions may prevent refugees returning to countries from which they have fled. A related concern is that, rather than promoting peace, criminal trials might work to entrench existing divisions in society. This point has been made in relation to the arrests and judgments of war criminals by the International Criminal Tribunal for Yugoslavia which, some suggest, led to an increase rather than a reduction in hostility between ethnic groups.[14]

A specific example of how friction between transitional justice and peace-building goals can manifest is evident in the case of demobilisation, demilitarisation and reintegration (DDR) programmes, which are often implemented as part of peacebuilding interventions. These programmes aim to remove weapons from former combatants and assist them to integrate into society through the provision of training, education and, often, material benefits. As some scholars have pointed out, DDR programmes and transitional justice mechanisms are oriented towards very different constituencies. While transitional justice is thought to be concerned with victims, DDR programmes focus on combatants and security. Given these differences, tensions may arise if the provision of reinsertion and reintegration of benefits for former combatants are high compared to victims' reparations programmes, or if beneficiaries of DDR benefits are perceived to be perpetrators of serious crimes during the conflict. These tensions emerged in Sierra Leone.[15] Conversely, as occurred in Timor-Leste, veterans may oppose reparations payments to victims who are perceived to have supported the 'wrong' side.[16]

The ability of transitional justice to contribute to long-term peace is also constrained by practical problems. For domestic trials to be effective, infrastructure and human resources must be available which is often rare in post-conflict situations. Judiciaries may also be weak or non-existent, there may be a lack of trained lawyers and judges, and legal systems may have collapsed. Moreover,

---

13 See Chandra Lekha Sriram, 'Justice as Peace? Liberal Peacebuilding and Strategies of Transitional Justice' (2007) 21(4) *Global Society* 579, 587.

14 James Meernik, 'Justice and Peace? How the International Criminal Tribunal Affects Societal Peace in Bosnia' (2005) 42(3) *Journal of Peace Research* 287.

15 Sharp, above n 5, 187–188. See also Rosalind Shaw, 'Linking Justice with Reintegration: Ex-Combatants and the Sierra Leone Experiment' in Rosalind Shaw and Lars Waldorf (eds), *Localizing Transitional Justice: Interventions and Priorities after Mass Violence* (Stanford University Press, 2010) 111, 113; Jeremy Ginifer, 'Reintegration of Ex-Combatants' in Mark Malan et al (eds), *Sierra Leone: Building the Road to Recovery* (Institution for Security Studies, 2003) 39.

16 Eva Ottendorfer, 'Contesting International Norms of Transitional Justice: The Case of Timor Leste' (2013) 7(1) *International Journal of Conflict and Violence* 32. See also Lia Kent, 'After the Truth Commission: Gender and Citizenship in Timor-Leste' (2016) 17(1) *Human Rights Review* 51.

criminal trials, even when successful, will only ever be able to address a small number of human rights violations by prosecuting a small number of individuals. There is furthermore the added issue that in resource-poor post-conflict settings, there is often competition over limited resources (or at the very least, the appearance of competition). Transitional justice processes may be criticised for being too expensive in the context of competing economic and social development priorities.

In recent years, a profound critique of the liberal assumptions that underpin both peacebuilding and transitional justice interventions has also been mounted. Contemporary peacebuilding is sometimes described as *liberal* (or neo-liberal) peacebuilding because it is based on the twin assumptions that liberally constituted societies are more peaceful than illiberal states, and that a sustainable peace will best be accomplished by fostering a liberal democracy (through periodic elections), functioning public institutions, and an open market economy.[17] Put simply, liberal peacebuilding might be thought of as based on an underlying narrative of 'transition' that suggests that 'weak failing, and conflict-prone states' can be 'relocated from a sphere of conflict to a sphere of peace through a process of political, social and economic liberalization'.[18]

One strand of the critique of liberal peacebuilding is concerned with the inappropriateness of promoting liberal democracy and market economics in volatile and unstable post-conflict societies. It is argued that sources of instability, which do not simply disappear once an international peacebuilding operation is in place, may be exacerbated by the introduction of initiatives to promote a state's rapid integration into a global economy.[19] This is particularly the case in societies that have little experience with market economies, and where the state itself may have limited power. In these fragile post-conflict environments, states may struggle to manage the inequalities and social dislocation that results from opening their markets to the global economy. Rapid political and economic liberalisation also has the potential to exacerbate social and political tensions, and to increase the likelihood of renewed violence.[20]

A second, related, strand of the critique of liberal peacebuilding is concerned with the ways in which policymakers tend to view peacebuilding interventions as comprising a standardised package of narrowly focused and externally devised

---

17 Edward Newman, Roland Paris and Oliver P Richmond, 'Introduction' in Edward Newman, Roland Paris and Oliver P Richmond (eds), *New Perspectives on Liberal Peacebuilding* (United Nations University Press, 2009) 11. See also Jeffery and Kim, above n 7.

18 Dustin Sharp, 'Emancipating Transitional Justice from the Bonds of the Paradigmatic Transition' (2015) *International Journal of Transitional Justice* 9 (1) 153.

19 Sriram, above n 13, 586.

20 Roland Paris, *At War's End: Building Peace after Civil Conflict* (Cambridge University Press, 2004) 5.

programmes that can be implemented in a top–down manner. This critique is applicable not only to peacebuilding interventions but to transitional justice measures (which increasingly comprise a key part of these interventions). Indeed, the extent to which transitional justice is based on a standardised 'tool-kit' package is evident in the way that post-conflict states are now 'expected, encouraged and even coerced'[21] to accept trials, truth commissions and other rule of law programmes, on the basis that this will help facilitate their 'transition' and transformation into peaceful, liberal democracies.

Critics argue that the standardised or 'one-size fits all' approach to transitional justice for peacebuilding is problematic in five key respects. First, it leads to a tendency for policymakers to promote their interventions as 'technical' interventions that are short term in nature and are transferable to a wide variety of places.[22] This approach pays little regard to local context, including the complex underlying economic, social and institutional legacies (including colonial legacies) that affect the ability of many post-conflict states to become stable democracies. Some of these legacies include deep-seated structural inequalities that often underlie, and contribute to, violent conflict and which do not end with the signing of a peace accord or the arrival of a UN peace mission. The tendency to overlook structural inequalities is exacerbated by the preoccupation of transitional justice mechanisms – and criminal justice processes in particular – with questions of *individual* accountability, which leads to the marginalisation of questions of social or distributive justice.

A second reason why standardised approaches to transitional justice are problematic is that they have a tendency to obscure the politics entailed in their establishment. Transitional justice interventions are the product of compromise, limited choice and conflicting policy agendas between and amongst international, national and local actors. This is no more evident than in the case of criminal prosecutions. Not only is a successful prosecutorial approach dependent on the willingness of post-conflict states to pursue high-profile perpetrators, but powerful Western states also exert a disproportionate influence over whether and how criminal prosecutions take place.[23] These political dynamics were apparent in Timor-Leste, where despite the UN's rhetoric about the need to bring those responsible for human rights violations to justice, there was little appetite among members of the UN Security Council for establishing an international criminal tribunal to prosecute Indonesian war crimes, in part because of Indonesia's status

---

21 Jelena Subotić, *Hijacked Justice: Dealing with the Past in the Balkans* (Cornell University Press, 2009) 21.

22 Lia Kent, *The Dynamics of Transitional Justice: International Models and Local Realities in East Timor* (Routledge, 2012) 31.

23 Rosemary Nagy, 'Transitional Justice as Global Project: Critical Reflections' (2008) 29(2) *Third World Quarterly* 275–289.

as a key ally of Western states in the so-called 'war on terror'. This led not only to the establishment of a hybrid tribunal that was hamstrung in its prosecutorial efforts, but also influenced the East Timorese leadership's prioritisation of 'development' goals over prosecutions.

Third, it is argued that standardised transitional justice interventions overlook questions of 'local ownership', undermining their legitimacy and therefore their ability to contribute to sustainable peace. The argument here is quite simply that if transitional justice interventions are perceived as imposed rather than as locally generated, they may be viewed as distant and foreign, and 'lose their legitimacy and efficacy'.[24] These dynamics have been particularly apparent in relation to the two international criminal tribunals, the International Criminal Tribunal for the former Yugoslavia (ICTY) and the International Criminal Tribunal for Rwanda (ICTR). As some studies have shown, accusations of bias continue to be made by parts of the population in Serbia and the Bosnian Republika Srpska against the ICTY, which is regarded as a distant mechanism imposed from outside.[25] Further exacerbating these issues has been the lack of communication between the ICTY and its local publics, and the fact that, during the first years of the ICTY's existence, trials and public declarations were published exclusively in English.[26]

Fourth, it is argued that the promotion of top–down institutionalised transitional justice interventions has the potential to overlook the extent to which conceptions of justice and peace vary across societies. There is growing awareness that transitional justice mechanisms transplanted into societies with different legal cultures, experiences and histories, and expectations and understandings of justice, may simply not be effective.[27] In societies where a large percentage of the population does not have access to formal state justice systems and relies upon informal systems of conflict resolution, issues such as collective wellbeing and compensation for victims might be valued over punishment of perpetrators through a formal justice process. Or it might simply be the case that transplanted transitional justice mechanisms remain inaccessible to the population and are not widely known. Another related concern is that in societies where resources are scarce, punishment by a formal justice system may be viewed differently than it is in well-resourced societies. In Rwanda, for example, locals complained

---

24 Chandra Lekha Sriram, Olga Martin-Ortega and Johanna Herman, 'Guidance Paper: Evaluating and Comparing Strategies of Peacebuilding and Transitional Justice' (Working Paper No. 2, Centre on Human Rights in Conflict, May 2009) 19.

25 See, e.g., Julie Mertus, 'Findings from Focus Group Research on Public Perceptions of the ICTY' (2007) 55(1) *Südosteuropa* 107–117; Martina Fischer and Ljubinka Petrovic-Ziemer, 'Dealing with the Past in the Western Balkans: Initiatives for Peacebuilding and Transitional Justice in Bosnia-Herzegovina, Serbia and Croatia' (Berghoff Report No. 18, Berghoff Foundation, 2013).

26 Mertus, above n 25.

27 See Lars Waldorf, 'Local transitional justice', in this volume.

that 'suspected war criminals are living better lives in their UN-standard prisons than the victims back home'.[28] Similar complaints have been heard in Timor-Leste, where it is commonly perceived that perpetrators 'become fat' in prison – normally a privilege of the rich.[29]

Finally, it is argued that a focus on institutionalised justice may undercut and potentially even stifle local ways of responding to conflict and building peace. This point has been made in relation to the Australian-led Regional Assistance Mission to the Solomon Islands (RAMSI). As described by Allen and Dinnen, the decision taken by RAMSI to devote a substantial amount of resources and energy to prosecuting alleged perpetrators of crimes committed during the 'tensions' led to a focus on individual culpability which, among other things, had the effect of leaving 'little scope for alternative approaches including those founded on local knowledge and practice'.[30] This oversight has led to ongoing tensions between the law enforcement approach espoused by RAMSI and locals who demand greater engagement with indigenous peacemaking.[31]

Case study A: Timor-Leste

The case of Timor-Leste not only illustrates the tensions that may arise between the pursuit of justice and peace goals, but also supports the critique of liberal peacebuilding. In the aftermath of the UN-sponsored referendum on self-determination in 1999, that brought a quarter of a century of oppressive Indonesian occupation of the territory to an end, the UN Security Council established the UN Transitional Administration for East Timor (UNTAET), in October 1999, to administer the territory until the nation gained its formal independence in 2002.

UNTAET encountered a challenging context in which much of the territory's infrastructure had been destroyed, over a thousand people had been killed during the violence of 1999 (and up to a third of the population had perished during the Indonesian occupation), there were no functioning courts or practising judges, and hundreds of thousands of refugees remained across the border in Indonesian West Timor. Moreover, centuries of colonialism and occupation had left a legacy of widespread impoverishment and mistrust amongst the population. To respond to these challenges, UNTAET was given an unprecedented state-building mandate. In accordance with liberal peacebuilding tenets,

---

28 Rami Mani, 'Rebuilding an Inclusive Political Community after War' (2005) 36(4) *Security Dialogue* 517.

29 Tanja Chopra, Christian Ranheim and Rod Nixon, 'Local-Level Justice under Transitional Administration: Lessons from East Timor' in Deborah Isser (ed), *Customary Justice and the Rule of Law in War-Torn Societies* (United States Institute for Peace, 2011) 119, 139.

30 Matthew Allen and Sinclair Dinnen, 'The North Down Under: Antinomies of Conflict and Intervention in Solomon Islands' (2010) 10(3) *Conflict, Security and Development* 299.

31 Ibid.

transitional justice – and, in particular, prosecutions – were promoted as necessary for sustainable peace. UNTAET established a specialised investigations unit and an internationalised or 'hybrid' tribunal known as the Special Panels for Serious Crimes (SPSC) that was mandated to hear cases of serious crimes.[32]

Despite UNTAET's stated emphasis on prosecutions, tensions soon emerged both within the UN, and between UNTAET and the East Timorese leadership, over the relative priority to be accorded to justice goals over other concerns, such as the need to ensure the security of Timor-Leste's borders, repatriate refugees and attend to the territory's urgent developmental needs. Geopolitical factors, such as Indonesia's power in the region and its strategic value to Western states in the so-called 'war on terror', also came into play in transitional justice decision-making. As a consequence, the hybrid SPSC was both politically compromised and under-resourced, and was unable to prosecute suspects located in the territory of Indonesia (among them, senior members of the Indonesian military).

UNTAET's initial approach to transitional justice also took little account of East Timorese experiences, understandings and expectations of justice, including the extent to which local dispute resolution practices remained widespread, and the state justice system was, for many in the rural areas, perceived as remote, cumbersome and inaccessible.[33] As a consequence, there was little local understanding of, or engagement with, the SPSC. Many of those who did come before the court as witnesses were frustrated that it did not respond to their desires for practical, economic assistance to address their ongoing material hardships, while the court's lack of an effective outreach strategy meant that few were aware of trial outcomes.[34]

Some two years later, however, UNTAET established a new, and more innovative, transitional justice mechanism. This was a truth commission, known as the Commission for Reception, Truth and Reconciliation (CAVR), which, among other things, initiated a community reconciliation process (CRP) that aimed to resolve some of the thousands of cases of 'less serious' crimes committed during 1999 that, it was increasingly recognised, the overstretched judicial system would have no hope of tackling.[35]

In comparison to the SPSC, the CRP has been praised for achieving a high degree of legitimacy amongst the population. Due to its proximity to local communities, its engagement of local leaders and its attempts to incorporate 'indigenous' dispute resolution practices, the CRP successfully integrated about 1400 perpetrators of minor crimes back into their communities. Yet, the CRP remained tethered to a short term state-building timetable that demanded quick

(continued)

---

32 Serious crimes were defined as genocide, war crimes, crimes against humanity, and torture, in addition to murder and sexual offences committed between 1 January and 25 October 1999. See UNTAET Regulation 2000/11, *On the Organization of Courts in East Timor*, UN Doc UNTAET/REG/2000/11 (6 March 2000) and UNTAET Regulation 2000/15, *On the Establishment of Panels with Exclusive Jurisdiction over Serious Criminal Offences*, UN Doc UNTAET/REG/2000/15 (6 June 2000).

33 Chopra, Ranheim and Nixon, above n 29, 119.

34 Kent, above n 22, 168–169.

35 This included cases of theft, minor assault, killing of livestock, arson, and the destruction of crops.

(continued)

results, which limited its effectiveness.[36] Building community awareness of, and trust in, the CRP process was slow, and by the time the CAVR concluded its work after two years of operation, there were thousands of people waiting to take part in reconciliation hearings who were unable to do so. Local trust in the CAVR was also eroded by the flaws of the SPSC, the lack of practical assistance provided to victims and the government's lack of interest in implementing the recommendations of the CAVR report (including its recommendation for a reparations programme).

In 2006, not long after Timor-Leste had been hailed a 'poster child' of successful UN peacebuilding, the country descended into violence. The 'crisis' of 2006, which stemmed from the government's dismissal of 594 soldiers who had left their barracks, soon became a lightning rod for other frustrated and disaffected groups to express their grievances, many of which were exacerbated by poverty and unemployment. Following the deaths of over 37 people, the displacement of over 150,000 people from their homes and the destruction of many houses, a new UN intervention was deployed to restore order.

The crisis highlighted the misguided nature of the assumption that international actors could transform Timor-Leste into a stable, liberal, democratic state within a two-and-a-half year period (and primarily through the introduction of Western style institutions of governance and justice). Certain aspects of UNTAET's peacebuilding intervention – namely its focus on embedding a free market model of development and promoting export production – had arguably also exacerbated some of the conditions in which the crisis took hold, for instance by raising the costs of basic goods and increasing food insecurity in rural areas. Although the UN's transitional justice approach had not itself promoted a free market model of economic development, like the peacebuilding intervention as a whole, it had paid little attention to continuing socio-economic injustices and underlying historical sources of tension and conflict. Rather, with the exception of the CAVR's CRP, it had promoted a politically compromised Western style justice system that had little local legitimacy.

Case study B: Sierra Leone

Like Timor-Leste, Sierra Leone was the subject of a transitional justice experiment that involved both a truth commission and a hybrid court. These mechanisms were promoted as a key aspect of the peacebuilding process that was initiated after more than a decade of civil war between the Revolutionary United Front (RUF) and the government of Sierra Leone. The conflict, which claimed the lives of tens of thousands of civilians, left thousands of others mutilated and impoverished, displaced about two million people, was layered upon decades of socio-economic marginalisation, poverty, unemployment, corruption and civil disenfranchisement. As in Timor-Leste, these conditions had been exacerbated by the legacies of colonialism.

---

36 See, e.g., Kent, above n 22, 96.

As in Timor-Leste, early peacebuilding efforts in Sierra Leone were accompanied by intense peace versus justice debates. These debates came to the fore in 1999, when the Government of Sierra Leone and the RUF signed the Lomé Peace Accord, which granted an unconditional blanket amnesty for all parties on condition that hostilities would cease. Although agreement was also reached for the establishment of a Truth and Reconciliation Commission (TRC) that would provide some degree of accountability for human rights abuses, given the scale of atrocities committed, the amnesty was viewed as profoundly unacceptable by international lawyers and justice advocates. Many national actors present at the Lomé negotiations argued, however, that a peace agreement would not be possible without some provision of amnesty for past crimes.[37] At the last moment, the UN representative to the peace negotiations included a handwritten note stating that the UN understood that the amnesty would not apply to international crimes of genocide, crimes against humanity, war crimes and other serious violations of international humanitarian law.[38]

Despite the signing of the Lomé agreement, the civil war dragged on for another two years, until the signing of the Abuja Protocols in 2001. At this point, the Sierra Leone government made a significant shift in its approach to questions of accountability, and formally requested the UN's help to establish a court to prosecute those responsible for human rights violations during the conflict.[39] The United Nations Mission in Sierra Leone (UNAMSIL) that had been established in 1999, helped to set up a hybrid tribunal, known as the Special Court for Sierra Leone (SCSL), and provided support for the TRC mandated in the Lomé accord. UNAMSIL also provided support for other peacebuilding activities, including the disarmament and demobilisation of ex-fighters, the repatriation of refugees, and the organisation of presidential and parliamentary elections.

Although the SCSL was given a mandate to try those 'most responsible' for human rights abuses during the armed conflict, as in the case of Timor-Leste, the court was constrained by geopolitical dynamics, which meant that there were serious omissions in terms of those prosecuted.[40] For instance, the then President Kabbah was not tried, despite his involvement as Minister of Defence throughout the conflict, and the roles of regional leaders Muammar Gaddafi and Blaise Compaoré were similarly overlooked. Another parallel with the Timor-Leste context was the lack of local input into the design and implementation of the SCSL, which fostered perceptions that the court was distant and irrelevant to the lives of ordinary Sierra Leoneans, and that it was driven by and served

(continued)

---

37 Priscilla Hayner, 'Negotiating Peace in Sierra Leone: Confronting the Justice Challenge' (Report, Centre for Humanitarian Dialogue and the International Center for Transitional Justice, December 2007) 6.

38 Ibid 10–11.

39 Mohamed Gibril Sesay and Mohamed Suma, *Transitional Justice and DDR: The Case of Sierra Leone: Research Brief* (International Center for Transitional Justice, 2009) 1.

40 Chris Mahoney, 'A Political Tool? The Politics of Case Selection at the Special Court for Sierra Leone' in Kirsten Ainley, Rebekka Friedman and Chris Mahony (eds), *Evaluating Transitional Justice: Accountability and Peacebuilding in Post-Conflict Sierra Leone* (Palgrave Macmillan, 2015) 77.

(continued)

foreign interests.[41] There was also, as in Timor-Leste, a disjuncture between the SCSL and popular understandings of justice. Many ordinary Sierra Leoneans prioritised 'forgetting' and 'compensation' over the prosecution of individuals, views that were reinforced by a lack of access to the formal justice system, fears of retaliation, and people's impoverished material conditions.[42]

The TRC, by contrast, has been praised for the 'definitive account' it delivered of the conditions and causes of the civil war. Funded by the UN's Office of the High Commissioner for Human Rights in Geneva, the TRC undertook a nationwide exercise in truth-telling between late 2002 to August 2003 that involved more than 500 individual hearings, 9,000 personal statements and nearly 200 written submissions from national or international institutions and NGOs. Yet a severe lack of resources constrained the TRC's visibility and effectiveness. In addition, some argue that the TRC, like the SCSL, promoted a culturally inappropriate model of truth-telling that was at odds with local justice priorities, desires for economic assistance, and local strategies for recovery and reintegration.[43]

The lack of complementarity between the SCSL and TRC on the one hand, and the DDR process on the other, further constrained the effectiveness of the transitional justice process. Although the DDR process (which disarmed 75,000 ex-fighters and provided them with reinsertion packages and skills training) had taken place concurrent with the transitional justice process, there was a discrepancy between the resources provided to ex-combatants compared to those provided to victims of the conflict. This gave rise to complaints from non-combatants that those who had committed human rights abuses received assistance while they did not receive reparations.[44] Ordinary people's ongoing experiences of poverty and marginalisation added fuel to local expressions of dissatisfaction with peacebuilding and transitional justice interventions. This discontent serves to highlight that the UN's focus on violations committed during the civil war and the reintegration of combatants has done little to address deep-seated structural inequalities, or meet popular demands for social or redistributive justice.[45]

10.5 Current positions

What conditions might need to be in place in order for transitional justice to contribute to building sustainable peace? Recently there have been calls within the

---

41 See Charles T Call, 'Is Transitional Justice Really Just?' (2004) 11(1) *Brown Journal of World Affairs* 101–113; Paul Jackson, 'Whose Justice in Sierra Leone? Power, Security and Justice in Post-Conflict Reconstruction' in Ainley, Friedman and Mahoney, above n 40.

42 See Tim Kelsall, *Culture under Cross Examination, International Justice and the Special Court for Sierra Leone* (Palgrave Macmillan, 2009).

43 See Rosalind Shaw, 'Memory Frictions: Localizing the Truth and Reconciliation Commission in Sierra Leone' (2007) 1 *International Journal of Transitional Justice* 183, 184.

44 Shaw, above n 15, 112–113.

45 Ibid 111.

scholarly and policy literature for better awareness of the shared goals of transitional justice, peacebuilding and development interventions. This, it is argued, is required to develop more coherent policy responses to address the array of interconnected challenges faced by post-conflict societies. Arguments have been mounted, for example, that peacebuilding interventions could be more 'justice sensitive'. For instance, DDR packages for ex-combatants could be designed in coordination with reparations packages for victims and do more to screen ex-combatants for human rights abuses. It has also been suggested that transitional justice interventions could do more to complement peacebuilding and development goals. For example, more could be done to reform and strengthen the capacity of domestic judicial systems, and to promote civic engagement on issues of accountability and justice. Important arguments are also emerging for the need of both trials and truth commissions to give more attention to the practical, material needs of victims.

As valuable as these suggestions are, developing better forms of coordination between transitional justice and peacebuilding programmes may not be enough to address the flaws of top–down, de-contextualised, interventions. Peter Uvin, writing of the post-conflict industry generally, observes that:

> There exists a deep imbalance between its far-reaching and ambitious aims and its limited resources and lack of knowledge. It appears as a giant, free-floating, machine, hovering, UFO-like, over a society, somehow totally out of touch and yet always present.[46]

Critiques such as these indicate that there may be a need for scholars and practitioners to engage in deeper forms of reflection about the adequacy, flaws and blind spots of liberal peacebuilding interventions. These reflections might, in turn, provide a basis for different kinds of conversations about both 'justice' and 'peace' that move beyond an emphasis on standardised approaches.

Recent scholarship is beginning to chart some creative ways forward in this regard. There are emerging calls for peacebuilders to pay more attention to the historical, political and cultural nuances of the contexts in which they are attempting to build peace. This is based on a recognition that, as Call and Cousens put it, 'without understanding something about how state–society relations have evolved, or who has power and how power works, any generic peacebuilding strategy is likely to be a poor fit'.[47] Others suggest that, as part of paying greater attention to local context, peacebuilders need also to pay attention

---

46 Peter Uvin, The Development/Peacebuilding Nexus: A Typology of Changing Paradigms (2002) 1(1) *Journal of Peacebuilding and Development* 12.

47 See Charles T Call and Elizabeth M Cousens, 'Ending Wars and Building Peace: Coping with Crisis' (Working Paper, International Peace Academy, March 2007) 13.

to the 'tensions, trade-offs and debates'[48] that may arise in any peacebuilding intervention, including the tensions between peace and justice. In other words, there appears to be a growing awareness that peacebuilding and transitional justice interventions need to be understood not as technical or neutral but as inevitably *political*. A recognition of this politics also requires acknowledging the power imbalance that inevitably exists in the peacebuilding context, in particular between the external actors and agencies that control (and provide much-needed funds for) peacebuilding programmes, and recipient populations.

It is not that all of these contradictions, tensions and power dynamics can necessarily be overcome. Greater awareness of the contingent, partial and political nature of peacebuilding might, however, allow more space for questions to be asked about 'whose peace (or whose justice)' is being built, 'based on whose priorities, to what ends, and who gets to decide'.[49] Issues of legitimacy are at the heart of these questions, as it is increasingly being recognised that top–down interventions that are introduced over and above national or subnational political spheres may only lead them to become 'internationalised but isolated from their societies'.[50] The focus on legitimacy reflects an emerging recognition that deliberations about questions of both justice and peace need to involve a wide section of society, not only 'elites', and that building a sustainable peace is contingent on the long-term political action of citizens and cannot be instituted from above.

Calls are also being made for an expansion of transitional justice goals to address not only human rights violations committed during times of 'conflict' but also the abuses and structural violence that often helped to precipitate conflict, and which contribute to ongoing instability.[51] Louise Arbour, the former UN High Commissioner for Human Rights, for instance, has called for an expansion of transitional justice to include a greater focus on economic, social and cultural rights. As she suggests, transitional justice must

> reach to – but also beyond – the crimes and abuses committed during the conflict . . . and it must address the human rights violations that pre-dated the conflict and caused or contributed to it. With these aims so broadly defined, transitional justice practitioners will very likely expose a great number of . . . violations of economic, social, and cultural rights.[52]

Any attempt to rethink liberal peacebuilding and transitional justice assumptions needs also to move beyond an exclusive preoccupation with the state and

---

48 Sharp, above n 5, 182.
49 Sharp, above n 18.
50 David Chandler, *Empire in Denial: The Politics of State-Building* (Pluto Press, 2006) 166.
51 See, e.g., Shaw, above n 15, 114.
52 See Louise Arbour, 'Economic and Social Justice for Societies in Transition' (Paper presented at Annual Lecture on Transitional Justice, New York University School of Law, 25 October 2006).

its institutions (including legal institutions) and consider peacebuilding and transitional justice from the 'bottom–up'. There are emerging calls for more attention to be given to the needs and priorities of communities affected by conflict, including socio-economic concerns such as job creation, welfare and basic social services. These issues are traditionally not prioritised by peacebuilders and transitional justice practitioners concerned with questions of formal justice and institution building.

Related arguments are emerging for peacebuilders and transitional justice practitioners to pay more attention to local conflict resolution practices. While many rightly caution against the romanticisation of these practices, which may have discriminatory impacts for less powerful members of society (for instance women, young people and ethnic minorities), there is nonetheless a growing recognition that citizens in post-conflict societies often turn to these practices in their efforts to reconstruct their lives. Local dispute resolution practices should therefore be taken seriously and should not be automatically placed in a secondary position to formal state mechanisms.

These insights do not provide a template for negotiating the complex questions, choices and trade-offs involved in building peace and pursuing justice in post-conflict societies. What they do suggest, however, is that many issues that have traditionally been relegated to the margins be brought into the foreground. Above all, by drawing attention to the fact that there are no 'quick fixes', they underscore the need to understand peacebuilding as a long-term, locally grounded process rather than a top-down externally imposed, technical project.

10.6 Summary

As transitional justice is increasingly considered to be an essential component of peacebuilding, there is a growing interest in exploring the potential connections between, and mutually reinforcing goals of, both fields. The argument is that a better awareness of the shared goals of transitional justice and peacebuilding, and a more coordinated approach to addressing these goals, will help deliver a more sustainable peace. The increasing enmeshment of transitional justice within peacebuilding has nonetheless also rendered transitional justice open to many of the critiques that have been mounted of liberal peacebuilding in recent years. A key aspect of this critique focuses on the liberal assumptions that underpin peacebuilding interventions, and which lead policymakers to view them as standardised packages of narrowly focused, technical and externally devised programmes that are transferable to a wide variety of places.

Critics argue that the 'one size fits all' approach to transitional justice for peacebuilding is problematic because it pays little regard to the local context including deep-seated structural inequalities that often underlie and contribute to violent conflict. It also obscures the politics of transitional justice, including the extent to which these interventions are often the product of compromise, limited choice and conflicting policy agendas. Questions of local ownership of transitional justice interventions are similarly overlooked, as are diverse conceptions of justice and peace, and local ways of responding to conflict. What these critiques highlight is that while it is important and necessary to develop more integrated approaches to peacebuilding and transitional justice, this in itself will be insufficient to address the top–down, de-contextualised nature of these interventions. Rather, there is a need for greater attention to questions of local and national legitimacy, and for the development of more holistic, 'bottom–up', responses to both peacebuilding and transitional justice.

10.7 Discussion and tutorial questions

1) Is justice necessary for a sustainable peace?

2) Where do the goals of peacebuilding and transitional justice converge, and where do they differ?

3) What conditions are necessary for transitional justice to contribute to building sustainable peace?

4) How might peacebuilders and transitional justice practitioners in Timor-Leste and Sierra Leone have engaged more effectively with the 'local context'?

Suggested reading

Ainley, Kirsten, Rebekka Friedman and Chris Mahony (eds), *Evaluating Transitional Justice: Accountability and Peacebuilding in Post-Conflict Sierra Leone* (Palgrave Macmillan, 2015).

The *Beyond Intractability Project*, the Conflict Information Consortium, University of Colorado ‹http://www.beyondintractability.org/essay/peacebuilding›.

Chopra, Tanya, Christian Ranheim and Rod Nixon, 'Local-Level Justice under Transitional Administration: Lessons from East Timor' in Deborah Isser (ed), *Customary Justice and the Rule of Law in War-Torn Societies* (United States Institute for Peace, 2011).

Kent, Lia, *The Dynamics of Transitional Justice: International Models and Local Realities in East Timor* (Routledge, 2012).

Mani, Rama, 'Rebuilding an Inclusive Political Community after War' (2005) 36(4) *Security Dialogue*.

Professionals in Humanitarian Assistance and Protection (PHAP), *Transitional Justice and Peacebuilding Processes* (July 2009) Peacebuilding Initiative ‹http://www.peacebuilding initiative.org/›.

Sharp, Dustin, 'Beyond the Post-Conflict Checklist: Linking Peacebuilding and Transitional Justice through the Lens of Critique' (2013) 14(1) *Chicago Journal of International Law*.

Sriram, Chandra Lekha, 'Justice as Peace? Liberal Peacebuilding and Strategies of Transitional Justice' (2007) 21(4) *Global Society*.

Sriram, Chandra Lekha, Jemima García-Godos, Johanna Herman and Olga Martin-Ortega (eds), *Transitional Justice and Peacebuilding on the Ground: Victims and Ex-Combatants* (Routledge, 2013).

United Nations Peacebuilding Commission ‹http://www.un.org/en/peacebuilding/›.

Suggested films

A Hero's Journey: Xanana Gusmao of East Timor (Directed by Grace Phan, Lux Lucis, 2006) [documentary on Xanana Gusmao that also explores the complex challenges of reconstruction and reconciliation in East Timor from Gusmao's perspective].

Fambul Tok [Family Talk] (Directed by Sarah Terry, Produced by Sara Terry, Libby Hoffman and Rory Kennedy, 2011) [documentary film about how Sierra Leoneans are building sustainable peace at the grassroots level].

Peace Versus Justice: A False Dilemma (Directed by International Center for Transitional Justice, 2011) ‹https://www.ictj.org/multimedia/video/peace-versus-justice-false-dilemma› [short multimedia clip on the ICTJ website on the peace versus justice debate].

Bibliography

Aggestam, Karin and Annika Björkdahl, 'Introduction: The Study of Justice and Durable Peace' in Karin Aggestam and Annika Björkdahl (eds), *Rethinking Peacebuilding: The Quest for Peace in the Middle East and the Western Balkans* (Routledge, 2013).

Allen, Matthew and Sinclair Dinnen, 'The North Down Under: Antinomies of Conflict and Intervention in Solomon Islands' (2010) 10(3) *Conflict, Security and Development*.

Ainley, Kirsten, Rebekka Friedman and Chris Mahony (eds), *Evaluating Transitional Justice: Accountability and Peacebuilding in Post-Conflict Sierra Leone* (Palgrave Macmillan, 2015).

Arbour, Louise, 'Economic and Social Justice for Societies in Transition' (Paper presented at Annual Lecture on Transitional Justice, New York University School of Law, 25 October 2006) ‹http://nyujilp.org/wp-content/uploads/2013/02/40.1-Arbour.pdf›.

Boutros-Ghali, Boutros, *An Agenda for Peace: Preventative Diplomacy, Peacemaking and Peace-Keeping*, UN Doc A/47/277-S/2411 (31 January 1992).

Call, Charles T, 'Is Transitional Justice Really Just?' (2004) 11(1) *Brown Journal of World Affairs*.

Call, Charles T and Elizabeth M Cousens, 'Ending Wars and Building Peace: Coping with Crisis' (Working Paper, International Peace Academy, March 2007).

Chandler, David, *Empire in Denial: The Politics of State-Building* (Pluto Press, 2006).

Chopra, Tanja, Christian Ranheim and Rod Nixon, 'Local-Level Justice under Transitional Administration: Lessons from East Timor' in Deborah Isser (ed) *Customary Justice and the Rule of Law in War-Torn Societies* (United States Institute for Peace, 2011).

de Greiff, Pablo and Roger Duthie (eds), *Transitional Justice and Development: Making Connections* (Social Science Research Council, 2009).

Fischer, Martina and Ljubinka Petrovic-Ziemer, 'Dealing with the Past in the Western Balkans: Initiatives for Peacebuilding and Transitional Justice in Bosnia-Herzegovina, Serbia and Croatia' (Berghoff Report No. 18, Berghoff Foundation, 2013).

Francis, David, 'Introduction: When War Ends: Building Peace in Divided Communities – Core Issues' in David Francis (ed), *When War Ends, Building Peace in Divided Communities* (Ashgate, 2012).

Ginifer, Jeremy, 'Reintegration of Ex-Combatants' in Mark Malan, Sarah Meek, Thokozani Thusi, Jeremy Ginifer and Patrick Coker (eds), *Sierra Leone: Building the Road to Recovery* (Institution for Security Studies, 2003).

Hayner, Priscilla, 'Negotiating Peace in Sierra Leone: Confronting the Justice Challenge' (Report, Centre for Humanitarian Dialogue and the International Center for Transitional Justice, December 2007).

ICTJ Research Unit, *Transitional Justice and Development: ICTJ Briefing* (International Center for Transitional Justice, 2009).

Jackson, Paul, 'Whose Justice in Sierra Leone? Power, Security and Justice in Post-Conflict Reconstruction' in Kirsten Ainley, Rebekka Friedman and Chris Mahony (eds), *Evaluating Transitional Justice: Accountability and Peacebuilding in Post-Conflict Sierra Leone* (Palgrave Macmillan, 2015).

Jeffery, Renee and Hun Joon Kim, 'Introduction: New Horizons: Transitional Justice in the Asia-Pacific' in Renee Jeffery and Hun Joon Kim (eds), *Transitional Justice in the Asia-Pacific* (Cambridge University Press, 2014).

Kaldor, Mary, *New and Old Wars: Organized Violence in a Global Era* (Polity Press, 2012, third edition, p.106 and Afterword).

Kelsall, Tim, *Culture under Cross Examination, International Justice and the Special Court for Sierra Leone* (Palgrave Macmillan, 2009).

Kent, Lia, 'After the Truth Commission: Gender and Citizenship in Timor-Leste' (2016) 17(1) *Human Rights Review*.

Kent, Lia, *The Dynamics of Transitional Justice: International Models and Local Realities in East Timor* (Routledge 2012).

Mahoney, Chris, 'A Political Tool? The Politics of Case Selection at the Special Court for Sierra Leone' in Kirsten Ainley, Rebekka Friedman and Chris Mahony (eds), *Evaluating Transitional Justice: Accountability and Peacebuilding in Post-Conflict Sierra Leone* (Palgrave Macmillan, 2015).

Mani, Rama, 'Rebuilding an Inclusive Political Community after War' (2005) 36(4) *Security Dialogue*.

Meernik, James, 'Justice and Peace? How the International Criminal Tribunal Affects Societal Peace in Bosnia' (2005) 42(3) *Journal of Peace Research*.

Mertus, Julie, 'Findings from Focus Group Research on Public Perceptions of the ICTY' (2007) 55(1) *Südosteuropa*.

Nagy, Rosemary, 'Transitional Justice as Global Project: Critical Reflections' (2008) 29(2) *Third World Quarterly*.

Newman, Edward, Roland Paris and Oliver P Richmond, 'Introduction' in Edward Newman, Roland Paris and Oliver P Richmond (eds), *New Perspectives on Liberal Peacebuilding* (United Nations University Press, 2009).

Olsen, Tricia D, Leigh A Payne and Andrew G Reiter, 'The Justice Balance: When Transitional Justice Improves Human Rights and Democracy' (2010) 32(4) *Human Rights Quarterly*.

Ottendorfer, Eva, 'Contesting International Norms of Transitional Justice: the Case of Timor Leste' (2013) 7(1) *International Journal of Conflict and Violence*.

Paris, Roland, *At War's End: Building Peace after Civil Conflict* (Cambridge University Press, 2004).

Professionals in Humanitarian Assistance and Protection (PHAP), *Transitional Justice and Peacebuilding Processes* (July 2009) Peacebuilding Initiative ‹http://www.peacebuilding initiative.org›.

Sesay, Mohamed Gibril and Mohamed Suma, *Transitional Justice and DDR: The Case of Sierra Leone: Research Brief* (International Center for Transitional Justice, 2009).

Sharp, Dustin, 'Beyond the Post-Conflict Checklist: Linking Peacebuilding and Transitional Justice through the Lens of Critique' (2013) 14(1) *Chicago Journal of International Law*.

Sharp, Dustin, 'Emancipating Transitional Justice from the Bonds of the Paradigmatic Transition' (2015) *International Journal of Transitional Justice* 9 (1).

Shaw, Rosalind, 'Memory Frictions: Localizing the Truth and Reconciliation Commission in Sierra Leone' (2007) 1 *International Journal of Transitional Justice*.

Shaw, Rosalind, 'Linking Justice with Reintegration? Ex-Combatants and the Sierra Leone Experiment' in Rosalind Shaw and Lars Waldorf (eds), *Localizing Transitional Justice: Interventions and Priorities after Mass Violence* (Stanford University Press, 2010).

Sriram, Chandra Lekha, 'Justice as Peace? Liberal Peacebuilding and Strategies of Transitional Justice' (2007) 21(4) *Global Society*.

Sriram, Chandra Lekha, Olga Martin-Ortega and Johanna Herman, 'Guidance Paper: Evaluating and Comparing Strategies of Peacebuilding and Transitional Justice' (Working Paper No. 2, Centre on Human Rights in Conflict, May 2009).

Subotić, Jelena, *Hijacked Justice: Dealing with the Past in the Balkans* (Cornell University Press, 2009).

UN Security Council, *The Rule of Law and Transitional Justice*, UN Doc S/2011/634 (12 October 2011).

UN Security Council, *The Rule of Law and Transitional Justice in Conflict and Post-Conflict Societies*, UN Doc S/2004/616 (23 August 2004).

UNTAET Regulation 2000/11, *On the Organization of Courts in East Timor*, UN Doc UNTAET/REG/2000/11 (6 March 2000).

UNTAET Regulation 2000/15, *On the Establishment of Panels with Exclusive Jurisdiction over Serious Criminal Offences*, UN Doc UNTAET/REG/2000/15 (6 June 2000).

Uvin, Peter, The Development/Peacebuilding Nexus: A Typology of Changing Paradigms (2002) 1(1) *Journal of Peacebuilding and Development*.

Waldorf, Lars, 'Just Peace? Integrating DDR and Transitional Justice' in Chandra Lekha Sriram, Jemima García-Godos, Johanna Herman and Olga Martin-Ortega, *Transitional Justice and Peacebuilding on the Ground: Victims and Ex-Combatants* (Routledge, 2013).

Wallensteen, Peter and Margareta Sollenburg, 'Armed Conflict 1989–1999' (2000) 37(85) *Journal of Peace Research*.

Chapter 11

Arts and transitional justice

Olivera Simić

11.1 Introduction

Experiencing artistic installations can be significant for transitional justice processes. Not only does an audience bear witness for harms done, but their presence also indicates public acknowledgement of crimes committed. This public acknowledgement is important for transitional justice: it is a break from the narrative of denial, which is often followed by strong feelings of shame and guilt for what has been done by group members. The process of re-humanisation of perpetrators is also necessary for any reconciliatory effort and rebuilding social relationships.[1] Art projects have been used as tools of transitional justice in countries on all continents to address atrocities committed by all kinds of non-democratic regimes. In the following chapter, we will explore the role of the arts in transitional justice processes. What is the power of art? Can art really make a difference in a community? Can it make a difference for those going through troubled times?

---

1 For example, a photo installation, *Entering the Tiger Zone* by Timothy Williams, endeavours to present perpetrators as humans rather than 'evil others': Timothy Williams, *Entering the Tiger Zone* (2015) University of Marburg <www.uni-marburg.de/konfliktforschung/Termine/entering-tiger-zone>. The aim of the exhibition is less about the everyday life of the perpetrators today, and more about their everyday life back in the 1970s and the dynamics that led to their participation in the Khmer Rouge massacres in Cambodia. Regarding the necessity for re-humanisation of perpetrators, see Phil Clark, *The Gacaca Courts, Post-Genocide Justice and Reconciliation in Rwanda: Justice without Lawyers* (Cambridge University Press, 2010) 42; David Bloomfield, Teresa Barnes and Luc Huyse (eds), *Reconciliation after Violent Conflict: A Handbook* (International Institute for Democracy and Electoral Assistance, 2003) 72; Geneviève Parent, 'Reconciliation and Justice after Genocide: A Theoretical Exploration' (2010) 5 *Genocide Studies and Prevention* 287.

11.2 Defining arts in transitional justice and its purpose

The field of transitional justice has only recently seen an upsurge of literature on the role of the arts in post-conflict societies, which has underscored that it is necessary to pay attention to 'the cultural and individual dimensions of transitional processes'.[2] There is general consensus among transitional justice scholars that judicial proceedings and accountability for human rights violations are necessary, but not sufficient to bring sustainable peace, democracy or reconciliation. The law is, according to several scholars, ineffective in bringing transformative change in social relations.[3] As Martha Minow argues, 'trials are not ideal'[4] and the law has limited capacity to capture and reflect people's experiences and incorporate them fully within the legal form. Trials, in large part, exclude the everyday experiences of those who have lived through an armed conflict or dictatorship.

Simply put, the law and prosecutions must be accompanied by social and institutional transformation in order to produce change in the affected society. In societies that have experienced mass human rights violations, very few people will seek justice before the courts and even fewer will qualify to obtain material reparation from the state. Many survivors will instead receive some form of symbolic reparation, such as an apology, while some will receive nothing at all. The necessity to document and memorialise crimes against humanity, in forums other than trials, thus becomes of paramount and enormous importance.[5] These other forms of symbolic reparations strive to achieve moral and not monetary satisfaction for survivors.[6]

Still, empirical studies show that analysis of reparations largely focuses on 'official state policy' towards individuals, mainly in the form of money, property or other forms of material reparations. Symbolic reparation may come not only in the form of an official apology, but also through artistic projects, and the potential of these for transformation and acknowledgement is still largely under-researched and under-theorised. For example, while recognising the importance of 'collective and symbolic forms of reparation [to] promote societal

---

2 Pablo de Greiff, 'On Making the Invisible Visible: The Role of Cultural Interventions in Transitional Justice Processes' in Clara Ramírez-Barat (ed), *Transitional Justice, Culture and Society: Beyond Outreach* (Social Science Research Council, 2014) 11, 14.

3 See, e.g., Laureen Snider, 'Towards Safer Societies: Punishment, Masculinities and Violence Against Women' (1998) 38 *British Journal of Criminology* 1.

4 Martha Minow, *Between Vengeance and Forgiveness: Facing History after Genocide and Mass Violence* (Beacon Press, 1998) 47.

5 Catherine Cole, 'Performance, Transitional Justice, and the Law: South Africa's Truth and Reconciliation Commission' (2007) 59 *Theatre Journal* 168, 169.

6 See Jemima García-Godos, Chapter 9, 'Reparations', this volume.

reconciliation', Olsen, Payne and Reiter exclude symbolic forms of reparation from their analysis 'because of the difficulties in finding full and systematic accounting' of a wide range of mechanisms.[7]

Although challenging for systematic research, symbolic reparation has been recognised as an important part of reparation packages. In its final report of 1998, the Reparation and Rehabilitation Committee of the Truth and Reconciliation Commission (TRC) in South Africa, for example, recommended reparations as necessary legal and moral obligations of the state to survivors of gross human rights violations, designed to 'restore human and civil dignity' and enable victims to come to terms with the past. According to the TRC report, symbolic reparations refer to measures that facilitate the 'communal process of remembering and commemorating the pain and victories of the past'.[8] Such measures, which are seen as mechanisms to restore the dignity of victims and survivors, may include, but are not limited to, exhumations, tombstones, memorials, monuments or the renaming of streets, parks, localities and public facilities.

Symbolic forms of reparation, according to Margaret Urban Walker, do not involve monetary transfer or transfer of property, but can be diverse, ranging from memorials to public apologies or educational projects.[9] According to her, *all* reparations have symbolic – that is, expressive or communicative – function. Likewise, Brandon Hamber notes that monetary reparation is also just another form of symbolic reparation which serves as a symbolic marker of redress and recognition.[10]

According to Walker, regardless of whether they are monetary or symbolic, all reparations are seen by victims as communicative gestures which produce real effects of moral, social, psychological and political kinds. Walker calls attention to the 'expressive' dimension of all types of reparations, which is the 'communicative act of expressing acknowledgement, responsibility, and intent to do justice'.[11] For many victims of political violence, it is precisely the denial of their victim status, and social and political silence about their victimisation, that are most difficult to bear.[12]

---

7 Tricia D Olsen, Leigh A Payne and Andrew G Reiter, *Transitional Justice in Balance: Comparing Processes, Weighing Efficacy* (United States Institute of Peace Press, 2010) 37.

8 Reparation and Rehabilitation Committee, Parliament of the Republic of South Africa, *Report* (1998) vol 6, part 2, 95.

9 Margaret Urban Walker, 'The Expressive Burden of Reparations: Putting Meaning into Money, Words, and Things' in Alice MacLachlan and Allen Speight (eds), *Justice, Responsibility and Reconciliation in the Wake of Conflict* (Springer, 2013) 205, 211.

10 Brandon Hamber, *Transforming Societies after Political Violence: Truth, Reconciliation and Mental Health* (Springer, 2009).

11 Margaret Urban Walker, 'Truth Telling as Reparations' (2010) 41 *Metaphilosophy* 529.

12 Brandon Hamber and Ingrid Palmary, 'Gender, Memorialization, and Symbolic Reparations' in Ruth Rubio-Marín (ed), *The Gender of Reparations: Unsettling Sexual Hierarchies While Redressing Human Rights Violations* (Cambridge University Press, 2009) 324, 364.

In that sense, artistic exhibitions become one of the various communicative acts that strive to bring forward survivors' experiences of armed conflict and political violence to a larger audience in order to break often entrenched silence and denial about past crimes. These artistic processes should be understood as a form of public recognition of survivors' and victims' suffering. The artworks strive to engage the public on multiple levels to create *potential* for confronting both injustice and historical narratives that need to be challenged. They can raise questions of justice, explore alternative historical narratives, give a voice to individual experiences far too often ignored, and ensure that these stories do not disappear altogether from the national memory. Artistic projects can also reach a much wider audience than legal justice ever can. As Chilean born artist Alfredo Jarr urged: 'Enough of you speaking to me and me speaking to me. Me applauding to you and you applauding to me. Let's get out, let's reach a larger audience'.[13] Theatrical performances, exhibitions and artistic installations can be created to be transportable, allowing for the possibility for them to be staged or displayed in isolated and remote areas, where the community may not necessarily engage with the media, internet and formal judicial language.

Artistic projects have the potential to break through silence, and to serve as a symbolic form of public acknowledgement and recognition that crimes happened. Such acknowledgement carries, as expressed by Haldemann, an 'idea of a "different kind of justice"', one that is less vindictive and state-centred and is more caring and responsive to human suffering'.[14] Art can foster 'precious sites of reflection', either collective or solitary, which in turn can allow creative and critical distance from the artwork.[15] Artistic installations may have a 'commemorative function' and represent some sort of 'temporary monuments'; they 'acknowledge that something has happened and have testimonial value and value of symbolic reparation'.[16] Art can facilitate negotiation among victims, parties responsible for wrongdoings, and their communities.[17] As a result, the audience is actively engaged in an act of moral reparation by participating in co-creating a 'shared understanding', with the capacity to produce empathy, space for insight and a public discussion forum about events and themes often pushed under the carpet by state officials.

---

13 Art21, Interview with Alfredo Jaar ('The Gramsci Trilogy', 11 March 2007) (online) <http://www. art21.org/texts/ alfredo-jaar/interview-alfredo-jaar-the-gramsci-trilogy>.

14 Frank Haldemann, 'Another Kind of Justice: Transitional Justice as Recognition' (2008) 41 *Cornell International Law Journal* 675.

15 Vikki Bell, *The Art of Post-Dictatorship: Ethics and Aesthetics in Transitional Argentina* (Routledge, 2014) 119.

16 Interview with Nataša Govedarica (Skype, 7 October 2013).

17 Urban Walker, above n 9, 222.

Acting upon this urge to turn to new languages and forms to address issues that are often silenced and unaddressed by the state authorities, artists have embarked on creating innovative arts projects in post-conflict/post-dictatorship countries, employing testimony, graphic arts, humour and cinema in order to respond to trauma and authoritarianism. Art projects assist recognition of past injustices, provide symbolic reparation and important unofficial counterparts for truth-finding, and enable improvement of under-represented groups.[18]

Artists look for different ways of communicating in order to reach a larger public, in order to make sense. When we say, for example, that 20,000 women had been raped, or every second woman, this can be meaningless because the statistics are too abstract. A strategy that artists often use is to reduce the scale to a single human being with a name, a story. This can help an audience identify with that person, and thus create conditions more conducive to empathy, solidarity and engagement with their story; to make space for dialogue, challenge indifference and inequality, and create intellectual involvement; in short, to reimagine justice.

11.3 Documentary theatre: using authentic testimonies and sources

Documentary theatre is a communicative act that strives to bring forward the stories of people's experiences of war and violence. It uses archival and authentic testimonies, collected in private settings and public legal spaces such as courtrooms. These testimonies may have been buried in official documents and archives or, too often, have not been archived at all. Documentary theatre takes people's experiences seriously, and has the capability to do so as an innovative medium that can capture an individual's journey in dealing with the past and the harm they have experienced. The use of archival material, including textual and visual documents, has a long history as a means of addressing broad social and political questions, histories of oppression and criminal justice systems, where the creative work of memory and the past through recollection and re-negotiation has been widely explored.[19] Artists recognise that a failure to respond to atrocity leaves survivors with frozen capacities to act, and produces wounded attachments to devastations, which can contribute to cycles of intergenerational transmission of trauma.[20]

---

18 Sanja Bahun, 'Transitional Justice and the Arts: Reflections on the Field' in Claudio Corradetti, Nir Eisikovits and Jack Volpe Rotondi (eds), *Theorizing Transitional Justice* (Ashgate, 2015) 153, 156.
19 Catherine Russell, *Experimental Ethnography: The Work of Film in the Age of Video* (Duke University Press, 1999); Jeffrey Skoller, *Shadows, Specters, Shards: Making History in Avant-Garde Film* (University of Minnesota Press, 2005).
20 Martha Minow, 'Breaking the Cycles of Hatred' in Nancy Rosenblum (ed), *Breaking the Cycles of Hatred: Memory, Law and Repair* (Princeton University Press, 2002) 14, 16.

Documentary theatre acknowledges and acts upon the need 'to reconceptual-ise transitional justice from the point of view of individual lived experiences'.[21] Such theatre is a site of social intervention that opens up a space for the re-negotiation of lived experiences, and also a site of practical endeavour that may advance justice for past violence. As Giovanna Zapperi notes, the appear-ance of women, for example, within documentary theatre can reveal things and events that have been repressed or overlooked. It can also remind us of the con-stitutive relationship between time and the image: it is when it is visualised that the past becomes recognisable and tangible.[22] The artists working with this form tend to believe that the focus on individual lives and experiences is something that needs to be captured, whereas – or because – macro historical and political events are often of importance to courts. This does not mean that context is irrel-evant, but that people's lives and experiences are at the forefront of their work.

The law, the courts and judges do not offer this kind of space or time or freedom of expression to survivors. They are interested in evidence, not in a story as such, and for the sake of evidence they will interrupt a witness when testimony is no longer deemed relevant. The rigidity and formalities that the rules of evidence and procedure require in the courtroom vanish in verbatim theatre. According to Dijana Milošević, documentary theatre is a specific form of theatre that uses

> testimonies, diaries, but also literature, visual art and music that speaks about the theme. It is the theatre that does not ask audience to 'judge' events and people because that is what courts must do. Art, and specifically theatre art, is able to record and revive the live word and the presence of the performers.[23]

Documentary theatre has become increasingly popular because it is capable of speaking with a live, everyday language about questions that audiences find dif-ficult to deal with. It offers provocation and controversy, which makes it attractive and topical in comparison with, for example, classical theatre. Documentary thea-tre encourages dialogue and publicly speaks about truths left unspoken, bringing to life personal narratives and memories, and often is the only public place where marginalised perspectives can be heard. It is a forum that is capable of keeping human experience alive and of encouraging rethinking, speaking up and learning, which may prevent repetition of wrongdoings.[24] Theatre plays a powerful role in

---

21 Romi Sigsworth and Nahla Valji, 'Continuities of Violence Against Women and the Limitations of Transitional Justice: The Case of South Africa' in Susanne Buckley-Zistel and Ruth Stanley (eds), *Gender in Transitional Justice* (Palgrave Macmillan, 2011) 115, 127.

22 Giovanna Zapperi, 'Woman's Reappearance: Rethinking the Archive in Contemporary Art – Feminist Perspectives' (2013) 105 *Feminist Review* 21.

23 Interview with Dijana Milošević (Skype, 12 January 2016).

24 Ibid.

this process of reckoning with the past, since artists have the power to speak out – and be heard – in the public domain.

Documentary theatre is a form often used by devised theatres such as Dah theatre (Serbia) and Yuyachkani (Peru). It is known also under the name of 'collaborative creation', since production of the show is a cooperative work between the director and actors. Devised theatre is an alternative to mainstream theatre. 'Devising' is a process in which the whole creative team develops a show collaboratively by sharing experiences, and exploring and experimenting with the nature of performance. Theatre companies will select their sources of inspiration such as a photograph, a poem, a fictional or non-fictional short story, a memory, interviews, or a question, and create a unique performance vocabulary informed by their source materials. They will articulate how their sources have informed process and product, form and content. The performances will often include movement, voice, visual image, sonic landscape, text and scenic environments that communicate style and aesthetics. Devising theatre strives to address challenges brought about by the cultural or socio-political changes of the time. These changes and theatre companies' preoccupations are reflected in the themes, form and content of the shows. The work they produce is not devised in a vacuum, but always reflects the broader context of society and culture, the world, its past and contemporary events.[25]

Case study A: Dah Theatre (Serbia)

Dah Theatre (Dah) was created in Belgrade by Dijana Milošević and Jadranka Anđelić in 1991, at the beginning of the fall of former Yugoslavia. At the time, Milošević and Anđelić were driven 'perhaps subconsciously, to oppose the destruction with creation; to create, in the midst of a world falling apart, a microcosmos of theatre'.[26] They had envisioned that their theatre would last for 15 to 20 years, but 25 years later Dah is still engaged in vital cultural work.

The war in the former Yugoslavia started in Slovenia and quickly spread to Croatia, Bosnia and Herzegovina (BiH), and later on Kosovo. The whole region was affected by it directly or indirectly. It was the war that brought the end of the one-party system (Communist Party) and saw almost 100,000 people dead, while approximately 8,000 are still missing. The region is still recovering from the destruction and mayhem that gripped the country between 1991 and 2001.

(continued)

25 For more on devised theatre, see, e.g., Alison Oddey, *Devising Theatre: A Practical and Theoretical Handbook* (Routledge, 1994).
26 Dubravka Knežević, 'Till the Last Breath' (1995) Sept–Dec *Scena* 5.

(continued)

Much has changed in the former Yugoslavia over the past two decades, but many challenges remain the same, including a lack of financial support for the work of theatre, and a determined denial of war crimes committed by one's own ethnic group. At the time when Dah was founded, there was no tradition of independent professional groups, no cultural understanding of what these groups were about, and no financial support to enable their existence. Dah, for its part, was a genuine pioneer: it introduced many radical new ideas, including a theatre lab, theatre workshops and actor's training. At the time, a civil war was raging in the former Yugoslavia – a war, for which the then Serbian government had an enormous responsibility. The circumstances for developing artistic projects could not have been less favourable. Paradoxically, it was precisely those circumstances that made the existence of Dah both intensely meaningful and culturally essential – the theatre's performances acted as a way of opposing the violence that engulfed all of the people living in the region at the time.

Although Dah does not define itself as documentary theatre, it uses this particular form in some performances to bring people's stories alive on the stage. Three performances that engage with the question of responsibility to the past – *Crossing the Line*, *Story about Tea* and *The Shivering of the Rose* – draw extensively on historical facts and documentary material. In *Crossing the Line*, documentary material is used, for the first time, throughout the entire performance, while *Story about Tea* incorporates, among other literature, documentary material about real-life war crimes committed in Štrpci.[27] Dijana Milošević, the director of Dah, commented on the importance of dealing with the past and acknowledging survivors' experiences. After *Crossing the Line* was performed in a small town in BiH she reported:

> I realised at one moment that the whole audience was weeping . . . once we finished the play, we received standing ovations and talked to [the] audience. I realised then how important it was for them to publicly hear their stories and in that way be acknowledged in their suffering.[28]

In *The Shivering of the Rose* Dah uses authentic testimonies of women from BiH, but also personal diaries and literature from Argentina and Chile. The performance deals with the post-traumatic memories of missing family members, especially women, who are their beloved ones. Dah positions itself as a theatre

---

27 Members of the Avengers (*Osvetnici*) military unit, commanded by Milan Lukić, with logistical support from Serbia, were responsible for the abductions and then murder of nineteen men on the Bosnian territory. Although Lukić was sentenced to twenty years of imprisonment by the International Court for the Former Yugoslavia (ICTY), his indictment did not include the massacre of nineteen men. Women in Black state that this situation exposes the limits of the ICTY. Only one person, Nebojša Ranisavljević, has been charged and convicted for this crime: Dušan Komarčević, 'Women in Black Remembered Abducted from a Train in Strpci: Those Who Committed the Crimes Remain at Large', *E-Novine* (online) 17 January 2016 <http://www.e-novine.com/drustvo/59890-Kreatori-zloina-dalje-slobodi.html> [trans of: 'Žene u crnom pamte otete iz voza u Štrpcima: kreatori zločina i dalje na slobodi'].

28 Olivera Simić and Dijana Milošević, 'Enacting Justice: The Role of Dah Theatre Company in Transitional Justice Processes in Serbia and Beyond' in Peter D Rush and Olivera Simić (eds), *The Arts of Transitional Justice: Culture, Activism, and Memory after Atrocity* (Springer, 2014) 99, 107.

that can open doors for the victims to seek justice, and as a space where people can reconsider their views. As a theatre, it employs techniques that allow the crossing of borders between the rational and the irrational, between reality and metaphor. These border-crossing techniques inherent to transformational theatre can at times open up a much larger space for potential reconciliation than formal justice mechanisms. Milošević sees Dah as fundamentally a truth-seeking mechanism:

> Art seeks to reveal the truth. We are a mechanism of truth. We create a space, where it is possible for truth to be heard. I see us, artists, as a consciousness of society. With our first performance, which was the anti-war performance in 1992 [*This Babylonian Confusion*], we came out on the streets and talked about the war at a time when it was forbidden to talk about it publicly in Serbia. We have a great need to talk about those things, which we are prohibited from talking about and about things that are happening; to talk about the things that we are obsessed with, things that bother us.

Figure 11.1 Maja Mitić, *The Shivering of the Rose*, Dah Theatre. Reproduced with permission of theatre director. Photographed by Una Škandro.

One of the most important transitional justice functions that theatre can offer is to inspire and encourage empathy and solidarity. Coming from Serbia and being of Serbian origin, the troupe wanted to express what was happening around them because of the personal urge felt by its members, and because Serbia's government, according to Milošević, had initiated the war. As Milošević stated:

> In our name the most unspeakable atrocities have been committed regardless of the other side's responsibility for the war. To us this

(continued)

(continued)

Figure 11.2 Maja Mitić, *The Shivering of the Rose*, Dah Theatre. Reproduced with permission of theatre director. Photographed by Una Škandro. Zašto! [Why!]

performance [*Crossing the Line*] was a path towards self-healing and reconciliation with our own people and with people from our former homeland. We are those, who were vulnerable, who felt guilty and who transformed our feeling of guilt into a feeling of responsibility. We are the ones who lived here and did not support what was happening, but our voices have not been heard. We had an enormous need for our voices to be heard in the name of all those people who had not agreed to and who didn't support what was happening. It is the power of theatre to give that voice, to give a voice to the voiceless.[29]

Case study B: Grupo Cultural Yuyachkani (Peru)

Peru's most important theatre collective, Grupo Cultural Yuyachkani, has been working since 1971 as an independent institution, and at the forefront of theatrical experimentation, political performance, and collective creation. 'Yuyachkani' is

---

29 Ibid 102.

a Quechua word that means 'I am thinking, I am remembering'. It is one of Latin America's oldest and most impressive activist theatre collectives, with a 45-year history of performing in reaction to, and in defiance of, politics in Peru. The theatre group has devoted itself to the collective exploration of embodied social memory, particularly in relation to questions of ethnicity, violence and memory in Peru. It is well known for embracing both cosmopolitan and indigenous forms of theatre, while addressing post-dictatorship and social issues in Latin America. Their work has a strong commitment to grassroots community issues, mobilisation, social justice and advocacy. Its members see the group and performance as a space for social interventions and self-reflection. One of their principal goals is a strong commitment to contribute to the development and strengthening of public memory.[30]

In the 1960s and 1970s, many Latin American countries were governed by military dictators, and Peru was no exception. The Peruvian Truth and Reconciliation Commission (TRC) was established in 2001 to examine abuses committed during the 1980s and 1990s, when Peru was plagued by the worst political violence in the history of the republic. The TRC focused on forced disappearances, massacres, human rights violations, terrorist attacks and violence against women; abuses that were committed by both the rebel groups and the military of Peru during the internal armed conflict. The TRC appointed many sectors of civil society as members, including scholars, journalists, sociologists, priests and artists.

To facilitate the truth-gathering process, as well as to publicly honour and remember the dead, five members of Yuyachkani travelled to the mountainous regions of the Andes most affected by the war. There, over a period of eight months, they held workshops, performed in the streets and participated in local demonstrations.[31] Through a range of performances and street-art installations, they converted ordinary streets and plazas into ritual spaces for reflection and remembrance. As Ana Correa, a Yuyachkani troupe member, reported,

> The Commission in Peru organised the meetings where families of the disappeared could come to testify . . . We met with people everywhere, in markets, public squares, churches . . . we emotionally supported people and families who suffered and testified . . . When they testified, I could really feel it . . . you can really feel these personal stories; you cannot get them out of your head, and you feel them in your guts, your soul while new questions keep coming up, questions that you keep asking yourself as a human being . . . I feel there is a bridge between families here, families that don't have their children or their parents. I feel I am an intermediary to tell them that here the memory flourishes and there is a justice . . .[32]

(continued)

---

30 For more, see, Yuyachkani Cultural Group, *Historia* <http://www.yuyachkani.org/historia.html>; Yuyachkani Cultural Group, *Historia del Grupo* <http://hemisphericinstitute.org/cuaderno/yuyachkani/ group.html>.

31 Salomón Lerner Febres, 'Memory of Violence and Drama in Peru: The Experience of the Truth Commission and the Yuyachkani Theater Group' (Speech delivered at the Just Performance: Enacting Justice in the Wake of Violence Symposium, Brandeis University, USA, 1–2 December 2011).

32 Yuyachkani Theatre Group 'Rosa Cuchillo' performed by Ana Correa, at Brown University's Brown International Advanced Research Institutes, 11 June 2013 <https://www.youtube.com/watch?v=i7U9NsRpjXcyoutube>. Accessed 13 November 2015.

(continued)

Figure 11.3 Ana Correa as Rosa Cuchillo. Reproduced with permission of the theatre group.

Figure 11.4 Ana Correa as Rosa Cuchillo. Reproduced with permission of the theatre group.

By listening and acting, Yuyachkani dignified the victims and their relatives and transformed the personal stigma of abuse into the collective trauma of a nation needing to heal. The troupe members heard stories and took testimonials from those in the audience who had come to testify. Similarly to Milošević, Ana Correa reflected on the socio-political situation in Peru at the moment she started working as an actress in the theatre:

> I started working in the theatre 30 years ago at [a] very special political moment in my country, at the time when military dictatorship started. I felt the need and desire to do something, to talk to people and to talk about my feelings of what was happening at that time.[33]

Devised theatres like Dah and Yuyachkani ask audiences to engage more actively with performance. The narratives they tell have no linearity and offer no solutions to complex issues, but include images, multiple stories and actions, often happening concomitantly. It is requested of audience members not to be passive, but to be 'active viewer[s], to be consumer[s], to reflect, to critically think'.[34] Such theatres also encourage free-thinking, because they bring to light stories that are silenced or taboo; talk about the importance of remembrance of the past; challenge the status quo; and offer opportunities to voice opposite, contradictory sides, and have these presented and heard. As such, devised theatre is more complex than classic theatre.

11.4 Photo exhibitions

With respect to photographs, Roland Barthes notes that they are always, to a certain extent, *momento mori*; the photographed images attest to what is already gone 'whether or not the subject is dead'.[35] Photographs, for Barthes, freeze the subject in a moment of the past. Walter Benjamin, Susan Sontag and Barthes, among others, refer to the ways in which photographic images 'haunt us', and thus pave the way for their use by artists in installation contexts to visualise the past. Photographic archives, according to Lerner, provide an 'invaluable source of information' and allow for reflection on pain and hope.[36] They have a

---

33 Ciudadaniasx: Intervenciones de Yuyachkani – Presentación de Ana Correa, 10 April 2012, <https://www.youtube.com/watch?v=YFtutxrICqk>.

34 Interview with Dijana Milošević, above n 23.

35 Roland Barthes, *Camera Lucida: Reflections on Photography* (Farrar, Straus and Giroux, 1981) 96.

36 Salomón Lerner Febres, 'Prefacio', Commission for Truth and Reconciliation, *In Order to Remember – A Visual Narrative of the Internal Conflict in Perú* [trans of: Comisión de la Verdad y Reconciliación, *Yuyanapaq: Relato Visual del Conflicto Armade Interno en el Perú*] (Fondo Editorial de la Pontificia Universidad Católica del Perú, 2003). See also the Museum of Memory and Human Rights <www.museodelamemoria.cl/expos/yuyanapaq-para-recordar/>.

demonstrative, didactic function that presents evidence, but they also appeal to our emotions by representing suffering and resistance. As Saona argues, 'images become a preferred form of testimonial, of truth-telling, because they seem to force the viewer to adopt the perspective of the eyewitness'.[37] Susan Sontag notes, 'even if they are only tokens . . . they still perform a vital function. The images say . . . Don't forget'.[38]

Case study C: Portraits of Reconciliation (Rwanda)

The photographers Pieter Hugo and Lana Mesić went to southern Rwanda and captured a series of unlikely, almost unthinkable images in many other post-conflict contexts. Most of these images present survivors and perpetrators standing or sitting close to each other with their bodies embodying what forgiveness and reconciliation mean to them today. For the 20-year commemoration of the 1994 genocide in Rwanda, a mini-exhibition of the project was on display in The Hague City Hall. Other exhibitions have taken place in The Hague next to the Peace Palace, the International Criminal Court, the Central Station and in the Het Nutshuis gallery. In late March 2015, the project was presented in Rwanda itself. The project has also been featured in Zagreb, New York, Tokyo and Kigali, and is accessible online.[39]

The people who agreed to be photographed are part of a continuing national effort towards reconciliation. They worked closely with the Association Modeste et Innocent (AMI), a non-profit organisation established in 2000 and known for its work in conflict resolution and the reconciliation process in Rwanda. AMI is recognised for bringing together former genocide perpetrators and genocide survivors for reconciliation by using a community-based approach.[40] In AMI's programme, a small group of perpetrators and survivors are counselled over a few months, culminating in the perpetrator's formal request for forgiveness. Atonement is a necessary precondition to forgiveness; acknowledgement of wrongdoing and regret is crucial for a restorative approach to justice that takes into account its communicative effects.[41] If forgiveness is granted by the survivor, the perpetrator and his family and friends typically bring a basket of offerings, usually food and sorghum or banana beer bread. The accord is sealed with song and dance.[42] Many of the victims and perpetrators are neighbours, living a close proximity to each other, often sharing and helping each other.

---

37 Margarita Saona, *Memory Matters in Transitional Peru* (Palgrave Macmillan, 2014) 51.
38 Susan Sontag, *Regarding the Pain of Others* (Picador, 2004) 115.
39 *The New York Times Magazine*, 'Portraits of Reconciliation', <http://www.nytimes.com/interactive/2014/04/06/magazine/06-pieter-hugo-rwanda-portraits.html?_r=0>.
40 Peace Direct, *Insight On Conflict: Association Modeste et Innocent (AMI)*, Peace Direct <www.insighton conflict.org/conflicts/rwanda/peacebuilding-organisations/ami/>.
41 Ibid.
42 Ibid.

Figure 11.5 François (left) and Epiphanie (right) ⓐ Pieter Hugo/Creative Court.

François said:

> I was in prison because I participated in the killing of her son. I went to her and ask[ed] for forgiveness as I was feeling disturbed in my mind, I could not let it rest if I didn't ask for her pardon. Now, we share everything. If she needs water, I fetch it for her. There is no suspicion between us, neither at night nor in the daytime. We have no problem with each other – we continue to live together. It is in this context that I asked for her pardon, and now we live in harmony.

Epiphanie reflected on her experience:

> He killed my child, then he came to ask me pardon. I immediately granted it to him because he did not do it by himself – he was haunted by the devil. I was pleased by the way he testified to the crime instead of keeping it in hiding, because it hurts if someone keeps hiding a crime he committed against you. Before, when I had not yet granted him pardon, he could not come close to me. I treated him like my enemy. But now, I would rather treat him like my own child.

Reflecting on their experiences and willingness to forgive and reconcile, Jean Pierre reported,

(continued)

(continued)

Figure 11.6 Jean Pierre Karenzi (left) and Viviane Nyiramana (right) ⓐ Pieter Hugo/Creative Court.

> My conscience was not quiet, and when I would see her I was very ashamed. After being trained about unity and reconciliation, I went to her house and asked for forgiveness. Then I shook her hand. So far, we are on good terms.

Viviane, pictured next to Jean Pierre, said,

> He killed my father and three brothers. He did these killings with other people, but he came alone to me and asked for pardon. He and a group of other offenders who had been in prison helped me build a house with a covered roof. I was afraid of him – now I have granted him pardon, things have become normal, and in my mind I feel clear.[43]

Reflecting on his experience during these photo shoots, Pieter Hugo stated that the relationship between victims and perpetrators varied widely. Some pairs arrived and sat together easily, others were willing to be photographed, but unable to go further. 'There are clearly different degrees of forgiveness . . . in the photographs, the distance or closeness you see is pretty accurate.'[44] While Hugo intervened in the positions of participants, Mesić asked the participants to

---

43 Rabiaâ Benlahbib, Pieter Hugo and Lana Mesić, *Rwanda 20 Years: Portraits of Reconciliation* (2014) 2 *Dar Lugar* 1 [trans of: *Ruanda 20 Años: Retratos de Reconciliación*].
44 Ibid.

think back to their moment of forgiveness, and if they felt comfortable in doing so, to recreate that moment for her. It is in her photographs that many of participants are touching each other, and some are even hugging.[45]

Case study D: *Yuyanapaq: Para Recordar* [*To Remember*] (Peru)

The Truth and Reconciliation Commission (TRC) in Peru produced *Yuyanapaq: Para Recordar*,[46] a photo exhibition resulting from the investigations of the TRC. The exhibition, which consists of 37 selected black and white photographs, was first staged by the TRC in 2003, and has been housed at the Museo de la Nación since 2009. The images are spread out through 27 rooms, and *in the final room, various audio tracks from the TRC hearings play in the background.*[47] The TRC has chosen this medium to convey facts and also combat the indifference of the general public. For the TRC members, photographs are invested with the capacity to affect viewers on cognitive and emotional levels.[48]

Case study E: *Ausencias* [*The Missing*] by Gustavo Germano (Argentina)

During the military dictatorship in Argentina from 1976 to 1983, nearly 30,000 people disappeared without trace. Argentine photographer Gustavo Germano restages snapshots of Brazilian and Argentine families whose loved ones are among the 'disappeared', people who were tortured and murdered by dictatorial regimes in Latin America from the 1960s to 1980s. He defines it as an exercise of reflection on temporality and as a threshold that brings viewers an illusory parallel dimension where a viewer can understand what the disappearance of a human being means. *Ausencias* strives to make visible those who are not; to display a history frozen in a space. The images powerfully convey the time that the victims of repression have missed in their life, and the time their family lived without enjoying their presence. Germano is a relative of a missing person. When he was eleven, his brother, Eduardo, who at that time was 18, was abducted and 'disappeared'. *Ausencias* has travelled throughout Europe and Latin America since 2007.[49]

(continued)

---

45 Rabiaâ Benlahbib, Pieter Hugo and Lana Mesić, *Rwanda 20 Years: Portraits of Reconciliation* (2014) 2 *Dar Lugar* 1 [trans of: *Ruanda 20 Años: Retratos de Reconciliación*].

46 Febres, above n 36.

47 Carolina A Miranda, *Remembering Peru's Internal Conflict: Yuyanapaq at the Museo Nacional in Lima* (8 June 2009) c-monster.com <http://c-monster.net/2009/06/08/yuyapanaq/>.

48 Saona, above n 37, 213.

49 Gustavo Germano, *Ausencias Argentina* (10 January 2016) Gustavo Germano Gallery <http://www.gustavo germano.com/>.

(continued)

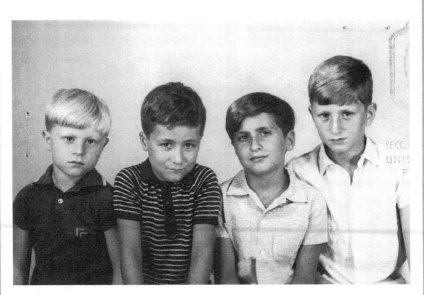

Figure 11.7 Gustavo Germano, *Ausencias*. Reproduced with permission of the photographer.

Figure 11.8 Gustavo Germano, *Ausencias*. Reproduced with permission of the photographer.

11.5 Points of debate and controversy

Artistic installations have limitations, in the sense that they can bring very modest transformation, while the larger transformation still needs to come from structural and legal reforms.[50] Nevertheless, art in the transitional justice context can serve as a gesture of political action against impunity and collective amnesia; an action which resists denial and acknowledges harm. Art is an important tool of symbolic justice that needs to be cherished and accounted for as a creative innovation to respond to past atrocity.

In artistic spaces, audiences may share time and physical space, opening up possibilities for dialogue and interaction, for sharing thoughts and feelings. As Susanne Karstedt argues, legal settings constrain such 'socioaffective mode of responses' and often disappoint victims.[51] However, while aesthetic experience as symbolic justice can 'subvert political power and re-create solidarity'[52], it can also narrate the past in a way that can become an obstacle towards a reconciliatory future. As Susanne Buckley-Zistel argues, transitional justice in post-conflict societies is always a political process, and we have to maintain a critical stance towards the political implications of its application.[53] As such, the arts need more interrogation and emphasis, as they have the potential to open or close space for critical reconsideration of memory work, which should 'reinforce the unification of citizens, not their division'.[54]

Artistic installations have the potential to create narratives that can strengthen or weaken the social fabric of the nation. They can create narratives of social trauma through aesthetic choices that privilege mutual negotiation of conflicting narratives, and appeal to recognition of different individual experiences with violence. However, they can also reinforce one particular narrative over others. This is important, since audiences are more prone to respond to this form of bearing witness than, for example, to courtroom testimony.

Aesthetic experience (both the production and the reception of art) may result in symbolic reparation and healing[55] of a particular victim subject or

---

50 Rubio-Marín, above n 12, 17.
51 Susanne Karstedt, 'The Emotion Dynamics of Transitional Justice: An Emotion Sharing Perspective' (2016) 8(1) *Emotion Review* 50, 53.
52 Ksenija Bilbija, Jo Ellen Fair, Cynthia E Milton and Leigh A Payne, *The Art of Truth-Telling about Authoritarian Rule* (The University of Wisconsin Press, 2005).
53 Susanne Buckley-Zistel, 'Transitional Justice in Divided Societies: Potentials and Limits' (Speech delivered at the 5th European Consortium for Political Research General Conference, Potsdam University, Germany, 10–12 September 2009).
54 Mirjana Spasovska, 'New Government, New History – New Divisions?', *Radio Slobodna Evropa* (online), 23 June 2012 [Trans of: 'Нова влада, нова историја – нови поделби?'] <www.makdenes.org/content/ article/24623301.html>.
55 Estelle Barrett, 'Reconciling Difference: Art as Reparation and Healing' (2003) 4 (1) *Double Dialogues* 1, 4 <http://www.doubledialogues.com/article/reconciling-difference-art-as-reparation-and-healing/>.

whole community. We can argue that arts may assist survivors' well-being and psychological healing. Aesthetic practices involve possible reconciliation of inner and outer conflicts. However, it would be naive to think that documentary theatre or any other form of art, on its own, can trigger significant change or by itself bring satisfaction to survivors. While it can serve as symbolic recognition of a victim's harm, and serve as a 'symbolic closure', it still needs to be accompanied by other initiatives.[56] Art alone cannot address the needs of the victims or communities who still strive to afford basic needs such as education, health care and housing.

According to one theatre activist, 'theatre . . . is very useful and effective means which would need to be accompanied by complementary means in order to mobilize society on transitional justice'.[57] Nola Chilton, a documentary theatre director from Israel, also has no illusions about what such theatre can do: 'it can't change very much, but it can at least bring people together'.[58] Similarly, Dijana Milošević notes,

> Devised theatre can open space for discussion about certain topics, but it would be naive to believe that it can make transformative changes . . . It can change individual lives of spectators, to empower them, to make them more proactive and in that way it can have wider effects, but without other social mechanisms, such as law, courts, human rights, economy, it cannot resolve any structural problems.[59]

Despite their growing numbers, projects of symbolic reparation still remain largely under-researched and under-theorised, not because they are unimportant, but because of the difficulty of finding systematic accounting for the wide range of processes involved.[60] As Simić and Daly argue, this may be in part because researchers do not have access to sites, local languages or adequate contact with local people to document such initiatives fully and accurately. In part, it may also be because civil society and local justice mechanisms have only recently received attention in the transitional justice literature, and in part because such mechanisms are often overlooked in researchers' analyses of reparations and reconciliation.[61]

56 Brandon Hamber and Richard Wilson, 'Symbolic Closure through Memory, Reparation and Revenge in Post-conflict Societies' (2002) 1 (1) *Journal of Human Rights* 35.

57 Nadia Siddiqui, Hadi Marifat and Sari Kuovo, 'Culture, Theatre and Justice: Examples from Afghanistan' in Rush and Simić, above n 28, 129.

58 Linda Ben-Zvi, 'Staging the Other Israel: The Documentary Theatre of Nola Chilton' (2006) 50(3) *The Drama Review* 42, 44.

59 Interview with Dijana Milošević (Skype, 12 January 2016).

60 Olsen, Payne and Reiter, above n 7, 37.

61 Olivera Simić and Kathleen Daly, '"One Pair of Shoes, One Life": Steps towards Accountability for Genocide in Srebrenica' (2011) 5 *International Journal of Transitional Justice* 477, 491.

11.6 Summary

Like all types of symbolic reparation, documentary theatre, photo exhibitions and other forms of artistic interventions cannot make significant individual or societal changes, but they can influence and contribute to transformation. For reparations to fully achieve their potential, it is necessary that corrective, rehabilitative social programmes are developed to meet the economic, social and psychological needs of victims, communities and society at large. Symbolic reparations such as, for example, the statue built in Shabunda which serves as a memorial to the suffering of women in war have been welcomed by women survivors of sexual violence in the Democratic Republic of Congo, but a clear preference was expressed for tangible benefits to address the more concrete needs of victims, to which a symbolic component might be attached.[62]

It would be naive to suggest that the arts alone can bring long-lasting peace, but artistic projects can provide a necessary means of reflection on the past or present, and ultimately, hope for the future. Such symbolic representations of what happened can help concretise a traumatic event, serve as focal points in the grieving process, and be a physical or visual representation of what was lost.[63] They can also aid recovery and help an individual to come to terms with the event over which they grieve while materialising society's willingness to do things differently.[64]

11.7 Discussion and tutorial questions

1) In what ways can art help societies overcome the legacy of human rights violations?

2) What is the responsibility of artists in relation to crimes committed in 'their name' (by their own group members)? What do you think of Milošević's statement about 'responsibility' that prompted her and Dah troupe members to act?

3) Do artists have the moral right to perform while people around them are suffering terribly?

4) Can art installations be a way of creating peace and bringing justice to the victims of war?

---

62 Read more about Shabunda Memorial in United Nations Office of the High Commissioner for Human Rights, *Report of the Panel on Remedies and Reparations for Victims of Sexual Violence in the Democratic Republic of Congo to the High Commissioner for Human Rights*, March 2011, 15–16, 22, 46. <http://www.refworld.org/docid/4d708ae32.html>.

63 Ibid.

64 Pablo de Greiff, 'Justice and Reparations' in Pablo de Greiff (ed), *The Handbook of Reparations* (Oxford University Press, 2006) 451–477.

5) What is the significance of documentary theatre in transitional justice processes?

6) Can photo exhibitions spark tensions rather than bring cohesion and unity among different communities? In what circumstances?

Suggested reading

A'ness, Francine, 'Resisting Amnesia: Yuyachkani, Performance, and the Postwar Reconstruction in Peru' (2004) 56 *Theatre Journal*.

Barat, Clara Ramírez (ed), *Transitional Justice, Culture and Society: Beyond Outreach* (Social Science Research Council, 2014).

Barnett, Dennis and Arthur Skelton, *Theatre and Performance in Eastern Europe: The Changing Scene* (Rowman and Littlefield, 2007).

Bisschoff, Lizelle and Stefanie van de Peer, *Art and Trauma in Africa: Representations of Reconciliation in Music, Visual Arts, Literature and Film* (IB Tauris, 2012).

Campbell, Colm and Catherine Turner, 'Utopia and the Doubters: Truth, Transition and the Law' (2008) 28 *Legal Studies*.

Cleveland, William, *Art and Upheaval: Artists on the World's Frontlines* (New Village Press, 2008).

Cohen, Cynthia, Roberto Gutiérrez Varea, Polly O Walker (eds), *Acting Together: Performance and the Creative Transformation of Conflict: Volume I: Resistance and Reconciliation in Regions of Violence* (New Village Press, 2011).

Cohen, Cynthia, Roberto Gutiérrez Varea, Polly O Walker (eds), *Acting Together: Performance and the Creative Transformation of Conflict: Volume II: Building Just and Inclusive Communities* (New Village Press, 2011).

Mengel, Ewald and Michaela Borzaga (eds), *Trauma, Memory, and Narrative in the Contemporary South African Novels* (Rodopi, 2012).

Milošević, Dijana, 'The Role of the Artist in the Dark Times' in Dennis Barnett and Arthur Skelton, *Theatre and Performance in Eastern Europe: The Changing Scene* (Rowman and Littlefield, 2007).

Möller, Frank, *Visual Peace: Images, Spectatorship, and the Politics of Violence* (Palgrave Macmillan, 2013).

Simić, Olivera, 'Breathing Sense into Women's Lives Shattered by the War: Dah Theatre Belgrade' (2010) 14 *Law Text Culture*.

Simić, Olivera, 'Stories We Tell: Documentary Theater, Performance and Justice in Transition' in Lavinia Stan and Nadya Nedelsky (eds), *Post-Communist Transitional Justice: Lessons from Twenty-Five Years of Experience* (Cambridge University Press, 2015).

Thompson, James, Jenny *Hughes* and Michael Balfour (eds), *Performance in Place of War* (University of Chicago Press, 2009).

Suggested films

For Those Who Can Tell No Tales (Directed by Jasmila Žbanić, Deblokada Produkcija, 2013).

Grbavica: Esma's Secret (Directed by Jasmila Žbanić, Dogwoof Pictures, 2006).

Other resources

Jarr, Alfredo, *The Rwanda Project: 1994–2000* (2006) Open Democracy ‹https:// www.open democracy.net/arts/rwanda_3412.jsp›.

Playback Theatre ‹http://www.playbacktheatre.org/›.

The Milk of Sorrow (Directed by Claudia Llosa, Generalitat de Catalunya, 2009).

Ubaldo, Rafiki, 'Temples of Memory: Rwanda', Temples of Memory ‹http://www. temples ofmemory.org/›.

Bibliography

Articles/books/reports

Bahun, Sanja, 'Transitional Justice and the Arts: Reflections on the Field' in Claudio Corradetti, Nir Eisikovits and Jack Volpe Rotondi (eds), *Theorizing Transitional Justice* (Ashgate, 2015).

Barthes, Roland, *Camera Lucida: Reflections on Photography* (Farrar, Straus and Giroux, 1981).

Bell, Vikki, The *Art of Post-Dictatorship: Ethics and Aesthetics in Transitional Argentina* (Routledge, 2014).

Benlahbib, Rabiaâ, Pieter Hugo and Lana Mesić, *Rwanda 20 Years: Portraits of Reconciliation* (2014) 2 *Dar Lugar* 1 [trans of: *Ruanda 20 Años: Retratos de Reconciliación*].

Ben-Zvi, Linda, 'Staging the Other Israel: The Documentary Theatre of Nola Chilton' (2006) 50(3) *The Drama Review*.

Bilbija, Ksenija, Jo Ellen Fair, Cynthia E Milton and Leigh A Payne, *The Art of Truth-Telling about Authoritarian Rule* (The University of Wisconsin Press, 2005).

Bloomfield, David, Teresa Barnes and Luc Huyse (eds), *Reconciliation after Violent Conflict: A Handbook* (International Institute for Democracy and Electoral Assistance, 2003).

Buckley-Zistel, Susanne and Ruth Stanley (eds), *Gender in Transitional Justice* (Palgrave Macmillan, 2011).

Clark, Phil, *The Gacaca Courts, Post-Genocide Justice and Reconciliation in Rwanda: Justice without Lawyers* (Cambridge University Press, 2010).

Cole, Catherine, 'Performance, Transitional Justice, and the Law: South Africa's Truth and Reconciliation Commission' (2007) 59 *Theatre Journal*.

Corradetti, Claudio, Nir Eisikovits and Jack Volpe Rotondi (eds), *Theorizing Transitional Justice* (Ashgate, 2015).

de Greiff, Pablo, 'On Making the Invisible Visible: The Role of Cultural Interventions in Transitional Justice Processes' in Clara Ramírez-Barat (ed), *Transitional Justice, Culture and Society: Beyond Outreach* (Social Science Research Council, 2014).

de Greiff, Pablo (ed), *The Handbook of Reparations* (Oxford University Press, 2006).

de Greiff, Pablo, 'Justice and Reparations' in Pablo de Greiff (ed), *The Handbook of Reparations* (Oxford University Press, 2006).

Fineman, Martha Albertson and Estelle Zinsstag (eds), *Feminist Perspectives on Transitional Justice* (Intersentia, 2013).

Haldemann, Frank, 'Another Kind of Justice: Transitional Justice as Recognition' (2008) 41 *Cornell International Law Journal*.

Hamber, Brandon, *Transforming Societies after Political Violence: Truth, Reconciliation and Mental Health* (Springer, 2009).

Hamber, Brandon and Ingrid Palmary, 'Gender, Memorialization, and Symbolic Reparations' in Ruth Rubio-Marín (ed), *The Gender of Reparations: Unsettling Sexual Hierarchies While Redressing Human Rights Violations* (Cambridge University Press, 2009).

Hamber, Brandon and Richard Wilson, 'Symbolic Closure through Memory, Reparation and Revenge in Post-conflict Societies' (2002) 1 (1) *Journal of Human Rights*.

Karstedt, Susanne, 'The Emotion Dynamics of Transitional Justice: An Emotion Sharing Perspective' (2016) 8 (1) *Emotion Review*.

Knežević, Dubravka, 'Till the Last Breath' (1995) Sept–Dec *Scena* 5.

Ling, Cheah Wui, 'Justice as Practiced by Victims of Conflict: Post-World War II Movements as Sites of Engagement and Knowledge' in Martha Albertson Fineman and Estelle Zinsstag (eds), *Feminist Perspectives on Transitional Justice* (Intersentia, 2013).

MacLachlan, Alice and Allen Speight (eds), *Justice, Responsibility and Reconciliation in the Wake of Conflict* (Springer, 2013).

Minow, Martha, 'Breaking the Cycles of Hatred' in Nancy Rosenblum (ed), *Breaking the Cycles of Hatred: Memory, Law and Repair* (Princeton University Press, 2002).

Minow, Martha, *Between Vengeance and Forgiveness: Facing History after Genocide and Mass Violence* (Beacon Press, 1998).

Oddey, Alison, *Devising Theatre: A Practical and Theoretical Handbook* (Routledge, 1994).

Olsen, Tricia D, Leigh A Payne and Andrew G Reiter, *Transitional Justice in Balance: Comparing Processes, Weighing Efficacy* (United States Institute of Peace Press, 2010).

Parent, Geneviève, 'Reconciliation and Justice after Genocide: A Theoretical Exploration' (2010) 5 *Genocide Studies and Prevention*.

Ramírez-Barat, Clara (ed), *Transitional Justice, Culture and Society: Beyond Outreach* (Social Science Research Council, 2014).

Reparation and Rehabilitation Committee, Parliament of the Republic of South Africa, *Report* (1998) vol 6, part 2.

Rosenblum, Nancy (ed), *Breaking the Cycles of Hatred: Memory, Law and Repair* (Princeton University Press, 2002).

Rubio-Marín, Ruth (ed), *The Gender of Reparations: Unsettling Sexual Hierarchies While Redressing Human Rights Violations* (Cambridge University Press, 2009).

Rush, Peter D and Olivera Simić (eds), *The Arts of Transitional Justice: Culture, Activism, and Memory after Atrocity* (Springer, 2014).

Russell, Catherine, *Experimental Ethnography: The Work of Film in the Age of Video* (Duke University Press, 1999).

Saona, Margarita, *Memory Matters in Transitional Peru* (Palgrave Macmillan, 2014).

Siddiqui, Nadia, Hadi Marifat and Sari Kuovo, 'Culture, Theatre and Justice: Examples from Afghanistan' in Peter D Rush and Olivera Simić (eds), *The Arts of Transitional Justice: Culture, Activism, and Memory after Atrocity* (Springer, 2014).

Sigsworth, Romi and Nahla Valji, 'Continuities of Violence Against Women and the Limitations of Transitional Justice: The Case of South Africa' in Susanne Buckley-Zistel and Ruth Stanley (eds), *Gender in Transitional Justice* (Palgrave Macmillan, 2011).

Simić, Olivera and Kathleen Daly, '"One Pair of Shoes, One Life": Steps towards Accountability for Genocide in Srebrenica' (2011) 5 *International Journal of Transitional Justice*.

Simić, Olivera and Dijana Milošević, 'Enacting Justice: The Role of Dah Theatre Company in Transitional Justice Processes in Serbia and Beyond' in Peter D Rush and Olivera Simić (eds), *The Arts of Transitional Justice: Culture, Activism, and Memory after Atrocity* (Springer, 2014).

Skoller, Jeffrey, *Shadows, Specters, Shards: Making History in Avant-Garde Film* (University of Minnesota Press, 2005).

Snider, Laureen, 'Towards Safer Societies: Punishment, Masculinities and Violence Against Women' (1998) 38 *British Journal of Criminology*.

Sontag, Susan, *Regarding the Pain of Others* (Picador, 2004).

Stan, Lavinia and Nadya Nedelsky (eds), *Post-Communist Transitional Justice: Lessons from Twenty-Five Years of Experience* (Cambridge University Press, 2015).

Urban Walker, Margaret, 'The Expressive Burden of Reparations: Putting Meaning into Money, Words, and Things' in Alice MacLachlan and Allen Speight (eds), *Justice, Responsibility and Reconciliation in the Wake of Conflict* (Springer, 2013).

Urban Walker, Margaret, 'Truth Telling as Reparations' (2010) 41 *Metaphilosophy*.

Zapperi, Giovanna, 'Woman's Reappearance: Rethinking the Archive in Contemporary Art – Feminist Perspectives' (2013) 105 *Feminist Review*.

Other

Art21, Interview with Alfredo Jaar ('The Gramsci Trilogy', 11 March 2007) <http://www.art21.org/texts/alfredo-jaar/interview-alfredo-jaar-the-gramsci-trilogy>.

Barrett, Estelle, 'Reconciling Difference: Art as Reparation and Healing' (2003) 4 *Double Dialogues* 1 <http://www.doubledialogues.com/article/reconciling-difference-art-as-re paration-and-healing/>.

Buckley-Zistel, Susanne, 'Transitional Justice in Divided Societies: Potentials and Limits' (Speech delivered at the 5th European Consortium for Political Research General Conference, Potsdam University, Germany, 10–12 September 2009).

Dominus, Susan and Pieter Hugo, 'Portraits of Reconciliation', *The New York Times* (online), 4 June 2014 <www.nytimes.com/interactive/2014/04/06/magazine/06-pieter-hugo-rwanda-portraits.html?_r=0>.

Febres, Salomón Lerner, 'Memory of Violence and Drama in Peru: The Experience of the Truth Commission and the Yuyachkani Theater Group' (Speech delivered at the Just Performance: Enacting Justice in the Wake of Violence Symposium, Brandeis University, USA, 1–2 December 2011).

Febres, Salomón Lerner, 'Prefacio', Commission for Truth and Reconciliation, *In Order to Remember – A Visual Narrative of the Internal Conflict in Perú* [trans of: Comisión de la Verdad y Reconciliación, *Yuyanapaq: Relato Visual del Conflicto Armade Interno en el Perú*] (Fondo Editorial de la Pontificia Universidad Católica del Perú, 2003).

Germano, Gustavo, *Ausencias Argentina* (10 January 2016) Gustavo Germano Gallery ‹http://www.gustavogermano.com/›.

Interview with Dijana Milošević (Skype, 12 January 2016).

Interview with Nataša Govedarica (Skype, 7 October 2013).

Komarčević, Dušan, 'Women in Black Remembered Abducted from a Train in Strpci: Those Who Committed the Crimes Remain at Large', *E-Novine* (online) 17 January 2016 ‹http://www.e-novine.com/drustvo/59890-Kreatori-zloina-dalje-slobodi.html› [trans of: 'Žene u Crnom Pamte Otete iz Voza u Štrpcima: Kreatori Zločina i Dalje Na Slobodi'].

Miranda, Carolina A, *Remembering Peru's Internal Conflict: Yuyanapaq at the Museo Nacional in Lima* (8 June 2009) c-monster.com ‹http://c-monster.net/2009/06/08/ yuyapanaq/›.

Museum of Memory and Human Rights ‹www.museodelamemoria.cl/expos/yuyanapaq-para-recordar/›.

Peace Direct, *Insight On Conflict: Association Modeste et Innocent (AMI)*, Peace Direct ‹www.insightonconflict.org/conflicts/rwanda/peacebuilding-organisations/ami/›.

Spasovska, Mirjana, 'New Government, New History – New Divisions?', *Radio Slobodna Evropa* (online), 23 June 2012 (Trans of:' Нова влада, нова историја - нови поделби?') ›www.makdenes.org/content/article/24623301.html›.

United Nations Office of the High Commissioner for Human Rights, *Report of the Panel on Remedies and Reparations for Victims of Sexual Violence in the Democratic Republic of Congo to the High Commissioner for Human Rights*, March 2011 ‹http://www.refworld.org/docid/4d708ae32.html›.

Williams, Timothy, *Entering the Tiger Zone* (2015) University of Marburg ‹www.uni-marburg.de/konfliktforschung/Termine/entering-tiger-zone›.

Yuyachkani Cultural Group, *Historia* ‹http://www.yuyachkani.org/historia.html›.

Yuyachkani Cultural Group, *Historia del Grupo* ‹http://hemisphericinstitute.org/cuaderno/ yuyachkani/group.html›.

Chapter 12

Memorials and transitional justice

Susanne Buckley-Zistel and Annika Björkdahl

12.1 Introduction[1]

The year 2015 was one full of commemorations: 100 years after the Armenian genocide, 70 years after the liberation of Auschwitz and 20 years after the genocide of Srebrenica. All three events are referred to as genocides, and all three events are remembered in the form of memorials. Memorials portray pain and suffering, sometimes figuratively, sometimes abstractly. They provide a place for public commemorations and quiet mourning. They seek to link the past to the present through continuously retelling what once happened. They serve as a reminder of people lost and pain endured.

Post-conflict memory landscapes embed and convey meaning, and are thus inexorably linked to the legacy of the conflict, to struggles over interpretations about the violent past and to the sites where remembering takes place. Constructing memorials after atrocities has become an important aspect of coming to terms with atrocities and thus forms a central component of transitional justice. This chapter takes a look at how memorials function in this context. In contrast to measures such as tribunals and truth commissions, memorials – and commemoration more generally – are a more recent acquisition in the repertoire of dealing with the past. Even though memorials have been around for a long time, connecting them to more constructive ways of coming to terms with the past, and promoting their establishment as part of transitional justice processes in post-violence societies is a relatively new phenomenon. Thus, this chapter

1 Susanne Buckley-Zistel is grateful for the senior fellowship of the Käte Hamburger Kolleg Global Cooperation Research at the University Duisburg-Essen, Germany, in the context of which this chapter was written. Annika Björkdahl appreciates the funding from the Swedish Research Council (D0017001) that made this research possible.

aims to address the following questions: What functions do memorials play in the transition to justice? Who engages with commemoration at memorials and for what ends? What are the ways in which memorials work in the context of transitional societies?

12.2 Key concepts, definitions, and approach

Memorials are material or virtual objects which serve to represent events or persons who should not be forgotten. In the context of transitional justice, the latter mainly refers to victims of human rights abuses during wars, ethno-political conflicts, repressive dictatorships, terrorist attacks, apartheid, as well as genocides. Their main objectives are based on a number of political and ethical assumptions such as providing an adequate site for mourning, holding perpetrators accountable, vindicating the dignity of victims, putting past wrongs right and contributing to reconciliation.

Memorials often employ a common aesthetic language communicating a key message: *We must not forget!* It is important to note, though, that memorials can never be an accurate replica of the past but only offer a particular interpretation of an event, which may be contested or subject to change over time. Nevertheless, they seek to fix and store the representation of the atrocity through turning it into a monument that prevails and is available to future generations, often with the intention to educate the youth and in doing so to prevent the recurrence of the atrocity. *Never Again* is thus a maxim of many sites. In this sense, memorials exist in the present to tell us something about the past while seeking to affect the future.

Memorials may be material and tangible, but they are also increasingly virtual and web-based, allowing for the participation of a larger group of activists in different geographic locations.[2] For Judy Barsalou, three forms of material memorials – as well as memorialisation – can be distinguished: authentic sites at the places where the atrocities occurred, constructed sites which may be anywhere and are often more abstract and conceptual, and activities such as commemorations and peace marches.[3] A number of different actors may initiate memorial

---

2 See, e.g., *Digital Monument to the Jewish Community in the Netherlands* (2001) Jewish Historical Museum <http://www.joodsmonument.nl/?lang=en>; Human Rights & Democracy for Iran, *Omid: A Memorial in the Defense of Human Rights in Iran* (2016) Abdorrahman Boroumand Foundation <https://www.iranrights.org/memorial>; *Korean War Veterans Digital Memorial* (2015) Korean War Legacy Foundation <http://www. kwvdm.org/>; *Lives of the First World War* (12 May 2014) Imperial War Museum <https://livesofthefirstworldwar.org/>.

3 Judy M Barsalou, 'Reflecting the Fractured Past: Memorialisation, Transitional Justice and the Role of the Outsiders' in Susanne Buckley-Zistel and Stefanie Schäfer (eds), *Memorials in Time of Transition* (Intersentia, 2014) 49.

sites ranging from civil society initiatives to national governments or international organisations. Erecting memorials, such as murals in Belfast, Northern Ireland, or on Cairo's Tahrir Square, Egypt, can be spontaneous and inexpensive, rendering it a suitable tool for community action.[4] The process can, however, also be very slow if the different parties involved – including different groups of victims – struggle over the form of, and meaning portrayed by, a memorial. For instance, the Memorial to the Murdered Sinti and Roma of Europe Murdered under the National Socialist Regime was inaugurated in 2012 in Berlin, after 20 years of intense debate about its message and aesthetic form.

In the context of transitional justice, memorials are often referred to as symbolic reparations, in contrast to material reparations such as financial compensation. This ties in with an increasing focus of norms on victims more generally, such as expressed by the Basic Principles and Guidelines on the Right to a Remedy and Reparation for Victims of Gross Violations of International Human Rights Law and Serious Violations of International Humanitarian Law by the United Nations.[5] Reparations are often also listed as an instrument of restorative justice since they seek to improve community relations, and recent truth commissions such as in Liberia and in East Timor have included the quest for memorials in their recommendations, alongside other mechanisms such as prosecution or institutional reform.[6]

Importantly, the way the past is depicted in a memorial depends on the particular experience of violence.[7] After dictatorship and political repression, where violence was mainly top–down and exercised by the government, in many cases a culture of impunity prevails, and information about the whereabouts of the disappeared remains concealed. In such a scenario, memorials often point at the absence of individuals, and where possible lobby groups or victims' associations construct them at authentic places such as prisons or torture centres. *Robben Island*, a former prison where Nelson Mandela was held during apartheid, or the torture centre Memorial Londres 38 in Santiago di Chile, from where many political activists were 'disappeared', serve to illustrate this tendency. Ethno-political conflicts where violence occurred between two social groups, in contrast, often either lead to the construction of memorials that reinforce the division of the

---

4 Brandon Hamber, Liz Ševčenko and Ereshnee Naidu, 'Utopian Dreams or Practical Possibilities? The Challenges of Evaluating the Impact of Memorialization in Societies in Transition' (2010) 4(3) *International Journal of Transitional Justice* 397.

5 Basic Principles and Guidelines on the Right to a Remedy and Reparation for Victims of Gross Violations of International Human Rights Law and Serious Violations of International Humanitarian Law, GA Res 60/147, UN GA, 60th sess, 64th plen mtg, Agenda Item 71(a), UN Doc A/Res/60/147 (adopted and proclaimed 16 December 2005) <www.unhcr.org/refworld/docid/4721cb942.html>.

6 Ereshnee Naidu, 'Memorialisation in Postconflict Societies in Africa: Potentials and Challenges' in Buckley-Zistel and Schäfer (eds), above n 3, 33.

7 Barsalou, above n 3, 52–55.

society by claiming an exclusive victim status, such as the Ovcara Memorial Center in Vukovar, Croatia, or to attempts to foster some form of mutual understanding and potential future reconciliation as exemplified by the Sierra Leone Peace Museum. If violence took on an extreme form to the point of annihilation, such as in the case of genocides, memorials often portray shock and horror, such as in many Rwandan memorials, and also on the Cambodian killing fields, through displaying human remains, including bones and skulls. One strategy here is to emphasise the enormity of the crime and the magnitude of the destruction.

12.3 Overview

It is not surprising that memorials have entered the field of transitional justice as potential mechanisms to deal with the legacy of a violent past. Since 1970 and 1980 there has been a *memory boom*,[8] in particular regarding the commemoration of the Holocaust and World War II, leading to what Daniel Levy has termed 'the memory imperative'.[9] Remembering has become a duty. This coincides with an important shift in the culture of remembrance away from commemorating war heroes who supposedly testify to a nation's strength and invincibility, such as depicted in memorials to fallen soldiers or to veterans. More recently, victims – chief carriers of the moral weight regarding the atrocities committed – have become the focus of attention of commemorations.[10] This is, for instance, central to the rising number of memorials built in the shape of so-called walls of names such as at the Potočari Memorial in Srebrenica, Bosnia, or walls with photographs such as at the Kigali Memorial Center, Rwanda, or the Tuol Sleng Genocide Museum, Cambodia. Through naming or depicting victims, they are identified as individuals, preventing their submersion in an anonymous and amorphous mass of people killed. The intention of naming is to give them back some dignity.

Transitional justice, too, has in recent years strengthened its focus on victims, leading to its almost natural conversion with the field of memory studies.[11] In its initial phase, the focus was mainly on perpetrators in order to identify and hold them accountable, not at least due to a strong focus on criminal prosecution. At present, victims are increasingly identified as target audiences of transitional justice, as well as its agents. The latter is apparent in the context of retributive

---

8 Jay Winter, 'Notes on the Memory Boom: War, Remembrance and the Uses of the Past' in Duncan Bell (ed), *Memory, Trauma and World Politics: Reflections on the Relationship between Past and Present* (Palgrave Macmillan, 2006) 61.

9 Daniel Levy, 'Changing Temporalities and the Internalization of Memory of Culture' in Yifat Gutman, Adam D Brown and Amy Sodaro (eds), *Memory and the Future: Transnational Politics, Ethics and Society* (Palgrave Macmillan, 2010) 18.

10 Ibid 62.

11 See also Andrew G Reiter, 'The development of transitional justice', this volume.

justice where victims now participate in criminal proceedings at the International Criminal Court, secondly in the context of restorative justice due to their active role in truth commissions, and also in the design and organisation of memorials and memorial sites.[12]

Parallel to the inclusion of victims in memorial processes, the aesthetic form of some memorials has changed, giving way to a new memorial culture. There has been a shift away from figurative depictions of strong heroic persons or national symbols – set in solid stone such as marble or granite, and leaving no room for interpretation – to more conceptual sites which encourage onlookers to think and reflect. Instead of dictating one particular interpretation of past events, they invite one to form one's own opinion, in a sense liberating and democratising remembrance. It is no longer the initiators or artists who dictate memory, but visitors may draw on their own personal experience to create meaning. Considering that memorials often make reference to repressive dictatorships, this form of liberating the mind is an important symbolic yet highly political step.

These more recent sites avoid solid structures and employ water features – with still water serving as a mirror to reflect visitors and the sky as in the State War Memorial in Perth, or running water pointing to the moving of time such as the 9/11 Memorial in New York. Gardens serve as places for seclusion and reflection (for example, the Sharpeville Memorial Garden or the Kigali Memorial Center in Rwanda), open spaces inviting opening minds, and narrow spaces transmitting the claustrophobic experience of death and destruction. Maya Lin's Vietnam Veterans Memorial in Washington, a gap in the ground reminiscent of an open wound, or Peter Eisenman's Memorial to the Murdered Jews of Europe in Berlin which consists of 2,711 narrowly assembled stelae (concrete blocks), serve to illustrate this trend. In and of themselves these sights have no symbolic significance which links them to the atrocities; it is the personal experience and interpretation of the visitor that matters.

It is important to note, however, that despite this recent trend, memorials with more imposing interpretations of the past abound, such as the Memorial in Commemoration of Famines' Victims in Ukraine. The above suggested memory culture, as expressed in the work of Lin, Eisenmann and others, should thus be read as a comment and criticism on authoritative memorials of past and present, which is why they are often referred to as counter-memorials. We shall return to this aspect again below.

---

12 Thorsten Bonacker, Anika Oettler and Christoph Safferling, 'Valorising Victims' Ambivalences in Contemporary Trends in Transitional Justice' in Thorsten Bonacker and Christoph Safferling (eds), *Victims of International Crimes: An Interdisciplinary Discourse* (Asser Press/Springer, 2013) 280.

12.3.1 Function of memorials

In the context of transitional justice, memorials fulfil different functions which – at the far end of the spectrum – may lead to a better understanding between the conflicting parties and an increase of knowledge about, and acknowledgement of, the crimes committed on one side, or a perpetuation of the division between the parties and a politicisation of remembrance on the other.[13] Regarding their positive impact, first, they may serve to (re-)establish the dignity of the victims through offering a gesture of symbolic reparation. This carries the message that individuals or groups are now accepted and respected by the respective society. In cases where victims were persecuted due to their faith, race or ethnic belonging, sexual orientation or political views, publicly acknowledging this aspect affirms this part of their identity.

Second, memorials have the potential to stimulate public debates about the crimes committed, including discussions about their causes and consequences, and in some cases also about the conditions to which victims of these human rights abuses are subjected at present, such as continued discriminating and marginalisation. They may turn into sites of conscience at which various interest groups can influence ongoing discussions and stimulate civil engagement to prevent similar atrocities being committed in the future.[14] This may be of great significance for societies in transition.

Third, from the perspective of transforming the conflict that caused the human rights abuses, it is occasionally intended that the memorial contributes to improving the relationship between the conflicting parties, and to some form of rapprochement between them. Some memorials provide spaces for encounter where people affected can share their experiences and views about past events in order to reduce divisions and strengthen commonalities. This is sometimes linked to promoting a form of memory which contributes to nation-building.[15]

So far, the function of memorials in the context of transitional justice has been portrayed in a rather positive way. Yet how about the situation in which the suffering of victims of human rights abuses is not publicly known, or is even subject to denial? In these cases, memorials are sites of resistance to a culture of impunity, and function as exclamation to draw attention to what is silenced, as depicted in the memorial to homosexuals elaborated in the next section. For affected groups this is often an important element in times of transition. Moreover, since the interpretation of the past may be contested by the parties to

---

13 See also Susanne Buckley-Zistel and Stefanie Schäfer, 'Memorials in Time of Transition' in Buckley-Zistel and Schäfer (eds), above n 3, 9.

14 Sebastian Brett et al, *Memorialization and Democracy: State Policy and Civic Action* (International Center for Transitional Justice, 2007) 7.

15 Timothy G Ashplant, Graham Dawson and Michael Roper (eds), *Commemorating War: The Politics of Memory* (Transaction Publishers, 2004) 7.

the conflict, memorials may turn into sites over which this contestation is fought out. The case of the memorial in Srebrenica discussed in the following pages serves to illustrate this point.

In addition to these public functions of memorials, they also serve a deeply private purpose as sites of bereavement and reflection.[16] For those left behind, they may turn into spaces where they feel close to their deceased or disappeared loved ones. Taking care of commemoration sites may then turn into a ritual which helps with the personal grieving process, similar to looking after the grave of a loved one.[17]

Bearing these functions in mind, the following section introduces two memorials which were erected in different contexts and which serve different functions. While the memorial in Srebrenica responds to a form of conflict that is legally defined as genocide, the memorial in Berlin is dedicated to victims of repression. While the first was established almost instantly, the second took more than 70 years to materialise.

Case study A: The Srebrenica-Potočari Memorial Centre

The Dayton Peace Accord marked the end of the war in Bosnia-Herzegovina (BiH) and the beginning of a transition to peace and justice. How to deal with the atrocities committed during the war, and how to address calls for justice has become contested in the deeply divided society of BiH. To acknowledge past sufferings, rehabilitate the dignity of victims and support personal griev-ing processes, a number of memorials have been erected. The largest and perhaps most renowned of them is the Srebrenica-Potočari Memorial Centre outside the small town of Srebrenica in eastern BiH, constructed to commemo-rate the genocide that took place there in July 1995 when more than 8,000 men and boys were killed by Bosnian Serb forces. The memorial addresses the absences brought about by sudden and violent killings – the losses of the embodied presence, participation in everyday life and relationships, emotional equilibrium among bereaved people and, ultimately, the memory of someone who once lived.

During the 1992–1995 war the town of Srebrenica was under siege. Due to imminent threats against its population it was designated by the UN as one of six 'safe areas' in BiH and protected by 400 Dutch peacekeepers. As a conse-quence, many Bosniaks sought refuge in the town to escape the ethnic cleansing that took place in eastern BiH, and the town's population increased dramatically. In 1995, the town was taken over by Bosnian Serb forces and many fled to

(continued)

---

16 Jay Winter, *Sites of Memory, Sites of Mourning: The Great War in European Cultural History* (Cambridge University Press, 1995) 3.

17 Julia Viebach, 'Alétheia and the Making of the World: Inner and Outer Dimensions of Memorials in Rwanda' in Buckley-Zistel and Schäfer (eds), above n 3, 89.

(continued)

the UN camp a few kilometres away in the village of Potočari. There, the UN peace-keepers watched as Europe's largest single war crime since World War II was committed. After being separated from their families by Bosnian Serb forces, some 15,000 men and boys fled through the woods trying to reach the town of Tuzla and the territory controlled by the Bosnian Army. The flood of Bosniaks out of Potočari has been called the *'put smrti'* – the journey of death – and Potočari became the site of the only war crime in Europe that has been defined as genocide since the Holocaust. Today, the town hosts the largest memorial in BiH in what is now the Serb-led entity Republika Srpska (RS).

The construction of the Srebrenica-Potočari Memorial Centre was con-tested from its inception. The first commemoration organised by a small group of surviving family members, mostly women, was held on 11 July 1999, when they gathered in Potočari and held a funeral service for the killed and missing. The materialisation of the memorial was largely influenced by the determined efforts of victim-advocacy groups such as the Mothers of Srebrenica, and followed by the support of international actors. Victims and survivors of the genocide fought hard for the memorial to be built in Srebrenica itself. Fierce opposition came from the nationalist Bosnian Serb political elite of whom many denied the genocide and obstructed the processes, and demanded such a memorial to be erected in the Federation of BiH, where Bosniaks today are the majority.[18] In 2000, after years of contestation, the High Representative Wolfgang Petritsch used his executive pow-ers to place the memorial outside Srebrenica at the Potočari base in accordance with the views of the victims and survivors of the genocide. The memorial was finally inaugurated by the then US president Bill Clinton on 20 September 2003.

Aesthetic language

The Memorial complex is composed of three parts. It is housed at the 'Battery Factory Potočari', which was used as a base by the Dutch battalion *Dutchbat*, but which is now reconstructed as a museum space, hosting the Memorial Room. The Cemetery includes a Memorial Wall where the names of the victims buried in the cemetery following the July 1995 genocide are inscribed. The number of killed and buried marks the entrance of the cemetery: '8,372' is inscribed on a block of marble, followed by an ellipsis indicating that this figure is not final as there are people still missing and unidentified.[19] So far 5,500 victims have been buried at the cemetery, each with a personalised tombstone with the name and the birth year of the dead, and a phrase from the Qur'an. A single wooden cross stands out at the grave of a Catholic inhabitant of the town who was killed during the genocide and thus buried in the cemetery in 2010 when his remains were recovered.

The hall, where approximately 4,000 refugees stayed for two days in July 1995 under deteriorating conditions, is dreary and depressing, cold and empty, except for two large black cubic constructions situated opposite each other in the middle of the building. In one of the two cubic spaces, there are 20 personal

---

18 Christian Braun, 'The Srebrenica-Potočari Memorial: Promoting (In)Justice?' in Buckley-Zistel and Schäfer (eds), above n 3, 189.
19 Ibid.

narratives displayed with a photo, a short life story and one personal belonging of a victim who is buried or still missing. These narratives reveal that it was not only combatants who were killed, as the stories include old men and children who could not have been combatants. In the other cubic space a 30 minute documentary film, 'A Cry from the Grave' by Muhamed Mujkić, a film maker from BiH, and the British director Leslie Woodhead, is screened.[20] The film provides a reconstruction of day-by-day events preceding and following the Srebrenica fall. It is based on the recordings made during the exhumation of mass graves, testimonies of the surviving families, testimonies of the Dutch peacekeepers, as well as original video recordings from July 1995. The row of pictures and posters with quotes, maps and court verdicts on the walls of the hall provides a framework to the narratives presented in the documentary and the personal stories on display. A quote from the International Criminal Tribunal to the former Yugoslavia (ICTY) verdict against the Serb General Radislav Krstić, which refers to the events that took place here as a 'genocide', attracts the attention of the visitors.[21] Out of 20 persons indicted for the Srebrenica event, final judgment has been issued against 15 accused to date. These do not include the case of the former Serbian President Slobodan Milošević, which was terminated following his death, or the ongoing cases such as the trials against Radovan Karadzic and Ratko Mladič. The genocide verdict has given Srebrenica a special status, and resonates with and reinforces the cosmopolitan meta-narrative of *Never Again*.

Figure 12.1 'Inside Memorial Room in Potočari-Srebrenica'. Photographed by Susanne Buckely-Zistel.

(continued)

---

20 Olivera Simić, 'Remembering, Visiting and Placing the Dead: Law, Authority and Genocide in Srebrenica' (2009) 13 *Law Text Culture* 273.

21 *Prosecutor v Radislav Krstić* (International Criminal Tribunal for the Former Yugoslavia, Records of Proceedings, Case No. IT-98-33, 1998–2004) <http://www.icty.org/case/krstic/4>.

(continued)

Stimulating public debate and awareness to prevent re-occurrence by emphasising victimhood

Apart from attempting to preserve the memory of genocide and define it as 'the site of memory', the purpose of the memorial is also to prevent similar atrocities from happening again, and reinforce the moral imperative of *Never Again*. Thus, the Memorial Centre aims to develop educational and research dimensions. A good example for this is the *Summer Research University Srebrenica-Potočari* initiated in 2010, which gathered around 15 participants in the first year. This annual three-week programme is aimed at postgraduates and researchers involved in Genocide Studies.

The Srebrenica-Potočari Memorial Centre is also central to the three-day commemorative 'peace march', an annual event that begins on the morning of 8 July in a field near the village of Nezuk. The participants then retrace the 110 kilometres trek made by the column of 15,000 Bosniak men and boys making their way through the hills, valleys, woods and villages where the column was ambushed and cut off, and where some 6,000 men and boys (out of the over 8,000 victims in total) perished en route to safety. It is a march to commemorate their suffering and their courage that ends at the Srebrenica-Potočari Memorial Centre. Some survivors from the original trek, Bosniaks of all generations, men and women, boys and girls, join the ranks, as do international tourists from across the globe. Much of the commemorative activities around the Srebrenica genocide involve movement into and across space, pilgrimages of remembrance to places weighted by the spectre of past violence.

Today, it still remains 'a highly contested site that plays a central role in the ongoing struggles around victim hegemony in the region at large'.[22] Nettlefield and Wagner note that wartime strategies that resulted in war crimes 'evolved into a post-war strategy to expunge their experiences of recent history through denial, distortion, and revision of facts'.[23] This affects not only Srebrenica survivors, but everyone in BiH, especially in the Republika Srpska (RS), but also in neighbouring Serbia where like in RS the genocide is still often denied.

The narratives presented in the memorial can not and do not seek to incorporate the Serbs, and are clearly targeted at Bosniak or international visitors. This is understandable since the people killed on the Potočari site were all Bosniaks (with the exception of very few Croats). The exclusion of the Bosnian Serb narratives of the war is why many local Serbs do not visit the memorial, and it is also why the Bosnian Serbs recently have established a small Memorial Room of their own in Srebrenica to commemorate those Bosnian Serbs that were killed in the nearby villages during the war.

Preserving the memory of the fall of the safe area of Srebrenica, and the genocide in its aftermath, is not reduced to the marking of 11 July or confined to Potočari. However, to identify one particular place as a site of memory raises some critical questions concerning what is remembered and what is

---

22 Johanna Mannergren Selimovic, 'Frictional Commemoration: Local Agency and Cosmopolitan Politics at Memorial Sites in Bosnia-Herzegovina and Rwanda' in Annika Björkdahl et al (eds), *Peacebuilding and Friction: Global and Local Encounters in Post-Conflict Societies* (Routledge, 2016).

23 Lara Nettlefield and Sarah Wagner, *Srebrenica in the Aftermath of Genocide* (Cambridge University Press, 2014).

forgotten. If some places are remembered and present in the spatial narrative of the past, there are other places that continue to be silenced, absent and forgotten. Other mass killings of Bosniaks and Croats have been covered by international and national media (daily press, national news), such as the one in Brčko for example, where an estimated number of victims in camp Luka reached 3,000; in the Omarska, Keraterm and Manjača concentration camps near Prijedor; and the killings of Serbs in small villages such as Bratunac and Celebici. They, however, do not draw as much attention as the Srebrenica commemorations.

One of the motivations behind the memorial was the necessity of finding out and offering the exact sequence of events, their time and spatial frame, proving culpabilities, punishing those responsible and keeping alive memories of the crime. In this regard, the memorial fully satisfies its primary function – fighting against oblivion.

Case study B: Memorial to the Homosexuals Persecuted under the National Socialist Regime

The Memorial to the Homosexuals Persecuted under the National Socialist Regime was designed by Michael Elmgreen and Ingar Dragset and inaugurated in Berlin on 27 May 2008. It was built following a decision of the German parliament in 1999 that a memorial for Holocaust victims should be established, and that all other victims of National Socialism should be commemorated as well. In 2003, parliament sealed the construction of the memorial and determined its location in the Tiergarten, right in the administrative yet also commercial centre of the city where it is easily accessible to tourists.

Persecution of homosexuality began with the takeover of National Socialism in 1933 when it was branded as aberrant and all clubs, associations and publishing houses were closed down.[24] In 1935, this obtained its legal basis in §175 of the German Criminal Code which condemned same-sex relations amongst men, leading to criminal prosecution of homosexuals. According to the plaque at the memorial site, approximately 50,000 men were sentenced and between 5,000 to 15,000 were deported to concentration camps where they had to wear a pink triangle called *Rosa Winkel* to mark their offence, and by implication their socially unacceptable sexual orientation, leading to their stigmatisation amongst other inmates.

Prior to the establishment of the Memorial to the Homosexuals in Berlin, there were a number of smaller initiatives since the 1960s–1970s, increasingly with reference to the *Rosa Winkel*.[25] After the German Federal President Richard

(continued)

---

24 Angelika von Wahl, 'How Sexuality Changes Agency: Gay Men, Jews, and Transitional Justice' in Susanne Buckley-Zistel and Ruth Stanley, *Gender in Transitional Justice* (Palgrave Macmillan, 2012) 204.

25 Thomas O Haakenson, '(In)Visible Trauma: Michael Elmgreen and Ingar Dragset's Memorial to the Homosexuals Persecuted under the National Socialist Regime' in Bill Niven and Chloe Paver (eds), *Memorialization in Germany since 1945* (Palgrave Macmillan, 2010).

(continued)

von Weizäcker publicly acknowledged in parliament in 1985 that homosexuals had also been victims of Nazi persecution, memorial sites in the former concentration camps Dachau and Sachsenhausen, as well as a full advent exhibition in Sachsenhausen in 2000, followed.[26] Since it was inaugurated 83 years after the beginning of National Socialism, there are hardly any detainees or concentration camp survivors left to use it as a site for personal grievance or reflection. Due to the temporal distance, moreover, the campaigns for its establishment were not driven by survivors themselves, as is often the case with memorials, but by members of the contemporary gay community, and by associations of homosexuals who were concerned about both discrimination in the past and in the present.

Aesthetic language

The memorial consists of a single, tall concrete stelae (block) with a small square window through which the visitor can watch a film depicting the kiss of a same-sex couple. Initially, it was a 90 second film of two men kissing, running in a loop. This was replaced temporarily by a film of other same-sex couples – both male and female – kissing interchangeably. The concealed screening of the same-sex kissing scenes render them visible and invisible at the same time; they are hidden from view by being inside the stelae, but they are nonetheless there.[27] This oscillation between presence and absence continues until today, as one of the artists states: 'Today we accept homosexuals, but we don't want to see them'.[28] The memorial thus draws past injustices into the present and serves as a symbol against current and future stigmatisation of homosexuals. The plaque next to the memorial offers a historical account of the persecution of homosexuals under National Socialism, both in German and in English, and declares that it serves as a 'lasting symbol against exclusion, intolerance and animosity towards gays and lesbians'.

Through using stelae, the aesthetic language of the memorial connects to Eisenman's Memorial to the Murdered Jews of Europe comprised of 2,711 stelae, just on the other side of the street, establishing a bond between various victims groups of National Socialism, and undermining discussions about competitive victimhood.[29] According to one of the artists '[i]t was the same suffering, the same history, but at the same time there were many differences'.[30] The repeated use of the stelae also draws attention to the obliteration of the plight of homosexuals in the decades following National Socialism – compared

---

26 Erik N Jensen, 'The Pink Triangle and Political Consciousness: Gays, Lesbians, and the Memory of Nazi Persecution' (2011) 11(1) *Journal of the History of Sexuality* 319, 336.

27 Haakenson, above n 25, 152.

28 Author's translation. Cited in Benjamin Drechsel and Fabian Pingel, 'Bilderstreit in der Endlosschleife' (2010) 3 *Politische Ikonographie* 1, 7.

29 Apart from that, the German homosexual community has avoided comparing its experience to the Jewish Holocaust, instead aligning itself with communists and socialists. Jensen, above n 26, 342.

30 'Remembering Different Histories: Monument to Homosexual Holocaust Victims Opens in Berlin', *Spiegel* (online) 27 May 2008 <http://www.spiegel.de/international/germany/remembering-different-histories-monument-to-homosexual-holocaust-victims-opens-in-berlin-a-555665.html>.

to other victims' groups who were able to stand up for their rights – as well as to the ignorance or discrimination they currently endure.

Re-establishing dignity, encouraging public debates

Re-establishing the dignity of victims was the key impetus behind the Memorial to the Homosexuals Persecuted under the National Socialist Regime. This was important regarding the period of National Socialism, but also because persecution did not end with its demise in 1945. In West Germany, §175 was applied until 1969, only completely lifted in 1994, and it took until 2002 to legally rehabilitate men who had been sentenced on its basis. Keeping the law after the end of National Socialism was unusual, since the Allies did not otherwise allow the retaining of laws which had increased in severity under the Nazis.[31] Some homosexuals even had to continue serving their sentence set under the regime. Moreover, between 1950 and 1969, over 100,000 legal investigations were opened and 59,316 men were sentenced for being homosexual.[32]

As a consequence, in the first decades after National Socialism there was a culture of silence around the persecution and prosecution of homosexuals. The continuing criminalisation and stigmatisation kept victims from coming forward to tell their stories or even to demand reparations. While Jews, Sinti and Roma where labelled victims of the Nuremberg Laws and were eligible for compensation – and other victims of fascism had access to some form of monetary and social rehabilitation – homosexuals, 'asocials', criminals, victims of euthanasia and forced sterilisation, and displaced persons had no right to claim reparations.[33] To finally gain some public recognition through the memorial was thus a major achievement. In this sense, the memorial serves as a belated sign of resistance in a former culture of impunity.

A further achievement of the memorial is to encourage public debates about past injustices. Against the backdrop of silence in the years following National Socialism it helps to draw their plight into the public realm. The main contention about the memorial was not and is not about its existence *per se*, but about who it is for. In its initial conception, the memorial was for gay men only, since they were singled out by §175, and there is very little record and evidence of lesbians being targeted during National Socialism and the ensuing decades. From a feminist perspective it was argued that women, too, were affected by the Nazi regime even though they were less frequently sentenced and arrested, and that women (as well as men) continue to suffer from homophobia today, again linking past and present.[34] The conceptual opening up of the memorial to both sexes led to heated debates about historical accuracy on the one hand, and the perpetual exclusion and invisibility of (homosexual) women in society on the other.

---

31 von Wahl, above n 24, 205.
32 Ibid.
33 Ibid.
34 Christiane Wilke, 'Remembering Complexity? Memorials for Nazi Victims in Berlin' (2013) 7(1) *International Journal of Transitional Justice* 136.

12.4 By way of conclusion

This chapter elaborates on how memorialisation, memorials and transitional justice are closely related. Often serving as a reminder of a tragic past, post-conflict societies establish memorials in order to prevent the recurrence of such tragedies. In this context, memorials are often regarded as having a positive impact on transitional justice processes. Yet, transitional justice in transitional societies is always a political process, and we have to maintain a critical stance towards the political implications of commemorating a past.

We should be aware that only certain memories, testimonies and events become part of the official narrative of the past and are thus to be commemorated, while others that challenge this narrative are to be forgotten. Memorials in such settings tend to provide the victors or power-holders with a mechanism of imagining a new nation through the narratives of the past that they disseminate. The memories reflected in and reproduced by such memorials are deeply contested, severely politicised and highly divisive, and as memorials are open to an infinite number of interpretations, they can readily slide into contested and contradictory narratives about history, specific events, victimhood and victory.[35] This in turn may be counterproductive to reconciliation and conflict transformation.

The creation of any memorial actively or potentially excludes those who do not subscribe to it, or who are embraced within the meanings attached to that memorial. Thus, the memoryscape of transitional societies often also includes counter-memorials as discussed above. In parallel to official memorialisation, memorials groups and individuals who feel excluded, silenced or forgotten initiate non-official, alternative, grassroots ways of representing the past. Such counter-memorials do not represent the 'right memory' but can become a collective social symbol with the ability to encapsulate and perpetuate certain identities, and claims may be established in resistance towards a uniform and exclusive memorialisation process.

Counter-memorials are important as they reveal the danger of uniform or hegemonic interpretations of the past and encourage multiple understandings of the past. Furthermore, by communicating narratives of the past to the public, memorials also introduce a new type of agent to the field of transitional justice in addition to victims and perpetrators – the visitor – and in doing so displace the dichotomy of victims and perpetrator, by not belonging to either group. More research focusing on such counter-memorials that represent resistance to official commemorations, and the bystander and the external gaze of the tourist,

---

35 Nicholas Saunder, 'Matter and Memory in the Landscapes of Conflict: The Western Front 1914–1999' in Barbara Bender and Margot Winer (eds), *Contested Landscapes: Movement, Exile and Place* (Berg, 2001).

is needed. One example is the Daniel Libeskind's Jewish Museum in Berlin in which he designed a museum with six voids built into the architecture to remind everybody who enters that no matter what they see of Jewish history (as exhibited in this museum), it is going to be disrupted, interrupted by the memory of the Holocaust. Another famous example is Maya Lin's Vietnam Veterans Memorial, which is a place where Vietnam veterans come to remember their fallen comrades, and where Americans can begin to remember how they received the veterans when they came back from Vietnam. It reflects America's loss, the divided American society, and the memorial reflects this ambivalence.[36]

Commemorative landscapes, particularly those which evoke the memory of war, are clearly gendered, as they produce and reproduce the experiences and narratives of men, and often silence women's interpretations of the war. Feminist scholars have raised the question: What role do commemorations and memorials play in dispelling or affirming the gender order in post-conflict contexts?[37] In transitional societies and in war-torn societies, male war heroes or war veterans are frequently commemorated, but the varied experiences of women often remain excluded or silenced in the construction of the meta-narratives of the past that is represented in the memorials. Thus there is an urgent need to discuss the gendered nuances of commemorations in transitional societies through a critical examination of commemorative material culture such as monuments and memorials.

Post-memory is another critical, yet under-explored aspect of the connection between memorialisation, memory and transitional justice. By handing down through the generations a version of events that reproduces identity and anchors memory in the site of the most intense experiences, memorials are key to transferring memory across generations and to intergenerational commemoration and remembering. Memorials such as the one in Srebrenica-Potočari risk fetishising the place as its name will forever be associated with genocide, and obscure a wider social memory capable of accommodating different recollections and interpretations.[38]

Clearly, memorials derive their importance from the ideas and values that are projected through them.[39] These ideas and values are not fixed in time and can

---

36 Yad Vashem Shoah Resource Center, *Holocaust Monuments and Counter-Monuments* (24 May 1998) International School for Holocaust Studies <http://www.yadvashem.org/ odot_pdf/ Microsoft%20Word%20-%203659.pdf>.

37 Hamzah Muzaini and Brenda SA Yeoh, 'War Landscapes as "Battlefields" of Collective Memories: Reading the Reflections at Bukit Chandu, Singapore' (2005) 12 *Cultural Geographies* 1288; Sara McDowell, 'Commemorating Dead "Men": Gendering the Past and Present in Post-Conflict Northern Ireland' (2008) 15(4) *Gender, Place & Culture* 335–354; Janice Jones Monk, "Gender in the Landscape: Expressions of Power and Meaning' in Kay Anderson and Fay Gale (eds), *Inventing Places: Studies in Cultural Geography* (Longham, 1992).

38 Brian Graham and Peter Howard, 'Introduction: Heritage and Identity' in Brian Graham and Peter Howard (eds), *The Research Companion to Heritage and Identity* (Ashgate, 2008).

39 Ibid.

be dissonant, and they can reject official historical narratives to present an alternative reading of place and memory. Due to their construction and representation of a particular past they acquire certain functions, as discussed in this chapter, and thus lend themselves to affecting societies in transition as central to the idea of transitional justice, yet both with negative and positive repercussions.

12.5 Summary

Memorials present an attempt to fixate and store memories. They are symbolic reparations and serve to remember past events or persons that should not be forgotten in the present, such as victims of war, of repressive dictatorships, of terrorist attacks, apartheid as well as genocide. The chapter demonstrates that memorials link the past, the present and the future. There has been a shift in commemorations from war heroes to victims, parallel to a shift in focus of transitional justice from perpetrators to victims. The chapter distinguishes between three forms of memorials: authentic sites at the place where atrocities were committed such as the Srebrenica-Potočari Memorial Centre, constructed sites that often are more abstract such as the Memorial to the Homosexuals Persecuted under the National Socialist Regime, and commemorations such as the peace march to Srebrenica-Potočari. Memorials can fulfil different functions such as rehabilitate the dignity of victims, stimulate public debates about past injustices, serve as a sign of resistance in a culture of impunity and break silences about past injustices, contribute to conflict transformation and aid the nation-building process by helping to construct shared collective identities, as well as provide a space for private reflection and mourning. We can also see that memorials are often contested in transitional societies as they represent a particular historical narrative of the past.

12.6 Discussion and tutorial questions

1) What forms do memorials take around the world, and what role does the form of a violent conflict – dictatorship, ethno-political war, genocide and so on – play in shaping the impact of memorials?

2) How do memorials reflect the object of commemoration such as victims or war heroes?

3) What is the role of memorialisation in dealing with the past?

4) What is the relationship between memorials and other transitional justice tools?

5) And how can memorials advance the goals of other transitional justice initiatives?

Suggested reading

Bell, Duncan (ed), *Memory, Trauma and World Politics: Reflections on the Relationship between Past and Present* (Palgrave, 2006).

Buckley-Zistel, Susanne and Stefanie Schäfer (eds), *Memorials in Times of Transition* (Intersentia, 2014).

Center for Non-Violent Action, *War of Memories: Places of Suffering and Remembrance of War in Bosnia-Herzegovina* (CNA, 2016).

Nettlefield, Lara and Sarah Wagner, *Srebrenica in the Aftermath of Genocide* (Cambridge University Press, 2014).

Young, James, *The Texture of Memory: Holocaust Memorials and Meaning* (Yale University Press, 1993).

Suggested film

Srebrenica – A Cry from the Grave (Directed by Leslie Woodhead, Antelope Productions, 2000) ‹https://www.youtube.com/watch?v=Fliw801iX84›.

Other resources

Digital Monument to the Jewish Community in the Netherlands (2001) Jewish Historical Museum ‹http://www.joodsmonument.nl/?lang=en›.

Human Rights & Democracy for Iran, *Omid: A Memorial in the Defense of Human Rights in Iran* (2016) Abdorrahman Boroumand Foundation ‹https://www.iranrights.org/mem orial›.

Korean War Veterans Digital Memorial (2015) Korean War Legacy Foundation ‹http://www. kwvdm.org/›.

Lives of the First World War (12 May 2014) Imperial War Museum ‹https://livesofthe firstworldwar.org/›.

Bibliography

Articles/books/reports

Ashplant, Timothy G, Graham Dawson and Michael Roper (eds), *Commemorating War: The Politics of Memory* (Transaction Publishers, 2004).

Barsalou, Judy M, 'Reflecting the Fractured Past: Memorialisation, Transitional Justice and the Role of the Outsiders' in Susanne Buckley-Zistel and Stefanie Schäfer (eds), *Memorials in Time of Transition* (Intersentia, 2014).

Bonacker, Thorsten, Anika Oettler and Christoph Safferling, 'Valorising Victims' Ambivalences in Contemporary Trends in Transitional Justice' in Thorsten Bonacker and Christoph Safferling (eds) *Victims of International Crimes: An Interdisciplinary Discourse* (Springer, 2013).

Braun, Christian, 'The Srebrenica-Potočari Memorial: Promoting (In)Justice?' in Susanne Buckley-Zistel and Stefanie Schäfer (eds), *Memorials in Time of Transition* (Intersentia, 2014).

Brett, Sebastian, Louis Bickford, Liz Ševčenko and Marcela Rios, *Memorialization and Democracy: State Policy and Civic Action* (International Center for Transitional Justice, 2007).

Buckley-Zistel, Susanne and Stefanie Schäfer, 'Memorials in Time of Transition' in Susanne Buckley-Zistel and Stefanie Schäfer (eds), *Memorials in Time of Transition* (Intersentia, 2014).

Drechsel, Benjamin and Fabian Pingel, 'Bilderstreit in der Endlosschleife' (2010) 3 *Politische Ikonographie* ‹http://edoc.hu-berlin.de/kunsttexte/2010-3/drechsel-benjamin-2/PDF/d rechsel.pdf›.

Graham, Brian and Peter Howard, 'Introduction: Heritage and Identity' in Brian Graham and Peter Howard (eds), *The Research Companion to Heritage and Identity* (Ashgate, 2008).

Haakenson, Thomas O, '(In)Visible Trauma: Michael Elmgreen and Ingar Dragset's Memorial to the Homosexuals Persecuted under the National Socialist Regime' in Bill Niven and Chloe Paver (eds), *Memorialization in Germany since 1945* (Palgrave Macmillan, 2010).

Hamber, Brandon, Liz Ševčenko and Ereshnee Naidu, 'Utopian Dreams or Practical Possibilities? The Challenges of Evaluating the Impact of Memorialization in Societies in Transition' (2010) 4(3) *International Journal of Transitional Justice*.

Jensen, Erik N, 'The Pink Triangle and Political Consciousness: Gays, Lesbians, and the Memory of Nazi Persecution' (2011) 11(1) *Journal of the History of Sexuality*.

Jones Monk, Janice, "Gender in the Landscape: Expressions of Power and Meaning' in Kay Anderson and Fay Gale (eds), *Inventing Places: Studies in Cultural Geography* (Longman, 1992).

Levy, Daniel, 'Changing Temporalities and the Internalization of Memory of Culture' in Yifat Gutman, Adam D Brown and Amy Sodaro (eds), *Memory and the Future: Transnational Politics, Ethics and Society* (Palgrave Macmillan, 2010).

McDowell, Sara, 'Commemorating Dead "Men": Gendering the Past and Present in Post-Conflict Northern Ireland' (2008) 15(4) *Gender, Place & Culture*.

Mannergren Selimovic, Johanna, 'Frictional Commemoration: Local Agency and Cosmopolitan Politics at Memorial Sites in Bosnia-Herzegovina and Rwanda' in Annika Björkdahl, Kristine Höglund, Gearoid Millar, Jair van der Lijn and Willemijn Verkoren (eds), *Peacebuilding and Friction: Global and Local Encounters in Post-Conflict Societies* (Routledge, 2016).

Muzaini, Hamzah and Brenda SA Yeoh, 'War Landscapes as "Battlefields" of Collective Memories: Reading the Reflections at Bukit Chandu, Singapore' (2005) 12 *Cultural Geographies*.

Naidu, Ereshnee, 'Memorialisation in Postconflict Societies in Africa: Potentials and Challenges' in Susanne Buckley-Zistel and Stefanie Schäfer (eds), *Memorials in Time of Transition* (Intersentia, 2014).

Nettlefield, Lara and Sarah Wagner, *Srebrenica in the Aftermath of Genocide* (Cambridge University Press, 2014).

Saunder, Nicholas, 'Matter and Memory in the Landscapes of Conflict: The Western Front 1914–1999' in Barbara Bender and Margot Winer (eds), *Contested Landscapes: Movement, Exile and Place* (Berg, 2001).

Simić, Olivera, 'Remembering, Visiting and Placing the Dead: Law, Authority and Genocide in Srebrenica' (2009) 13 *Law Text Culture*.

Viebach, Julia, 'Alétheia and the Making of the World: Inner and Outer Dimensions of Memorials in Rwanda' in Susanne Buckley-Zistel and Stefanie Schäfer (eds), *Memorials in Time of Transition* (Intersentia, 2014).

Von Wahl, Angelika, 'How Sexuality Changes Agency: Gay Men, Jews, and Transitional Justice' in Susanne Buckley-Zistel and Ruth Stanley (eds), *Gender in Transitional Justice* (Palgrave Macmillan, 2012).

Wilke, Christiane, 'Remembering Complexity? Memorials for Nazi Victims in Berlin' (2013) 7(1) *International Journal of Transitional Justice*.

Winter, Jay, *Sites of Memory, Sites of Mourning: The Great War in European Cultural History* (Cambridge University Press, 1995).

Winter, Jay, 'Notes on the Memory Boom: War, Remembrance and the Uses of the Past' in Duncan Bell (ed), *Memory, Trauma and World Politics: Reflections on the Relationship between Past and Present* (Palgrave Macmillan, 2006).

Other

Basic Principles and Guidelines on the Right to a Remedy and Reparation for Victims of Gross Violations of International Human Rights Law and Serious Violations of International Humanitarian Law, GA Res 60/147, UN GA, 60th sess, 64th plen mtg, Agenda Item 71(a), UN Doc A/Res/60/147 (adopted and proclaimed 16 December 2005) ‹www.unhcr.org/refworld/docid/4721cb942.html›.

Prosecutor v Radislav Krstić (International Criminal Tribunal for the Former Yugoslavia, Records of Proceedings, Case No. IT-98-33, 1998–2004) ‹http://www.icty.org/case/krstic/4›.

'Remembering Different Histories: Monument to Homosexual Holocaust Victims Opens in Berlin', *Spiegel* (online) 27 May 2008 ‹http://www.spiegel.de/international/germany/ remembering-different-histories-monument-to-homosexual-holocaust-victims-opens-in-berlin-a-555665.html›.

Yad Vashem Shoah Resource Center, *Holocaust Monuments and Counter-Monuments* (24 May 1998) International School for Holocaust Studies ‹http://www.yadvashem.org/ odot_pdf/Microsoft%20Word%20-%203659.pdf›.

Chapter 13

Measuring the success (or failure) of transitional justice

Andrew G Reiter

13.1 Introduction

As the previous chapters have demonstrated, transitional justice mechanisms are complex, time-consuming, and often expensive. The UN has spent nearly $2 billion to date on the International Criminal Tribunal for the former Yugoslavia (ICTY) that was created in 1993.[1] Reparations programmes can be costly for societies emerging from war and needing to rebuild. Likewise, vetting programmes often remove skilled officials from government at the very crucial moment when the best and brightest are needed to help the country move forward. Moreover, many transitional justice processes are extremely controversial, leading to intense public debates, protests, and even violence. In 1998, military officers assassinated a commissioner of Guatemala's truth commission just two days after its final report was released.[2] Argentina experienced a series of military revolts following high-profile trials in the aftermath of its transition to democracy in 1983.[3] It comes as no surprise, then, that policymakers want to know that transitional justice actually works and is thus worth the costs; and many policymakers, non-governmental organisations (NGOs), and academics have attempted to evaluate the relative success of transitional justice mechanisms.

This chapter proceeds by first outlining three distinct levels of analysis at which transitional justice can be evaluated: the micro, or individual level; the meso, or institutional level; and the macro, or national level. It then surveys

---

1 Robert M Hayden, *From Yugoslavia to the Western Balkans: Studies of a European Disunion, 1991–2011* (Brill, 2013) 278.

2 Raúl Molina Mejía, 'The Struggle against Impunity in Guatemala' (1999) 26(4) *Social Justice* 55, 64.

3 Leigh A Payne, *Uncivil Movements: The Armed Right Wing and Democracy in Latin America* (Johns Hopkins University Press, 2000) 51–100.

attempts to measure the success of transitional justice on all three levels of analysis. It pays particular attention to the methods used, the overall conclusions drawn from existing studies, and the limitations of research in this area of transitional justice. Finally, the chapter concludes with a reflection on what it means for transitional justice policies to be successful, and whether we can or should evaluate these initiatives in the same ways in which we evaluate other political and social policies.

13.2 How do we know if transitional justice works?

Measuring the success of transitional justice can occur at roughly three distinct levels of analysis, each with its own strengths and weaknesses. First and foremost, researchers focus on the micro or individual level and study how people experience and perceive transitional justice efforts. A high-profile trial may be lauded, but will have little impact if victims do not feel justice was served. Reparations programmes may look good from the outside, but are the lives of individual victims being improved? We can also study whether individual victims and perpetrators feel healed or atoned after participating in various transitional justice mechanisms, and how societal attitudes change over time. In examining the individual level, researchers conduct interviews, focus groups, and surveys of victims, perpetrators, and members of society as a whole in places where transitional justice was pursued to gauge their perceptions of events and to understand their individual experiences. Survey work is also important for attempting to assess levels of reconciliation, ideally being used to track societal attitudes over time and across groups within society.

Second, there is an acknowledgement that transitional justice mechanisms vary significantly in quality. A trial that ends in a verdict metes out more justice than legal proceedings that fail to finish. Some reparations programmes provide more aid to victims than do others. Some truth commissions are cursory reviews of past events, while others are thorough and highly participatory investigations. In examining the success of transitional justice at this meso or institutional level, researchers strive to collect detailed information on the many specific judicial proceedings, laws, programmes, and institutions related to transitional justice. They often compile this information in qualitative datasets that are publicly available, or publish qualitative narratives in the form of books, articles, or reports. The goal at this level is to assess whether or not transitional justice mechanisms carried out their work as intended and achieved their stated objectives.

Yet those engaged in transitional justice also want to know if these mechanisms achieve larger, long-term, societal goals such as peace and reconciliation.

Indeed, policymakers often pursue these mechanisms precisely because of the view that they are a necessary component of transitioning from war to peace and from authoritarianism to democracy, and because of the promise that they will aid divided societies in reconciling differences and learning to live side-by-side without violence. At this macro or national level we can examine, for example, whether countries that pursue particular transitional justice mechanisms are more peaceful or democratic than similar countries that did not. This can take the form of qualitative case studies that comparatively trace the pathways of similar countries, or quantitative analyses of larger datasets of countries that rely on statistical techniques to control differences and similarities between cases, and isolate the effects of transitional justice.

Finally, some researchers – particularly international relations scholars – take this macro level a bit further and attempt to examine the impact of transitional justice at the global or international level. Countries do not pursue transitional justice mechanisms in isolation, but look to past experiences of other countries and respond to pressures from powerful states, international organisations, and influential non-governmental organisations. Over time, we might see global norms emerge, whereby certain approaches to past human rights violations become expected and other approaches become scorned or even taboo. Here researchers typically quantitatively examine global trends in the use of transitional justice mechanisms over time, often coupled with case studies that demonstrate why policymakers pursued particular mechanisms.

In all three levels of analysis, one important question confronts researchers: How long do we have to wait? A key trial verdict or the release of a truth commission report can quickly change the narrative within a country and discredit long-standing myths maintained by former perpetrators. The process of participating in a truth commission or local justice process can be cathartic for victims and perpetrators. The impact of transitional justice might then be seen almost immediately. Yet democracies take time to consolidate, countries need to be at peace for a sufficient time before we can say that they have avoided renewed war, and reparations are intended to improve the lives of victims over the long term. It may then take years or even decades to be able to fully assess whether transitional justice has been successful in achieving these lofty goals. Finally, for the emergence of international norms and for a goal like reconciliation, it may take many generations to truly be able to determine whether transitional justice has worked. The difficult state of race relations in the United States, 150 years after the Civil War and the end of slavery, for example, demonstrates that well-entrenched prejudices and structural inequalities are extremely difficult to overcome. We should not then expect instant improvements from societies emerging from repression and genocide in the late twentieth and early twenty-first centuries.

13.3 The micro or individual level: recognition, reparation, and reconciliation

Transitional justice aims, first and foremost, to recognise past wrongs, repair damages, and bring about reconciliation to divided societies. Scholars and policymakers, therefore, focus much of their research at the local community or individual level. Do victims feel as though transitional justice efforts have effectively recognised their experiences, have these initiatives improved their livelihoods, and have views between perpetrator and victim communities changed as a result? Answering these questions at the micro level typically requires methodologies that are in-depth and intensive, including ethnographic research, focus groups, interviews, and surveys.

Truly understanding the needs and priorities of victims, and how transitional justice mechanisms resonate in societies requires researchers to immerse themselves within the populations. Ethnographers and forensic anthropologists observe individuals and groups, conduct extensive on-the-ground interviews, and aim to bring out a local perspective in their analysis. In a study of victim communities in Guatemala, for example, Victoria Sanford affirms that truth and justice are vital for community healing and successfully transitioning from authoritarian rule. Yet she emphasises that redress for past human rights goes beyond trials and official commissions, and that exhumations of mass graves, collective remembering, and public mourning are also crucial to helping society heal.[4]

Conducting surveys is also a central focus of micro level research. Doing so allows researchers to gain insight into the diverse experiences of those affected by periods of human rights violations. Indeed, we may not know the extent of victimhood in a case or understand who exactly victims are until we conduct surveys. Surveys can also reveal the needs of victims, and their preferences and priorities for how transitional justice mechanisms should address them. Moreover, surveys are vital in attempting to assess the impact of transitional justice on reconciliation, enabling researchers to gauge societal attitudes and views on national and regional identity. The most effective survey designs gather a range of data about participants, including gender, ethnicity, and location, along with their responses to detailed questions about transitional justice specifically. The Reconciliation Barometer Project and the West African Transitional Justice Project are two well-known examples of efforts to conduct broad surveys across time in post-conflict societies.[5]

---

4 Victoria Sanford, *Buried Secrets: Truth and Human Rights in Guatemala* (Palgrave Macmillan, 2003).

5 Kim Wale, *Confronting Exclusion: Time for Radical Reconciliation, SA Reconciliation Barometer Survey: 2013 Report* (Institute for Justice and Reconciliation, 2013) <http://reconciliationbaro meter.org/wp-content/uploads/2013/12/IJR-Barometer-Report-2013-22Nov1635.pdf>; David Backer and Anu Kulkarni, *West African Transitional Justice Project* <https://www.wm.edu/as/government/research/undergraduateresearch/watj/ index.php>.

The overall result of micro level research can be a clear picture of variations in how transitional justice mechanisms are perceived by and impact individuals. It may be the case, for example, that a trial remains unknown throughout most of the country, or that key segments of the population feel as though a verdict was too lenient, leading us to question whether the trial should be considered successful in achieving its primary goal of delivering justice. In Cambodia, for example, the government established a hybrid tribunal with the United Nations – the Extraordinary Chambers in the Courts of Cambodia – to bring former members of the genocidal Khmer Rouge regime that ruled from 1975 to 1979 to trial. Yet a population-based survey conducted in 2010 demonstrated that many Cambodians were unaware of the trial, and that a strong majority (83 per cent) felt that the government should be focusing on improving the everyday lives of its citizens rather than delving into the past.[6]

Research can also help to determine how widespread knowledge of a truth commission is, whether a final report has actually been accessed by victims and members of the population at large, and what the overall perception is of the commission's work. If citizens view the commission as being biased, then its results will have less impact no matter how robust its operations were. An evaluation of Sierra Leone's Truth and Reconciliation Commission, for example, found that its restorative approach to justice clashed with local conceptualisations of justice, leading to negative views of its work by many citizens in the country.[7] We can also assess whether victims and their families actually received the money and benefits that were promised to them when reparations programmes were established, and whether or not they feel their lives were improved because of it. The reparations programme in Malawi, for example, has been lauded by politicians aiming to show that they are addressing past human rights violations, but heavily criticised by victims who complain of incomplete compensation, poor communication, and favouritism.[8] In some cases, reparations programmes, no matter how generous, can be perceived as 'blood money' and rejected by victims. The Madres of the Plaza de Mayo in Argentina, for example, split into two organisations, in part over the issue of reparations, when some members rejected government compensation for their missing children, 'since to accept reparation

---

6 Phuong Pham, Patrick Vinck, Mychelle Balthazard and Sokhom Hean, *After the First Trial: A Population-Based Survey on Knowledge and Perceptions of Justice and the Extraordinary Chambers in the Courts of Cambodia* (Human Rights Center, University of California, Berkeley, 2011) <https://www.law.berkeley.edu/files/HRC/ Publications_After-the-First-Trial_06-2011.pdf>.

7 Gearoid Millar, 'Local Evaluations of Justice through Truth Telling in Sierra Leone' (2011) 12(4) *Human Rights Review* 515.

8 Diana Cammack, 'Reparations in Malawi' in Pablo de Greiff (ed), *The Handbook of Reparations* (Oxford University Press, 2006) 215.

is to acknowledge death'.[9] Yet in other cases small sums or symbolic reparations bring with them a level of recognition that dramatically changes how victims feel about government and society – and only micro level research can uncover these differences.

Research at the micro level also aims to uncover local meanings of success for transitional justice. A broad concept like 'reconciliation' can have different meanings in different cultures, and scholars argue that we cannot measure the effectiveness of transitional justice in bringing about reconciliation until we come to terms with what it means to local people in the communities affected by violence. In examining the impact of the South African Truth and Reconciliation Commission, for example, Antjie Krog has emphasised the importance of the concept of '*ubuntu*', or 'interconnectedness-towards-wholeness', in how victims understand forgiveness and reconciliation.[10] There is thus a view that we must strive to understand and consider local and individual views of concepts such as peace, reconciliation, apology, and reparation to be able to assess the effectiveness of transitional justice mechanisms.

With all research at the micro level, timing is important. Some researchers attempt to investigate the impact of transitional justice immediately, to minimise the effect of other factors that can influence individual views. Yet others stress the need for waiting and thus gaining a longer-term retrospective from individuals. Ideally, surveys and interviews are conducted repeatedly over time, allowing researchers to track any important changes.

Overall, micro level research is an important component in assessing the success of transitional justice. Only by tapping into community and individual views and understandings of transitional justice mechanisms, can we truly comprehend their success. We may find that mechanisms that appear to be working well are having little impact on the ground, or that they are impacting different communities and individuals in divergent ways. Moreover, micro level research can cause us to reassess how we should even approach the question of how to measure success.

Yet there are significant limitations to micro level research, beyond the practical barriers of the cost and time necessary to conduct studies at the individual level. First, it can be difficult for researchers to figure out who to interview or survey in the first place. Typically there are not convenient lists of victims for researchers to use, and researching particular groups can introduce bias – the composition of one refugee camp, for example, could be drastically

---

9 Brandon Hamber and Richard A Wilson, 'Symbolic Closure through Memory, Reparation and Revenge in Post-Conflict Societies' (2002) 1(1) *Journal of Human Rights* 35, 45.

10 Antjie Krog, '"This Thing Called Reconciliation . . . " Forgiveness as Part of an Interconnectedness-Towards-Wholeness' (2008) 27(4) *South African Journal of Philosophy* 353, 353.

different than others, leading to skewed conclusions about victimhood in a country. Researchers also need appropriate language skills and well-connected local contacts, and may need to overcome hesitation on the part of communities to open up about sensitive issues to outsiders. Second, this type of research relies on self-reported data, and individuals can recall past events incorrectly, and misunderstand crucial concepts or questions, especially given the difficulty of translating particular concepts such as truth and justice across cultures. Lastly, micro level research fails to address the larger institutional and national level goals of transitional justice mechanisms. National improvements in human rights protections and democratic freedoms may not always be perceptible by individuals. Or perhaps a vetting programme is not well received or understood by the local population, but is extremely effective at removing human rights abusers from office. Micro level research can thus be complemented by research at the meso and macro levels respectively.

13.4 The meso or institutional level: justice, truth, and reform

Above the micro or individual level, researchers evaluate transitional justice at the meso or institutional level by conducting institutional assessments of specific mechanisms themselves. Here the task is to examine the creation and functioning of transitional justice mechanisms such as courts, truth commissions and reparations programmes. How effectively are they designed and how well do they carry out their intended tasks?

States pursue many trials for former perpetrators, but a sizeable number never reach a verdict. The trial of Slobodan Milošević at the ICTY, for example, failed to issue a verdict prior to his death in 2006; and despite many days under house arrest, Augusto Pinochet was never convicted of any crime in Spain or Chile prior to this death in 2006. The success of a trial can, therefore, be partially measured by whether the prosecution was completed, a verdict was rendered, and a sentence was imposed. Others would go even further to define success as guilty verdicts only, and measure that success by the extent of the sentence, viewing long prison sentences as a better outcome than 'slaps on the wrist' in the form of fines or short jail time. Those investigating the success of transitional justice also take breadth into consideration. A country that has witnessed hundreds of trials of former members of its authoritarian regime, like Argentina or Greece, could be considered more successful in pursuing justice than those who pursue only a few token trials. In other words, how comprehensive were the trial proceedings and how effective were they at meting out justice to perpetrators of human rights violations? There has been extensive work at this meso level into trials in Latin America, with major NGOs and academic institutions tracking and analysing prosecutions in key cases, including Argentina, Chile, and Peru.[11] The major international tribunals have also received significant attention from researchers.

Likewise, governments often announce commissions to investigate past human rights violations, but the success of many in doing so is unclear. At times, these announcements are political posturing and the commissions that are created never complete their work, by design or due to lack of funding and support. Yet other commissions conclude their investigations and release public reports. Researchers typically assess the success of truth commissions along two dimensions: robustness and output. The robustness of a commission can be measured by how well it was funded and staffed, and the breadth of its mandate. More comprehensive commissions with greater resources and more investigatory powers are considered stronger or more successful. Regarding output, researchers ask whether the commission produced a final report of its findings, whether that report was made public, and whether that report named the names of individual perpetrators. In addition, researchers examine the recommendations truth commissions make in their final reports – such as reparations programmes and institutional reforms – and whether they are in turn implemented by the government. Overall, more robust truth commissions can uncover a more detailed and respected truth about past atrocities, and where the findings are public and recommendations are implemented, truth commissions represent a greater deterrent and should be more successful in preventing future crimes. Some researchers also contend that victim participation in the truth commission process is an important component for measuring its success. The ability for victims to testify and tell their stories can be cathartic and thus can make the commission more successful in bringing reconciliation to society. The most emblematic academic work in this area is Priscilla Hayner's book, which examines the similarities and differences and varying levels of success across 40 truth commissions used around the world.[12]

Like truth commissions, reparations programmes vary considerably on how robust they are and on their output.[13] Those that cover a larger percentage of victims and provide more substantial awards are generally considered more successful than minimal efforts to provide primarily symbolic funds to isolated victim groups. Moreover, some reparations programmes function more effectively than others. Scholars thus ask how well programmes are publicised and what types of outreach are undertaken, how easily victims can file claims, and how efficiently and fairly decisions are made. Finally, timing is important when analysing this

---

11 Cath Collins, Lorena Balardini and Jo Marie Burt, 'Mapping Perpetrator Prosecutions in Latin America' (2013) 7(1) *International Journal of Transitional Justice* 8.

12 Priscilla Hayner, *Unspeakable Truths: Transitional Justice and the Challenge of Truth Commissions* (Routledge, 2nd ed, 2011).

13 de Greiff, Pablo (ed), above n 8.

mechanism as well. Victims should receive reparations in a timely manner so as to allow them to improve their livelihoods. Programmes that drag on for many years without compensating victims are considered less successful. Similarly, vetting programmes that apply to the government and military widely may be viewed as qualitatively better than the purging of a handful of high-ranking officials, though researchers also attempt to account for the procedural fairness of the process in evaluating this mechanism.[14]

With respect to amnesties, measures of success vary considerably and research at this meso level has used several important criteria.[15] Those that are debated by legislative bodies or informed by public referenda are considered more legitimate than other amnesties enacted unilaterally by executive decree, particularly if they are done so by non-democratic governments. With amnesties, breadth is generally treated in the opposite fashion as with other mechanisms. Here scholars typically view the most successful amnesties as those that are narrow – complying with international law and requiring recipients to comply with certain conditions (for example, participation in disarmament, demobilisation, and reintegration programmes) to obtain their benefits – though the most successful amnesties typically cover both sides in a conflict – the government and the rebel groups challenging the government – rather than simply the state's own forces.

Overall, research at the meso or institutional is typically done through qualitative case studies, often buttressed by on-site observation of mechanisms in action, extensive archival research, and interviews with politicians and bureaucrats associated with the creation and operation of the transitional justice efforts. Research at this level is invaluable at providing a clear picture of how transitional justice mechanisms are operating and determining how successful they are at carrying out many of their tasks. Yet there are also major limitations. A focus on institutional effectiveness can ignore variations in impact and perceptions at the individual level. In other words, a mechanism may look great 'on paper' but have had less than the expected impact on the ground. In addition, by focusing on each mechanism, studies at this level can overlook how they fit into the transitional experience and comprehensive transitional justice efforts undertaken by countries. It is difficult to assess a mechanism's overall contribution to larger goals like peace and democracy without understanding how it complements or complicates other transitional justice initiatives. Research at the macro level can aid in answering these larger questions.

---

14 Alexander Mayer-Rieckh and Pablo de Greiff (eds), *Justice as Prevention: Vetting Public Employees in Transitional Societies* (Social Science Research Council, 2007).

15 Louise Mallinder, *Amnesty, Human Rights and Political Transitions: Bridging the Peace and Justice Divide* (Hart Publishing, 2008).

13.5 The macro or national level: peace, democracy, and human rights

While micro and meso level studies can reveal a great deal about how well particular transitional justice mechanisms work and touch people's lives, they tell us little about the overall value of transitional justice endeavours to countries emerging from conflict or authoritarianism. Scholars and policymakers alike now champion transitional justice as a necessary and vital undertaking for states to successfully overcome past legacies of violence.[16] As transitional justice competes with other important tasks for transitioning states, such as economic development, it is important to know if transitional justice really does help to contribute to stronger democracies, improved human rights records, and more peaceful societies.

Early approaches to studying these effects at the national level were comparative case studies. Researchers selected anywhere from several to a dozen or more cases that shared similarities. Often the cases were from the same region or experienced similar types of transitions during the same period. Yet the cases differed in their use of transitional justice and in the state of their democracy and human rights protections today. This allowed researchers to look for relationships between choices and these important outcomes. The methods used here were largely qualitative, relying on process-tracing transitional justice events over time in each case, and the outcomes were usually subjective, based on the researcher's knowledge of the cases, though some studies used external measures from other sources. One important work, for example, examined nineteen cases of democratic transition across Europe, Latin America, and South Africa.[17] Another compared the effects of transitional justice across 32 post-conflict countries.[18] While important contributions that began to highlight national level impact, the studies were limited in their scope. Even the largest of those studies covered only a small, unrepresentative sample of the overall number of countries that have used transitional justice, and were therefore unable to make broad conclusions about the effects of mechanisms.

More recently, there has been a proliferation of quantitative studies drawing on cross-national databases of transitional justice mechanisms. Scholars first collect information on what mechanisms countries around the world have used, then use various statistical techniques to see if there are any correlations

---

16 United Nations, 'Guidance Note of the Secretary-General: United Nations Approach to Transitional Justice' (10 March 2010).

17 Alexandra Barahona de Brito, Carmen González-Enríquez and Paloma Aguilar (eds), *The Politics of Memory: Transitional Justice in Democratizing Societies* (Oxford University Press, 2001).

18 Jack Snyder and Leslie Vinjamuri, 'Trials and Errors: Principle and Pragmatism in Strategies of International Justice' (2003–04) 28(3) *International Security* 5.

between those choices and measures of peace, democracy, and human rights, controlling for other factors that might explain those outcomes. The Transitional Justice Database Project, Post-Conflict Justice Dataset, and Transitional Justice Research Collaborative, are some of the most prominent examples of cross-national databases on multiple transitional justice mechanisms.[19] These studies are notable for their scope. They can reveal the existence of global trends and patterns that other studies are unable to show, and are able to make more general statements about the effectiveness of transitional justice that may be skewed by smaller studies of cases that may, in reality, be outliers.

The findings of these works to date, however, have been mixed. Studies have found conversely that trials and truth commissions are both positive for human rights, that truth commissions have a negative effect on democracy and human rights, that trials and amnesties when used in combination are the most beneficial, and that transitional justice has little effect on levels of peace.[20] These inconsistencies are due in part to some significant limitations in this type of research. To statistically test for the effectiveness of transitional justice, scholars typically use very blunt measures of mechanisms – for example, whether a country used a truth commission or not – ignoring significant variations in their type and quality. Moreover, the outcomes of interest are drawn from other existing datasets, all of which have their own inherent flaws. To measure a country's level of democracy in a given year, for example, most scholars use the 20-point 'Polity Score' from the Polity IV dataset maintained by the Center for Systemic Peace, which ranges from –10 (fully autocratic) to 10 (fully democratic).[21] Yet many in the field have questioned whether the dataset accurately captures the aspects of a regime necessary to assess its level of democracy.[22] Scholars also disagree on how to define mechanisms and how to select which cases to include (having different methodologies to determine which countries experienced transitions to democracy, for example), leading to very different sets of data to examine the same questions. Finally, the element of time is contested here. Does it make sense to examine levels of democracy and human rights records for countries five years after they

---

19 Tricia D Olsen, Leigh A Payne and Andrew G Reiter, 'Transitional Justice in the World, 1970–2007: Insights from a New Dataset' (2010) 47(6) *Journal of Peace Research* 803; Helga Malmin Binningsbø et al, 'Armed Conflict and Post-Conflict Justice, 1946–2006: A Dataset' (2012) 49(5) *Journal of Peace Research* 731; *Transitional Justice Research Collaborative* (September 2012) Transitional Justice Data <www.transitional justicedata.com>.

20 Oskar NT Thoms, James Ron and Roland Paris, 'State-Level Effects of Transitional Justice: What Do We Know?' (2010) 4(3) *International Journal of Transitional Justice* 329.

21 Monty Marshall and Keith Jaggers, *Polity IV Project: Political Regime Characteristics and Transitions 1800–2013* (6 June 2014) Systemic Peace <http://www.systemicpeace.org/polity/polity4.htm>.

22 See, e.g., Kristian S Gleditsch and Michael D Ward, 'Double Take: A Reexamination of Democracy and Autocracy in Modern Polities' (1997) 41(3) *Journal of Conflict Resolution* 361.

transitioned to democracy? Ten? Twenty? How long does a country have to avoid renewed civil war to be able to say that it has achieved peace?

While these limitations will never be completely overcome, quantitative cross-national studies are becoming more reliable. New data collection efforts are producing more nuanced measures of transitional justice mechanisms, and statistical techniques are becoming far more sophisticated. Most importantly, even where these types of studies are limited, they serve as valuable direction pointers for researchers working at the micro and meso levels of analysis, identifying key variables that should be studied further, and highlighting case studies that would be valuable to the field.

Some scholars have further broadened this national level approach to examine global trends in transitional justice use and impact. In doing so, they ask two primary questions. First, are there patterns or trends in state behaviour that suggest the presence of global transitional justice norms? Second, are those new norms successful in creating a global deterrent that is improving human rights and preventing atrocity?

As discussed in Chapter 2, several international relations scholars, most prominently Kathryn Sikkink, have argued that a justice cascade now exists in the world, whereby states are increasingly holding perpetrators of human rights violations accountable for their actions. Some of the evidence for this centres on the advent of UN-led criminal tribunals following the end of the Cold War, the creation of the International Criminal Court, and the prominence of new doctrines, such as the Responsibility to Protect, in international political and legal discourse. Yet much of the argument is buttressed by quantitative analysis of global databases of transitional justice mechanisms. Using a global database of judicial proceedings for individual criminal responsibility for past human rights violations, Sikkink demonstrates a dramatic increase in the pursuit of justice around the world beginning in the early 1990s.[23] There is debate, however, within the scholarly community on the extent of this trend. There have been far more countries transitioning to democracy since the early 1990s, and so some of the global increase in the number of trials may simply be due to there being more opportunities for trials – the rate by which transitioning countries pursue prosecutions may not have changed as much over time as we assume. In addition, by counting all years in which prosecutions are underway, the database perhaps exaggerates the rise of justice, and different databases, focusing on verdicts only, find less of an increase.[24] Moreover, analysis of databases of amnesty laws also

---

23 Kathryn Sikkink, *The Justice Cascade: How Human Rights Prosecutions Are Changing World Politics* (Norton, 2011).

24 Tricia D Olsen, Leigh A Payne, and Andrew G Reiter, *Transitional Justice in Balance: Comparing Processes, Weighing Efficacy* (United States Institute of Peace Press, 2010).

finds an upsurge in recent decades, a trend that would seem to stand in opposition to the norms behind the justice cascade.[25] A new collaborative research project, based on the creation of a new global database of transitional justice mechanisms, is currently underway with the aim of shedding more light on these issues.[26]

Assessing the extent to which the rise of accountability has served as a global deterrent is even more difficult. As discussed above, evidence about the impact of transitional justice on peace, democracy, and human rights within individual countries is mixed. Moreover, the extension of this to the global level is part of a socialisation process that admittedly will require time, even a generation or more, to take hold. Researchers are, however, beginning to examine recent downward trends in war and improvements in human rights, and transitional justice may be one component of a larger set of factors working together to make the world less violent.[27]

Case study: The impact of transitional justice in Guatemala

In 1954, Guatemalan President Jacobo Árbenz was deposed in a US-sponsored military coup. A series of conservative and anti-Communist military governments followed, leading to armed resistance from the left. By the mid-1960s a full-fledged civil war had developed. In the early 1980s fighting between a new military regime, led by General Efraín Ríos Montt, and the now united Guatemalan National Revolutionary Unity rebels intensified, with the military engaging in a 'scorched-earth pacification campaign' against the rural, predominantly Mayan, population. Forced disappearances were widespread, and it is estimated that the conflict left up to 200,000 people dead or missing. A slow transition to democracy began in 1986, and a peace agreement formally ended the conflict a decade later in 1996.

Following the end of the conflict and the transition to democracy, transitional justice efforts were widespread. The peace accords included the Law on National Reconciliation, which provided an amnesty for both sides of the conflict for all crimes except genocide and other serious crimes against humanity under international law. The accords also created the Commission for Historical Clarification to investigate crimes committed during the civil war. It began operation in 1997 and produced a final report in February 1999. Later, in 2004 a major reparations programme, the National Reparations Commission, was created, with the goal of awarding nearly $500 million in payments to victims. In addition, a DNA databank has been established to help identify remains to return them to their families. Trials were sporadic for the first decade following the end of the war, but have picked up in recent years, including a high-profile conviction of

(continued)

---

25 Mallinder, above n 15.
26 *Transitional Justice Research Collaborative*, above n 19.
27 Joshua S Goldstein, *Winning the War on War: The Decline of Armed Conflict Worldwide* (Dutton, 2011).

(continued)

Montt for genocide in 2013, though the ruling was subsequently overturned by the Constitutional Court.[28]

There has been a corresponding amount of research into whether or not all of these transitional justice initiatives have been successful. At the macro level, research has generally highlighted Guatemala's success. There have been no authoritarian reversals, measures of democracy illustrate significant improvement from the mid-1980s to present, human rights protections have improved moderately, and the peace agreement has remained intact and there has been no renewed warfare. Moreover, the truth commission was influential throughout Latin America, and Montt became the first former head of state to be convicted of genocide in his own country, suggesting that Guatemala is adding its own streams to the rising justice cascade.

At the meso and micro levels, however, the assessment of Guatemala's transitional justice has been more mixed. The truth commission was received well by the human rights community in Guatemala, and its hard-hitting final report revealed the true extent of the conflict that had been downplayed by the government, and stated clearly that genocide had been perpetrated.[29] Yet Priscilla Hayner notes that it led to few prosecutions, no subsequent vetting programmes, and despite the eventual disbanding of some security forces most of its recommendations remain unimplemented.[30] Likewise, the new Human Rights Ombudsmen office created following the conflict has been criticised for being ineffective,[31] and the need for a retrial of Montt demonstrates the lack of judicial reform to date.

Moreover, scholars studying local initiatives at social reconstruction have criticised these national transitional justice mechanisms, noting that it is 'not clear how much difference these efforts – while necessary – have made in people's daily experience'.[32] They contend that national-level efforts have failed to capture the meaning of the conflict for those affected by the violence, and argue that national transitional justice programmes need to more effectively complement local efforts to heal the deeply divided society. The reparations programme in particular has been criticised for not being sufficiently locally contextualised.[33] The outcomes used at the macro level miss the fact that Guatemala is now dominated by criminal gangs and has one of the highest homicide rates in the world,

---

28 Elizabeth Malkin, 'Guatemalan Court Overturns Genocide Conviction of Ex-Dictator' *New York Times* (online), 20 May 2013 <http://www.nytimes.com/2013/05/21/world/americas/guatemalas-highest-court-overturns-genocide-conviction-of-former-dictator.html?_r=0>.

29 Christian Tomuschat, 'Clarification Commission in Guatemala' (2001) 23(2) *Human Rights Quarterly* 233.

30 Hayner, above n 12, 281.

31 Michael Dodson and Donald W Jackson, 'Horizontal Accountability in Transitional Democracies: The Human Rights Ombudsman in El Salvador and Guatemala' (2004) 46(4) *Latin American Politics and Society* 1.

32 Laura J Arriaza and Naomi Roht-Arriaza, 'Weaving a Braid of Histories: Local Post-Armed Conflict Initiatives in Guatemala' in Rosalind Shaw and Lars Waldorf (eds), *Localizing Transitional Justice: Interventions and Priorities after Mass Violence* (Stanford University Press, 2010) 205, 206.

33 Lieselotte Viaene, 'Life Is Priceless: Mayan Q'eqchi' Voices on the Guatemalan National Reparations Programme' (2010) 4(1) *International Journal of Transitional Justice* 4.

and that at the local level society remains deeply divided. Most researchers conclude that Guatemala is certainly better off today for engaging in its varied transitional justice efforts, but that its journey to truly reconcile from its past is just beginning.

13.6 Is doing something better than nothing?

As the discussion in this chapter should have made clear, despite a variety of approaches and methods, existing studies on the impact of transitional justice have been mixed and unconvincing. More rigorous research and new methodological approaches will certainly help, and mixed-method and multi-level research will provide the fullest picture of transitional justice processes. In addition, the passing of time will allow for follow-up interviews, longitudinal surveys, and a greater number of observations for statistical models. In the future, we will thus be able to say more about the extent to which transitional justice works than we can today.

Yet we may always be destined to feel unsatisfied with the ability of transitional justice to accomplish its goals. In part, this may be due to the goal or outcome-oriented view of transitional justice held by most researchers and policymakers. McAdams contends that transitional justice may be better conceptualised as a 'process in which the outcome is uncertain but the undertaking is valued in itself'.[34] In other words, we may not ever truly achieve justice or truth or reconciliation. Transitional justice may never be over or completed. Yet the process of wrestling with the past itself may be positive, indeed vital, for democratic societies. In this view, transitional justice may work simply by continually being pursued.

13.7 Summary

Evaluating the impact of transitional justice has become a central goal of scholars and policymakers. In assessing whether or not transitional justice works, researchers focus on a variety of outcomes at three distinct levels of analysis. At the individual or micro level, researchers use ethnographic studies, interviews, and surveys to determine how specific mechanisms impact the lives of victims and perpetrators, how they are perceived by different segments of the population, and the extent to which they alter views and bring about reconciliation within the society at large. At the meso or institutional level, researchers use a variety of qualitative and quantitative methods to evaluate the quality of specific

---

34 A James McAdams, 'Transitional Justice: The Issue That Won't Go Away' (2011) 5(2) *International Journal of Transitional Justice* 304, 312.

transitional justice mechanisms and to assess whether or not they achieve their stated goals. Finally, at the macro or national level, studies of transitional justice impact typically rely on quantitative, statistical methods to determine if particular choices are correlated with long-term success on measures of democracy and human rights. Some researchers have also begun to examine global trends in transitional justice and the possibility that new norms are successful in improving democracy and human rights worldwide. Each approach has its strengths and weaknesses, and research on transitional justice impact overall is hindered by the difficulty of defining and measuring important concepts like democracy and reconciliation. Even if convincing evidence of transitional justice impact remains elusive, however, there may still be important reasons to pursue these mechanisms in post-conflict and post-authoritarian societies.

13.8 Discussion and tutorial questions

You are proposing a new study to determine if a transitional justice mechanism works. Select one mechanism, perhaps something that has been in the news recently, one on which you are conducting research, or one from course readings.

1) What outcomes are you most interested in seeing if this mechanism produces? What level of analysis is this? How would you define or measure this outcome?

2) What kind of research would you have to conduct to see if the mechanism has been successful? Briefly outline what your study would look like.

3) What are the limitations of your approach? What other types of research might be useful to complement your study?

Suggested reading

Palmer, Nicola, Julia Viebach, Briony Jones, Zoe Norridge, Andrea Grant, Alisha Patel, Leila Ullrich, Djeyoun Ostowar and Phyllis Ferguson, *Transitional Justice Methods Manual: An Exchange on Researching and Assessing Transitional Justice* (Swisspeace and Oxford Transitional Justice Research, 2013) ‹http://www.swisspeace.ch/fileadmin/user_upload/ Media/Publications/TJ_Methods_Manual_homepage.pdf›.

Thoms, Oskar NT, James Ron and Roland Paris, 'State-Level Effects of Transitional Justice: What Do We Know?' (2010) 4(3) *International Journal of Transitional Justice*.

van de Merwe, Hugo, Victoria Baxter and Audrey R Chapman (eds), *Assessing the Impact of Transitional Justice: Challenges for Empirical Research* (United States Institute of Peace Press, 2009).

Suggested film

Seeking Truth in the Balkans (Directed and Produced by Erin Lovall and June Vutrano, 2014, available at http://www.seekingtruthinthebalkans.com/home.html).

Bibliography

Arriaza, Laura J and Naomi Roht-Arriaza, 'Weaving a Braid of Histories: Local Post-Armed Conflict Initiatives in Guatemala' in Rosalind Shaw and Lars Waldorf (eds), *Localizing Transitional Justice: Interventions and Priorities after Mass Violence* (Stanford University Press, 2010).

Backer, David and Anu Kulkarni, *West African Transitional Justice Project* ‹https://www. wm. edu/as/government/research/undergraduateresearch/watj/index.php›.

Binningsbø, Helga Malmin, Cyanne Loyle, Scott Gates and Jon Elster, 'Armed Conflict and Post-Conflict Justice, 1946–2006: A Dataset' (2012) 49(5) *Journal of Peace Research*.

Cammack, Diana, 'Reparations in Malawi' in Pablo de Greiff (ed), *The Handbook of Reparations* (Oxford University Press, 2006).

Collins, Cath, Lorena Balardini and Jo Marie Burt, 'Mapping Perpetrator Prosecutions in Latin America' (2013) 7(1) *International Journal of Transitional Justice*.

de Brito, Alexandra Barahona, Carmen González-Enríquez and Paloma Aguilar (eds), *The Politics of Memory: Transitional Justice in Democratizing Societies* (Oxford University Press, 2001).

de Greiff, Pablo (ed), *The Handbook of Reparations* (Oxford University Press, 2006).

Dodson, Michael and Donald W Jackson, 'Horizontal Accountability in Transitional Democracies: The Human Rights Ombudsman in El Salvador and Guatemala' (2004) 46(4) *Latin American Politics and Society*.

Gleditsch, Kristian S and Michael D Ward, 'Double Take: A Reexamination of Democracy and Autocracy in Modern Polities' (1997) 41(3) *Journal of Conflict Resolution*.

Goldstein, Joshua S, *Winning the War on War: The Decline of Armed Conflict Worldwide* (Dutton, 2011).

Hamber, Brandon and Richard A Wilson, 'Symbolic Closure through Memory, Reparation and Revenge in Post-Conflict Societies' (2002) 1(1) *Journal of Human Rights*.

Hayden, Robert M, *From Yugoslavia to the Western Balkans: Studies of a European Disunion, 1991–2011* (Brill, 2013).

Hayner, Priscilla, *Unspeakable Truths: Transitional Justice and the Challenge of Truth Commissions* (Routledge, 2nd ed, 2011).

Krog, Antjie, '"This Thing Called Reconciliation . . . " Forgiveness as Part of an Interconnectedness-Towards-Wholeness' (2008) 27(4) *South African Journal of Philosophy*.

McAdams, A James, 'Transitional Justice: The Issue That Won't Go Away' (2011) 5(2) *International Journal of Transitional Justice*.

Malkin, Elizabeth, 'Guatemalan Court Overturns Genocide Conviction of Ex-Dictator' *New York Times* (online), 20 May 2013 ‹http://www.nytimes.com/2013/05/21/ world/americas/ guatemalas-highest-court-overturns-genocide-conviction-of-former-dictator.html?_r=0›.

Mallinder, Louise, *Amnesty, Human Rights and Political Transitions: Bridging the Peace and Justice Divide* (Hart Publishing, 2008).

Marshall, Monty and Keith Jaggers, *Polity IV Project: Political Regime Characteristics and Transitions 1800–2013* (6 June 2014) Systemic Peace ‹http://www.system icpeace.org/ polity/polity4.htm›.

Mayer-Rieckh, Alexander and Pablo de Greiff (eds), *Justice as Prevention: Vetting Public Employees in Transitional Societies* (Social Science Research Council, 2007).

Mejía, Raúl Molina, 'The Struggle against Impunity in Guatemala' (1999) 26(4) *Social Justice*.

Millar, Gearoid, 'Local Evaluations of Justice through Truth Telling in Sierra Leone' (2011) 12(4) *Human Rights Review*.

Olsen, Tricia D, Leigh A Payne and Andrew G Reiter, 'Transitional Justice in the World, 1970–2007: Insights from a New Dataset' (2010) 47(6) *Journal of Peace Research*.

Olsen, Tricia D, Leigh A Payne and Andrew G Reiter, *Transitional Justice in Balance: Comparing Processes, Weighing Efficacy* (United States Institute of Peace Press, 2010).

Payne, Leigh A, *Uncivil Movements: The Armed Right Wing and Democracy in Latin America* (Johns Hopkins University Press, 2000).

Pham, Phuong, Patrick Vinck, Mychelle Balthazard and Sokhom Hean, *After the First Trial: A Population-Based Survey on Knowledge and Perceptions of Justice and the Extraordinary Chambers in the Courts of Cambodia* (Human Rights Center, University of California, Berkeley, 2011) ‹https://www.law.berkeley. edu/files/HRC/Publications_ After-the-First-Trial_06-2011.pdf›.

Sanford, Victoria, *Buried Secrets: Truth and Human Rights in Guatemala* (Palgrave Macmillan, 2003).

Sikkink, Kathryn, *The Justice Cascade: How Human Rights Prosecutions Are Changing World Politics* (Norton, 2011).

Snyder, Jack and Leslie Vinjamuri, 'Trials and Errors: Principle and Pragmatism in Strategies of International Justice' (2003–04) 28(3) *International Security*.

Thoms, Oskar NT, James Ron and Roland Paris, 'State-Level Effects of Transitional Justice: What Do We Know?' (2010) 4(3) *International Journal of Transitional Justice*.

Tomuschat, Christian, 'Clarification Commission in Guatemala' (2001) 23(2) *Human Rights Quarterly*.

Transitional Justice Research Collaborative (September 2012) Transitional Justice Data ‹www.transitionaljusticedata.com›.

United Nations, 'Guidance Note of the Secretary-General: United Nations Approach to Transitional Justice' (10 March 2010).

Viaene, Lieselotte, 'Life Is Priceless: Mayan Q'eqchi' Voices on the Guatemalan National Reparations Programme' (2010) 4(1) *International Journal of Transitional Justice*.

Wale, Kim, *Confronting Exclusion: Time for Radical Reconciliation, SA Reconciliation Barometer Survey: 2013 Report* (Institute for Justice and Reconciliation, 2013) ‹http://reconciliationbarometer.org/wp-content/uploads/2013/12/IJR-Barometer-Report-2013-22Nov1635.pdf›.

Chapter 14

Doing the fieldwork: well-being of transitional justice researchers[1]

Olivera Simić

14.1 Introduction

> Although I know that it is terribly unprofessional, I have held hands with my inter-
> viewees and wept openly with them – if a woman is talking about her experience
> being gang-raped, or about her child being abducted, how can I remain passively
> un-engaged? I know there's a fine line about emotional engagement in this kind
> of work, but I can't figure out where that line is and how to properly negotiate it.[2]

Transitional justice research involves critical examination of difficult topics that
can raise ethical and methodological issues for researchers. Empirical research
is a common approach to transitional justice studies in the field, yet researchers'
accounts of the tensions that can arise when undertaking research in politically
sensitive environments are largely missing from the scholarly literature. This
chapter aims to introduce you to the myriad ways in which researching sensitive topics may affect researchers, and to bring attention to strategies used by
researchers to negotiate these challenges. The chapter concludes with some suggestions for improving the well-being of researchers when working with difficult
topics in the field.

Although a relatively young field of inquiry, we know that transitional
justice has received significant attention from anthropologists, psychologists,
lawyers, and others interested in understanding and critically evaluating how

---

1 This is a revised and updated version of papers that first appeared as Olivera Simić,
  'Feminist Research in Transitional Justice Studies: Navigating Silences and Disruptions in the
  Field' (2016) 17(1) *Human Rights Review* 95 and Olivera Simić, '"Doing the Research I Do Has Left
  Scars": Challenges of Researching in Transitional Justice Field' *Transitional Justice Review*
  (forthcoming, 2016).
2 Female participant in the study I conducted about well-being of researchers in February 2015.

individuals and societies deal with past human rights abuses in societies in transition to democracy and the rule of law. Yet despite the significant number of qualitative research studies that have been undertaken on mechanisms and actors, scant attention has been paid to the personal challenges posed by the research process in transitional, conflict and post-conflict contexts.[3] As in other social science fields, transitional justice research 'stories' have been 'treated lightly' and left to be 'told informally',[4] over conference dinners and coffee breaks, rather than framed as methodological issues demanding serious and systematic consideration.

As Stephen Tomsen notes in relation to the limited extent that personal stories are shared amongst researchers in the field of criminology:

> Over dinner and late drinks at research conferences, many of us have realised that others have shared similar difficulties that are sharpened in the case of qualitative studies. Yet these are mostly not articulated, discussed or theorised . . . even the strong contemporary criminological interest in emotions and criminal justice issues has not done much to reverse this collective silence . . .[5]

Similarly, Kimberly Theidon suggests that 'the dinner party moment became a leitmotif' for researchers who conduct research on violence. She talked to researchers about their strategies of emotional and psychological self-care while in the field, and also upon returning and writing their research. Theidon recalls a story of a colleague who was doing well for a long time after his return from Bosnia and Herzegovina (BiH) where he conducted one hundred interviews about the Srebrenica massacre. When asking him a question about his strategies of self-care, Theidon noted that, 'he found himself welling up, bursting into tears, sobbing. He . . . has been caught off guard.'[6]

---

3 Valuable contributions in identifying challenges in conducting qualitative research in difficult circumstances come from other fields of study, in particular anthropology. For some good reflections on the difficulties of research in conflict and post-conflict, see, e.g., Gearoid Millar, *An Ethnographic Approach to Peacebuilding: Understanding Local Experiences in Transitional States* (London, Routledge, 2014); Dyan Mazurana and Karen Jacobsen (eds), *Research Methods in Conflict Settings: A View from Below* (Cambridge: Cambridge University Press, 2013); Chandra Lekha Sriram et al (eds), *Surviving Field Research: Working in Violent and Difficult Situations* (Routledge, 2009); Carolyn Nordstrom and Antonius CGM Robben (eds), *Fieldwork Under Fire: Contemporary Studies of Violence and Survival* (University of California Press, 1995).

4 For more, see Raymond M Lee and Elizabeth A Stanko (eds), *Researching Violence: Essays on Methodology and Measurement* (Routledge, 2003) 4.

5 Stephen Tomsen, 'Foreword: The Collective Remembering of the Stories of Qualitative Criminology' in Lorana Bartels and Kelly Richards (eds), *Qualitative Criminology: Stories from the Field* (Hawkins Press, 2011) v, vii.

6 Kimberly Theidon, '"How Was Your Trip?" Self-Care for Researchers Working and Writing on Violence' (Working Paper on Research Security No. 2, Social Science Research Council, April 2014) 1.

For many researchers, being on guard may be an important coping strategy that allows them to distance themselves from the research topic and its subjects, but once they return from the field it may be harder to compartmentalise their experiences. They will try to do it to protect their families and friends from the details of what they have heard or seen, but it would not be possible to keep those experiences at bay all the time. Sometimes a sound, smell or memory will bring up uninvited memories.[7]

Silence about the various obstacles that scholars have encountered during their qualitative research process has become a feature of the transitional justice field. Where sensitive issues are divulged in the research process, it is important for the researcher to understand the possible effects upon themselves as the recipient of that information. Heather McCosker, Alan Barnard, and Rod Gerber state that the minimisation of harm to the researcher is a significant ethical consideration, and that researchers must be able to debrief where research and data may impact the psychological and physical health of all participants.[8] This chapter aims to bring some of these issues to the fore.

14.2 Difficulties of researching violence and its effects on emotional well-being

While an increasing number of academics and researchers seek to analyse causes and responses to atrocities, they may not be well prepared to undertake fieldwork in politically and economically fragile and unstable societies. It is common for qualitative researchers to report on the context they are studying by taking detailed field notes about the setting and the interviews they have conducted.[9] However, it is less common for these researchers to report on personal challenges they have encountered during the research process. Researchers of transitional justice processes often must pay close attention to painful human experiences and listen to stories of intense suffering and injustice which may personally affect them. They may need to see the world through another person's eyes,[10] which can require techniques for navigating and absorbing life stories that can be deeply disturbing. While researchers are expected to maintain a certain detachment from

---

7 Ibid.
8 Heather McCosker, Alan Barnard and Rod Gerber, 'Undertaking Sensitive Research: Issues and Strategies for Meeting the Safety Needs of All Participants' (2001) 2(1) *Forum: Qualitative Social Research* Art 22, 1, 2–6.
9 Virginia Dickson-Smith, Erica Lyn James, and Pranee Liamputtong, *Undertaking Sensitive Research in the Health and Social Sciences: Managing Boundaries, Emotions and Risks* (Cambridge University Press, 2008) 38.
10 Jenny Fleming, 'Learning to Work Together: Police and Academics' (2010) 4(2) *Policing* 139.

their participants, they must weight this against the empathy required to grasp the world from another's perspective.[11]

Research in conflict and/or post-conflict societies often confronts fieldworkers with difficult questions[12] by disturbing their basic expectations, hopes and assumptions. Although Academic Ethics Committees will normally act as gatekeepers as part of a systematic effort to protect from harm the researchers and the individuals and/or groups who form the research sample,[13] researchers frequently find themselves facing challenges that are difficult to predict and/or manage on the ground.

In such complex political environments, researchers need to take particular care of their personal well-being and that of their interviewees, who may belong to highly vulnerable and stigmatised groups, such as victims of genocide, rape, torture or other war crimes. Researchers are expected to be experts in the context they research, with all of its laden complexities, including navigating the contested divisions between 'victims' and 'perpetrators'. A lack of local language skills or social networks can heighten the risk of 'being instrumentalized and unconsciously becoming the voice' of either non-state actors or government.[14]

Max Weber was among the first to write about personal involvement in research. He maintained that social scientists need to be clear about their own ideas and values, and how these will affect their work.[15] While one may argue that all researchers 'are to some degree connected to, or part of, the object of their research',[16] some topics of research are more sensitive than others. For some researchers, sensitive research is considered to connote a study that has emotional, political and social implications. Joan Sieber and Barbara Stanley define socially sensitive research as:

[s]tudies in which there are potential consequences or implications, either directly for the participants in research or for the class of individuals represented by the research. Such studies may lead to a shift in public policy and it might also affect people's attitude towards a particular group.[17]

11 Antonius CGM Robben, 'The Politics of Truth and Emotion among Victims and Perpetrators of Violence' in Antonius CGM Robben and Jeffrey A Sluka (eds), *Ethnographic Fieldwork: An Anthropological Reader* (John Wiley & Sons, 2nd ed, 2012). See also Roy F Ellen (ed), *Ethnographic Research: A Guide to General Conduct* (Academic Press, 1984) 227.
12 Sarah MH Nouwen, '"As You Set Out for Ithaka": Practical, Epistemological, Ethical, and Existential Questions about Socio-Legal Empirical Research in Conflict' (2014) 27(1) *Leiden Journal of International Law* 227.
13 McCosker, Barnard and Gerber, above n 8, 1–14.
14 Maria-Joëlle Zahar, 'Fieldwork, Objectivity and Academic Enterprise' in Sriram et al, above n 3, 256.
15 Max Weber, *Methodology of Social Sciences* (Free Press, 1949).
16 Charlotte Aull Davies, *Reflexive Ethnography: A Guide to Researching Selves and Others* (Routledge, 2nd ed, 2008) 3.
17 Joan E Sieber and Barbara Stanley, 'Ethical and Professional Dimensions of Socially Sensitive Research' (1988) 43(1) *American Psychologists* 49.

Claire Renzetti and Raymond Lee define a sensitive research topic as one that is 'intimate, discreditable or incriminating'.[18] Lee puts forward another definition of sensitive research that encompasses the topic, the consequences, the situation and any number of other issues that may arise, by saying that sensitive research is 'research which potentially poses a substantial threat to those who are or have been involved in it'.[19] This definition suggests that sensitive research has the potential to impact all of the people involved, including the researchers, since qualitative researchers immerse themselves in the settings they are studying. Researchers form personal interactions and connections with participants of their research, which may affect them in various ways. Indeed, undertaking sensitive research may leave researchers, as Claire Melrose contends, 'feeling methodologically vulnerable . . . because of emotional and anxiety challenges . . . that may arise in this context'.[20]

Lee proposes that sensitive research can be seen as threatening in three broad areas. The first of these areas is 'intrusive threat', which deals with areas that are 'private, stressful or sacred'.[21] As Rebecca Campbell writes 'our emotions influence our research, and our research can affect us emotionally'.[22] It is important to examine the feelings and emotional impact that research has on researchers since it can provide us with a deeper intellectual understanding of the social phenomenon we analyse.[23] The second type of threat is a 'threat of sanction', which relates to studies of deviance and involves the possibility that research may reveal information that is stigmatising or incriminating in some way. The third type of threat that may be imposed by sensitive research is a 'political threat'.[24] This refers to the 'vested interests' of the powerful in society, and in these situations researchers may trespass into areas that involve some sort of social conflict.

Tsai argues that political sensitivity is always a challenge for the researcher doing fieldwork in non-democratic and transitional systems, especially when doing surveys and quantitative research. She notes that not only are more research topics likely to be politically sensitive in these systems, but in trying to collect precise and unbiased data, researchers are often doing what the government, and

---

18 Claire M Renzetti and Raymond M Lee (eds), *Researching Sensitive Topics* (SAGE Publications, 1993) ix.

19 Raymond M Lee, *Doing Research on Sensitive Topics* (SAGE Publications, 1993) 4.

20 Margaret Melrose, 'Labor Pains: Some Considerations on the Difficulties of Researching Juvenile Prostitution' (2002) 5(4) *International Journal of Social Research Methodology* 333, 338.

21 Lee, above n 19, 4.

22 Rebecca Campbell, *Emotionally Involved: The Impact of Researching Rape* (Routledge, 2001) 15.

23 Ibid.

24 Lee, above n 19, 4.

sometimes certain members of that population, would like to prevent.[25] Jelena Subotić provides a profound personal account of threats she received after publicly speaking about the politics in Serbia over Kosovo's self-proclaimed independence. Her experience demonstrates the necessity as she puts it, 'to look more systematically at how researchers' identities – as perceived by their informants and their critics – define the analytical tools and barriers to research'.[26]

Sensitive research may leave researchers who are working with particularly traumatic materials subject to a degree of vicarious traumatisation, in which they may begin to experience the effects of traumatisation themselves.[27] Researchers who work in the field often undertake empirical studies with highly vulnerable populations, and their time can be demanding and challenging, testing the researchers' emotional and psychological well-being.[28] Their repeated exposure to traumatic stories, materials and images can produce symptoms similar to those of the trauma victims they research about.

Case study A: Researchers' experiences

The purpose of the study I conducted in February 2015 was to find out about the range of emotional challenges faced by researchers in the transitional justice field while undertaking empirical research in the field.[29] I used an email-questionnaire as the primary data collection method. The interest expressed in the research project was overwhelming. While questionnaires are often plagued by low response rates, in a span of only five days I received 35 responses. In total, I received 29 full responses to the questionnaire. The distribution of gender was 23 female and six male participants. Participants were based in Australia (5), the USA (3), the UK (8), Germany (2), Sweden (1), Macedonia (2), Hungary (1), Croatia (2), India (1), South Africa (2), Rwanda (1) and Canada (1). Participants came from the fields of psychology, politics, anthropology, sociology, gender studies and law. Some of the participants were early career, while others had over 20 years of experience researching sensitive topics. All of the researchers, apart from one, conduct qualitative studies with vulnerable groups and spend considerable time undertaking fieldwork.

25 Lily L Tsai, 'Quantitative Research and Issue of Political Sensitivity in Rural China' in Allen Carlson et al (eds), *Contemporary Chinese Politics: New Sources, Methods, and Field Strategies* (Cambridge University Press, 2010) 246.

26 Jelena Subotić, 'No Escape from Ethnicity? Confessions of an Accidental CNN Pundit' (2010) 43(1) *PS: Political Science & Politics* 115, 120.

27 Laura J Schauben and Patricia A Frazier, 'Vicarious Trauma: The Effect on Female Counsellors Working with Sexual Violence Survivors' (1995) 19(1) *Psychology of Women Quarterly* 49.

28 Dinka Čorkalo Biruški, 'Etički Izazovi Kvalitativnih Istraživanja u Zajednici: Od Planiranja do Istraživačkog Izvještaja' (2014) 21(3) *Ljetopis Socijalnog Rada* 93.

29 For full details of the study, see Simić, '"Doing the Research I Do Has Left Scars": Challenges of Researching in Transitional Justice Field', above n 1.

Perhaps not surprisingly, a majority of researchers reported that their research affects them emotionally. All participants wrote about diverse emotions that their research settings produce:

I currently feel that my research mostly affects me emotionally. Many of the accounts of conflict-related sexual violence in general . . . are oftentimes extremely graphic and explicit, which obviously often leaves horrific impressions . . .

I collect women's oral narratives to capture women's unique experiences in doing justice . . . These women's . . . knowledge and experiences . . . makes me humble, respectful and privileged but also angry leaving me with a great feeling of inadequacy and despair as I watch ongoing injustices . . . I try to stay attuned to the lived realities of these women which in turn affects me emotionally and politically.

[A]spects of my research affect me emotionally . . . I would find it hard to write about without feeling affected by the material . . .

I am currently working with rape victims . . . It is a subject that I have wanted to tackle for a long time but somehow I never felt emotionally 'ready' . . . It is not easy and I often think about the people I have spoken to. Sometimes, and particularly when I am alone at night, I do become very emotional . . .

I am . . . engaging in the field with people who have lived through terrible events and often suffered personally, including through the loss of close family. This does have an emotional impact on me . . .

I spent one year researching transitional justice issues in post-genocide Rwanda which affected me a great deal emotionally . . .

I see a lot of pain and suffering. The often times very gruesome stories these individuals share evoke a variety of emotions in me: sadness, anger, frustration, hopelessness to name but a few . . . I also have a lot of very bad dreams in which I re-live the stories people tell me, experiencing their stories first-hand . . .

As Arditti et al argue, 'the distance between researchers and participants is dissolved, *their experience becomes our experience*' [emphasis in original], eliciting profound and very real emotion.[30] In the transitional justice field, the emotional well-being of a qualitative researcher is important to consider given the sensitive nature of the topic, as well as the intimate and intensive nature of some qualitative methods, which may increase risk of harm.[31] These concerns for the

(continued)

---

30 Joyce A Arditti et al, 'The Role of Emotions in Fieldwork: A Self-Study of Family Research in a Correction Setting' (2010) 15(6) *Qualitative Report* 1387, 1388.

31 Kelly Richards and Lorana Bartels, 'The Story Behind the Stories: Qualitative Criminology Research in Australia' in Bartels and Richards, above n 5, 1, 5.

(continued)

participants were echoed by the majority of participants in the study who felt a great responsibility of care for their own participants. Some expressed concerns about the potential re-traumatisation of participants:

> I also struggle with the fact that many of the people I interview have already told their stories to many different organisations and there is a certain level of fatigue about this. Some people have told me bluntly that they do not wish to be interviewed (a decision I am always respectful of).

> Emotionally I often found it hard to sit with people who told their stories from the war(s) . . . and to decide when I should stop them in order not to risk retraumatisation . . .

The researchers struggled as to whether their questions could harm people by asking them to recount traumatic events, and whether participants answering questions on sensitive subjects were being endangered.[32] While this has been well recognised in relation to participants[33] it has rarely been discussed in relation to researchers. Similar views were echoed by some of the participants in the study. For example, one participant commented, 'the concern is disproportionately for the participants in the research and not for the researcher'. The literature in qualitative research has acknowledged the emotional risk for participants, but there is little evidence providing understanding of researchers' emotions.[34] However, the acknowledgement and awareness of one's own emotions is important for both participants and researchers. As another participant noted, 'The fact that I am conscious of my strong feelings . . . makes me able to be respectful of the research participants and their views.'

Participants in the study reported using various strategies to protect themselves from emotional exhaustion by negotiating the topics they research: perhaps purposively changing or modifying topics or methods so they are easier to deal with emotionally, or taking a break from research with physical exercises such as long walks. Others find it harder to break from their research and seek professional help, and one researcher reported that she may leave academia all together. Sharing insights into the risks of doing sensitive research is important, and can help develop strategies into how to cope with some of the challenges. One strategy that may be used to assist with dealing with emotions is a debriefing with the researcher after fieldwork is completed. Such a debriefing will allow the researcher to share feelings and discuss any challenges they may have encountered.

---

32 Lee and Stanko (eds), above n 4, 2.

33 McCosker, Barnard and Gerber, above n 8, 1–14.

34 Gill Hubbard, Kathryn Backett-Milburn and Debbie Kemmer, 'Working with Emotion: Issues for the Researcher in Fieldwork and Teamwork' (2001) 4(2) *International Journal Social Research Methodology* 119.

14.3 'Covering up' our emotions

Researchers such as Ruth Wilkins often reported feeling frustrated by the lack of discussion of the emotional nature of qualitative research: 'I consulted the approved academic and methodologic texts and was astonished at the intellectual cover-up of emotion . . . in the name of expert or academic knowledge.'[35] Betty Ferrell argues that a qualitative consciousness implies that emotions emerging in the field serve to strengthen the research process because feeling is a way of knowing, but researchers in social sciences are not necessarily encouraged to write about them.[36]

There are many reasons why researchers would be reluctant to talk about the personal costs of doing research. One of the most common concerns is that if researchers openly express emotion, their research may be seen as too emotional and subjective, thus devaluing their research.[37] There are tensions between, on the one hand, the normative professional requirement of being an objective observer, and on the other, intellectually honest interrogation of a researcher's emotions while doing research. Researchers may fear breaching the norms of their discipline, and may fear for their reputation: that they are undermining their competency and objectivity; that their research is not 'real' and denounced as 'subjective'. In the field of international law and politics, reflexivity is rare, and while socio-legal research may be more open to reflexivity, peer reviewers often discourage reflexive accounts.[38] Marcia Bellas argues that there are explicit codes of conduct in academia that led to assumption that:

> At first glance, research appears to involve little emotional labor relative to teaching and service. This perception stems from the strong association between science and objectivity, as well as the view that emotions are an impediment or contaminant to the scientific process.[39]

Researchers are expected to write about the facts, the theories and the methods, but not about the personal, ethical and political characteristics of research.[40]

---

35 Ruth Wilkins, 'Taking It Personally: A Note on Emotion and Autobiography' (1993) 27(1) *Sociology* 93–94.

36 Betty Ferrell, 'Ethical Perspectives on Pain and Suffering' (2005) 6(3) *Pain Nursing Management* 83, 89.

37 Sherryl Kleinman, 'Fieldworkers' Feelings: What We Felt, Who We Are, How We Analyze' in William B Shaffir and Robert A Stebbins (eds), *Experiencing Fieldwork: An Inside View of Qualitative Research* (SAGE Publications, 1991) 184.

38 I have experienced such discouragement in a recent peer review of my book proposal. See also Charli Carpenter, '"You Talk of Terrible Things So Matter-of-Factly in This Language of Science": Constructing Human Rights in the Academy' (2012) 10(2) *Perspectives on Politics* 363.

39 Marcia L Bellas, 'Emotional Labor in Academia: The Case of Professors' (1999) 561 *The Annals of the American Academy of Political and Social Science* 96, 104.

40 Nouwen, above n 12, 227; Matthew Lockwood, 'Facts or Fictions? Fieldwork Relationships and the Nature of Data' in Stephen Devereux and John Hoddinott (eds), *Fieldwork in Developing Countries* (Lynne Rienner Publishers, 1992) 164.

Qualitative researchers in the transitional justice field do not readily turn their analytical lenses inwards to reflect on their ethical and methodological journeys and interactions from a personal perspective. The rare few who do disclose in a reflexive way expose themselves to the possibility of being 'accused' of limiting their findings. An even smaller number of academics engage in autobiographical reflection, sometimes due to privacy issues or to avoid the risk of being criticised for 'self-indulgence and intellectually sloppy work' which has, as Letherby argues, 'some basis in reality'.[41] Due to this largely entrenched discourse, personal feelings have often been censored or dismissed in scientific research.[42] Such views are echoed by one participant:

> I was presenting a paper at a large international conference and someone asked me what it was like, as a researcher, to do research on X topic. I started describing how it felt and found myself engulfed by emotion and tears rolling down my cheeks. I remember looking up and no one made eye contact with me, no one said anything and there was silence – people avoided me and I felt in some way that I/ my reaction represented something that shouldn't exist or that I should have been stronger and just buried it.[43]

Partially due to pressure to be perceived as objective scholars, and partially due to the emotional effects that research has on them, many scholars struggle with balancing their personal and professional lives. Learning how to set up boundaries is important for creating a safe space around you, and in that way we stave off burnout.[44] It is not uncommon for researchers after years researching and writing on violence to become overwhelmed with a sense of powerlessness and hopelessness. A few colleagues of mine told me about their decision to stop researching certain topics because they felt disappointed seeing continuation of injustices they have been trying to 'prevent' with their work. Some researchers also feel 'guilt' for not being able to help some of their interlocutors who live in difficult conditions. The feeling of relative privilege that many researchers enjoy is often coupled with this feeling of powerlessness.[45]

---

41 Gayle Letherby, 'Dangerous Liaisons: Auto/Biography in Research and Research Writing' in Geraldine Lee-Treweek and Stephanie Linkogle, *Danger in the Field: Risks and Ethics in Social Research* (Routledge, 2000) 91, 109.

42 Emma Wincup, *Residential Work with Offenders: Reflexive Accounts of Practice* (Ashgate, 2001).

43 See Case Study, 'Researchers' Experiences', in this chapter. For full study see Olivera Simic, '"Doing the Research I Do Has Left Scars": Challenges of Researching in the Transitional Justice Field', above n 1.

44 Theidon, above n 6, 8.

45 Ibid 9.

14.4 Researching in transitional justice contexts

It is important to document and discuss experiences of researchers in the transitional justice field who work on sensitive issues and in contested environments. So far, there has been a lack of systematic research in ethics and methodologies used by researchers in the field. Many of these accounts are informed by informal exchanges of shared experiences with scholars working on sensitive issues. However, while these informal encounters and conversations between researchers are important, the implications of these issues for qualitative research, researchers and research processes merit more serious attention. More space needs to be created for such conversations to take place.

It is important to extend theoretical understanding of transitional justice methods and ethics, and intertwine the academic and theoretical with the personal and subjective. Here the academic self is studied to gain understanding of what it means and what it takes to conduct research in transnational contexts. These insights are important since they can foreshadow issues that may be preventing researchers from pursuing research on certain topics or with particular vulnerable groups. For example, negotiation of well-being may affect the subjects of research, whose voices as a result may be either silenced or reinforced. Lack of support for researchers may mean that some researchers, as some participants in my study self-reported, decide intentionally to cease researching their original ideas or may modify their research projects. As a consequence, they may decide not to invest their expertise where it is direly needed, which in turn may affect the quality and/or quantity of the research and policy-making in countries in transition.

Rather than fixating on objectivity, transitional justice – as a social and human science – should allow for greater, explicit emotional intrusion by a researcher. This would allow the researcher to contribute to deeper levels of analysis of the context in which they research and also allow them to connect their personal observations and stories to wider issues within and outside the discipline. These stories may illuminate the social and political context in which transitional justice researchers work. Situating the stories of researchers of transitional justice within a broader context can help us gain in-depth understanding of the specificities of societies that go through transition. In that sense, studying the personal emotional challenges of researchers is not just a goal to capture emotional and evocative content, but can provide a framework for developing a broader analysis of a given post-conflict, post-dictatorship society.

If we agree that our emotions can influence our research, then not acknowledging them can introduce dangers, since our research can directly feed into policy and law reforms in countries in transition. Paradoxically, the potential significance of our contributions may make us even more resistant to looking inward and speaking about the difficulties we encounter in our work. In contrast to those whose research is focused on difficult themes in peaceful democracies, such as sexual violence or homicide, researchers working in transitional societies may feel more vulnerable and more helpless and hopeless. In the contexts in which transitional justice scholars work, the rule of law is often in its infancy if it exists at all, and the kinds of institutions and non-governmental organisations that should support victims simply do not exist, or if they do, they are extremely underfunded and precarious. In such circumstances structures to provide emotional support to researchers or victims are scarce.

This lack of support has, unfortunately, led to some researchers 'burning out', either leaving research altogether or turning their attention to topics that they perceive as less intrusive and 'dangerous'. There is a need for researchers involved in transitional justice fieldwork to receive systematic support from their respective institutions. Universities and research institutions have a duty of care to ensure that their research staff are not harmed by their participation in research. However, while postgraduate students have regular consultations with supervisors to this effect, experienced researchers usually do not have regular formal supervision and support.

Understanding how emotions can have a negative or positive impact on research, how they might affect our work, and 'who we become as a result' is important.[46] Informal peer or mentor support groups, and regular meetings to discuss the methodological and emotional challenges of qualitative research on sensitive topics could also be considered to minimise the risk to researchers' wellbeing. To approach the issue seriously, universities and research institutions need to put in place systematic provisions for the support of all researchers, whether early career or senior, part-time or full-time.

The study I had undertaken underscores the need and demand for transitional justice researchers to organise conferences and workshops dedicated to issues of ethics and methodology. It may also be possible to develop an online blog that would allow researchers to exchange their experiences from their fieldwork. Doctoral students and early career scholars would benefit from mentors who would guide them through issues that they could encounter in the field and assist in locating a scholar, researcher or organisation in the field that could provide necessary psychological and other support. As reported by the participants of my study, researchers are generally left to their own devices to find solutions to the difficulties they face. Ignoring and repressing feelings may endanger the wellbeing of researchers while also producing distortion of data, rather than clarity.[47]

---

46 Arditti et al, above n 30, 1407.
47 Geraldine Lee-Treweek, 'The Insight of Emotional Danger: Research Experiences in a Home for Older People' in Lee-Treweek and Linkogle, above n 41, 128.

14.5 Why should our stories matter?

The difficulties that I faced, and complexities of doing sensitive research in a deeply divided ethno-nationalist context such as Bosnia and Herzegovina made me think more deeply about the personal risks and costs that transitional justice scholars face. It also reminded me of the necessity that we as researchers 'become aware of our own research activities as *telling ourselves a story about ourselves*' [emphasis in original].[48] Writing about scholars' personal experiences reveals knowledge that has been subjectively constructed. It brings subjective elements into critical analysis of theoretical constructs which may serve as an 'impetus, example and frame' through which researchers can identify sites and opportunities for strategic interventions.[49]

Publishing about our own fieldwork experiences not only humanises the field but also bridges the gap between 'subjects' and 'researchers'. Those scholars who are at the same time 'insiders' and 'outsiders' have not only a unique perspective to offer, but also play an important role in bridging the false dichotomy of 'subjective' and 'objective' researchers. They bring an original contribution of an insider-outsider transitional justice researcher's story that forms unique storied knowledge. They also occupy the dual role of researcher and researched, and are able to turn their gaze both inward and outward.[50]

In my writing I have been inspired and instructed by feminist scholars who have simply refused to accept the dichotomy between the personal and political – critical race theorists such as Patricia Williams and Mari Matsuda, to name a few, who have incorporated first person narratives into their discussions of the law. These and others scholars departed from the academic convention of speaking in the impersonal, 'universal' voice and related incidents they themselves had experienced. As Susan Brison, a scholar, philosopher and a woman who has herself experienced rape and attempted murder writes:

> Some may consider such first-person accounts in academic writing to be self-indulgent, but I consider them a welcome antidote to scholarship that, in the guise of universality, tends to silence those who most need to be heard.[51]

Autobiographical researchers' narratives can help us to map out and unpack the unique journeys of transitional justice scholars and activists. They provide us

---

48 Frederick Steier, *Research and Reflexivity* (SAGE, 1993) 3 (emphasis in original).

49 Louise Morley and Val Walsh, *Breaking Boundaries: Women in Higher Education* (Taylor and Francis, 1995) 1.

50 Loreen N Olson, 'The Role of Voice in the (Re)Construction of a Battered Woman's Identity: An Autoethnography of One Woman's Experience of Abuse' (2004) 27(1) *Women's Studies in Communication* 1, 6.

51 Susan J Brison, *Aftermath: Violence and the Remaking of a Self* (Princeton University Press, 2002) 6.

with important insights into the trajectories underpinning the researching process, and how particular events and moments in time have provided critical junctures in the course of research. Such moments are significant and may indeed be central to the researcher–participant relationship within which the data is elicited and recounted. They are also significant since they can and do influence a particular form of knowledge production.

By being reflexive, researchers not only tell us of the impact of their work on their personal and professional life but they also communicate the relevance and vigour of their work. I believe that by sharing their narratives surrounding research ethics and methodology, scholars add to the value, transparency and impact of their research in multiple ways. Using my own research experience, I explored elsewhere what it takes to do sensitive feminist research with a group of women who are considered an out-group, unpopular victims, non-authentic and non-ideal victims, by a researcher (me) who is at the same time an insider and outsider, and who seeks to disrupt the popular and mainstream discourse that recognises only one victim and one perpetrator in the fragile and ethnically divided country of BiH; a country in which divisions are still very strong, and where no one who thinks outside the box is particularly welcomed.

14.6 Conclusion

While empirical studies are regularly undertaken in the transitional justice field, there is a dearth of research into researchers' perspectives of the methodology and ethics of their research. Minimising the risk to the well-being of those who undertake sensitive research is of paramount importance to the field. It has been acknowledged that it is necessary to validate serious consideration of a transitional justice researcher's well-being during the research process and to signal the complex difficulties that may be encountered during the research process. In this way, it is hoped that researchers can learn from each other and from their 'mistakes', and become better informed and more reflexive scholars.

Similar experiences are to be found with researchers working broadly on sensitive topics, such as health, domestic or child violence and abuse. Some of these common ethical and methodological concerns are inherent in researching sensitive topics and can hardly be avoided. However, certain concerns are unique to transitional justice scholars, who not only work on sensitive issues, but do so in vulnerable socio-political contexts with a high degree of risk to personal safety. Rather than leaving transitional justice researchers to cope with the difficulties they encounter on their own, universities and research institutions should develop programmes of support. As I suggested in this chapter, perhaps informal peer and mentor support groups could be established.

This introductory chapter does not pretend to offer all solutions and outline all methodological and ethical concerns, but serves as an initial contribution and thought-starter about 'the stories behind the stories' of empirical research undertaken in the transitional justice field. It seeks to dismantle the thinking that stories behind research are trivial or essentially personal with no value for the larger researcher community.

14.7 Discussion and tutorial questions

1) Why is there scant study of the methods and ethics of research in the transitional justice field?

2) What are some of the issues that researchers in transitional justice studies need to deal with when conducting their research?

3) What are some of the effects of the research on the emotional well-being of researchers?

4) How do you understand the term 'vicarious trauma'?

5) What are some of the things you can do in order to prepare well for a field trip in politically unstable societies?

6) What are some of the things you can do in order to prepare yourself for reading/writing/interviewing highly vulnerable groups of people?

Suggested reading

Buckley-Zistel, Susanne, 'Ethnographic Research after Violent Conflicts: Personal Reflections on Dilemmas and Challenges' (2007) 10 *Journal of Peace, Conflict & Development*.

Clark, Janine N, 'Fieldwork and Its Ethical Challenges: Reflections from Research in Bosnia' (2012) 34 *Human Rights Quarterly*.

Nouwen, Sarah MH, '"As You Set Out for Ithaka": Practical, Epistemological, Ethical, and Existential Questions about Socio-Legal Empirical Research in Conflict' (2004) 27(1) *Leiden Journal of International Law*.

Rogers-Brown, Jennifer B, 'More Than a War Story: A Feminist Analysis of Doing Dangerous Fieldwork' in Vasilikie Demos and Marcia Texler Segal (eds) *At the Center: Feminism, Social Science and Knowledge (Advances in Gender Research, vol 20)* (Emerald Group Publishing, 2015).

Simić, Olivera, 'A Tour to a Site of Genocide: Mothers, Borders and Bones' (2008) 9(3) *Journal of International Women's Studies*.

Wamai, Njoki, 'First Contact with the Field: Experiences of an Early Career Researcher in the Context of National and International Politics in Kenya' (2014) 6(2) *Journal of Human Rights Practice*.

Bibliography

Arditti, Joyce A, Karen S Joest, Jennifer Lambert-Shute and Latanya Walker, 'The Role of Emotions in Fieldwork: A Self-Study of Family Research in a Correction Setting' (2010) 15(6) *Qualitative Report*.

Bartels, Lorana and Kelly Richards (eds), *Qualitative Criminology: Stories from the Field* (Hawkins Press, 2011).

Bellas, Marcia L, 'Emotional Labor in Academia: The Case of Professors' (1999) 561 *The Annals of the American Academy of Political and Social Science* 96.

Biruški, Dinka Čorkalo, 'Etički Izazovi Kvalitativnih Istraživanja u Zajednici: Od Planiranja do Istraživačkog Izvještaja' (Ethical Challenges of Qualitative Research in Community: From Planning to Reporting) (2014) 21(3) *Ljetopis Socijalnog Rada*.

Brison, Susan J, *Aftermath: Violence and the Remaking of a Self* (Princeton University Press, 2002).

Buckley-Zistel, Susanne, 'Ethnographic Research after Violent Conflicts: Personal Reflections on Dilemmas and Challenges' (2007) 10 *Journal of Peace, Conflict & Development*.

Campbell, Rebecca, *Emotionally Involved: The Impact of Researching Rape* (Routledge, 2001).

Carlson, Allen, Mary E Gallagher, Kenneth Lieberthal, and Melanie Manion (eds), *Contemporary Chinese Politics: New Sources, Methods, and Field Strategies* (Cambridge University Press, 2010).

Carpenter, Charli, '"You Talk of Terrible Things So Matter-of-Factly in This Language of Science": Constructing Human Rights in the Academy' (2012) 10(2) *Perspectives on Politics*.

Clark, Janine N, 'Fieldwork and its Ethical Challenges: Reflections from Research in Bosnia' (2012) 34 *Human Rights Quarterly*.

Davies, Charlotte Aull, *Reflexive Ethnography: A Guide to Researching Selves and Others* (Routledge, 2nd ed, 2008).

Demos, Vasilikie, Marcia Texler Segal (eds), *At the Center: Feminism, Social Science and Knowledge (Advances in Gender Research, vol 20)* (Emerald Group Publishing, 2015).

Devereux, Stephen and John Hoddinott (eds), *Fieldwork in Developing Countries* (Lynne Rienner Publishers, 1992).

Dickson-Smith, Virginia, Erica Lyn James, and Pranee Liamputtong, *Undertaking Sensitive Research in the Health and Social Sciences: Managing Boundaries, Emotions and Risks* (Cambridge University Press, 2008).

Ellen, Roy F (ed), *Ethnographic Research: A Guide to General Conduct* (Academic Press, 1984).

Ferrell, Betty, 'Ethical Perspectives on Pain and Suffering' (2005) 6(3) *Pain Nursing Management*.

Fleming, Jenny, 'Learning to Work Together: Police and Academics' (2010) 4(2) *Policing*.

Hubbard, Gill, Kathryn Backett-Milburn, and Debbie Kemmer, 'Working with Emotion: Issues for the Researcher in Fieldwork and Teamwork' (2001) 4(2) *International Journal Social Research Methodology*.

Kleinman, Sherryl, 'Fieldworkers' Feelings: What We Felt, Who We Are, How We Analyze' in William B Shaffir and Robert A Stebbins (eds), *Experiencing Fieldwork: An Inside View of Qualitative Research* (SAGE Publications, 1991).

Lee, Raymond M, *Doing Research on Sensitive Topics* (SAGE Publications, 1993).

Lee, Raymond M and Elizabeth A Stanko (eds), *Researching Violence: Essays on Methodology and Measurement* (Routledge, 2003).

Lee-Treweek, Geraldine, 'The Insight of Emotional Danger: Research Experiences in a Home for Older People' in Geraldine Lee-Treweek and Stephanie Linkogle, *Danger in the Field: Risks and Ethics in Social Research* (Routledge, 2000).

Lee-Treweek, Geraldine and Stephanie Linkogle, *Danger in the Field: Risks and Ethics in Social Research* (Routledge, 2000).

Letherby, Gayle, 'Dangerous Liaisons: Auto/Biography in Research and Research Writing' in Geraldine Lee-Treweek and Stephanie Linkogle, *Danger in the Field: Risks and Ethics in Social Research* (Routledge, 2000).

Lockwood, Matthew, 'Facts or Fictions? Fieldwork Relationships and the Nature of Data' in Stephen Devereux and John Hoddinott (eds), *Fieldwork in Developing Countries* (Lynne Rienner Publishers, 1992).

McCosker, Heather, Alan Barnard and Rod Gerber, 'Undertaking Sensitive Research: Issues and Strategies for Meeting the Safety Needs of All Participants' (2001) 2(1) *Forum: Qualitative Social Research* Art 22.

Mazurana, Dyan and Karen Jacobsen (eds), *Research Methods in Conflict Settings: A View from Below* (Cambridge University Press, 2013).

Melrose, Margaret, 'Labor Pains: Some Considerations on the Difficulties of Researching Juvenile Prostitution' (2002) 5(4) *International Journal of Social Research Methodology*.

Millar, Gearoid, *An Ethnographic Approach to Peacebuilding: Understanding Local Experiences in Transitional States* (London, Routledge, 2014).

Morley, Louise and Val Walsh, *Breaking Boundaries: Women in Higher Education* (Taylor and Francis, 1995).

Nordstrom, Carolyn and Antonius CGM Robben (eds), *Fieldwork Under Fire: Contemporary Studies of Violence and Survival* (University of California Press, 1995).

Nouwen, Sarah MH, '"As You Set Out for Ithaka": Practical, Epistemological, Ethical, and Existential Questions about Socio-Legal Empirical Research in Conflict' (2014) 27(1) *Leiden Journal of International Law*.

Olson, Loreen N, 'The Role of Voice in the (Re)Construction of a Battered Woman's Identity: An Autoethnography of One Woman's Experience of Abuse' (2004) 27(1) *Women's Studies in Communication*.

Renzetti, Claire M and Raymond M Lee (eds), *Researching Sensitive Topics* (SAGE Publications, 1993).

Richards, Kelly and Lorana Bartels, 'The Story Behind the Stories: Qualitative Criminology Research in Australia' in Lorana Bartels and Kelly Richards (eds), *Qualitative Criminology: Stories from the Field* (Hawkins Press, 2011).

Robben, Antonius CGM, 'The Politics of Truth and Emotion among Victims and Perpetrators of Violence' in Antonius CGM Robben and Jeffrey A Sluka (eds), *Ethnographic Fieldwork: An Anthropological Reader* (John Wiley & Sons, 2nd ed, 2012).

Robben, Antonius CGM and Jeffrey A Sluka (eds), *Ethnographic Fieldwork: An Anthropological Reader* (John Wiley & Sons, 2nd ed, 2012).

Rogers-Brown, Jennifer B, 'More Than a War Story: A Feminist Analysis of Doing Dangerous Fieldwork' in Vasilikie Demos, Marcia Texler Segal (eds) *At the Center: Feminism, Social Science and Knowledge (Advances in Gender Research, vol 20)* (Emerald Group Publishing, 2015).

Schauben, Laura J and Patricia A Frazier, 'Vicarious Trauma: The Effect on Female Counsellors Working with Sexual Violence Survivors' (1995) 19(1) *Psychology of Women Quarterly*.

Shaffir, William B and Robert A Stebbins (eds), *Experiencing Fieldwork: An Inside View of Qualitative Research* (SAGE Publications, 1991).

Sieber, Joan E and Barbara Stanley, 'Ethical and Professional Dimensions of Socially Sensitive Research' (1988) 43(1) *American Psychologists*.

Simić, Olivera, 'A Tour to a Site of Genocide: Mothers, Borders and Bones' (2008) 9(3) *Journal of International Women's Studies* 320.

Simić, Olivera, 'Feminist Research in Transitional Justice Studies: Navigating Silences and Disruptions in the Field' (2016) 17(1) *Human Rights Review*.

Simić, Olivera, 'Doing the Research I Do Has Left Scars' *Transitional Justice Review* (forthcoming, 2016).

Sriram, Chandra Lekha, John C King, Julie A Mertus, Olga Martin-Ortega and Johanna Herman (eds), *Surviving Field Research: Working in Violent and Difficult Situations* (Routledge, 2009).

Steier, Frederick, *Research and Reflexivity* (SAGE, 1993).

Subotić, Jelena, 'No Escape from Ethnicity? Confessions of an Accidental CNN Pundit' (2010) 43(1) *PS: Political Science & Politics*.

Theidon, Kimberly, '"How Was Your Trip?" Self-care for Researchers Working and Writing on Violence' (Working Paper on Research Security No. 2, Social Science Research Council, April 2014).

Tomsen, Stephen, 'Foreword: The Collective Remembering of the Stories of Qualitative Criminology' in Lorana Bartels and Kelly Richards (eds), *Qualitative Criminology: Stories from the Field* (Hawkins Press, 2011).

Tsai, Lily L, 'Quantitative Research and Issue of Political Sensitivity in Rural China' in Allen Carlson, Mary E Gallagher, Kenneth Lieberthal and Melanie Manion (eds), *Contemporary Chinese Politics: New Sources, Methods and Field Strategies* (Cambridge University Press, 2010).

Wamai, Njoki, 'First Contact with the Field: Experiences of Early Career Researcher in the Context of National and International Politics in Kenya' (2014) 6(2) *Journal of Human Rights Practice*.

Weber, Max, *Methodology of Social Sciences* (Free Press, 1949).

Wilkins, Ruth, 'Taking It Personally: A Note on Emotion and Autobiography' (1993) 27(1) *Sociology*.

Wincup, Emma, *Residential Work with Offenders: Reflexive Accounts of Practice* (Ashgate, 2001).

Zahar, Maria-Joëlle, 'Fieldwork, Objectivity and Academic Enterprise' in Chandra Lekha Sriram, John C King, Julie A Mertus, Olga Martin-Ortega and Johanna Herman (eds), *Surviving Field Research: Working in Violent and Difficult Situations* (Routledge, 2009).

Index